MW00579770

SLAVE SHIPS
AND SLAVING

BARTERING FOR SLAVES ON THE GUINEA COAST
From a colored lithograph in the Macpherson Collection

SLAVE SHIPS AND SLAVING

George Francis Dow

with an introduction by
Capt. Ernest H. Pentecost, R.N.R.

DOVER PUBLICATIONS, INC.
Mineola, New York

Published in Canada by General Publishing Company, Ltd., 895 Don Mills Road, 400-2 Park Centre, Toronto, Ontario M3C 1W3.

Published in the United Kingdom by David & Charles, Brunel House, Forde Close, Newton Abbot, Devon TQ12 4PU.

Bibliographical Note

This Dover edition, first published in 2002, is an unabridged republication of the work originally published by The Marine Research Society, Salem, Massachusetts, in 1927.

Library of Congress Cataloging-in-Publication Data

Dow, George Francis, 1868–1936.
    Slave ships and slaving / George Francis Dow ; with an introduction by Ernest H. Pentecost.
        p. cm.
    Originally published: Salem, Mass. : Marine Research Society, 1927.
    Includes bibliographical references and index.
    ISBN 0-486-42111-2 (pbk.)
    1. Slave-trade—Africa, West. I. Title.

HT1322 .D6 2002
380.1'44'0966—dc21

2001054900

Manufactured in the United States of America
Dover Publications, Inc., 31 East 2nd Street, Mineola, N.Y. 11501

PREFACE

THE infamous deeds of the pirates alone excepted, there is no blacker page in the story of the sea than that which records the voyages of the slave ships. Captivated in tribal wars and kidnapped in times of peace, uncounted millions of negroes were closely stowed in the holds of all kinds of sailing craft and carried to the West Indies and America to be sold as slaves to work the sugar plantations. The cruelty and horror of "the middle passage"—the voyage from the Guinea coast—can never be told in all its gruesome details. It is enough to recall that the ships were always trailed by man-eating sharks.

The slaving trade was also the grave of many of the seamen who engaged in it, for the African coast reeked with fevers and other fearful diseases and those who escaped the infection and ophthalmia of "the middle passage," on reaching the West Indies frequently opened their own graves by unrestrained drinking of new rum. Many masters of slave ships were cruel and overbearing by nature; the trade exacted its toll; and cruelty inflicted upon slaves was easily transferred to equally helpless seamen.

The ships of America and the principal maritime nations of Europe were engaged in this trade for centuries and few voices were raised in protest until after the revolutions in the American colonies and in France, when a new conception of personal freedom began to gain ground. Even after the traffic in human flesh was prohibited by law, for many years, or until the market failed, slave ships surreptitiously collected their cargoes and ran the blockade of naval vessels keeping guard on eastern and western coasts.

This volume does not attempt to give a history of the African slave trade; it would require many volumes to do justice to the subject. It merely presents an account of the trade as conducted at different times and by different nations and is a piece of narrative and description and not a history of events. The Introduction has been written by Captain Pentecost, a British officer in the Naval Reserve, now retired after a long and varied service at sea, during which he gathered a knowledge of slaving from the lips of those formerly engaged in the trade. He also placed at our disposal certain printed and illustrative material which has been utilized in the preparation of this volume. Thanks are also due to Mr. A. G. H. Macpherson of London, England, from whose unrivaled collection of pictures and engravings relating to ships and the sea most of the plates in this volume have been reproduced.

TABLE OF CONTENTS

ILLUSTRATIONS

TO THE READER

READ this book and visions see
 Of Afric land and tropic sea;
Of beaches wide where great waves roar,
 Where sea birds scream and vultures soar;
Of lofty palms that bow and sigh
 And cast their shade where slavers lie;
Of steaming forests and calm lagoons,
 And swelt'ring blacks in barracoons;
Of brutal captains and negro kings,
 And dusky belles in anklets and rings;
Of muddy rivers where black craft hide
 Among the mangoes—at anchor ride;
Of brig and schooner, snow and ship,
 Casting from shore with anchor atrip;
Filling away for the Western World
 With cargoes below oft-times hurled
To feed the ravenous water brutes
 Which ever cruise on the slavers' routes;
Of idle ships on a sea asleep
 Along the line where the latitudes meet;
Of a western land where "Cotton was King"
 And the markets were busy when the slavers were in.

ERNEST H. PENTECOST.

INTRODUCTION

"NEXT to a pirate give me a slaver," said the boy. A sky pilot in charge of a bethel in a far eastern port, finding that prayers, sermons and psalms were not sufficient to keep his sea-faring flock on the course he wished them to steer, reinforced his efforts with moral stories, which he read to them when the day drew towards those hours during which "Himself" of the lower regions is said to be most active. Instead of his reinforcement having the desired effect, he was grieved to see his congregation soon reduced to a penniless few; the rest he had good reason to fear were frequenting those haunts from which he had wrought to keep them. The poor padre, at last realizing that he was losing ground in his fight with evil, sought the advice of an ancient seafarer, who, when he heard of the sort of stories the parson had read to his brother seamen, said, "Parson, read 'em yarns about pirates, slavers and highwaymen and you'll soon have a full bethel."

Although pirates, slavers and highwaymen were what in our childhood we would have described as "naughty, wicked, bad men," kindly Time having clothed those lewd fellows with a mantle of romance they but ill deserve, we now love to read of their destructive adventures.

There is no record of either pirates or highwaymen ever having been regarded as persons following an honest calling; whereas, the slave trade, until the early part of the nineteenth century, was a perfectly legitimate business and those engaged therein were considered as respectable as any other traders. Man, being by nature a slaver, it is quite probable that in those far-away days when he carried a lanyard fast to his stern, some unfortunate animal was forced to carry the end of it for him, when he was making a passage.

The Spaniards, ten years after their discovery of the West India isles, sent out negro slaves to do the hard work in their new possessions for which the original inhabitants were found to be unfit. Although all the maritime nations of Europe engaged in the western slave trade, the English, according to some authorities, during the two and a half centuries they were engaged in that traffic, took more than double the number of negroes from the coast of Africa than all other nations combined.

Life was ever cheap in teeming Africa, where the process of reproduction was both rapid and continuous, and Nature exercised her "right of might" without let or hindrance. The working of that unchangeable law, "eat and be eaten," was there apparent on every hand.

In the account of Capt. John Lok's voyage to Guinea, in 1555, the negroes are described as "a people of beastly living, without a God, lawe, religion, or common wealth, and so scortched by the heat of the sunne, that in many places they curse it when it riseth."

In 1568, Capt. John Hawkins helped three negro kings take a town of negroes, and the narrator, John Hartop, says: "We took and carried thence for traffique to the West Indies five hundred negroes. The three Kings drove seven thousand negroes into ye sea at low water, at the point of the land, where they were all drowned in the ooze, for they could not take their canoes to save themselves."

Capt. William Snelgrave's book, *A New Account of Some Parts of Guinea and the Slave Trade*, published in 1734, contains interesting information about negro life and death. The captain says: "I have in my younger years traded to many places in this tract especially at Old Callabar, where, in the year 1704, I saw a sad instance of barbarity. The King of the place, called Jabrue, being fallen sick, he caused, by the advice of his priests, a young child about ten months old, to be sacrificed to his god, for his recovery. I saw the child after it was killed, hung on the bough of a tree, with a live cock tied near it, as an addition to the ceremony."

In 1727, Captain Snelgrave, with other white men, visited the camp of the King of Dahome a few weeks after that chief had conquered the people of Whidaw. Soon after their arrival at the camp, a messenger came to them, desiring them to go to the King's gate. "Accordingly we went," says the captain, "and on our way saw two large stages on which were heaped a great number of dead men's heads, that afforded no pleasing sight or smell. Our interpreter told us they were the heads of four thousand of the Whidaws who had been sacrificed by the Dahomes to their God." The white men saw other gruesome sights including the sacrifice of many men, women and children. Their interpreter told them that the "head of the victim was for the King, the blood for the Fetiche, and the body for the People."

And so down through time the killing went on until the bloody shambles found at Benin when the British took that place in 1897.

The number of Africans taken to the Americas and West Indies, during the three and a half centuries of the slave traffic to those countries, was probably small compared with the number violently done to death in various ways in that steamy coastland of blood, lust and tomtoms. The writer when a boy in a South African port, met an old man who had lived with the Zulus for many years. When asked what the Zulus reckoned their losses in men to have been at the battle of Isandhlwana, he replied, "The Zulus don't keep any account of their men, but are very careful to do so of their cattle, which they, like many other African tribes, think more valuable than their own kind."

Captain Snelgrave, a slaver of great experience, offers a few words in justification of the trade.

"As for the manner how those people became slaves, it may be reduced under these several heads.

"1. It has been the custom among the negroes, time out of mind, and is so to this day, for them to make slaves of all the captives taken in war. Now, before they had an opportunity of selling them to white people, they were often obliged to kill great multitudes, when they had taken more than they could well employ in their own plantations, for fear they should rebel and endanger their master's safety.

"2. Most crimes among them are punished by mulcts and fines; and if the offender has not wherewithal to pay his fine, he is sold for a slave. This is the practice of the inland people, as well as of those on the sea side.

"3. Debtors who refuse to pay their debts, or are insolvent, are likewise liable to be made slaves; but their friends may redeem them. And if they are not able and willing to do it, then they are generally sold for the benefit of their creditors. But few of these come into the hands of the Europeans, being kept by their country-men for their own use.

"4. I have been told, that it is common for some inland people to sell their children for slaves, tho' they are under no necessity for so doing; which I am inclined to believe. But I never observed that the people near the sea coast practise this, unless compelled thereto by extream want and famine, as the people of Whidaw have lately been.

"Now, by these means it is that so many negroes become slaves, and more especially by being taken captives in war. Of those the number is so great, that I may safely affirm, without any exaggeration, that the Europeans of all nations, that trade to the coast of Guinea, have in some years, exported at least seventy thousand. And tho' this may no doubt be thought at first hearing, a prodigeous number; yet, when 'tis considered how great the extent of this coast is, namely from Cape Verd to Angola, which is about 4000 miles in length; and that polygamy is allowed in general among them by which means the countrys are full of people, I hope it will not be thought improbable that so many are yearly exported from thence.

"Several objections have often been raised against the lawfulness of this trade, which I shall not here undertake to refute. I shall only observe in generall, that tho' to traffic in human creatures, may at first appear barbarous, inhuman and unnatural, yet, the traders herein have as much to plead in their own excuse, as can be said of some other branches of trade, namely, the advantage of it; and that not only in regard of the merchants, but also of the slaves themselves, as will appear from these following reasons.

"First, it is evident, that abundance of captives, taken in war, would be inhumanely destroyed, was there not an opportunity of desposing of them to the Europeans. So that at least many lives are saved, and great numbers of usefull persons kept in being.

"Secondly, when they are carried to the plantations, they generally live much better there, than they ever did in their own country; for as the planters pay a great price for them, 'tis their interest to take care of them.

"Thirdly, the English plantations have been so much improved, that 'tis almost incredible, what great advantages have accrued to the nation thereby; especially to the Sugar Islands, which, lying in a climate near as hot as the coast of Guinea, the negroes are fitter to cultivate the lands there than white people.

"Then as to the criminals amongst the negroes; they are by this means effectually transported, never to return again; a benefit we very much want here.

"In a word, from this trade proceed benefits, far outweighing all, either real or pretended mischiefs and inconveniences, and let the worst that can be said of it, it will be found, like all other earthly advantages, tempered with a mixture of good and evil."

Judged by the ethics of today, however, the slave trade was wrong, and cannot be defended even by the law of economics, of which it was the result.

The philanthropic frenzy of the abolitionists, few of whom had ever seen a slave ship with her cargo aboard, created, by their exaggerated statements, a wrong impression of the conditions aboard such craft, which usually were among the cleanest and best found merchantmen afloat. The common conception of the treatment of slaves aboard slavers, previous to the abolition of the slave trade, is very different from what it really was. In reality the slaves were much better cared for than free white emigrants and other poor passengers were until the second decade of the nineteenth century.

The reason for this difference in favor of the slaves is not far to·
seek. As in the cattle trade, the healthier the cargo, the greater
the profit; whereas in the case of the poor white passengers, who
had to pay their passage money before embarking, the sooner they
died, the better for the shipowner.

In support of the above statements, the following is quoted from
Notes on the West Indies, by George Pinckard, M.D., London,
1806. Doctor Pinckard's work was written in 1795-1796 in the form
of letters to a friend.

"It will be quite within your recollection how long, and how I
have wished to visit the ships trading to Africa and to witness per-
sonally the manner of treating those poor beings of sable skin, who
are torn from their native home by the iron hand of commerce, to
be transported to a home of slavery; and you will be pleased to
learn that in this wish, I have had an early opportunity of being
gratified.

"A slave ship belonging to North America, and bound to Savannah in Georgia, had arrived from the coast of Guinea just before
we came into harbour [Barbadoes] and was lying very near to us,
with a cargo of negroes on board. Fearing she might sail for America
and being unwilling to lose the first occasion that offered, of ad-
ministering to a curiosity which beat strong in our breasts, Master
Cleghorn and myself took off a boat, the morning after we came to
anchor, and went to visit the Guinea man. We considered ourselves
fortunate in finding both master and mate of the ship disposed to
shew us every civility, and to indulge us in ready reply to the questions which our curiosity suggested. . . .

"The cargo consisted of a hundred and thirty slaves, of whom
two-thirds were males and one-third females. The two sexes were
kept seperate by a partition, or bulk-head, built from side to side,
across the ship; alloting the waist to the men and to the women,
the quarterdeck. A great majority of them were very young, being
from ten to eighteen years of age. We were pleased to observe that
an air of cheerfullness and contentment prevailed among them. In a

few only we remarked despondency, and dejection of countenance. Both sexes were without apparel, having only a narrow band of blue cloth put around the waist, and brought to fasten before, so as to serve the office of the fig-leaf worn by our first parents in the fruitful garden of Eden.

"As we walked through the different groups of them, they fixed their eyes upon us, with seeming curiosity, and some of the boys, like those of fairer skin, were inclined to be playful and to exhibit youthful tricks. One or two of the females, unchecked by the reserve of education, occasionally glanced an expressive look or displayed a significant gesture. Many of them had marks upon the skin, which appeared to have been made by a cutting instrument. These, we learned, were distinctive of the nation to which they had belonged. Some had their teeth cut, or filed to sharp points, giving them a very hideous and canine appearance. They looked well fed and healthy, although some of them had an eruption, called the 'Cra-Cra,' upon the skin.

"Their sleeping berths were the naked boards. Divided into two crowded parties they reposed, during the night, upon the bare planks below—the males on the main deck—the females upon the deck of the aft cabin. In the day time they were not allowed to remain in the place where they had slept, but were kept mostly upon the open deck, where they were made to exercise, and encouraged by the music of their loved banjor, to dancing and cheerfulness. We saw them dance and heard them sing. In dancing they scarcely moved their feet, but threw about their arms and twisted and writhed their bodies into a multitude of disgusting and indecent attitudes. Their song was a wild and savage yell, devoid of all softness and harmony, and loudly chanted in harsh monotony.

"Their food is chiefly rice which they prepare by plain and simple boiling. At the time of messing they squat around the bowl in large bodies, upon their heels and haunches, like monkeys, each putting his paw into the platter to claw out with his fingers. We saw several of them employed in beating the red husks off the rice, which was done by pounding the grain in wooden mortars, with wooden pestles, sufficiently long to allow them to stand upright while beating in mortars placed at their feet. This appeared to be a labour of cheerfulness. They beat the pestle in time to the song and seemed happy; yet nothing of industry marked their toil, for the pounding was performed by indolently raising the pestle and then leaving it fall by its own weight.

"I am most happy to conclude my report of this visit by informing you that we discovered no marks of those horrors and cruelties said to be practised on board the ships occupied in this sad traffic of human flesh; and which are represented as so frightfully augmenting the manifold ills of slavery. Chains, stripes, and severities did not seem to have been in the catalogue of means employed in conveying these poor Africans to their American masters. Our minds, necessarily, suffered in contemplating the degrading practices of civilized beings towards the less cultivated heathen of their species; but the eye was not shocked by the abuses of tyranny and inhumanity. The comfort and health of the slaves was promoted with every care.

"Being fond of washing in cold water, they were encouraged to the free use of it; and their persons, as well as the whole ship, were kept remarkably clean. They were plentifully fed; and, in the day time, were dispersed about the ship so as to be prevented, as much as possible, from assembling together in close, unwholesome crowds. Mirth and gaiety were promoted among them; they were roused to bodily exercise and care was used to divert their minds from dwelling upon their change of state and loss of home: and I may truly say, that a more general air of contentment reigned among them than could have been expected. While many were dancing and singing and playing together, others were giving their assistance in working the ship; and, we even learned that several of them had made themselves highly usefull on the passage and were already becoming expert sailors. They all seemed to regard the master of the vessel more in affection than fear; and although strictly obedient, they did not at all appear to be under the influence of terror. Crowded in some degree, they, necessarily must be, particularly in the place where they slept; but every attention was paid to prevent the injury which might derive from it and to keep them in health.

"We went down below to see their place of repose where the hard planks form one common bed and each individual employed his arm as his pillow. The men could not stand between decks, without stooping, and when they lay down the boards were so closely spread that it was scarcely possible to set a foot between their naked bodies. They were always taken upon deck early in the morning and the sleeping berth was thoroughly cleaned and washed; but still it was highly offensive to European olfactories and plainly indicated, that were it not for the great attention paid to cleanliness and ventilation, disease must inevitably be generated. Their nakedness is, perhaps, their best security; for although they had neither bedclothes nor personal covering, nor any kind of baggage, or furniture in the place, we perceived that all the cleaning and airing employed could not subdue the stench created by their sleeping together in such crowded heaps. Although they are fond of washing, and seem to have some sense of personal cleanliness, they have none of cleanliness of place nor of common decency, for, notwithstanding the strictest injunction against it, they cannot always be prevented from the filthy habit of depositing their natural excretions upon the spot where they sleep. . . .

"The next day after our visit to the American slaveship, an opportunity offered of seeing one of our own nation, a Liverpool Guinea-man, a ship of much greater burden, fitted out expressly for the trade, with a sufficient number of hands and of guns on board to protect her against the enemy's privateers and calculated for a cargo of five hundred slaves. We were taught to believe that we should find the negroes much better accommodated in this, than in the American ship; but we could not observe that the superiority was either great or striking. Although the vessel was larger, the number of slaves was more than proportionally greater. In other respects the accommodations were nearly equal. The Liverpool ship was kept remarkably clean; but the American was not less so and, between the deck, the American ship was the most commodious, being higher and having more room in proportion to the cargo, from which the slaves had the advantage of being less close and confined during the night.

"The difference in point of health is peculiarly striking between the troops convoyed in transports from England and the slaves brought in Guinea ships from Africa. Perhaps, from the present mode of conducting slave ships, might be derived some useful hints for the management of our transports. The slaves are much more crowded than the soldiers, yet far more healthy. It becomes us, therefore, to ascertain the cause of this and I much suspect that it will be found in the difference of treatment and accommodation. According to the present method of conducting them, I might venture it as an opinion that a Guinea ship would carry—with less danger of disease being generated among them—a cargo of slaves more than thrice as numerous as a transport would carry of soldiers."

Professor Edward Ashworth Ross says in his *The Old World in the New:* "Were the Atlantic dried up today, one could trace the path between Europe and America by the cinders from our steamers; in the old days it would have revealed itself by human bones."

The conditions of oversea passage then brought about a shocking elimination of the weaker. The ships were small and crowded, the cabins close, and the passage required from six to ten weeks. "Between decks," writes a colonist, "there can hardly a man fetch his breath by reason there ariseth such a funk in the night that it causeth putrification of the blood and breedeth disease much like the plague."

William Penn urged in a circular, that those who came over should keep as much upon deck as might be, "and to sprinkle vinegar about the cabin." The ship on which he came over lost a third of her passengers by smallpox.

In 1639, the wife of the Governor wrote that the ship on which she came out had been "so pestered with people and goods; so full of infection that after a while they saw little but throwing people overboard." One vessel lost 130 out of 150 souls. One sixth part of three thousand Germans sent over in 1710 perished during a voyage that lasted from January to June. No better fared a shipload of Huguenot refugees in 1689,—a ship that left Rotterdam, with 150 Palatines and landed fewer than fifty after a voyage of twenty-four weeks. In 1738, "malignant fever and flux" left only 105 out of 400 Palatines. In 1775, a brig reached New York having lost 100 Highlanders during the passage. It was estimated that between the years 1750 and 1755, 2,000 corpses were thrown overboard from ships plying out of Rotterdam. In 1756, Muhlenberg thus describes the horrors of the passage. "During the voyage there is aboard these ships terrible misery, stench, fumes, vomiting, many kinds of sickness, fever, dysentery, scurvy, mouth rot, and the like. All of which come from sharply salted food and meat; also from very bad and foul water, so that many die miserably. . . . Many hundred people necessarily perish in such misery and must be cast into the sea. The sighing and crying and lamenting on board the ship continues night and day."

The excellent regulations for the preservation of health on board slavers continued until the trade was declared illegal by the various nations engaged therein, after which it was carried on by smugglers, a set of piratical scoundrels, the riffraff of the maritime nations. The slaves were no longer carried in comfortable, broad-beamed, bluff-bowed craft, but in sharp-built, fast vessels with comparatively small deck and hold space, aboard of which the poor negroes often suffered hardships, disease and death. These craft were driven for all they were worth in all sorts of weather, especially when being chased, which made it frequently necessary to batten the hatches down. Under such conditions the state of the living cargo must have been terrible indeed. One no longer hears of slaves helping to work the ship or of their being taught the use of arms to assist their white masters to defend themselves.

In an old book of voyages there is an account of the voyage of the French slaver *Le Rodeur*, of 200 tons burden, which sailed from the port of Havre for the river Calabar, on the coast of Africa, where she arrived and anchored at Bonny, March 14, 1819. During a stay of three weeks she obtained 160 negroes and sailed for Guadaloupe on April 6th. The following authentic account of this voyage, intended for the eye of his mother, was kept by a lad of twelve, named J. B. Romaigne. He was the son of a planter of Guadaloupe and had been sent out as a passenger in *La Rodeur*, under the especial care of the captain. This document is highly valuable for its simplicity and for the light it throws upon the human heart in circumstances that seem to baffle observation.

I

"It is now just a week since we sailed; but, indeed, it is not my fault that I have not sooner sat down to write. The first two days I was sick, and the other five were so stormy that I could not sit at the table without holding. Even now we are rolling like a great porpoise yet I can sit very well and keep the pen steady. Since I am to send you what I do without copying it over again at the end of the voyage, I shall take what pains I can; but I hope, my dear mother, you will consider that my fingers are grown hard and tarry with hauling all day on the ropes, the Captain being determined, as he says, to make me a sailor. The Captain is very fond of me and is very good-tempered; he drinks a great deal of brandy; he is a fine, handsome man and I am sure I shall like him very much.

II

"I enquired of the Captain today, how long it would be before we should get to Guadaloupe; and he told me we had a great distance to go before we should steer that way at all. He asked how I should like to have a little black slave and I said very well; that I was to have plenty of them at Guadaloupe. He asked me what I could do with them. 'Feed them,' I said. 'That is right,' said the

Captain; 'it will make them strong. But you will make them work won't you?' added he. 'Yes, to be sure,' said I. 'Then I can tell you you must flog them as well as feed them.' 'I will,' said I, 'it is what I intend, but I must not hurt them very much.' 'Of course not maim them,' returned he, 'for then they could not work; but if you do not make them feel to the marrow, you might as well throw them into the sea.'

III

"Since we have been at this place, Bonny Town in the Bonny river, on the coast of Africa, I have become more accustomed to the howling of these negroes. At first, it alarmed me, and I could not sleep. The Captain says that if they behave well they will be much better off at Guadaloupe; and I am sure, I wish the ignorant creatures would come quietly and have it over. Today, one of the blacks whom they were forcing into the hold, suddenly knocked down a sailor and attempted to leap overboard. He was caught, however, by the leg by another of the crew, and the sailor, rising up in a passion, hamstrung him with a cutlass. The Captain, seeing this, knocked the butcher flat upon the deck with a handspike. 'I will teach you to keep your temper,' said he, with an oath. 'He was the best slave in the lot.' I ran to the main chains and looked over; for they had dropped the black into the sea when they saw that he was useless. He continued to swim, even after he had sunk under water, for I saw the red track extending shoreward; but by and by, it stopped, widened, faded, and I saw it no more.

IV

"We are now fairly at sea again, and I am sure my dear Mother, I am heartily glad of it. The Captain is in the best temper in the world; he walks the deck, rubbing his hands and humming a tune. He says he has six dozen slaves on board, men, women and children, and all in prime marketable condition. I have not seen them, however, since we set sail. Their cries are so terrible that I do not like to go and look down into the hold. At first, I could not close my eyes; the sound froze my very blood; and, one night, jumping up in horror, I ran to the Captain's state-room. The lamp shone upon his face; it was as calm as marble, he slept profoundly, and I did not like to disturb him.

V

"Today, word was brought to the Captain, while we were at breakfast, that two of the slaves were dead, suffocated, as was supposed, by the closeness of the hold; and he immediately ordered the rest should be brought up, gang by gang, to the forecastle, to give them air. I ran up on deck to see them. They did not appear to me to be very unwell; but these blacks, who are not distinguished from one another by dress, are so much alike one can hardly tell.

"However, they had no sooner reached the ship's side, than first one, then another, then a third, sprang up on the gunwale, and darted into the sea, before the astonished sailors could tell what they were about. Many more made the attempt, but without success; they were all knocked flat to the deck, and the crew kept watch over them with handspikes and cutlasses till the Captain's pleasure should be known with regard to the revolt.

"The negroes, in the meantime, who had got off, continued dancing about among the waves, yelling with all their might, what seemed to me a song of triumph, in the burden of which they were joined by some of their companions on deck. Our ship speedily left the ignorant creatures behind; their voices came fainter and fainter upon the wind; the black head, first of one, then of another, disappeared; and then the sea was without a spot; and the air without a sound.

"When the Captain came up on deck, having finished his breakfast, and was told of the revolt, his face grew pale, and he gnashed his teeth. 'We must make an example,' said he, 'or our labour will be lost.' He then ordered the whole of the slaves in the ship to be tied together in gangs and placed upon the forecastle, and having selected six, who were known to have joined in the chorus of the revolters and might thus be considered as the ringleaders, he caused three of them to be shot, and the other three hanged, before the eyes of their comrades.

VI

"Last night I could not sleep; cold sweats broke over my body. I thought the six negroes were passing to and fro through the cabin, and looking in at the door of the Captain's stateroom. The Captain, I could hear, was sound asleep, and this made me more afraid. At last I began to pray so loud, that I awoke him, and he asked me, what was the matter. 'I am saying my prayers,' said I. 'That is a good boy,' replied he, and, in an instant he was as sound asleep as before.

VII

"The negroes, ever since the revolt, were confined closely to the lower hold and this brought on a disease called ophthalmia, which produced blindness. The sailors, who sling down the provisions from the upper hold, report that the disease is spreading frightfully and today, at dinner, the Captain and the surgeon held a conference on the subject. The surgeon declared that, from all he could learn, the cases were already so numerous as to be beyond his management; but the Captain insisted that every slave cured was worth his value and that it was better to lose a part than all. The disease, it seems, although generally fatal to the negro, is not always so. The patient is at first blind; but some escape, eventually, with the loss of one eye or a mere dimness of vision. The result of the conversation was, that the infected slaves were to be transferred to the upper hold and attended by the surgeon the same as if they were white men.

VIII

"All the slaves and some of the crew are blind. The Captain, the surgeon, and the mate are blind. There is hardly enough men left, out of our twenty-two, to work the ship. The Captain preserves what order he can and the surgeon still attempts to do his duty, but our situation is frightful.

IX

"All the crew are now blind but one man. The rest work under his orders like unconscious machines; the Captain standing by with a thick rope, which he sometimes applies, when led to any recreant by the man who can see. My own eyes begin to be affected; in a little while, I shall see nothing but death. I asked the Captain if he would not allow the blacks to come up on deck. He said it was of no use; that the crew, who were always on deck, were as blind as they; that if brought up, they would only drown themselves, whereas, if they remained where they were, there would, in all probability, be at least a portion of them salable, if we had ever the good fortune to reach Guadaloupe.

"We rolled along on our dreadful pain, with no other steersman than fate; for the single individual of the crew who was our last hope and stay, had added a thousand fold to the calamity of his fellows by sharing in it himself.

"You cannot comprehend our situation. It will not do to figure yourself tossing on the black and midnight deep, with not a star to cheer you, and not a hand to help; for even then you could see; you could see the glitter of the waters and the white crest of the wave and half see, half conjecture, the form of the objects around you. In the midst of all, you would at least possess an absolute conviction that, in a few hours more, a new sun would rise out of the ocean, a new morning dawn upon the world.

"Our night was not like that of the sea, the darkness of which is mingled with light like the faint memory of day and relieved by the certainty of approaching morning. We were blind, stone blind, drifting like a wreck upon the ocean and rolling like a cloud before the wind. The Captain was stone blind, yet had hopes of recovering his sight, while most of the others were in despair. A guard was continually placed, with drawn swords, at the store room, to prevent the men getting at the spirit-casks and dying in the frenzy of intoxication. Some were cursing and swearing from morning till night, some singing abominable songs; some kissing the crucifix and making vows to the blessed saints. A few lay all day long in their hammocks, apparently content to starve rather than come abroad for food. For my part, I snatched at anything I could get to eat; cookery was unthought of. I thought myself fortunate when I was able to procure a cupfull of water to soften a biscuit as dry and as hard as a stone.

X

"Mother, your son was blind for ten days, although now so well as to be able to write. I can tell you hardly anything of our history during that period. Each of us lived in a little dark world of his own, peopled by shadows and phantasms. We did not see the ship, nor the heavens, nor the sea, nor the faces of our comrades.

"Then there came a storm. No hand was upon the helm, not a reef upon the sails. On we flew like a phantom ship of old, that cared not for wind or weather, our masts straining and cracking; our sails bursting from their bonds, with a report like that of musketry; the furious sea one moment devouring us up, stem and stern, and the next casting us forth again, as if with loathing and disgust. Even so did the whale cast forth the fated Jonah. The wind, at last, died moaningly away, and we found ourselves rocking, without progressive motion, on the sullen deep. We at length heard a sound upon the waters, unlike that of the smooth swell which remained after the storm, and our hearts beat with a hope which was painful from its suddenness and intensity. We held our breath. The sound was continued; it was like the splashing of a heavy body in smooth water; and a simultaneous cry arose from every lip on deck and was echoed by the men in their hammocks below and by the slaves in the hold.

"Our cry was answered! We shouted again, our voices broken by sobs, and our burning eyes deluged with tears. Our shout was still answered; and, for some minutes, nothing was heard but an interchange of eager cries.

"The Captain was the first to recover his self-possession, and our voices sank into silence when we heard him speak the approaching vessel with the usual challenge.

" 'Ship Ahoy! Ahoy! What ship?'

" 'The *Saint Leon* of Spain. Help us for God's sake!'

" 'We want help ourselves,' replied our Captain.

" 'We are dying of hunger and thirst. Send us on board some provisions and a few hands to work the ship and name your own terms.'

" 'We can give you food, but we are in want of hands. Come on board of us and we will exchange provisions with you for men,' answered our Captain.

" 'Dollars! dollars! We will pay you in money, a thousand fold; but we cannot send. We have negroes on board; they have infected us with ophthalmia, and we are all stone-blind.'

"At the announcement of this horrible coincidence, there was a silence among us, for some moments, like that of death. It was broken by a fit of laughter, in which I joined myself; and, before our awful merriment was over, we could hear, by the sound of the curses which the Spaniards shouted against us, that the *St. Leon* had drifted away.

"This vessel, in all probability, foundered at sea, as she never reached any port.

XI

"The man who preserved his sight the longest, recovered the soonest; and to his exertions alone, under the providence of God and the mercy of the blessed saints, is it owing that we are now within a few leagues of Guadaloupe, this twenty-first day of June 1819. I am myself almost well. The surgeon and eleven more are irrecoverably blind; the Captain has lost one eye; four others have met with the same calamity; and five are able to see, though dimly, with both. Among the slaves, thirty-nine are completely blind and the rest blind of one eye or their sight otherwise injured.

"This morning the Captain called all hands on deck, negroes and all. The shores of Guadaloupe were in sight. I thought he was going to return God thanks publicly for our miraculous escape.

" 'Are you quite certain,' said the mate, 'that the cargo is insured?'

" 'I am,' said the Captain. 'Every slave that is lost must be made good by the underwriters. Besides, would you have me turn my ship into a hospital for the support of blind negroes? They have cost us enough already. Do your duty.'

"The mate picked out thirty-nine negroes who were completely blind, and, with the assistance of the rest of the crew, tied a piece of ballast to the legs of each. The miserable wretches were then thrown into the sea."

The Abolitionist party was probably older and stronger in Great Britain than in any other country and it was there that the press gang flourished for centuries and was not abolished until long after the slave trade. By that unjust system multitudes of free-born British seamen were condemned to a life in many respects worse than that of the negro slave. On board men-of-war, life was unnatural and the discipline such that it would have broken the spirits of others than hard-bitten sailormen. Orators howled and poets sang in aid of the poor Africans torn from their native shore, but devil a word was said or sung for the victims of the press. Had their dusky brothers, like the impressed sailors, stood in the breach between them and their enemy, they would have done their best to keep them there as long as the menace to their smug comfort existed.

ERNEST H. PENTECOST.

SLAVE SHIPS AND SLAVING

CHAPTER I

THE GUINEA COAST

THE slave coast of West Africa lies between the river Senegal, just north of Cape Verde, and the Congo River country, six degrees south of the equator. It is a low-lying coast, with many sandy beaches, though much of it is bordered by deltalands, covered with poisonous swamps, through which wind the uncounted channels of small rivers that penetrate the country. There are few harbors and the trader must find an anchorage inside the bar at the mouth of some river or lay offshore, at safe distance, while trade is carried on in canoes and boats that ride the long rollers pounding on the beach. A country well populated by negroes, it supplied for nearly four centuries the slave labor required by the West Indies and the two Americas,—a trade inseparable from cruelty, disease and death. Goree and Gambia,—the Gold Coast and the Tooth Coast,—Whidah, Old Calabar and Bonny, are some of the names that have a suggestive meaning in connection with the abhorrent trade in human flesh.

Not long after the gulf of Guinea was discovered by Portuguese navigators and at least two decades before Columbus sailed from Palos, a slave market was set up at Lisbon at which negroes from the Guinea coast were sold to any who would buy. It was the Moors who had told the Portuguese of the black-skinned people living in great numbers to the south of the great desert,—a race cursed of God and predestined as slaves.

By 1502, the first shipload of Africans had been landed at Hispaniola, to work in the mines, and the slave-bearing fleet plied to and from the Guinea coast very nearly up to the time of the abolition of slavery in Brazil, in 1888.

At first, the slave vessels bargained with the negroes in villages near the coast for such slaves, gold or wax as they might be able to supply. It usually followed that a ship must sail along the coast for some distance, picking up a few negroes at one place and a little ivory or gold at another. At some stops no slaves or ivory would be found and it required a long time to pick up a decent cargo. The coast was pestilential for the European and the trade with the treacherous negroes was exceedingly dangerous. Soon the plan was adopted of planting small settlements of Europeans at intervals along the slave coast, defended by forts, sometimes of considerable size and strength. These were called slave factories and it was the business of the factor or commander to negotiate with the negroes and stimulate them to activity in organizing slave-hunting expeditions. As the slaves were brought in from the back country, they would be purchased by barter and then housed and guarded in sheds or warehouses, known as barracoons, until the arrival of slave ships.

Factories of this kind were planted by the English, French, Dutch and Portuguese, all along the western coast, from Cape Verde to the Congo. The location usually chosen was near the mouth of some river, so as to tap easily the slave supply up country. Sometimes, however, a small island, offshore, was selected on which to build a factory, because it was cooler and a more healthful spot.

The walls of the larger forts enclosed a considerable space of ground, on which were built barracks, storehouses for merchandise and sheds for the slaves. The huts of the negroes employed in the service of the factory, would be outside the walls of the fort, but under the protection of its guns. The principal fort of the English was Cape Coast Castle, on the Gold Coast, and not far away was St. George del Mina, erected by the Portuguese, but later falling into the hands of the Dutch. The French built Fort Louis at the mouth of the Senegal and also a fort on Goree, an island near Cape Verde. Fort James was on the Gambia and there were important forts at Anamaboe, Accra and Whidah. Most of these forts mounted from fifty to sixty guns and were not only impregnable to the negroes, but capable of standing a regular siege by a European force.

Under the command of the governor or commandant were sol-

CAPE COAST CASTLE, THE PRINCIPAL ENGLISH SETTLEMENT ON THE GOLD COAST
From a colored aquatint by J. Hill, published in 1806, in the Macpherson Collection

THE GUINEA COAST ABOUT THE YEAR 1700

From the map in Churchill's *Collection of Voyages*, engraved by R. W. Seale

diers employed in the service of the company, and a number of clerks, mechanics and junior factors, the latter in charge of the traffic with the interior towns. These men would ascend the rivers in small sailing vessels or armed boats and exchange European manufactures for slaves, gold dust and ivory furnished by the negroes. Sometimes they would open a sort of shop or trading post in a populous town and remain there for several months at the pleasure of the local king or chief. Many of these men were outcasts at home or destitute of means and therefore willing to engage to go to the coast of Africa where they knew they could lead a life of comparative indolence, with little or no restraint. There they might indulge nearly every human passion with utter freedom, whether it be confirmed drunkenness or unrestrained intercourse with negro girls. They knew that the deadly climate was likely to claim them eventually, so it was "a short life, and a merry one" for many an outcast free of home ties.

The soldiers in the forts seldom were called upon for active duty and spent their time in smoking, drinking palm wine and gaming. In fact, much of the time they were physically unfit for any service and within two years after their arrival on the Coast, they would be carried off by fever or dissipation. A stranger, on visiting one of these African forts, felt that there was something both horrible and ludicrous in the appearance of its garrison, for the soldiers appeared ghastly, debilitated and diseased, and their tattered and soiled uniforms, resembling each other only in meanness and not in color, suggested the thought that these men were a band of drunken deserters or starved and maltreated prisoners of war.*

Sir John Hawkins was the first Englishman to transport slaves from the Guinea coast to America. This was in 1562, and his prosperous voyage which "brought great profit to the adventurers," led to other similar ventures. In 1618, King James granted a charter to a stock company to trade with Guinea, but private adventurers

* John Howison, *European Colonies*, 2 vols., Edinburgh, 1821.

and interlopers broke in upon the preserves of the company and forced the trade open.

In 1662, another exclusive company was chartered with the king's brother, the Duke of York, at its head, and this company undertook to supply the English plantations with three thousand slaves annually. It was known as the "Company of Royal Adventurers of England for Carrying on a Trade to Africa," and for a year or two traded successfully and brought gold dust to England in such quantity that King Charles II ordered the minting of a new gold coin, of the value of twenty-one shillings, to be known as a *guinea*. These coins, made of the gold imported by the African Company, had, in its honor, a small elephant under the bust of the King, as a mark of distinction, done, it is said, to encourage the importation of gold. In 1664, the Dutch admiral, De Ruyter, captured the Guinea forts of the company, including Cormentyn Castle, and a number of ships, so that its losses amounted to over £200,000, which eventually forced the company to surrender its charter.

In 1672, the Royal African Company was chartered and for over a century conducted a more or less successful trade with the Guinea coast. It encouraged the English manufacture of several kinds of woolen and cotton goods and opened up a considerable market for Sheffield wares. The importations were elephant's teeth, dye woods, wax and gold dust, the latter reaching England in such quantity that forty or fifty thousand guineas would be minted at a time. But the dominating feature of the trading operations of the company was the advantageous purchase of negroes in Guinea, to be carried to the American colonies and there sold into slavery, the return cargo being muscovado sugar to supply the expanding English market.

In 1790, the number of forts and factories established on the coast was about forty; fourteen belonging to the English, fifteen to the Dutch, three to the French, four to the Portuguese and four to the Danes; and it has been estimated that the number of negroes sold or kidnapped into slavery, annually, about that time, could not fall far short of one hundred thousand, while an estimate of the total number carried away into slavery, previous to the year 1800, shows that African mothers provided about thirty million victims for the slave ships.

The ship trading on the slave coast discovered that the manner of trade varied with the locality. On coming to anchor in the river Gambia, opposite James Fort, a boat was sent ashore to announce the arrival to the alkaide or chief of the town, who at once came aboard to receive the anchorage money. This was ten gallons of liquor for the king, two iron bars for the alkaide and perhaps a few bottles of wine, beer or cider for presents. After a detention of four to seven days, the king would send his people to receive his custom, amounting to the value of 140 iron bars in merchandise. Later, the ship was supplied with a first and second linguist, two messengers and six or more butlers. The first linguist served as interpreter between the broker, who sold the slaves for the owner, and the factor, trader or master of the ship. The second linguist acted as interpreter for an officer of the ship, either in the tender, long-boat or factory on shore. The messengers were employed in looking out for trade on shore,—slaves, ivory, gold, provisions, etc. and for carrying letters to and from vessels, factories, etc. The butlers were employed to row in boats, cut wood, water the ship, in fact, were hired to preserve the health of the ship's crew, by saving them from exposure to the sun on board and the damps on shore.

Thus provided, the ship proceeded up river for about one hundred leagues to Yanamaroo, in the kingdom of Yancy, where more liquor was supplied for an anchorage and then the messengers were sent out to the principal people, for twenty or thirty miles around, soliciting slaves and trade. The tender or long-boat would also be dispatched farther up the river with merchandise for trade. It was at this port that ships generally began and finished their trading.

The slaves sold by these blacks were for the most part prisoners of war. But not infrequently men would sell their own children or the children of neighbors, that they had kidnapped,—stolen is perhaps a better word. Some slaves were also brought from a distance but usually when offered were in poor and weak condition.

The linguist would bring the slave broker on board or to the factory, who would inquire what price the master of the ship was willing to pay for a slave and the commission he was to receive and this was never settled until the broker had visited all the factories and every ship in port. Having no better offer, the broker would then bring on board the owner of the slaves, who examined the merchandise offered, agreed upon the articles and then sent for the slaves, who would be examined by the ship's surgeon. If approved, the owner would then be paid the merchandise he had selected, less one bar of iron, duty for the king. Men slaves would then be put in irons on the main deck; boys on the main deck, not ironed; and women and girls, not ironed, on the quarter deck. The broker was then given his commission, which completed the transaction.*

Much of the ivory obtained there had been picked up in the woods and having laid out in the rain and wind for some time was for the most part scurfy and hollow.

The northern coast of the gulf of Guinea is divided into particular sections which, in order, have been named the "Grain Coast," extending from Cape Mount to Cape Palmas, a country producing much rice and maize (Indian corn); the "Ivory or Tooth Coast," extending from Cape Palmas to the river Lagos, and formerly having a considerable trade in elephant ivory; the "Gold Coast," between Assinee and the river Volta, so named for the large amounts of gold dust obtained there, which came from the mountains and streams at the north; and lastly, the "Bight of Benin," lying between Cape St. Paul's and Cape Formosa, which clasps within its curve, the "Slave Coast" and the coast of Whidah and Lagos, in former times much resorted to by slavers and pirates.

Cape Coast Castle, the principal English fort in slaving days,

* *Report to the House of Lords on the Abolition of the Slave Trade*, 2 vols., London, 1789.

guarded a part of the Gold Coast and behind it was the Fantee and Ashantee country, which supplied great numbers of slaves for the American market. The castle was built near the sea and not only was dominated by three hills, not far behind it, but its location was only nine miles from the Castle of St. George at Mina, belonging to the Dutch, and only a short mile distant was Fredericksburg, a Danish fort. The only landing place was a small sandy flat just under the castle, on which the blacks could run their canoes without danger of splitting. The agent general of the "Royal Company of Africa,"* who spent much time at Cape Coast Castle, remarked upon the unhealthfulness of the place notwithstanding the rocky shore and the surrounding high land. He wrote:

"Their fondness for their beloved liquor punch, is so great, even among the officers and factors, that, whatever comes of it, there must be a bowl upon all occasions, which causes the death of many of them. . . . I have often represented to some of the principal men how to live more regularly, viz., to abstain from the black women, whose natural hot and lewd temper soon wastes their bodies, to drink moderately, especially of brandy, rum, and punch; and to avoid sleeping in the open air at night, as many, when heated with debauchery, do, having nothing on but a shirt, thinking thus to keep cool, but, on the contrary, they murder themselves; for nothing is more pernicious to the constitution of Europeans, than to lie in the open air, as I have been sufficiently convinced by experience. I always kept to my bed, as well as I could well bear it, and both night and day wore a dressed hare's skin next to my bare stomach, for above two years together, which kept it in good disposition and helped digestion very much; though I must say it was sometimes, and especially in the excessive hot nights, very troublesome and occasioned much sweating. The air, though not so cold, is much

* John Barbot, "Description of North and South Guinea," in Churchill's *Collection of Voyages*, London, 1746.

thinner and more piercing than in England, and corrodes iron much faster.

"The Castle has a lofty wall around it and had no fresh water except what is saved in a very large cistern, during the rains, which supplies both the garrison and shipping. In order to destroy Guinea worms, ship masters are accustomed to put two or three spoonsful of quick lime into each water cask filled from the cistern."

The inland negroes supplied the market with fruit, corn and palm wine, the maize or Indian wheat being produced in such quantity that much was sold to shipping and to blacks from other parts. The country was also very rich in gold and slaves, many of the latter coming from a considerable distance in the interior. The Fantees and Ashantees were esteemed most highly and were more hardy than the inland blacks.

Anamaboe, an important roadstead, lies a few leagues to the east of Cape Coast Castle. It was formerly a point at which slaves were to be had in considerable number and the road was generally full of shipping. The blacks were a clever and villainous people and frequently adulterated their gold so the trader must narrowly watch all transactions. The town was located on a sandy beach, strewn with rocks, close to the sea, the surf being so heavy that ships' boats could not land and all trade was carried on in the canoes of the natives.

At Accra, further to the eastward, the coast is bolder, with a good landing and plentiful supplies of provisions, and gold of the purest refinement. This country usually was at war with neighboring nations and accordingly had many prisoners to sell into slavery, so that sometimes a ship happening on the coast at just the right time, could obtain a lading of slaves in a fortnight and at a very low cost.

The use made by the natives of European manufactures obtained in trade is interestingly described by John Barbot, in his account of Guinea.

"The broad linen serves to adorn themselves, and their dead men's sepulchers within; they also make clouts thereof. The narrow cloth to press palm-oil; in old sheets they wrap themselves at night from head to foot. The copper basins to wash and shave, the Scotch pans serve in lieu of butcher's tubs, when they kill hogs or sheep; from the iron bars the smiths forge out all their weapons and country and household tools and utensils. Of friezes and perpetuanas they make girts four fingers broad, to wear about the waist, and hang their sword, dagger, knife, and purse of money or gold, which they commonly thrust between the girdle and their body. They break Venice coral into four or five parts, which afterwards they mould into any form, on whetstones, and make strings or necklaces, which yield a considerable profit. Of four or five ells of English or Leyden serges they make a kind of cloth to wrap about their shoulders and stomach. Of chintzes, perpetuanas, printed calicoes, tapseils and nicanees, are made clouts to wear round their middles. The wrought pewter, such as dishes, basons, porringers, &c. serve to eat their victuals out of. Muskets, firelocks, and cutlaces they use in war. Brandy is most commonly spent at their feasts. Knives to the same purposes as we use them. With tallow they anoint their bodies from head to toe, and even use it to shave their beards, instead of soap. Venice bugles, glass beads and contacarbe serve all ages and sexes, to adorn their heads, necks, arms and legs, and sarsaparilla is used by such as are infected with the venereal disease."

Lying to the eastward of the Gold Coast is a stretch of country known as the Slave Coast, because the whole trade there was confined to slaves, there being very little gold. It extends from the river Volta to Jackin. The country is flat and low, rising gradually as it runs up inland, and landing along the coast is difficult, not to say dangerous, because of the terrible surf, which at nearly all times of the year cannot be passed without great hazard. From April to July, which is the rainy season, the waves run so high that whoever ventures to land should mind the saying "he ought to have two lives who ventures." The bar-canoes, however well manned, were frequently overset with loss of goods and also lives, for the waters swarm with monstrous sharks, sometimes thirty feet long, that soon make way with any man who happens to fall near them. These sharks usually swim in company and when a dead slave was thrown overboard, one shark would bite off a leg, another an arm, while others would sink down with the body; and all this happened in much less time than it takes to describe the gruesome feast. Great numbers of sharks always followed the course of slave ships, as if they knew that one or more bodies would be thrown, daily, to their ravenous jaws.

As the slaves came down to the coast from Dahomey and the inland country, they were put into a large shed, built for that purpose, near the beach, and when brought out for sale, the ship's surgeons would carefully examine every bit of their anatomy down to the smallest member, men and women alike being stark naked. Those found to be sound would be set aside and soon after be branded, with a hot iron, on the breast (later it was more customary to brand on the shoulder) with the mark of the company or the individual trader, so as to prevent the natives from substituting slaves in poorer condition. Care was usually taken that the women should not be burned as deeply as the men. The branded slaves would then be returned to the shed and sometimes it would be two or more weeks before the surf would be low enough to make it safe to send them off to the slave ships anchored in the roadstead. They were always stripped of every rag of clothing before they entered the bar-canoes and as they stepped into the canoe, a native priest standing by would strew sand over their heads to exorcise the evil spirit and preserve them from being overset in the passing through the rollers.

To trade on the Slave Coast, particularly after the king of Dahomey had subjugated the coast tribes, necessitated much ceremony and many presents, to say nothing of the employment of numerous retainers and servants. The king must be paid his customs at the outset. Then came the hire of the factory house and the canoes and

CHRISTIANSBORG, THE DANISH SETTLEMENT ON THE GOLD COAST
From the engraving by J. Hill, published in 1806, in the Macpherson Collection

ELMINA, ON THE GOLD COAST, NEAR CAPE COAST CASTLE

From a colored aquatint published about 1830, in the Macpherson Collection

canoemen and it was customary to hire a conductor to take care of the goods brought up from the beach and also the slaves going down to the canoes. Two brokers or interpreters were required; two boys for servants; a doorkeeper and a boy, to serve at the tent on the beach; a messenger to carry to the king the news of the ship's arrival and the captain's compliments; a gong beater, to announce the opening of trade; a trunk keeper, to take care of the slaves while on shore; six water rollers; a woman to bring water; and a washer-woman.

Fees must also be paid to the viceroy, who came with his people to receive the captain and conduct him to the fort,—usually a Spanish hat, a piece of silk, a cask of flour and another of beef or pork. The captain of the waterside, at the ship's departure, was given a piece of cloth and an anker of brandy; and there was a fee for putting up a tent on the beach. Porters had to be hired and there were other expenses for entertainment, so that the preliminary costs of lading a slave ship, on this coast, about the year 1790, amounted to a value of about £368; and about the same time slaves were costing five ounces of gold, or £10, apiece.

This entire coast from the river Sherboro, just south of Sierre Leone, to the river Benin, at New Calabar (which is the part of Africa with which Europeans were best acquainted previous to the year 1800),—in all this tract of at least fifteen hundred miles of seacoast, there is not one navigable river, bay or harbor, into which a ship can enter; nor is there one river or creek into which a sailing boat can go above ten miles from the sea. Very few creeks will even admit a boat and not one on the Gold Coast, except at Chama and Mines. The entire shoreline, almost in every part, is difficult of access, because of the heavy surf that breaks upon the beach and it is only possible to land in a light canoe and even in that way it is frequently impracticable for many days together. In many places near the shore there is scarcely water enough for even a canoe and the waves break so fiercely and there is so wide a stretch of broken water, that all communication between shipping and the shore is frequently interrupted for weeks at a time, and seldom can a landing be effected with safety. At the easterly end of the Bight of Benin, the entire coast is inhospitable and very little frequented and for the most part is drowned occasionally by the sea or the heavy rains in August and September.*

A very important part of the coast, in old slaving days, was Calabar, Old and New, and the Bonny River. Ships of considerable burden could anchor on the hard, sandy ground, in eight fathoms, in the river at New Calabar and also at Bonny and as these towns tapped an extensive back-country, they traded in slaves in large numbers. As New Calabar was badly afflicted with mosquitoes, shipping usually lay at anchor near Foko Point. The blacks living there, through frequent contact with Europeans, were of a more civilized sort than elsewhere along the coast, and half a dozen vessels would sometimes lie at anchor in the river at one time. From 12,000 to 15,000 slaves were exported annually from this locality, during a long period of years, the English, French and Dutch participating in the trade. These slaves were brought down the rivers from market towns, a hundred and more miles away, having originally come from a considerable distance in the interior. Some of them undoubtedly were prisoners of war, but many were kidnapped by raiding parties or sold into slavery because of crime or the necessity of relatives, and not infrequently in consequence of debt.

The black traders of Calabar and Bonny came down the rivers with slaves about once a fortnight. There would be twenty or thirty canoes come down at a time, and sometimes even more, and each canoe would carry twenty to thirty slaves. The arms of some of the men would be tied with grass rope and a man who happened to be stronger than common might also be pinioned above the knee. In this condition the slaves would be thrown into the bottom of the canoes, where they would lie, able to move but slightly, sometimes in great pain and often almost covered with water. On landing, they

* *New Sailing Directions for the Coast of Africa*, London, 1799.

would be taken to the trader's sheds, where they would be fed, rubbed down with palm oil and made up for sale.

"Bonny River is a noble stream, spacious and deep and wider than the Thames in Sea Reach. The land is low and covered with lofty cocoanut, palm tree, pine, plantain and banana trees. On the north side is the kingdom of Benin and on the south, Bonny, independent of each other. New Calabar can be seen here at the distance to the northwest. Plenty of palm wine is made (or rather got) here, for they have only to make an incision in the top of a tree in the evening, hang a calabash under it, and in the morning it will be full. It is of a whitish color and tastes like cider.

"Our slaves had two meals a day, one in the morning consisting of boiled yams and the other in the afternoon of boiled horse-beans and slabber sauce poured over each. This sauce was made of chunks of old Irish beef and rotten salt fish stewed to rags and well seasoned with cayenne pepper. The negroes were so fond of it that they would pick out the little bits and share them out; but they didn't like the horse-beans.

"The brandy that we brought out for trade was very good but the darkies thought it was not hot enough and didn't bite—as they called it; therefore, out of every puncheon we pumped out a third of the brandy, put in half a bucketful of cayenne pepper, then filled it up with water and in a few days it was hot enough for Old Nick, himself, and when they came to taste it, thinking that it was from another cask, they would say 'Ah, he bite.' "*

In some of the following chapters will be found detailed accounts of trading at Calabar and Bonny, the procuring of slaves and what happened during the voyage to the West Indies.

About twenty-five leagues to the east of Bonny River is Old Calabar, where ships formerly made fast to large trees on the river bank and traded for provisions and slaves. The climate is very un-

* William Richardson, *A Mariner of England*, London, 1908.

healthy and as trade there went on very slowly in time it came to be a place to avoid.

About ten leagues farther to the eastward is the Rio del Rey, which formerly supplied many slaves and some fine, large elephant's tusks. But the country has no fresh water except what the blacks collect from the tops of their houses when it rains and the river has much thick, foggy weather. An old English pilot wrote of this river:

"Here an European must look out for himself, for the inhabitants are so subtly mischievous that you'll be betrayed before you are aware; and they are so barbarously cruel, that the parents sell their children, the husband his wife, one brother and sister the other, and in decency and order are scarce a degree above the beasts. This description was written in the last century and we don't find that the inhabitants are altered in the least since that time."*

South of the Rio del Rey lies the country of the Cameroons, a tall, lusty people, who carried on some trade with Europeans; the Gaboon River, a good place for trade and also for cleaning and refitting vessels; Loango, a rich and important kingdom, whose people worked in metal and were more civilized than the nations to the north of them; and lastly, the great region about the Congo River, its trade, in former times, largely controlled by the Portuguese.

The slave trade was abolished by law by Great Britain in 1807; by Denmark in 1812; by Holland in 1814; by France in 1818; and by Spain in 1820, after the receipt of a subsidy of £400,000 from Great Britain, but the prohibition was a farce as far as the Spanish authorities were concerned, and the trade in slaves from West Africa to Cuba and Porto Rico was only checked by the vigilance of British and French cruisers. The United States, in its southern part, was vitally interested in slavery, but the slave trade with the African Coast was abolished in 1807. Portugal abolished

---

* *New Sailing Directions for the Coast of Africa*, London, 1799.

the slave trade in 1830 and received therefor a subsidy from Great Britain, but as a matter of fact, the export of slaves from Portuguese Africa did not really come to an end until Brazil abolished slavery in 1888.

To enforce the suppression of the African slave trade Great Britain sent her war vessels to the West Coast and later, as treaties were entered into with other countries, the activities of her blockading vessels did much to lessen the number of negroes carried overseas.

In 1820, the United States sent three war vessels to the African coast to aid in the suppression of the slave trade; but the appropriation of $100,000 made by Congress in 1819, for enforcing the Act, was reduced to $50,000 in 1823, and soon after was reduced to a few ineffective thousands.

In 1842, by the Ashburton treaty with Great Britain, the United States engaged to keep on the Coast of Africa a "sufficient and adequate" naval force for the suppression of the slave trade, and after that a small squadron was kept on the African station.

The blockading fleets had a long coastline to cover. One by one the well-known slave factories were destroyed and one by one the slaving fleet grew smaller. The gulf of Guinea, because of the character of its coastline, was soon free of traders, and debarred from using the Spanish settlements on or off the Cameroons coast, the slave traders of nineteenth-century Cuba and Brazil established themselves on the Rio Pongo, a no-man's land northwest of Sierra Leone. There came the Fulah traders from the Mandingo and upper Niger countries; the adjoining rivers and islands of Portuguese Guinea also fed a similar slave trade, and it was some time before the slave depots at Rio Pongo and Bobama were broken up by the joint action of British and French gunboats.

The Cuban ships then found their way to the eastern side of the Sierra Leone colony, to the Gallinas lagoon and the river Sulima,*

* Johnston, *The Negro in the New World*, New York, 1910.

along the unclaimed "Grain Coast," now Liberia, and from 1822 to 1839 an average of five thousand slaves were shipped annually to Cuba, Porto Rico, South Carolina, Georgia and Brazil, from this one locality alone. Pedro Blanco, a native of Malaga, was the leading spirit of this slaving factory and one of his principal lieutenants was Theodore Canot, a French seaman.* Blanco lived near the Gallinas lagoon, with a large harem, surrounded by every luxury that money could buy in Europe or America. His drafts were as promptly cashed in Cuba, London or Paris as on the West African coast. He employed large numbers of negroes as paid watchers or spies, and from a hundred lookouts along the beach and on the islands of the lagoon, they scanned the horizon for the approach of British cruisers. By their signals they saved incoming or outgoing slave ships from capture. In 1839, Blanco retired from the trade with a fortune of nearly a million sterling and at last ended his days quite pleasantly on the Italian Riviera.

The slave-trading factories on the coasts of Sierra Leone and Liberia had all been destroyed by about 1847, but slave smuggling was carried on from inland stations, by prearranged connections, for long years after, although not on so large a scale as before. A lading of negroes, from the interior, would be brought to the coast and concealed at a place agreed upon. On a certain day or not long after, a vessel would appear off the beach and display a recognized signal. Immediately the negroes would be rushed to the shore and carried aboard in canoes and the ship's boats and four hours later a distant sail on the horizon was the only visible reminder of another trade in human flesh.

Cruisers were active and so were the slave smugglers, for the profits were enormous. In 1858, a citizen of Savannah, Georgia, proposed an expedition to the coast of Africa, for "a cargo of African apprentices to be bound for the term of their natural lives,"

* Mayer, *Captain Canot; or Twenty Years of an African Slaver,* New York, 1854.

and estimated the costs at $300,000 and the net profits at $480,000, which did not include the value of the steamer, already paid for. It is a significant fact that during the year 1859, only two years before the Civil War, according to the annual report of the Secretary of the Navy, eleven slavers were captured by United States war vessels.

CHAPTER II

SIR JOHN HAWKINS, SLAVE TRADER

THE first Englishman to engage in the slave trade between the Guinea coast and America was Capt. John Hawkins, a younger son of Capt. William Hawkins of Plymouth, who was trading on the coast of Brazil as early as 1630, "in a tall and goodlie ship of his owne." Young Hawkins was born in 1532 and also followed the sea. He made several voyages to the Canary Isles and while there formed a trade alliance with a Spanish merchant, Pedro de Ponte, of Teneriffe, who suggested to him the feasibility of a trade in negro slaves to be obtained in the gulf of Guinea and sold to the sugar planters in the Spanish West Indies. Between voyages Hawkins made inquiry of his father and others as to the conditions existing in the West Indies, but his principal source of information was found among the traders in the Canaries. He was assured that negroes were greatly desired in Hispaniola (Haiti) and that they might easily be had on the African coast. Pedro de Ponte agreed to furnish a pilot familiar with Spanish America and the state of the trade there and Hawkins finally decided to make a trial of the venture.

He returned to London from his last Canary voyage, in the summer of 1562, and at once laid the project before his father-in-law, Benjamin Gonson, the Treasurer of the Admiralty, who thought so well of it that Thomas Lodge, the governor of the Russia Company and a member of the Grocer's Company; Alderman Lionel Ducket, an enterprising merchant who afterwards became Lord Mayor of London; Sir William Winter, and several others were interested and "became liberal contributors and adventurers in the action."* These men were venturers in the full meaning of the word, for no Eng-

* Hakluyt, *The principal Navigations, Voyages, and Discoveries made by the English Nation,* London, 1589.

lish fleet had yet entered into the commercial field in the New World long monopolized by Spain. Any prudent Englishman could easily forecast trouble with that mighty power in case the proposed voyage was carried out to a conclusion.

Forty-five years before this date, Charles V had formally licensed the importation of negro slaves into the West Indies. In 1551, 17,000 licenses for slave importation from Africa to the West Indies were offered for sale by the Spanish government and two years later a monopoly of the African slave trade was granted for seven years obligating an importation of 23,000 negroes. It was this monopoly that Captain Hawkins proposed to break and only bold men became shareholders in his venture.

In the fall of 1562, three "private" ships were fitted out,—the *Solomon*, of one hundred and twenty tons burden, the *Swallow*, of one hundred tons, and the *Jonas*, a bark of only forty tons. The vessels were manned by less than a hundred men, "for feare of" sickness and other "inconveniences, whereunto men in long voyages are commonly subject," and with a cargo of English goods aboard, the little fleet set sail in October, 1562, and laid a course for the island of Teneriffe, where Captain Hawkins "received friendly intertainement" at the hands of Senor de Ponte and his friends.

"From thence hee passed to Sierra Leona, upon the coast of Guinea, which place by the people of the country is called Tagarin, where he stayed some good time, and got into his possession, partly by the sword and partly by other meanes, to the number of 300 negroes at the least, besides other merchandises, which that Country yeldeth. With this praye he sailed over the Ocean sea unto the Island of Hispaniola, and arrived first at the port of Isabella: and there hee had reasonable utterance of his English commodities, as also of some part of his Negroes, trusting the Spaniards no further than by his owne strength he was able still to master them. From the port of Isabella he went to Porte de Plata, where he made like sales, standing always upon his gard: from thence also hee sailed to

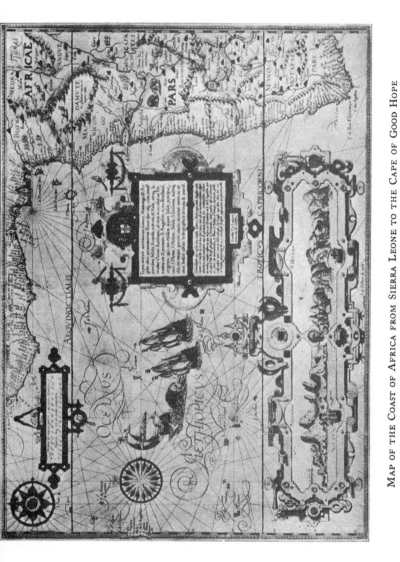

Map of the Coast of Africa from Sierra Leone to the Cape of Good Hope
From an original by Arnoldus F. a Langren, engraved in 1599, in the Macpherson Collection

Dutch Ships Trading on the Guinea Coast. From De Bry's "Voyages," 1601

(A) Ship. (B) Negro merchants. (C) How goods are passed from the canoes to the shore. (D) Where the merchants have to pay a tax to the chief. (E) Canoe being carried up the beach.

Monte Christi;* another port on the north side of Hispaniola, and the last place of his touching, where he had peaceable trafique and made vent of the whole nomber of his Negroes: for which he received in those 3 places, by way of exchange, such quantity of merchandise, that he did not onely lade his owne 3 shippes with hides, ginger, sugers, and some quantitie of pearles, but he fraighted also two other hulkes with hides and other like commodities, which he sent to Spaine. And thus leaving the Island, hee returned and disimboked,† passing out by the Islands of the Caycos,‡ without further entring into the Bay of Mexico, in this his first voyage to the West India, and so with prosperous successe and much gaine to himselfe and the aforesaid adventurers, he came home and arrived in the moneth of September 1563."§

In attempting to dispose of part of his gains in Spain, Hawkins displayed an almost incredible assurance. He professed to rely on old commercial treaties between the two countries, but when his second in command arrived in Cadiz, the cargoes were promptly seized and half of the profits of the venture were thus lost. Moreover, an order was at once dispatched to the West Indies absolutely forbidding any future trade with English vessels.

The success of Captain Hawkins' first slaving voyage was so great that he had no difficulty in obtaining powerful backing for a second interloping venture. Even the queen became a shareholder and lent the expedition the *Jesus of Lubeck*, a vessel of seven hundred tons that had been bought for the English navy, by Henry VIII, from the Hanse traders of Lubeck. Elizabeth's stake in the venture may be judged from the fact that the *Jesus* was valued at £4,000, about £40,000 in present day values.

* Isabella, Port Plata and Monte Christi were all ports on the north shore of Hispaniola, or St. Domingo.

† Disimboked: *i.e.,* went into the main ocean.

‡ The Caicos bank, north of St. Domingo.

§ Hakluyt, *The principal Navigations, Voyages, and Discoveries made by the English Nation*, London, 1589.

The slaving fleet of four vessels, consisting of the *Jesus*, 700 tons; the ship *Solomon*, 140 tons; the bark *Tiger*, 50 tons; and the pinnace *Swallow*, 30 tons, supplied with ordnance and well victualled and manned by 170 men, sailed from Plymouth, Oct. 18, 1564, bound for Teneriffe and the information that Senor de Ponte might be able to furnish.

The sailing orders, governing the southerly voyage, were as follows:

"The small shippes to be always a head and a weather of the *Jesus*, and to speake, twise a day with the *Jesus*, at least.

"If in the day the Ensigne bee over the poope of the *Jesus*, or in the night two lights, then shall all the shippes speake with her.

"If there be three lights aboord the *Jesus*, then doth she cast about.

"If the weather be extreme, that the small shippes cannot keep companie with the *Jesus*, then all to keep companie with the *Solomon*, and foorthwith to repaire to the Island of Teneriffe, to the Northward of the road of Sirroes.

"If any happen to any misfortune, then to shewe two lights and to shoote off a piece of Ordnance.

"If any loose company, and come in sight again, to make three yawes [*veerings of the ship*] and strike [*lower*] the Myson [*the mizzen sail*] three times.

"Serve God daly [*have daily prayers*], love one another, preserve your victuals, beware of fire, and keepe good companie [*the fleet keep together*]."

When only three days out a great storm arose and continued for a day and a night so that the little fleet lost company and Hawkins put into the port of Ferrol, on the Spanish coast, to refit. While here, the brigantine *Minion*, one of Queen Elizabeth's ships, came in with news of a disaster that a few days before had befallen her consort, the *Merlin* of London.

"Through the negligence of one of her gunners, the powder in the gunners' roome was set on fire, which with the first blast struck out her poope, and therewithall lost three meen, besides many sore burned (which escaped by the Brigantine being at her sterne), and immediately, to the great losse of the owners and mose horrible sight to the beholders, she sanke before their eyes."

Captain Hawkins' fleet reached Teneriffe early in November and after coming to anchor in the port of Adecia he hoisted out his ship's pinnace and went ashore proposing to send word of his arrival to Senor de Ponte, who lived at Santa Cruix, twenty leagues distant. As the boat neared the share, a company of some eighty men, armed with harquebusses, halberts, pikes, swords and targets, suddenly appeared and disputed his landing. Hawkins at once cried out that he was a friend of Senor de Ponte, to whom he desired to send a letter, and the commander "put his men aside." Two days later Senor de Ponte arrived and "gave him as gentle entertainment as if he had been his own brother."

The ships reached Alcatraz island, off the African coast and south of the river Gambia, early in December, after various adventures. One day, on the voyage down the coast, the ship's pinnace, with two men in her, sailing beside the *Jesus*, by the neglect of the men was overset. The wind was high and before the ship could be brought about, the overturned pinnace was out of sight and there was small hope of her recovery. But Captain Hawkins, "having well marked which way the pinnesse was by the Sunne, appointed 24 of the lustiest rowers in the greate boat to rowe to windewards and so recovered, contrary to all men's expectations, both the pinnesse and the men sitting upon the keele of her."

While riding at anchor at Alcatraz island, the two barks went to another island and landed eighty men in armor for the purpose of capturing slaves. But the negroes were wary and fled into the woods "leaping and turning their tailes, that it was most strange to see and gave us great pleasure to behold them," wrote John Sparke, a gentleman adventurer who accompanied Hawkins on this voyage.*

As his men were unable to find the towns where these negroes lived, Hawkins continued his southerly course and three days later, on the 12th of December, 1564, came to anchor at an island called Sambula. The negroes living there were Sapies, and three years before they had been conquered by the Samboses (the modern Sambos), a tribe that lived beyond Sierra Leone. The men of the fleet were kept busy going ashore every day to capture the negroes, burning and spoiling their towns, and many were taken, none of whom, however, turned out to be of the Sambos tribe. They had fled to the mainland at the first alarm.

On the beach were found about fifty canoes,—dugouts about twenty-four feet long and three feet wide, having a beak head and carved sides painted in red and blue. These were able to carry twenty to thirty men, the rowers standing upright. Sparke comments that four rowers and a steersman, in one of these canoes, could make as good time as a pair of oars in a wherry, in the Thames at London.

By the 21st of December, the raiding parties had taken all the negroes they could find and had also carried on board as much fruit, rice and other food as they could stow, so on that day the fleet made sail for the river called Callowsa, the Portuguese being located there about twenty leagues from the sea. Hawkins left his two ships at the mouth of the river and going up trafficked with the Portuguese and three days later started on his return with two caravels loaded with negroes.

Misfortune befell him, however, on the way down the river, for the Portuguese had told him of a negro town called Bimba, located near the river bank, where there was a great quantity of gold and only forty men and a hundred women and children. Captain Hawkins and his men were in high spirits over their success thus far and

* Hakluyt, *The principal Navigations, Voyages, and Discoveries made by the English Nation*, London, 1589.

sighting an easy capture of an additional hundred slaves, to say nothing of the gold known to be in the village, forty armed men, with Portuguese guides, were landed at the indicated point. The men had been ordered to keep together for mutual protection and offense, but on reaching the negro village the company broke up into ones and twos in a mad search for the gold. In the midst of the ransacking of the houses some two hundred negroes fell upon them and many of Hawkins' men were wounded and all driven back to the boats in confusion, where several were drowned and others perished in the deep ooze.

"Thus wee returned backe," wrote Sparke, "somewhat discomforted, although the Captaine in a singular wise manner, with countenance very cheerful outwardly, as though he did little weigh the death of his men, nor yet the great hurt of the rest, although his heart inwardly was broken in pieces for it, done to this ende, that the Portingals, being with him, should not presume to resist against him, or take ocasion to put him to further displeasure or hindrance, for the death of our men: having gotten by our going ten Negroes and lost seven of our best men, whereof Master Field, Captaine of the *Solomon*, was one, and we had 27 of our men hurt."

The barks and the caravels reached the ships at the mouth of the river on the 28th of December and two days later the fleet set sail for Taggarin, across the river from where now stands Freetown, the capital of the Sierra Leone, where a colony of liberated slaves was founded in 1791 by Englishmen. From here the two barks and both the boats went into a river called the Casseroes and brought back negroes. The *Swallow* also went up the river "about her traffik, where they saw great townes of the Negroes, and Canoes that had three score men in a peece: there they understood of the Portingals, of a great battell, betweene them of the Sierra Leona side, and them of Taggarin: they of Sierra Leona had prepared 300 canoes to invade the other. The time was appointed not past 6 daies after our departure from thence, which we would have seene, to the intent we might have taken some of them, had it not been for the death and sickness of our men, which came by the contagiousness of the place, which made us to haste away."

The ships had difficulty in watering while lying here. Soon after anchoring, the empty water casks were put ashore and filled with water to season them, intending afterwards to fill with fresh water. While the men were ashore, some of them at their boats, they were set upon by negroes and a number were wounded. The negroes also cut the hoops from twelve of the water butts, which was a serious loss considering the water supply required for so many people during the voyage to the West Indies. Again, just before sailing, some of the *Solomon's* men went ashore at night to fill water casks and just as they were ready to leap on land they espied a negro standing on a rock with nine or ten others behind him, who immediately disappeared among the rocks. This put fear into the hearts of the sailors and they returned at once to the ship. The next day it was learned from the Portuguese, that the king of Sierra Leone had designed to capture some of the sailors. "But God, who worketh all things for the best, would not have it so, and by him wee escaped without danger, his name bee praysed for it," afterwards wrote John Sparke.

The slaving fleet set sail for the West Indies on Jan. 19, 1565, and during the voyage was becalmed for twenty-eight days, to say nothing of experiencing contrary winds and a tornado or two. As the store of fresh water was none too great, before long both Englishmen and negroes were pinched "and that which was worst, put us in such feare that many never thought to have reached to the Indies, without great death of Negroes and of ourselves; but Almightie God, who never suffereth his elect to perish, sent us the sixteenth of Februarie, the ordinarie Breese, which is the Northwest wind, which never left us till we came to an Island of the Cannybals, called Sancta Dominica, where we arrived the ninth of March." They came to a desolate part of the island where the men were unable to find fresh water, save some rain water that remained in a puddle in a dale, "whereof we filled for our Negroes."

A week later, Margarite, an island off the coast of Venezuela, was reached, where they obtained meat and supplies from the alcade, but the Spanish governor would have nothing to do with them and sent a caravel to the viceroy with news of their arrival. Word came back forbidding all traffic and soon all the inhabitants of the town, including the governor, abandoned their homes and fled to the mountains. With plenty of fresh supplies and a full cargo of negro slaves aboard, the fleet set sail for Cumana, on the Spanish main, where they found soldiers newly arrived and so were not able to sell a negro. "A marvelous goodly watering place," was found about two leagues from Cumana, where fresh water came into the sea and where black-haired Indians, wearing no beards, came aboard bringing cakes made of a "kinde of corne called Maize, in bigness of a pease, the eare whereof is much like to a teasell, but a span in length, having thereon a number of graines." They also brought hens, potatoes and pineapples which were traded for beads, pewter, whistles, glasses, knives and other trifles.

On March 28, 1565, the fleet again set sail and the next day passed near the island of Tortuga and two days later Captain Hawkins, sailing near the coast in the pinnace belonging to the *Jesus*, saw many Caribs on the shore and made in to trade with them, narrowly escaped capture—"as God would have it." On April 3d, he reached Burboroata, near the present town of La Guaira, in Venezuela, where by a show of strength and persuasive guile he was permitted to bring his ships into the harbor and also to obtain from the Spanish officials a license to sell thirty "lean and sicke Negroes which he had on his shippe like[ly] to die upon his hands, having little or no refreshing for them."

The sale of these negroes went on slowly. The Spaniards claimed that the price asked was too high, and Hawkins "shewed his writings what he paid for his Negroes, declaring also the great charge he was at in his shipping and men's wages." Another grievance was the customs charge amounting to thirty ducats on each slave (about £66, in modern money). The governor would not abate this amount so Hawkins showed his teeth and with "one hundred men well armed with bowes, arrowes, harquebusses and pikes, hee marched to the towne wardes, and beying perceived by the Governor, hee straight with all expedition sent messengers to know his request." When told that 7½ per cent duty was enough and if it was not granted that Hawkins and his men "would displease" them, the governor quickly sent word that "all things should bee to his content."

While at anchor here a French slaver, the *Green Dragon* of Havre, Captain Bontemps, arrived from the Guinea coast with news that he had been driven off by Portuguese galleys before completing his cargo of slaves; that Capt. David Carlet with his supercargo and a dozen sailors had been taken prisoners and accounts of other misadventures, of loss of men and great lack of fresh water that had occurred, "which was most sorrowful for us to understand," wrote Master Sparke.

Curaçao was reached on the 6th of May, where they had difficulty in finding an anchorage. Here they trafficked for hides "and found great refreshing both of beefe, mutton and lambes," the flesh being so abundant that when they brought the hides the flesh was given to them so that "the worst in the ship thought scorn not onely of mutton, but also of sodden lambe, which they disdained to eate unrosted."

Rio Hache, on the coast of what is now Bolivia, was reached on the nineteenth and the Spanish authorities denying Hawkins a license to trade he replied, that "seeing that they had sent him this for his supper, hee would in the morning bring them as good a breakfast." When morning came he shot off a whole-culverin, to summon the town, and with a hundred men in armor, rowed towards the shore. In his great boat were two brass falcons and in the bow of each of the other boats were small cannon called "double-bases." Drawn up on the beach were thirty horsemen and about one hundred and fifty foot soldiers "making great bragges with their cries," but a round from the two falcons "put them in no small feare," so that "they broke their arraie and fell flatte to the grounde," and then "dispersed themselves." Hawkins landed his men and began marching on the town, which brought out the Spanish treasurer, in great fear, who granted all demands and "so we made our traffique quietly with them," continues the narrative.

While lying in the river they saw many "crocodiles" and lost a negro who was carried away by one as he was filling water casks by the river bank. "His nature is ever when he would have his praie, to crie and sobbe like a Christian bodie, to provoke them to come to him and then he snatcheth at them, and thereupon came this proverbe that is applied unto women when they weepe, *Lachryma Crocodili,* the meaning whereof is, that as the Crocodile when he crieth, goeth about most to deceive, so doth a woman most commonly when she weepeth."

Having disposed of his entire cargo of negroes, Captain Hawkins set sail on May 31st for the island of Jamaica, proposing there to complete his cargo of hides, but mistaking the island for Hispaniola he ran by to the leeward and was unable to get up again by reason of the force of the current, so the little fleet made for Santa Cruz on the island of Cuba, which also was overpassed and thereby was lost a rich profit on a great store of hides to be had at either place. Storms and contrary winds in time brought on great want of fresh water. On the 16th of June, the Isle of Pines was reached, where they "reasonably watered" from brackish pools of rainwater found near the shore and made haste to get away from the exposed anchorage. Scarcely were the anchors weighed and foresails set than a storm swept down on them and one of the barks was obliged to cut her cable in hawse in order to save herself.

After passing Cape St. Antonio, at the westerly end of Cuba, they sailed to the westward, "to fetch the wind," and also to take advantage of the current which brought them in sight of the Dry Tortugas on July 5th, where they loaded a pinnace with birds and took many turtles; also finding many turtle's eggs which "they did eat very sweetly." An effort was then made to reach the harbor at Havana, but it was passed in the night and with a short store of water, so that "every man was contented to pinch his own bellie," a course was set for the Florida coast. The little fleet, swept along by the Gulf Stream, made rapid northing and after one or two mishaps reached the river of May, now the St. Johns, where a Huguenot colony had been established three years before. Captain Hawkins found the settlement greatly weakened and with only a small supply of food. He sold them twenty barrels of meal, four pipes of beans and other necessaries and also the fifty-ton bark, for which he received seven hundred crowns.

The homeward voyage was continued on July 28, 1565, and was prolonged by contrary winds, so that victuals were scanted. On August 23d they were on the bank off Newfoundland, in one hundred and thirty fathoms. A great many cod were caught here, which relieved their distress. A week later two French fisherman were spoken and more fish were obtained in exchange for Spanish gold and silver; "but they, not looking for anything at all, were glad in themselves to meete with such goode intertainement at sea, as they had at our handes. After which departure from them, with a good large winde the 20 of September we came to Padstow in Cornewall, God be thanked, in safetie, with the losse of 20 persons in all the voyage, and profitable to the venturers of the said voyage, as also to the whole Realme, in bringing home both golde, silver, pearles and other jewels great store. His name therefore be praised for evermore, Amen."

CHAPTER III

THE VOYAGE OF THE SHIP *HANNIBAL* OF LONDON, IN 1693

IT WAS my misfortune, as well as many others, this last war with
France, in my voyage home from Venice and Zant, in the *William* of two hundred tons and twenty guns, to fall into the
clutches of three great French men of war of seventy guns each, in
the soundings, about sixty leagues S.W. from Cape Clear in Ireland.
There being so great an inequality in our strength, and no hopes of
escaping, I thought it prudence to submit without any resistance,
and not have my men killed and wounded to no purpose; for they
had five hundred men each, and I but thirty in all; therefore I was
forced to let might overcome right, and upon summons by a shot
athwart our fore foot, from the *Crown*, of seventy brass guns,
which came first up with us, to strike our ensign and become their
prize.*

After my return to England, I was for some time destitute of
imployment, until Sir Jeffrey Jeffreys, Knt., out of his extraordinary
generosity and good will to me, understanding that the ship *Hannibal* of four hundred and fifty tons, and thirty-six guns, was to be
sold, gave me orders to buy her. Having done this he was pleased
to deposit the money for her presently out of his own pocket; and
after, by his interest, to bring in his worthy brother, John Jeffreys,
Esq.; Sam. Stanyer, Esq.; then sub-governor of the African company, and some other eminent merchants, to be part-owners with
me, and then to recommend me and the ship to the Royal African
Company of England; from whom, upon his account I found ac-
ceptance. Being entered into their service, on a trading voyage to
Guinea, for elephant's teeth, gold, and negro slaves; and having the

* This early narrative of a slaving voyage has been abstracted from Capt.
Thomas Phillips' "Journal," printed in Churchill's *Collection of Voyages*, vol. VI,
London, 1746.

needful cargoes on board wherewith to purchase them, as well as supplies of merchandise, stores, &c. for the company's castles and factories; my business being compleated at London, I took boat for Gravesend the fifth of September in the year 1693, and got on board about eleven at night, with money to pay my men their river-pay, and one month's pay advance-money, as per agreement.

Sunday the 10th in the morning, we broke ground from Gravesend, and drove with the ebb to the upper end of the Hope, where we chop'd to an anchor, and in the evening I went up to Gravesend.

Tuesday the 12th. This morning about three o'clock we got under sail, with a brave gale at W. At nine we were past the Nore, where we drove till one in the evening, waiting for water, at which time we bore away for the red sand, and about four got through the narrow, and at six anchored off the North Foreland, in nine fathom water.

Wednesday the 13th. At four this morning we got up our anchors, with the wind at S.W. and after several tacks, about eleven we came to an anchor in the Downs, in eight fathom water. We were detained in the Downs with every blustering weather and contrary winds until the twenty-fifth of October when the wind veering to the north, we got up our anchors, and about seven in the evening were under sail. At noon the next day we saw the isle of Wight, bearing north-west. We got our anchors up, and our ship clear for the sea, and removed two of our guns that were open in the waist into the after-ports in the great cabin.

Friday the 27th. From yesterday noon till twelve this day we have had a brave topsail gale from north to north-east, steering away west. We run from four in the evening yesterday, 112′ west, by the best computation I could make, for our log-line breaking in the night, we lost our log and were forced to make guess-work. We saw many ships on all sides, but spoke with none, except one Portuguese of two-hundred tons, bound from Oporto to London, laden with wine, for some quantities of which commodity we had a great desire to traffick with him; but it blowing so hard, and night being come on,

PROSPECT OF THE CUSTOM HOUSE, LONDON, IN 1714, WITH SHIPPING OF THE PERIOD
From an engraving by John Harris, in the Macpherson Collection

NEGRO SLAVES FROM LOANGO, AFRICA

From an engraving in Stedman's *Narrative of an Expedition to Surinam*, London, 1796

hinder'd our design, so that we bid him farewell, and left him to proceed on his voyage, as we did on ours. Unbent our cables, and clap'd on house-boards, clear'd our ship, and appointed by men their quarters in case of engaging an enemy, having seventy men belonging to the ship, and thirty-three of the African company's passengers, for their castles in Guiney, so that we made in all, men and boys, a hundred and three.

Wednesday the first. At three this morning, the mate that had the watch came to acquaint me that they discover'd four strange ships with lights to windward of us. When I came upon deck I perceiv'd one with a light standing as we did, upon which we got our half ports off,—chests and hammocks up, and order'd every man to their several quarters, to get them clear for an engagement. About eleven, being clear day, we had all things in order, and ready for a fight, at which time I plainly saw four tall ships with all sails set standing directly with us. I am sure they were men of war of sixty and seventy guns each, as near as I could discover through my glass, but of what nation I could not tell, tho' we had great reason to believe them French, our frigats seldom or never cruising so far to the S. and W. They stood towards us with all sails set in a line, upon which I made a signal, by hoisting and lowering my ensign four times, to give notice to Capt. Shurley of our new companions, and crowded with all sails to speak with him, he being about a mile distant upon my lee bow, and the only one of our fleet then in company, we having lost the rest last night and the night before. When I came up with him it blew so hard that we could not hear each other, tho' we had good speaking-trumpets, therefore we were forced to endeavour to understand one another by signs, by which I perceived that he was of my opinion, that since they were so many, not to stand the brunt with them, two to one being odds at football, we being deep loaden merchant ships, and they frigats, built and fitted only for fight, but rather to go away large, and endeavour, by often varying our course, to lose them, it blowing very hard at S. and being thick dirty weather, which was likely to continue and increase, which I was not sorry for, since I do verily believe it saved us a French voyage; therefore we hal'd up our mainsails, clapt the helm aweather, and bore away under foresail and maintopsail, with two reefs in, upon the cap, W.N.W. and N.W. till nine, handed maintopsail, and went away N.W. till ten, having lost sight of the ships that pursued us e'er since we went large. At eleven, it blowing a hard storm, having very thick weather and grown sea, lest we should lose each other, Capt. Shurley brought to under a mizen; my foresail being up I went to do the like, but in haling out our mizen the strap of the sheet-block broke, so that e'er we could brail him up he was by the violence of the gale split to pieces, which occasion'd us to lower the yard down and unbend him, upon which the ship labouring much for want of sail, found it convenient to set the mainsail, and having got the tack aboard, e'er we could gather the sheet aft we split the mainsail, and were forced to hale down the yard and furl him, and bear away before the wind N. and N. by W. with only the bunt of our foresail loose. In furling our main-sail one of our seamen, John Southern, being careless of himself, fell off the yard-arm and was drown'd, which I was extremely sorry for, but it was beyond human power to save him, it blowing a mere fret of wind, and a very great sea, and having no sails to command the ship.

Tuesday the 2d. From twelve yesterday until two in the evening, we went away N. with our bare poles, running four miles an hour; at which time, having brought to a new mizen and reef'd him, we hoisted the yard and set him, and brought her to under a mizen, then unbent our mailsail that was split, and with much pains and trouble, we bent another; and having reef'd him we furl'd him; About four we furl'd our fore-sail snug, and hoisted the mizen stay-sail, to keep the ship to, and her head upon the sea, she labouring most dreadfully. At twelve last night the violence of the storm being abated, we set the main-sail, and lay under it and mizen till daylight; when having righted up the ship a little, to my great trouble and surprise, we found that our fore-mast was sprung about three feet above the partners in the forecastle; the crack being very large, and opening above an inch upon every rent of the ship, which, to see, made my heart ake; we found it likewise upon searching, to be almost rotten to the heart in that place; whereupon I sent for my officers, to consult what was most proper to be done upon this unexpected accident, and how best to secure him; but finding some of them begin to urge that there was no proceeding on so long a voyage with such a mast, and that it was convenient to bear up for Plymouth, while we were so near it, to furnish ourselves with another, I thought it convenient to quash this motion in the bud, and declar'd I was resolv'd to proceed on my voyage, though I should be forced to go with a jury-mast, rather than return again to England; and forthwith order'd my carpenters to go to work to secure him, by paying four new capston bars of good oak, and nine feet long each, round him, where he was sprung, and spike them very well, and afterwards clapt four good wooldings upon him, which I was in hopes would sufficiently secure him, we every day approaching nearer a fair weather country; and when our carpenters had done what I had order'd them, it seem'd very firm, and did not complain all the voyage after. In crowding yesterday morning with maintop-sail to speak with Capt. Shurley, upon sight of the four strange ships, we wrench'd the head of our main-mast; and this morning set some men to woold the hull of the maintop-mast, to the head of the main-mast, to keep him fast, else the cap would slue much where the head of the mast was wrung.

Saturday the 18th. This morning we found out that one of the Royal African Company's soldiers, for their castles in Guiney, was a woman, who had enter'd herself into their service under the name of John Brown, without the least suspicion, and had been three months on board without any mistrust, lying always among the other passengers, and being as handy and ready to do any work as any of them; and I believe she had continued undiscover'd till our arrival in Africa, had not she fallen very sick, which occasion'd our surgeon to visit her, and order'd her a glister, which when his mate went to administer, he was surpriz'd at what he discovered, which occasion'd him to make a farther inquiry, which, as well as her confession, manifesting the truth of her sex, he came to acquaint me of it, whereupon, in charity, as well as in respect to her sex, I order'd her a private lodging apart from the men, and gave the taylor some ordinary stuffs to make her woman's cloaths; in recompence for which she prov'd very useful in washing my linen, and doing what else she could, till we deliver'd her with the rest at Cape Coast castle. She was about twenty years old, and a likely black girl.

Wednesday the 22d. About four o'clock in the morning it being day-light, Pico Tenerif bore due east of us, at which time being near Oratava road, we discern'd two sail between us and the shore, one of which we perceived to be a ship, and the other seem'd a barca longa; in a short time we saw the ship standing off to us, with all sails set, whereupon we tack'd off to the N. to have time to put our ship in a posture of defence, in case she prov'd an enemy, and with all expedition got our hatch ports off, our chests and hamocks up, our close quarters up, guns and small arms all ready, and about twelve we were every way clear and ready for an engagement, at which time we furl'd our main-sail, and handed all our small sails, flung our arms, clapp'd on our stoppers, our puddings, and plattings under our parrels, and being but little wind hal'd up our fore-sail, and lay by for the ship that was so earnest to speak with us.

Thursday the 23d. From noon yesterday we had but faint small breezes of wind until three in the evening, at which time the ship that stood after us was got within random gun-shot of us, appearing a fine long snug frigate; so that now we no longer doubted but she was an enemy, therefore letting fly my colours, we fir'd a shot athwart his fore foot; upon which he shew'd an English ensign; but for all his cheat we knew what he was, and were in all kinds ready to give him his welcome, we jogging easily under our fighting sails till four, at which time, being within carbine shot of us, he run out his lower tier of guns (which I did not expect, nor was well pleased to see) nine of each side, and struck his false

colours, and hoisted the French white sheet. I perceiv'd he was resolv'd to pluck a crow with me; therefore, after drinking a dram,
and encouraging all, order'd all my men to their guns, to behave
themselves courageously, and expected his broad-side, which when
within pistol-shot, he gave us, and his volley of small shot. We return'd his civility very heartily with ours; after which he shot a-head
of us, and brought to, and fell along our larboard side, and gave us
his other broad-side, as we did him; then each of us loaded and
fired as fast as we could, until ten o'clock at night, when his foretop
mast came by the board; then he fell astern of us, and made the
best of his way to lee-ward, with his boat towing a-head, and took
his leave of us. We gave him a levet with our trumpets, and what
guns we had loaded, to bid him farewell, being heartily glad to be
rid of such a troublesome guest. I was extremely glad that by God's
assistance we defended the ship, though she was most miserably
shatter'd and torn in her mast and rigging, having had eleven shot
in our main mast, three quite through him, and several lodg'd in
him and gaul'd him standing three or four inches deep; eight shot
in our fore-mast, two quite through; our main-top shot to pieces;
our main-topmast splinter'd half away; our mizen yard shot in two
pieces; our sprit-sail, top-mast jack, and jack staff, shot away; our
ancient staff shot by the board, so that had no colours flying most
part of the ingagement but the king's pendant, which, by authority
of my letter of mart, I fought under; we had several shot through
our yards, with much more too long to insert. As to the rigging, I
know not how to begin or end with it, it was so tore by long bars of
iron they fired; our main shrouds we were forced to knot in fourteen places, and had but one shroud standing of the larboard side
when Monsieur tow'd off. We knotted our fore shrouds, in nine
places; our main-top chain and main tie were shot to pieces, so that
the yard hung wholly by the parrel and pudding: our stay, sheets
and tacks were shot in several places; and of the running rigging
few or none escaped their small shot, which flew very thick; we had
not above thirty shot placed in our hull, four of which were under

water; he fired very high for the most part, at our mast, yards and rigging, to bring our mast by the board, and had we had a top-sail gale, they must have all gone away; but it was our good fortune to have smooth water (a thing not common in that place), and little wind, until we had opportunity, by stoppers, preventers, knotting and splicing, to secure them indifferently. We fired low all into his hull, and loaded our low guns (which were all demiculverin) constantly with both double and round shot, and our quarter deck guns with round shot, and tin cases full of musket bullets, so that we must certainly have killed him a great many men; our three boats and booms were shot thro' in many places; and we had a suit of sails quite spoil'd, some being shot thro' like strainers. We had five men kill'd outright, and about thirty-two wounded; among the last was my brother, my gunner, carpenter, and boatswain; the carpenter had his arm shot off, and three others their legs; five or six of my best men were dreadfully blown up by their carelessness in laying the lighted matches among some cartridges of powder; our harper had his scull fractur'd by a small shot; the rest are but slight small shot and splinter wounds, and bruises,—and hope will do all well; our surgeon, Mr. William Gordon, being a diligent man, and an excellent artist in his profession. The fight lasted six hours, from four till ten o'clock, being all that while within pistol shot, little wind, and small water, and firing as fast as both sides could load our guns. We often gave them huzza's during the engagement, and they would answer with *Vive le roys;* but when he towed away under our stern his note was changed, for I never heard such dreadful screeching and howling as was on board of him, so that he must needs have a great many men wounded. I judged him to be about 48 guns, and a man of war. After he left us we steered W. by S. with a small gale at N.E. and spent all the night in fixing our rigging as well as we could, to be in some posture to receive him, if he should incline to have another bout with us in the morning; but our men being tired all day, and the best of them kill'd or wounded, we could do but little, tho' they had all the encouragement that I could give them and as much punch as they would drink. This morning, when it was light, we saw the enemy about three leagues distance, standing to the northward from us, having, I presume, had his belly-full the night before, and which, without fallacy, I was very glad of, not desiring to have any more to do with such a quarrelsome fellow.

Friday the 24th. These twenty-four hours we have spent in knotting our shrouds, and fixing our other rigging as well as we could; knotted our main shrouds in fourteen places, and the fore-shrouds in nine, and after set them up very tort, to secure our poor shattered mast; we were forced to keep our chain-pump and both hand-pumps constantly going, to keep the ship free, she making a great deal of water, through the four shot holes rec'd under water, which we could not come at to stop effectually by reason of the sea. This day we lived on bread and cheese and punch, not being able to dress any meat, by reason our hearth and furnaces were shot thro', which our armourer was about mending. We had a hogshead of brandy shot in our lazaretta, whose loss we much regretted. The poor ship looked miserably with her shot rigging dangling about, and as full of splinters as a carpenter's yard full of chips.

Sunday the 26th. Yesterday in the evening we set up our shrouds tort again, the heat of the weather and the drawing of the knots having much slackened them; our shot mizen-yard being splic'd and fish'd, we bent a new mizen to him, and got him up and set him; we unbent our foresail (which had thirty large shot-holes thro' him, some half-yard wide, done with the long bars of iron they fired, and innumerable musket-shot holes) and brought to another; we woolded three large crows to the foremast, to succour a great gaul about eight inches deep which he had received in the engagement, about ten foot above the forecastle; set our carpenters to work about mending the shot-holes in our bolts.

Monday the 27th. Yesterday's evening our carpenters spent in mending the bottom of our yaul, so that now we have one boat that will swim, ready to be hoisted out upon any sudden accident of a man's falling overboard, or the like. We kept our pumps constantly plying, to free the ship, in which the Royal African Company's soldiers did us good service in the day-time. This morning, as soon as it was clear light, we saw a ship upon our weather bow, bearing of us S. by W. distance about a league, standing as we did; immediately we called up all hands to put the ship in a fighting posture, and in truth our men were very dextrous at it, so that we were clear for a fight in less than an hour's time (being improved by the last engagement). In about half an hour after we were every where ready, we perceived her to hale close upon a wind, crowding with all the sail she could towards the Barbary coast. She seemed to us a good ship, and I do believe it might be Capt. Daniell in the *Mediteranean*, bound to Angola. When we saw him shun us we kept on our own course being not very desirous to force a quarrel, having so lately been well bang'd, tho' all our men that were unwounded were very resolute to give him a rough salute, had he had any thing to say to us; he keeping still close hal'd, about twelve o'clock was out of sight. We then put our half ports on again, unflung our yards, and got off our close quarters, and set our carpenters about mending the rest of our boats. This false alarm hinder'd the paying of our tropick bottles. This day our bag-piper's leg was cut off a little below the knee.

Saturday the 2d. From noon yesterday until six in the evening we steered along the island of St. Jago, at which time took in our small, and hal'd up our low sails, and stood to the E. off, under our topsails only, Santa Mayo then bearing E.N.E. distance five leagues. At ten we braced our fore-topsail to the mast, and lay by for daylight to get into the harbour of Praya, to rift our ship; at six in the morning made sail and stood in for the port, and about ten we got in. We rid somewhat more than a cable's length from each shore, and about a mile from the bottom of the bay, which is fine and sandy, with a large cocoanut orchard near the water side.

Sunday the 3d. Yesterday we unbent the main-sail; and having lowered the yard, got it fore and aft, in order to splice a piece ten foot long to the starboard yard-arm, where it was broke. About three o'clock this morning got our guns over, and gave the ship a heel to port, in order to stop our leaks on the starboard side, where we received three shots under water afore the chestree. Our carpenters spent till two in the evening in stopping them, our men in the mean time giving the ship a scrub as low as they could; then we heeled the ship the other way, and found a very large shot-hole in the larboard-bow, about a foot under water. Our carpenters spent the rest of the day in stopping that, and righted the ship before night. About nine this morning I went with some of my officers to pay my respects to the governor at St. Jago town, having our trumpets in the pinnace's head.

After we had rowed about seven miles, we came about a point into the bay near the town. We run our boat ashore right against the gate; where being landed, and seeing only a few negroes and children, our trumpets sounded a levet, which soon brought an officer down to us, who conducted us to the governor's palace at the upper part of the town; where we saw no body but negro women, who talked to us many smutty English words, making lascivious undecent gestures with their bodies, which were all naked, excepting a little clout about their waste, hanging down to the middle of the thigh.

We were informed that the governor was at church; but our trumpets had alarmed him so, that we had not waited long ere he appeared, advancing towards us at the head of the congregation. There were two young captains and the priest accompanied him, his horse being led after him in pretty good equipage. When he was come where we were, we saluted him with our hats, which he and his company returned very courteously. Then he desir'd us to walk in, and led us thro' a court into a large hut, with an iron balcony facing the sea, towards which it had a fine prospect. After we were seated I acquainted him we were come to pay our respects to him, and gave him an account of our voyage, and what induced us to put into his port, desiring he would permit us to furnish ourselves with what fresh water and provisions we had occasion for. He replied, That since he was perswaded we were upon an honest account, we might furnish ourselves with what e'er the island afforded; which favour I thankfully acknowledged. I fancied him all this time a little uneasy by reason he saw so many of my officers and passengers with me, and that he had an inclination to give me some treat, but that he was afraid they would devour him; therefore calling one of them to me, I whispered him to go with the rest and take a walk for an hour; which they soon did, making their excuse to the governor, that they had a desire to see the town, which he was not backward to grant them, none remaining with me but my brother.

Soon after they were gone, we had a napkin laid, and a loaf of good white bread; then he went into the next room and brought out a box of marmalad, and a square case bottle half full of Madeira wine in which he drank to me; but had it not been out of perfect civility, I had rather have pledged him in water; for it was so thick, foul and hot, that it had like to have made me commit an indecency in his excellency's presence; but having laid a foundation of good punch in the morning aboard, it fortified my stomach so as that I had power to contain myself. Afterwards I gave him an invitation to come and dine aboard our ship, where he should find a cordial welcome, as well as all due respect. He received the invitation kindly, but assured me, that he had not been on board any ship since he had been governor there, and that if he were inclined to go, the inhabitants would lose their lives ere they would permit him, lest any harm should befal him, or tricks be put upon him, as there have been on some governors of these islands, by pirates and privateers, who when they have got them aboard, have carried them away if they did not forthwith give orders to bring them such a quantity of provisions as they demanded, for which they would pretend to give a bill of exchange payable at London, but drawn upon John-a-Nokes, or the pump at Algate, as Avery's bill was to the governor of St. Thomas's isle.

Monday the 4th. This day our carpenters spliced a piece to the main-yard, and clap'd two good iron hoops and two wooldings up it. We unbent our shot topsails, and brought others to the yards; fitted our shatter'd main-stay, sent the longboat for water, of which she filled sixteen punchions. We had fine weather, and a curious easy gale at N.E. In the morning I went ashore at the cod of the bay, which I found covered with ragged merchants; some with oranges, lemons, cocoa-nuts, pine apples, bananas, &c. Here one with a couple of small hens in his hand, there another with a little monkey upon his knee; a little farther, one with a goat betwixt his legs, another near him with a hog tied to his arm, and our seamen so busy trafficking with them for old ragged shirts, drawers, or any other moveables (for nothing came amiss) that the trade was very brisk and diverting. After we had pleased ourselves some time with this rag market, we walked up the hill to deliver the cheese I had promised the governor, which I intrusted with the before-named old officer, presenting himself with another. Here I met with a gentleman of the island who was come on purpose to offer to supply me with what provisions I wanted, and to take what money I could muster, and the rest in goods for it. I gave him orders for fifteen goats, ten sheep, four hogs, sixty hens, five hundred oranges, and five hundred lemons, which he promised should be ready at the seaside in the morning. The negroes here go naked, except a cloth about their middles, and a roll of linen the women wear about their heads. The cloaths they wear are of cotton, and chequered or striped with blue. I have been told they make great quantities of these cloaths to sell, being much esteemed, and a very good commodity upon the Gold Coast in Guiney; but for my part I saw none but what the women wore; neither did any body mention or offer any such to me for sale.

Tuesday the fifth. This morning, according to promise, I found the provision we had bespoke at the water-side, which we bought very reasonably, and paid for them three pounds in Spanish money which I had picked up among my officers, and the rest in muskets, coral, and painted linen. I went and took leave of the old officer, intending to go no more ashore, and about noon returned aboard, where our men were busy setting our shrouds well up fore and aft. Our carpenters had sawed a spare maintopmast we had into two halves, with which this morning they fished the foremast, which was very crazy. After having fayed and spiked the fishes, they clap'd four good wooldings upon them. We got up our low yards, and made all clear to sail next morning. Last night Thomas Cronow, an honest stout Welshman, one of our sailors, died of his wounds received in the late engagement, one of his legs being carried off about the ancle, and half his other foot by the same shot. He was rowed some distance from the ship and his body committed to the deep.

Wednesday the 6th. This morning at four we got our stream anchor and hauser aboard, then having loosed and hoisted our top-sails, hove up our small bower, and stood out to sea, with the wind at N.E., a fine fresh gale.

Thursday the 7th. Yesterday in the evening we cleaned all fore and aft between decks; and having covered the gratings close with tarpaulins, we burnt three buckets of tar to keep the ship wholesome and prevent infection and distempers. We hoisted in our pinnace and yaul; and having clap'd the boat rope and a hauser upon the longboat, towed her astern. We unbent our cables, got up our an-chors, clap'd on house-boards, and took up one reef in our top-sails.

Saturday the 23rd. From noon yesterday we steer'd along shore for Cape Mounseradoe, with a small gale of wind. At daylight, we saw the cape, and soon after descried three vessels riding at anchor under it; one of which seem'd a large ship. We not knowing what they might be, made our ship clear, and order'd all things ready for a battle, when we perceived a boat, rowing off towards us, who hav-ing discover'd what we were, came aboard us, being the pinnace of the *East India Merchant*, Captain Shurley, my consort, who had sent her to intreat me to put in there to his assistance, he having, off the cape, had his fore-mast and fore-yard split to pieces, with a thunder-bolt, and his fore-topgallant-sail set on fire by the precedent flash of lightning. I intended to wood and water at Junco, about twelve leagues more to the E. where is a good river, and plenty of wood; but understanding this disaster that had befallen Captain Shurley, I alter'd my resolution, and made all the way I could to get into Mounseradoe road, which, with the sea breeze, I did, and about four in the evening let go my anchor in eight fathom water. We found the other two vessels to be one Gubbins, an interloper, come from Barbadoes, chiefly laden with rum, to trade for gold and slaves, of which I bought about 500 gallons of him cheap, and sold it to good advantage. The other vessel was the *Stanier* sloop, with M. Colker on board her, who was agent of Cherborough, and came thence to trade along the coast for teeth, &c.

The people here are civil and courteous, but great beggars, the king and cappashires continually haunting us for dashes (which is their word for presents). Here is store of good rice, and cheap, which they brought us in abundance; and for our better conveniency of trading with them, as well as to lodge our carpenters that lay ashore in the nights to cut wood, we erected two tents with old sails, upon the spit of sand at the mouth of the river. The chief commodity we traded for was rice, of which I bought about five tuns, paying mostly for it in booges or cawries, which are the goods they chiefly esteem, for a pint of which we could buy 30 lb. of rice. The other goods they approved of were iron bars and red Welsh plains; but they had nothing considerable to trade with us for them. We bought some fowls of them which they call "Cocadecoes," being not bigger than our English chickens, and eat dry. We also purchas'd some limes, wild oranges, pine apples, and two or three small goats. They had a few small elephants teeth, but not worth our regard.

The 28th came in here Capt. John Soans, in the *Jeffry;* and having supply'd himself with some wood, water, and rice, set sail again for the Bight, on Thursday the 3d of Jan. having left with me a packet of letters directed for Sir Jeffry Jeffreys, to be forwarded to Europe, with the first conveniency. Agent Colker, set sail for Sherberow in the 5th, and Gubbins, in the Barbadoes interloper, the same morning for the Gold Coast, by whom I sent letters to the African Company's three chief merchants at Cabo Corse Castle, signifying my agreement with the company to slave upon the Gold Coast, and bespeaking their diligence in procuring what numbers they could for me against my arrival there, with what else was needful. I was forced to stay here ten days after I had compleated my business, for Capt. Shurley to refit his ship, which at length being done, we both set sail with the morning breeze, on the 9th of Jan. 1693/4 for the coast. The negroes of this place, express'd a great affection for the English, and as much hatred to the French; two of them took Capt. Shurley's and my name, assuring us their next sons should be called so.

Saturday the 13th. Yesterday till about four in the evening, being off the river of Sestos, we came to an anchor in nine fathom water. This morning I went ashore in my pinnace with some goods to trade, and Capt. Shurley sent his with his purser in her, being so ill that he could not go himself.

About eight miles up the river is the town where king Peter their monarch lives; but I could not spare time to go and visit him, and in truth had no great inclination to venture so far in a boat, having been informed that the negroes here are very treacherous and bloody, as some of our European traders have found to their cost. The goods in demand here are brass kettles, pewter basons of several sizes, boogas or cowries, freezes, Welsh plains, red and blue, knives, &c., some of each of which we carried ashore; but they had nothing to traffick with us for them, except a few little calves teeth (for so they call the young elephants) which were not worth our notice, and which they held very dear. We bought some hens, limes, and oranges; were offer'd some rice, but much dearer than we bought at Mounseradoe, where we had supply'd ourselves.

Sunday the 14th. Finding no trade to encourage our stay at Sestos, we got up our stream-anchor this morning, and set sail with a small gale at W.

Monday the 15th. From noon yesterday we steer'd along shore till two in the evening, at which time came several canoos aboard us from Sanguin river, where the Grain or Malagetta coast begins. They brought us pepper, or, as they call it, Malagetta, which is much like our Indian pepper and for ought I know, as good. It was brought in ozier baskets. I bought 1000 weight of it at one iron bar (value in England three shillings and six pence) and a dashy of a knife or two to the broker. The reason of our buying this pepper is to give it to our negroes in their messes to keep them from the flux and dry belly-ach, which they are very incident to.

Tuesday the 16th. At noon this day we were off of Wappo, whence came off to us more canoos, with Malagetta to sell, of which I bought three hundred weight for three two-pound pewter basons. We might have bought much more, but having enough for our purpose, we turn'd them ashore, and pursue'd our course.

Wednesday the 17th. Yesterday my poor brother grew very ill and delirious; and notwithstanding all the endeavours used by my own and Capt. Shurley's doctor for his recovery, about three in the evening this day he took his leave of this troublesome world, and left me full of affliction for the loss of him. He had been sick of a malignant fever about eight days, and many of my men lay ill of the same distemper.

January the 18th. Having yesterday doubled Cape Palmas, about five in the evening we came to an anchor in nineteen fathom water, where we rode till six this morning. We got under sail, when the coffin being ready, the deceas'd was nailed up therein; and our pinnace being hoisted out, he was lower'd into her, and myself, my doctor and purser went in her to bury him, the colours of our own ship and *East-India Merchant* being lowered half-mast down, our trumpets and drums sounding and beating, as is customary upon such melancholy occasions. We row'd the corpse about ¼ of a mile from the ship to seaward; and the prayers of the church being read, I help'd to commit his body to the deep, which was the last office lay in my power to do for my dear brother. Then the *Hannibal* fired sixteen guns at ½ minute distance of time, which was the number of years he had lived in this uncertain world; and the *East-India Merchant* fired ten guns.

Sunday the 21st. At six we weigh'd anchor, and stood along to the east. About ten came two canoos aboard us from Caba-la-ho, and were follow'd by several others with stores of good teeth, which invited us to come to anchor; but ere the negroes in the canoos would come aboard, they required that the captain of the ship should come down the out side of the ship, and drop three drops of the sea water into his eye, as a pledge of friendship, and of safety for them to come aboard; which I very readily consented to and perform'd, in hopes of a good market for their large fair teeth, which I had a longing desire to purchase. Then they came aboard, but seeing so many men on deck, were mistrustful, and went into their canoos again. I was much concerned at their fearfulness, and with much persuasion prevailed on them to return, which they did, and having given each that came in a good coge of brandy, I shewed them some of my commodities, and they brought in some teeth. I was astonished when first they came near the ship, to hear no other speech come from them but "Qua, Qua, Qua, Qua," like a parcel of ducks; from which I presume this teeth coast hath had the appellation of Quaquaa coast, it reaching from Cape Palmas to Bassam Picolo, where was the first gold I meet with. I have no where upon the coast met with the negroes so shy as here, which makes me fancy they have had tricks played them by such blades as Long Ben, alias Avery, who have seiz'd them and carried them away. The goods they most covet are pewter basons, the larger the better, iron bars, knives, and large screw'd pewter jugs, which they did much affect.

Saturday the 27th. At two in the evening yesterday we got up our anchors, and sailed along shore until six, when came a four-hand canoo aboard us from Bassam, assuring us of good trade of gold and slaves in the morning, if we would anchor, and that they would stay with us all night, which we permitted them, hoisting up their canoo in the tackles, and let go our anchors in fourteen fathom water. In the morning those aboard fell to trade, of whom I took thirty-six achies of gold in fatishes for pewter and iron bars.

Sunday the 28th. The negroes yesterday promised us a good trade this day if we stay'd. Accordingly this morning came aboard of me two canoos, of which I took sixteen ounces of gold in fatishes, for iron bars, pewter, and knives, viz. for one iron bar 1½ achy, for a dozen of knives, one achy, for a four-pound pewter bason, one achy, with several knives for dashes to those that traded briskly. Here the negroes are not so well skilled in trade as upon the Gold Coast, for we could put the bank-weights upon them; but to lee-ward, on the Gold Coast, they knew our Troy weights as well as ourselves, and have weights of their own, which they compare ours with. Like-wise at this place goods yield a better price than among our factories to leeward, by reason that here they can't supply themselves at all times as they can there; therefore when they have an opportunity of ships passing by, they buy what they want, tho' they give a better price for it; but they have but small quantities of gold to trade with.

Wednesday the 31st. Last night I was taken with a violent racking pain the right side of my head; and Capt. Shurley being very ill of a fever, sent for Mr. Gordon, my doctor, to have his advice. On Sunday the pain in my head increased, and I was taken with a dimness in my eyes, that I could not see ten yards off, and a dizziness in my head, that I could not stand nor walk without assistance.

Wednesday the 13th, in the morning we got under sail, and having doubled Cape Apollonia, in the evening we came to an anchor at Axem in eight fathom water, about two miles from the Dutch fort. Here we had but little trade, therefore after we got aboard we weigh'd, and stood along shore till night, when anchored in 18 fathom water, a-breast the Brandenburg fort, near Cape Tres Puntar.

The 20th in the morning Capt. Shurley and I went ashore to our castle at Succandy, where we found the factor, Mr. Johnson, in his bed raving mad, cursing and swearing most wretchedly at us, not

in the least knowing Capt. Shurley, tho' he had a long former acquaintance with him. I pity'd from my soul this poor man, who had
plunged himself into this condition thro' resentment of an affront
put upon him by one Vanbukeline, the copeman or merchant of the
Mine-castle, which, as we were informed by his second (who was a
young lad, and had been a bluecoat-hospital boy) was as follows:
One Taguba, a noted negro woman in Cape Corce town, being got
with child by some of the soldiers of our castle there, was brought
to bed of a Malatto girl, who growing to be about 11 years old,
Mr. Johnson a factor, then at Cabo Corce, had a great fancy for her,
and purposed to take her for his wife (as they take wives in Guiney); and about that time he being removed to Succandy, to be
chief factor, to make sure of the girl, took her there to live with
him till she was of age fit for matrimonial functions, using much
tenderness and kindness to her, and taking great pleasure and satisfaction in her company for two or three years. When she was grown
man's meat, and a pretty girl, Vanbukeline by bribes and presents
corrupted her mother Taguba, and prevailed with her to go to Succandy, and under pretence of making a visit to her daughter, to
steal her away and bring her to him, he having ordered a swift
canoo to lie ready under the Dutch fort at Succandy for that end.
The mother accordingly came, and having been kindly treated by
Mr. Johnson, who suspected nothing, went with her daughter to
take a walk, and being come near the canoo that lay perdue, the
canoo men took hold of her and put her per force into it, her
mother following, and carried them both away to the Mine-castle,
and delivered the young one to Vanbukeline, who soon cracked that
nut which Mr. Johnson had been so long preparing for his own
tooth. When I dined with the Dutch general at the Mine, I saw
her there, being brought in to dance before us, very fine, bearing
the title of madam Vanbukeline. This, and some other old differ-
ences between that Dutchman and he, did so disturb and vex him,
that it threw him into distempers, and quite turned his brain. We
were entertained by the young second as well as he could; and

about three in the evening we went aboard. I have been informed since my being here, that the adjacent negroes, instigated by Van-bukeline and the Dutch general, had in the night surprized and seiz'd the fort, cut Johnson the factor to pieces, and plundered all the goods and merchandise.

On the 27th in the afternoon we came to an anchor in Cape Corce road in eight fathom water, and saluted our castle with 15 guns, which they returned. The merchandise and stores we brought for the castle, we sent in our longboat as near the shore as she dare go, and the canoos came and unlade her; which being flat bottom'd, play upon the sea until they perceive a smooth, then with violence run themselves ashore, take out the goods, and launch off again. We landed out of the *Hannibal*, at this place, thirty soldiers for the company, in as good health as we received them aboard in England; but in two months time that we lay here to complete our business, they were near half dead, and scarce enough of the survivors able to carry their fellows to the grave.

The commodities that are most in demand upon the Gold Coast, are blue and red perpetuanoes, pewter basons of several sizes, from one to four pound weight, old sheets, large Flemish knives, iron bars, cases of spirits, blue sayes, if well dyed, and coral, if large and of a good colour. These goods will seldom or never fail of a good market. I also carried there on account of the African company, muskets, niconees, tapseals, baysadoes, brass kettles, English carpets, Welsh plains, lead bars, firkins of tallow, powder, etc. None of which did answer expectation, being forced to bring back to England a great part of them; and those we sold were at a very low rate.

Near the great gate of the castle is a dungeon for the confinement of heinous malefactors, such as murderers, traitors, &c. till an opportunity presents to send them into England to be tried, and receive the rewards of their villainy. Which dark apartment one of my trumpeters whose name was William Lord, hansel'd; for being ashore drinking punch with some of the inferior officers of the cas-

tle, there happened a difference between him and one of the ser-
jeants, who gave him a challenge to meet him with his sword near
the redoubt, which the trumpeter promis'd, and was as good as his
word; and both lugging out, it was the serjeant's chance to be thrust
into the belly; upon which he resign'd his sword, begg'd his life,
and sunk down. Upon knowledge whereof at the castle, the trumpeter was seized and clap'd into the dungeon, which as soon as I
understood, I desir'd the agents that their surgeon and mine might
visit the serjeant, search his wound, and consult the consequence
thereof, if mortal or not, which they freely agreed to; and in about
an hour after the surgeons return'd, and made their report, both
concurring that it was not mortal nor dangerous, the sword having
only passed about five inches, glancing into the abdomen, without
going thro' the belly, or injuring any of the entrails. Whereupon
the trumpeter was releas'd; who, after thanks given the agents,
immediately repair'd aboard the ship, as his best asylum, where he
was out of the reach of their power.

But though he was so lucky this time, yet I suspect a halter will
be his fate; for, tho' a stout fellow, he was a most dissolute wicked
wretch; and for his villainies and irregularities aboard, I was forced,
at St. Thomas's island, to clap him in irons, hands and feet, and
keep him so upon my poop eight weeks till my arrival at Barbadoes,
where I purpos'd to put him on board one of his majesty's men of
war that knew how to handle such refractory sparks; but upon his
seeming repentance and earnest intreaty I was prevail'd upon to
forbear, to my great vexation afterwards; for he soon got ashore
there, and run away from my ship, concealing himself in some of
the idle houses in Bridgetown, till, by his extravagancies, he had not
only spent all his wages, but run so far in debt, that he could have
no longer entertainment or credit; whereupon he enter'd himself on
board a small New-England frigat of twenty guns, and an excellent
sailer, which some Barbadoes merchants bought and mann'd, and
fitted out warlikely, and brought Colonel Russell, the governor to
be part-owner with them, who gave her his commission. The pre-

tence of her voyage was for Madagascar to purchase negroes; but as I privately understood then, and since have been well assured, her design was for the Red Sea, to make the best of her market with the Mogul's ships, which having done, and bought a few negroes for a colour, she might boldly and safely return to Barbadoes with her treasure, as long as the governor was interested, and a party concerned, and so near of kin to the English admiral. I sold a certain judge and merchant there then, a large parcel of fire-arms for her use, more than was customary or necessary for such a small vessel to carry only for her defence on a trading voyage. What became of her since I know not.

At Cabo Corce we took in part of the Indian corn ordered us for the provision of our negroes to Barbadoes, the allowance being a chest which contains about four bushels for every negro. Having landed all the castle cargo, which took us up a great deal of time, the *East-India Merchant* and our ship having each 300 tons of goods, and no boats to load it in but our own longboats, which could not work both at the same time, and sometimes the sea so high, that we could do nothing for six or seven days together, the canoos not being able to come off to fetch the goods, which occasion'd our long stay here, together with filling our water, disposing of our windward cargo as much as we could, the castle refusing to take the remainder ashore on any terms, settling accounts with the company's chief merchants, taking corn aboard, &c. All which having at length effected, on the 24th of April, about five in the evening, I took my leave of the company's worthy factors here, who had heap'd upon me abundance of civilities during my stay with them, and whose candour I shall always gratefully remember, as well as that of all the honest gentlemen of our nation upon this whole coast, who endeavour'd to out-vie each other in their favours and kind entertainments of us in their several factories, being over-joy'd at our arrival, and no less troubled and concern'd for our departure. But go we must; and accordingly, after a great many reciprocal endearments, I wish'd them all a merry Christmas, and took boat, having two chests of gold for the African Company in London, with me, in her.

When we came aboard we got in the chests of gold, and hoisted our pinnace upon the booms, but were acquainted by my mate, that when he came to an anchor with the small bower in the tornado, bringing up the ship, the cable broke, so that he was forced to let go the best bower, by which we rid all night.

April the 25th. This morning we took our leave of the castle, paying our respects with fifteen guns, which they return'd, it being too late to salute them last night. About eight o'clock sent our long-boat on the buoy to weigh the small bower anchor, and get him aboard, but he was so settled in the ground with the tornado, that in heaving a strain the buoy-rope broke, and the boat drove to lee-ward. We afterwards sent our boats with a tow-line and double-headed shot to sweep for him, but to no purpose, for they could not find him all day, therefore were forced to leave him behind. Captain Shurley got into Animabo this day, but the seeking for our anchor hinder'd us.

The 26th at six in the morning we hove up our best bower, and stood to the E. for Animabo. About nine o'clock we were abreast Anishen, which is a thatch'd house, where our African Company have a small factory, and lies about a league short of Animabo, where about ten o'clock we arriv'd and anchor'd in seven fathom water, about a mile and half off shore, the castle bearing N.W. which we saluted with seven guns, and were return'd the same. We moor'd our ship with ketch-anchor and hauser; and after dinner I went ashore to Mr. Searle, the factor here, to know where and when we should send for the corn assign'd us here by the chief merchants at Cape Corce, there being not enough to supply us there, and therefore we were to call for the rest at this place and Aena, to complete our quantity of 700 chests each. Mr. Searle immediately order'd what quantity he had to be deliver'd us when-ever our boats came for it, and entertain'd us very lovingly till night, when Capt. Shurley and I went aboard. Animabo lies in the

The Dutch Castle Cormantine, near Anamaboe on the Gold Coast
From an engraving in Ogilby's *Africa*, London, 1670

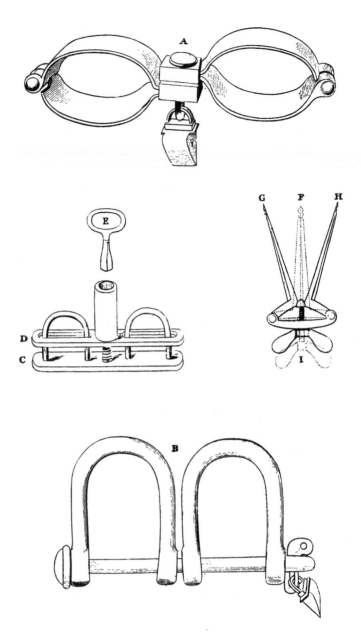

(A) Hand-Cuffs for Slaves. (B) Leg Shackles. (C-E) Thumb Screws.
(F-H) "Speculum Oris," to Open Closed Jaws.
From Clarkson's *Abolition of the Slave Trade*, London, 1808

kingdom of Fantine and is a pretty large town; the Negro inhabitants are accounted very bold and stout fellows, but the most desperate treacherous villains, and greatest cheats upon the whole coast, for the gold here is accounted the worst, and most mix'd with brass, of any in Guinea; it lies about four leagues to the east of Cabo Corce. Our castle is pretty strong, of about eighteen guns, where we were very kindly entertain'd by Mr. Searle some days, and by Mr. Cooper at Aga on other days. Aga is a small thatch'd house, about half a mile to the east from Animabo on the sea-shore, having little or no defence except a few muskets. It has a large yard and fine pond for ducks. Mr. Cooper, the factor, who is a very ingenious young gentleman, gave us a cordial reception, having the company of his wife (as he call'd her) to dine with us, as we had of Mrs. Searl's at Animabo, being both Mulattos, as was Mr. Ronon's at Cabo Corce. This is a pleasant way of marrying, for they can turn them off and take others at pleasure; which makes them very careful to humour their husbands, in washing their linen, cleaning their chambers, &c. &c. and the charge of keeping them is little or nothing.

We lay at Animabo until the 2d day of May, when Captain Shurley and I having each of us got off 180 chests of corn, fill'd two boats of water, and dispos'd of what we could of the remainder of our windward cargo, we took leave of Mr. Searle and Mr. Cooper, and got up our anchors, and stood to the E. along shore about two leagues distant; and at night came to an anchor in fifteen fathom water.

May the 3d. This morning we got under sail, and stood along shore for Winiba. We had several canoos come off, which occasion'd our lying by often in hopes of trade, but found little, they wanting gold. At eight in the evening we anchor'd, lest we should out-shoot our port.

May the 4th. This morning at eight made sail, and at eleven came to an anchor at Winiba in nine fathom good ground; and having moor'd ship after dinner, went ashore to see for our canoos, which

Mr. Nicholas Buckerige, the factor here, had promis'd to procure us for our use at Whidaw.

Here we got each of us one five-hand canoo, and set our canoo-men and carpenters to work to fit them with knees and timbers to strengthen them. We hal'd our long-boat ashore and trimmed him, being leaky and much worm-eaten. We fill'd some water, and cut good store of fire-wood, by the queen's permission. This queen is about fifty years old, as black as jet, but very corpulent. We went with Mr. Buckerige to pay our respects to her under a great tree where she sat. She received us very kindly, and made her attendants dance after their manner before us. She was very free of her kisses to Mr. Buckerige, whom she seemed much to esteem; and truly he deserved it from all that knew him, being an extraordinary good-humoured and ingenious gentleman, and understood this country and language very well. We presented her with an anchor of brandy each, and some hands of tobacco, which she received with abundance of thanks and satisfaction, and so bid her good night. She was so extremely civil before we parted, to offer each of us a bed-fellow of her young maids of honour while we continued there, but we modestly declined her majesty's proffer, and that night lay ashore with Mr. Buckerige. Next day we were forced to keep a fast; for the cook being dressing of dinner, among which there was a young pig roasting at a quick fire, the flame of it reached the dry palm branches that thatch'd the kitchen, which immediately took fire and spread so in an instant, that, in less than a quarter of an hour, our dinner and kitchen were converted to ashes.

Our business being compleated at Winiba by the 9th instant, we went aboard and got our ships under sail for Acra, Mr. Buckerige going my passenger, to pay a visit to Mr. Bloome the factor there. Capt. Shurley has been long sick of a flux and fever, and is now very ill, and I troubled with violent convulsions in my head, that I can get no sleep without opiates, and so giddy that I cannot walk without assistance. We stood along shore all day with an early sail to the east, and at night came to an anchor in 14 fathom water, with our stream-anchor and cable, which we have chiefly used along the whole coast for the easiness of weighing him.

The next day arrived at Acra two Danish ships of 26 guns a-piece; as they passed by our ships they saluted us with nine guns each, which we returned, and they came to an anchor about a mile to the east of us. They were sent on purpose from Denmark to compound with the black general for the surrendering of their fort, and to settle it again, for which end they had brought with them a governor, soldiers, provisions, ammunition, merchandize, &c. They made some propositions to the black general while we were here, but his demands were so exorbitant that they would not comply with them; tho' since I understood that the fort was delivered to them, and having resettled it, went for Whidaw to purchase slaves, and in their voyage thence to the West Indies, put into the island of Princes for water, where Avery, the pirate fell in with them, fought, took, plundered, and burnt them, which was the unhappy end of their voyage. The poor Danish general went from us aboard his countrymen, but not without reluctancy, and fear of being harshly treated in Denmark; but it seems Long Ben (as they called that rogue Avery) prevented that.

Captain Thomas Shurley, commander of the *East India Merchant*, my consort, departed this life here, having been long sick of a fever and flux. He was handsomely buried in Acra castle, a la Soldado, his own ship firing guns at half a minute distance, during the time the corpse was rowing ashore. Mr. Bloome, myself, Mr. Buckerige, and the chief of the Dutch factory, held up the pall. After he was buried, according to the service of the church of England, his own ship fired 30 guns, the *Hannibal*, 26, Acra fort, 20, and the Dutch and Black's fort, 16 each: He was very averse to making a will, and took it amiss when I urged him to it; he left the command of his ship to his first mate, Mr. Clay, and as to his own concerns, said his purser, Mr. Price, knew how all lay.

May the 20th. This morning about nine o'clock we arrived at Whidaw, being about sixty leagues from Acra to the east, and let go our anchor in eight fathom water, about two miles off shore, and moor'd with our stream anchor right against the landing place, a little to the west of the great thick tuft of trees that looks like a barn, and other trees at the east end of it, making like a tower. This day got our canoos and all things else ready, in order to go ashore to-morrow to purchase our slaves.

May the 21st. This morning I went ashore at Whidaw, accompany'd by my doctor and purser, Mr. Clay, the present captain of the *East India Merchant*, his doctor and purser, and about a dozen of our seamen for our guard, arm'd, in order here to reside till we could purchase 1300 negro slaves, which was the number we both wanted, to compleat 700 for the *Hannibal*, and 650 for the *East India Merchant*, according to our agreement in our charter-parties with the Royal African Company; in procuring which quantity of slaves we spent about nine weeks, during which time what observations my indisposition with convulsions in my head, &c. would permit me to make on this country, its trade, manners, &c. are as follows, viz.

Whidaw, or Quedaw, lies in the latitude of 6° 10′ N. latitude, being the pleasantest country I have seen in Guiney, consisting of champaigns and small ascending hills, beautified with always green shady groves of lime, wild orange, and other trees, and irrigated with divers broad fresh rivers, which yield plenty of good fish; towards the sea-shore it is very marshy, and has divers large swamps.

Our factory, built by Captain Wiburne, Sir John Wiburne's brother, stands low near the marshes, which renders it a very unhealthy place to live in; the white men the African Company send there, seldom returning to tell their tale; 'tis compass'd round with a mud wall, about six foot high, and on the south-side is the gate; within is a large yard, a mud thatch'd house, where the factor lives, with the white men; also a storehouse, a trunk for slaves, and a place where they bury their dead white men, call'd, very improperly, the hog-yard; there is also a good forge, and some other small houses: To the east are two small flankers of mud, with a few popguns and harquebusses, which serve more to terrify the poor ignorant negroes than to do any execution. While we were here the factor made a wide deep ditch, round the factory, and had my carpenters to make a draw-bridge over it, which has render'd it now pretty secure; for before it was enterable every rainy time, the walls being washed down, and when the rains were over, built up again. And here I must observe that the rainy season begins about the middle of May, and ends the beginning of August, in which space it was my misfortune to be there, which created sickness among my negroes aboard, it being noted for the most malignant season by the blacks themselves, who, while the rains last, will hardly be prevail'd upon to stir out of their huts, and myself and the poor men found it so by dear experience, the rains that fall down then being more like fountains than drops, and as hot as if warmed over a fire.

The factory is about 200 yards in circumference, and a most wretched place to live in, by reason of the swamps adjacent, whence proceed noisome stinks, and vast swarms of little flies, call'd musketoes, which are so intolerably troublesome, that if one does not take opium, laudanum, or some other soporifick, 'tis impossible to get any sleep in the night; and that one I lay there was the most uneasy that I ever felt, for I had not lain down above an hour in the factor's bed, but I was so vex'd and tormented by those little malicious animals, that I was forced to get up again, and dress myself, put gloves on my hands, and tie a handkerchief over my face till day-light, which notwithstanding these troublesome devils would sting thro; and the place so stung would be much inflam'd, and rise into a knob, much provoking the exercise of a man's nails; and had king James the first, been there some time, he would have been convinc'd that scratching where it itches was not the greatest pleasure in the world, as 'tis said was his opinion.

The best means I could find to allay the inflammation, was to rub the parts affected with lime-juice, or vinegar, which, tho' for the present it produced a smart, the ease it gave, in a short time, made abundant recompence; therefore to shun the spirit of this cursed little flie as much as we can, as well as to give us some cool air (that which is confin'd in a close place in this country, appearing as intensely hot to an European, as if he suck'd in the heat at the mouth of an oven in England), we have negro boys to fan us all night with large fans made of skins.

This factory, feared as 'tis, proved very beneficial to us, by housing our goods which came ashore late, and could not arrive at the king's town where I kept my warehouse, ere it was dark, when they would be very incident to be pilfer'd by the negro porters which carry them, at which they are most exquisite; for in the day-time they would steal the cowries, altho' our white men that attended the goods from the marine watched them, they having instruments like wedges, made on purpose to force asunder the staves of the barrels, that contain'd the cowries, whereby the shells dropt out; and when any of our seamen that watch'd the goods came near such porters, they would take out their machine, and the staves would insensibly close again, so that no hole did appear, having always their wives and children running by them to carry off the plunder; which with all our threats and complaints made to the king, we could not prevent, tho' we often beat them cruelly, and piniar'd some, but it was all one, what was bred in the bone, &c. whatever we could do would not make them forbear.

The factory prov'd beneficial to us in another kind; for after we had procured a parcel of slaves, and sent them down to the sea-side to be carry'd off, it sometimes proved bad weather, and so great a sea, that the canoos could not come ashore to fetch them, so that they returned to the factory, where they were secured and provided for till good weather presented, and then were near to embrace the opportunity, we sometimes shipping off a hundred of both sexes at a time.

We had our cook ashore, and eat as well as we could, provisions being plenty and cheap; but we soon lost our stomachs by sickness, most of my men having fevers, and myself such convulsions and aches in my head, that I could hardly stand or go to the trunk without assistance, and there often fainted with the horrid stink of the negroes, it being an old house where all the slaves are kept together, and evacuate nature where they lie, so that no jakes can stink worse; there being forced to sit three or four hours at a time, quite ruin'd my health, but there was no help.

When we were at the trunk, the king's slaves, if he had any, were the first offer'd to sale, which the cappasheirs would be very urgent with us to buy, and would in a manner force us to it ere they would shew us any other, saying they were the Reys Cosa, and we must not refuse them, tho' as I observed they were generally the worst slaves in the trunk, and we paid more for them than any others, which we could not remedy, it being one of his majesty's prerogatives. Then the cappasheirs each brought out his slaves according to his degree and quality, the greatest first, &c. and our surgeon examined them well in all kinds, to see that they were sound wind and limb, making them jump, stretch out their arms swiftly, looking in their mouths to judge of their age; for the cappasheirs are so cunning, that they shave them all close before we see them, so that let them be never so old we can see no grey hairs in their heads or beards; and then having liquor'd them well and sleeked with palm oil, 'tis no easy matter to know an old one from a middle-aged one, but by the teeths decay. But our greatest care of all is to buy none that are pox'd, lest they should infect the rest aboard; for tho' we separate the men and women aboard by partitions and bulk-heads, to prevent quarrels and wranglings among them, yet do what we can they will come together, and that distemper which they call the yaws, is very common here, and discovers itself by almost the same symptoms as the *Lues Venerea* or clap does with us; therefore our surgeon is forc'd to examine the privities of both men and women with the nicest scrutiny, which is a great slavery, but what can't be omitted. When we had selected from the rest such as we liked, we agreed in what goods to pay for them, the prices being already stated before the king, how much of each sort of merchandize we were to give for a man, woman, and child, which gave us much ease, and saved abundance of disputes and wranglings, and gave the owner a note, signifying our agreement of the sorts of goods; upon delivery of which the next day he receiv'd them; then we mark'd the slaves we had bought in the breast, or shoulder, with a hot iron, having the letter of the ship's name on it, the place being before anointed with a little palm oil, which caused but little pain, the mark being usually well in four or five days, appearing very plain and white after.

When we had purchased to the number of 50 or 60, we would send them aboard, there being a cappasheir, intitled the captain of the slaves, whose care it was to secure them to the waterside, and see them all off; and if in carrying to the marine any were lost, he was bound to make them good to us, the captain of the trunk being oblig'd to do the like, if any run away while under his care, for after we buy them we give him charge of them till the captain of the slaves comes to carry them away: There are two officers appointed by the king for this purpose, to each of which every ship pays the value of a slave in what goods they like best for their trouble, when they have done trading; and indeed they discharg'd their duty to us very faithfully, we not having lost one slave thro' their neglect in 1300 we bought here.

There is likewise a captain of the sand, who is appointed to take care of the merchandise we have come ashore to trade with, that the negroes do not plunder them, we being often forced to leave goods a whole night on the sea shore, for want of porters to bring them up; but notwithstanding his care and authority, we often came by the loss and could have no redress.

When our slaves were come to the sea-side, our canoos were ready to carry them off to the longboat, if the sea permitted, and he convey'd them aboard ship, where the men were all put in irons, two and two shackl'd together, to prevent their mutiny, or swimming ashore.

The negroes are so wilful and loth to leave their own country, that they have often leap'd out of the canoos, boat and ship, into the sea, and kept under water till they were drowned, to avoid being taken up and saved by our boats, which pursued them; they having a more dreadful apprehension of Barbadoes than we can have of hell, tho' in reality they live much better there than in their own country; but home is home, &c. We have likewise seen divers of them eaten by the sharks, of which a prodigious number kept about the ships in this place, and I have been told will follow her hence to Barbadoes, for the dead negroes that are thrown over-board in the passage. I am certain in our voyage there we did not want the sight of some every day, but that they were the same I can't affirm. We had about 12 negroes did wilfully drown themselves, and others starv'd themselves to death; for 'tis their belief that when they die they return home to their own country and friends again.

The best goods to purchase slaves here are cowries, the smaller the more esteemed; for they pay them all by tale, the smallest being as valuable as the biggest, but take them from us by measure or weight, of which about 100 pounds for a good man-slave. The next in demand are brass neptunes or basons, very large, thin, and flat; for after they have bought them they cut them in pieces to make anilias or bracelets, and collars for their arms, legs and necks. The other preferable goods are blue paper sletias, cambricks or lawns, caddy chints, broad ditto, coral, large, smooth, and of a deep red, rangoes large and red, iron bars, powder and brandy.

With the above goods a ship cannot want slaves here, and may purchase them for about three pounds fifteen shillings a head, but near half the cargo value must be cowries or booges, and brass basons, to set off the other goods that we buy cheaper, as coral, rangoes, iron, &c. else they will not take them; for if a cappasheir sells five slaves, he will have two of them paid for in cowries, and one in brass, which are dear slaves; for a slave in cowries costs us above four pounds in England; whereas a slave in coral, rangoes, or iron, does not cost fifty shillings; but without the cowries and brass they will take none of the last goods, and but small quantities at best, especially, if they can discover that you have good store of cowries and brass aboard, then no other goods will serve their turn, till they have got as much as you have; and after for the rest of the goods they will be indifferent and make you come to their own terms, or else lie a long time for your slaves, so that those you have on board are dying while you are buying others ashore; therefore every man that comes here, ought to be very cautious in making his report to the king at first, of what sorts and quantities of goods he has, and be sure to say his cargo consists mostly in iron, coral, rangoes, chints, &c. so that he may dispose of those goods as soon as he can, and at last his cowries and brass will bring him slaves as fast as he can buy them; but this is to be understood of a single ship: or more, if the captains agree, which seldom happens; for where there are divers ships, and of separate interests, about buying the same commodity they commonly undermine, betray, and out-bid one the other; and the Guiney commanders' words and promises are the least to be depended upon of any I know who use the sea; for they would deceive their fathers in their trade if they could.

The road where our ships ride is very good and clean ground, and gradual soundings. The best anchoring is in eight fathom water, against a great tuft of trees that make like a barn, about a mile and a half off the shore, on which there runs such a prodigious swell and surf, that we venture drowning every time we go ashore and come off, the canoos frequently over-setting, but the canoo-men are such excellent divers and swimmers, that they preserve the lives of those they have any kindness for, but such as they have any displeasure to they will let shift for themselves, therefore 'tis very prudent for all commanders to be kind and obliging to them, their lives lying in their hands, which they can make them lose at pleasure, and impute all to accident, and they could not help it; and there are no amends to be had.

The canoos we buy on the Gold Coast, and strengthen them with knees and weather-boards fore and aft, to keep the sea out, they plunging very deep when they go against a sea. They are made of the trunk of the cotton tree hollow'd, from a two hand to a twelve hand canoo, the largest being not above four foot broad, but twenty-eight or thirty foot long. Those that are most fit for the use at Whidaw, are five hand or seven hand canoos; of which each ship that buys many slaves ought to carry two, for they are very incident to be staved by the great sea when they overset, and here is none for supply, and without them there is no landing or coming off for goods or men.

The canoo-men we bring from Cape Corce, being seven in number, of which one is boatswain, and is commonly one of the most skilful canoo-men in Guiney; he commands the rest, and always steers the canoo, and gives his orders to the rest, when to row or when to lie on their paddles, to watch a smooth or shun a great sea they see coming. Their pay is certain and stated, half of which we pay them in gold at Cape Corce; and the rest in goods when we have done with them at Whidaw; 'tis also customary to give them a canoo to carry them back, and cut up the other for fire-wood, unless an opportunity offers to sell it, which is very rare. They lost us six or seven barrels of cowries, above 100 bars of iron, and other goods, by the oversetting of the canoos in landing them, which we could never recover, or have the least satisfaction for, but were forced to give them good words, lest they should, in revenge, play us more such tricks. We kept two men ashore here constantly to fill water, which lay and eat at the factory, which fill'd our small hogsheads in the night, and roll'd them over the sand to the sea-side, ready to raft off in the morning, before the sea breeze came in, which is the only time, we having no other way to get it off but by rafting, and in hauling off to the longboat the great sea would often break our raft, and stave our cask, whereby we lost a great many.

The longboat was chiefly employ'd in bringing water aboard, which we started into our butts in the hold, and sent the small cask ashore again next morning, of which we had two gangs on purpose. We had a little deal yaul which did us great service in bringing off cows, hogs, staves, letters, &c. from the canoos, with only two boys in her.

When our slaves are aboard we shackle the men two and two,

while we lie in port, and in sight of their own country, for 'tis then
they attempt to make their escape, and mutiny; to prevent which we
always keep centinels upon the hatchways, and have a chest of small
arms, ready loaden and prim'd, constantly lying at hand upon the
quarter-deck, together with some granada shells; and two of our
quarter-deck guns, pointing on the deck thence, and two more out
of the steerage, the door of which is always kept shut, and well
barr'd. They are fed twice a day, at 10 in the morning, and 4 in the
evening, which is the time they are aptest to mutiny, being all upon
deck; therefore all that time, what of our men are not employ'd in
distributing their victuals to them, and settling them, stand to their
arms; and some with lighted matches at the great guns that yaun
upon them, loaden with partridge, till they have done and gone
down to their kennels between decks. Their chief diet is call'd
dabbadabb, being Indian corn ground as small as oat-meal in iron
mills, which we carry for that purpose; and afterwards mix'd with
water and boil'd well in a large copper furnace, till 'tis as thick as a
pudding. About a peckful of which in vessels, call'd crews, is allow'd to 10 men, with a little salt, malagetta, and palm oil, to relish.

They are divided into messes of ten each, for the easier and better
order in serving them. Three days a week they have horse-beans
boil'd for their dinner and supper, great quantities of which the
African Company do send aboard us for that purpose. These beans
the negroes extremely love and desire, beating their breast, eating
them, and crying "Pram! Pram!" which is, "Very good!" They are
indeed the best diet for them, having a binding quality, and consequently good to prevent the flux, which is the inveterate distemper
that most affects them, and ruins our voyages by their mortality. The
men are all fed upon the main deck and forecastle, that we may have
them all under command of our arms from the quarter-deck, in case
of any disturbance; the women eat upon the quarter-deck with us,
and the boys and girls upon the poop. After they are once divided
into messes, and appointed their places, they will readily run there
in good order of themselves afterwards. When they have eaten their

victuals clean up (which we force them to for to thrive the better), they are order'd down between decks, and every one as he passes has a pint of water to drink after his meat, which is serv'd them by the cooper out of a large tub, fill'd beforehand ready for them. When they have occasion to ease nature, they are permitted by the centinels to come up, and go to a conveniency which is provided for that purpose, on each side of the ship, each of which will contain a dozen of them at once, and have broad ladders to ascend them with the greater ease.

When we come to sea we let them all out of irons, they never then attempting to rebel, considering that should they kill or master us, they could not tell how to manage the ship, or must trust us, who would carry them where we pleased; therefore the only danger is while we are in sight of their own country, which they are loath to part with; but once out of sight out of mind. I never heard that they mutiny'd in any ships of consequence, that had a good number of men, and the least care; but in small tools where they had but few men, and those negligent or drunk, then they surpriz'd and butcher'd them, cut the cables, and let the vessel drive ashore, and every one shift for himself. However, we have some 30 or 40 Gold Coast negroes, which we buy, and are procur'd us there by our factors, to make guardians and overseers of the Whidaw negroes, and sleep among them to keep them from quarrelling, and in order, as well as to give us notice, if they can discover any caballing or plotting among them, which trust they will discharge with great diligence; they also take care to make the negroes scrape the decks where they lodge every morning very clean, to eschew any distempers that may engender from filth and nastiness. When we constitute a guardian, we give him a cat of nine tails as a badge of his office, which he is not a little proud of, and will exercise with great authority. We often at sea, in the evenings, would let the slaves come up into the sun to air themselves, and make them jump and dance for an hour or two to our bag-pipes, harp, and fiddle, by which exercise to preserve them in health; but notwithstanding all our endeavour, 'twas my hard fortune to have great sickness and mortality among them.

Having bought my complement of 700 slaves, viz. 480 men and 220 women, and finish'd all my business at Whidaw, I took my leave of the old king and his cappasheirs, and parted, with many affectionate expressions on both sides, being forced to promise him that I would return again the next year, with several things he desired me to bring from England; and having sign'd bills of lading to Mr. Peirson, for the negroes aboard, I set sail the 27th of July in the morning, accompany'd with the *East India Merchant*, who had bought 650 slaves, for the island of St. Thomas, from which we took our departure, on August 25th, and set sail for Barbadoes.

We spent in our passage from St. Thomas to Barbadoes two months eleven days, in which time there happened such sickness and mortality among my poor men and negroes, that of the first we buried 14, and of the last 320, which was a great detriment to our voyage, the Royal African Company losing ten pounds by every slave that died, and the owners of the ship ten pounds ten shillings, being the freight agreed on to be paid them by the charter-party for every negro delivered alive ashore to the African Company's agents at Barbadoes; whereby the loss in all amounted to near 6500 pounds sterling. The distemper which my men as well as the blacks mostly died of, was the white flux, which was so violent and inveterate, that no medicine would in the least check it; so that when any of our men were seized with it, we esteemed him a dead man, as he generally proved. I cannot imagine what should cause it in them so suddenly, they being free from it till about a week after we left the island of St. Thomas. And next to the malignity of the climate, I can attribute it to nothing else but the unpurg'd black sugar, and raw unwholesome rum they bought there, of which they drank in punch to great excess, and which it was not in my power to hinder, having chastised several of them, and flung over-board what rum and sugar I could find; and was forced to clap one Lord, our trumpeter, in irons, for his being the promoter of their unseasonable carousing bouts, and going in one of his drunken fits with his knife to kill the boatswain in his bed, and committing other enormities; but tho' he remained upon the poop day and night in irons for two months, without any other shelter than the canopy of heaven, he was never troubled with any sickness, but made good the proverb, "That naught's never in danger," or "that he who is born to be hang'd," &c. I have given some account of him elsewhere, therefore shall say no more here.

The negroes are so incident to the small-pox, that few ships that carry them escape without it, and sometimes it makes vast havock and destruction among them; but tho' we had 100 at a time sick of it, and that it went thro' the ship, yet we lost not above a dozen by it. All the assistance we gave the diseased was only as much water as they desir'd to drink, and some palm-oil to anoint their sores, and they would generally recover without any other helps but what kind nature gave them.

One thing is very surprizing in this distemper among the blacks, that tho' it immediately infects those of their own colour, yet it will never seize a white man; for I had several white men and boys aboard that had never had that distemper, and were constantly among the blacks that were sick of it, yet none of them in the least catch'd it, tho' it be the very same malady in its effects, as well as symptoms, among the blacks, as among us in England, beginning with the pain in the head, back, shivering, vomiting, fever, &c. But what the smallpox spar'd, the flux swept off, to our great regret, after all our pains and care to give them their messes in due order and season, keeping their lodgings as clean and sweet as possible, and enduring so much misery and stench so long among a parcel of creatures nastier than swine; and after all our expectations to be defeated by their mortality. No gold-finders can endure so much noisome slavery as they do who carry negroes; for those have some respite and satisfaction, but we endure twice the misery; and yet by their mortality our voyages are ruin'd, and we pine and fret ourselves to death, to think that we should undergo so much misery, and take so much pains to so little purpose.

I deliver'd alive at Barbadoes to the company's factors 372, which being sold, came out at about nineteen pounds per head one with another.

Having got aboard near 700 hogsheads of sugars, at nine and ten shillings per hundred freight for Muscovadoes, and 11 for Clay'd; some cotton at 2 *d.* per lb. and ginger at 8 *s.* per cent. we got all clear to sail against the 2d of April, the *Tiger* man of war being then ready to carry Colonel Kendal to England, and to take under her convoy such ships as were ready to sail at that time, of which there were small and great about 30, seven of which were merchant-men of 28 guns and upwards each, and were order'd by Capt. Sherman to make the line of battle, in case we met an enemy, he being pleased to appoint me, in the *Hannibal,* to lead on the star-board tack, and Capt. Buttrom in the *Faulkenburg,* on the larboard tack, in case of engaging, while himself kept the centre; and the other ships of the line were disposed for seconds. Colonel Kendal having disengaged himself from the multitude of gentlemen that came to attend him, and wish him a good voyage, the 2d of April in the evening got aboard the *Tiger,* with a discharge of all the cannon round the town; and the third, in the evening, we set sail for England, with the *Chester* man of war in our company, which Colonel Cothrington, the general of the Leeward Islands, had sent from Antigua to Barbadoes, to strengthen our convoy, till we were past Diseada, upon advice he had receiv'd, that there was a squadron of French men of war from Martinico, waiting for us thereabouts.

Wednesday the 3d. Yesterday about four in the evening we got under sail, and stood out of Carlisle bay, and then laid our fore topsail to the mast, and drove to leeward to wait for the rest of the fleet: At seven were abreast the hole. We had great popling sea, but little wind at night, till this day noon.

Friday the 19th. In the morning 'twas my unhappiness to be seized with violent convulsions in my head, together with a vertigo, so that I could not stand, and all things I look'd on turn'd round. The vertigo was much allay'd soon, but the convulsions continued so severe upon me, that I was forced for most part to keep my bed, till we made the island of Scilly, which was upon the 22d of May, in which time the hearing of my left ear was much impair'd, I having lost the hearing of my right ear upon the coast of Guiney, by a former fit. And now, having none to look after me (my doctor having died of the plague in Barbadoes), my deafness increased daily.

When I came to London, thro' the kindness and good-will of my friends and acquaintance, who were sorry to see me return in that condition, I was advised to a great many applauded physicians, who all pretended they would cure my deafness. I went under the care of several of them, who were the most celebrated in that famous city, by whose orders I was tormented by the apothecaries, with doses of nasty physick every day, for four or five months time, and butcher'd by the surgeons with blisters, issues, setons, &c. and spent about 100 guineas among them, without receiving a farthing benefit; wherefore I did conceive it more prudence to bear my deafness as contentedly as I could, than any longer to undergo so much misery and charge to no purpose; accordingly I shook hands with the doctors, and being rendered unfit for my employment by my deafness, I settled my affairs in London, took my leave of it, and came down to Wales, among my relations in Brecknock, my native town, there to spend the rest of my life as easily as I can, under my hard misfortune.

CHAPTER IV

THE SLAVING VOYAGE OF THE *ALBION-FRIGATE* OF LONDON

THIS narrative of a voyage to New Calabar River, or Rio Real, on the Coast of Guinea, is taken from the journal kept by Mr. James Barbot, the supercargo, and part owner with other adventurers of London, in the *Albion-Frigate*, of 300 tons and 24 guns, a 10 per cent ship.*

We sailed from the Downs, on the thirteenth of January, 1698-9, and arrived before Madeira island, the third of February, whence we proceeded immediately after we had got some wine and refreshments aboard. On the tenth, we built up our sloop on our deck and the same day, in the night-time, a whale gave a violent shock to the ship, rising from the deep, exactly under our keel and about the middle of it, and afterwards plunging with a great noise. The man at the helm affirmed he could not move it any way for above a minute.

In the latitude of twelve degrees, five minutes north, we saw two sails and later hail'd one of them, which proved to be a Londoner, one Fleet, commander, who came aboard us and said he had been three days from the river Gamboa, steering for the Gold Coast of Guinea. That afternoon we were surrounded by large shoals of porpoises or sea hogs, and caught one with the cramp iron.

On the 25th of February, we anchored before Sestro river where we stayed for nearly a month getting in wood, water, rice, malaguette, fowls and other refreshments and provisions. King Peter was still alive and well, but we got few elephant's teeth because they were held very dear. On the 7th of April we came before Axim, the first Dutch fort on the Gold Coast and the next day anchored before the Prussian fort, Great Fredericksburgh, where

* Churchill's *Collection of Voyages*, vol. V, London, 1746.

the Prussian general received us very civilly, but told us he had no occasion for any of our goods. Trade everywhere on that coast was at a stand by reason of the vast number of interlopers and other trading ships and also because of the wars among the natives. The fort was a very handsome fortress mounted with about forty guns. The general told me that six weeks before, on his return from Cape Lopez to Tres-Pontas, he had been assaulted by a pirate, who was forced to let him go, being too warmly received; and that there were two or three other pirates cruising about that cape.

On the tenth, a small Portuguese ship anchored by us; the master, a black, said that he was three weeks from St. Tome, and that about three months before, he saw there, four tall French ships coming from the Coast of Guinea, loaded with slaves, mostly at Fida. Those ships were sent by the French King with a particular commission to purchase slaves to indemnify the freebooters of St. Domingo, for their pretensions to the booty taken formerly at Cartagena, by Mess. De Pointis and Du Casse, in lieu of money, and thereby engage them to return to St. Domingo and push on their settlement there, which they had abandoned.

The blacks near the fort, through malice, had diverted the channel of the fresh water ashore, to hinder us taking any, of which we complained to the Prussian general, who thereupon gave orders to let us have water. He also lent us some of his bricklayers to set up our copper aboard, for our slaves, beforehand. We had abundance of our men sick and several already dead, the weather being intolerably scorching hot, and we could get hardly any provisions save a few goats, very dear. From the Portuguese captain we had one goat, one hog, and seven chickens for five akies in gold. Here we also had the fortune to discover that above one hundred pounds worth of horse-beans, we had bought at London, for subsisting our slaves, during the voyage, were quite rotten and spoiled, for want of being well stowed and looked after ever since.

On the 17th of April, we were before Mina castle and found seven sail in the road, three or four of them tall ships, among which,

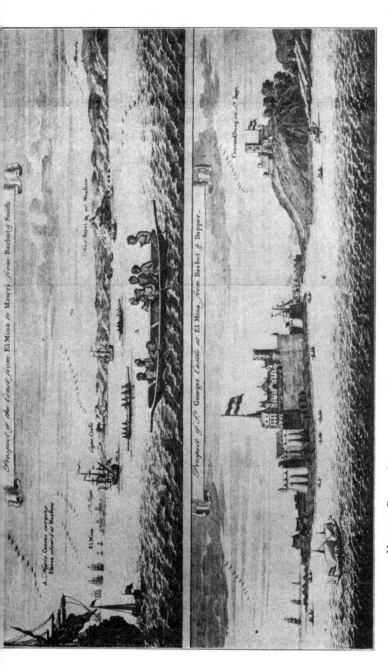

NEGROES BEING CARRIED OUT TO A SLAVE SHIP; AND CASTLES ON THE GOLD COAST
From an engraving in Churchill's *Collection of Voyages*, London, 1756

THE CEREMONY OF "CROSSING THE LINE"

From an engraving in Drake's *Collection of Voyages*, London, 1771

two frigats, each of about thirty guns and a hundred and thirty men, cruizers at the coast, who had taken three interlopers of Zealand, one of which carried thirty-six guns, who having made a brave resistance, the commander was to be tried for his life. One of the frigates having been already two years at the Coast, was ready to return home, with a thousand marks of gold.

On the twenty-first we set sail, saluting the castle with seven guns, and anchored at Anamaboe where we purchased with much trouble and at a very dear rate, a quantity of Indian wheat and sold many perpets and much powder. We paid three akies for every chest of corn, but having lost all our large stock of horse-beans, we were forced to get corn at all rates. Here the blacks put a great value upon perpets, in painted wrappers; oil-cloths with gilt leads, with large painted arms of England. We bought a boat load of fuel at three akies for each hundred billets, very dear wood.

On the fifteenth, we arrived at Acra and anchored about a league and a half from shore. Here we stayed for eleven days, trading for gold, slaves and some few teeth; diverting ourselves by turns, with the English, Dutch and Danish commanders of the forts, but more intimately with Mr. Trawne, the Danish chief, who had his lady with him. On making sail, as we worked our small bower aboard, both cable and buoy-rope breaking, we were forced to sail, leaving the anchor behind, which was hitched among the rocks at the bottom. We had purchased sixty-five slaves along the Gold Coast, besides gold and elephants' teeth and after saluting the three European forts, each with nine guns, we steered for New Calabar to buy more slaves, being followed by our small sloop under sail.

On this passage we met with much heavy weather having continually a high sea, dismal dark, and very cold days and nights, being as raw a cold as in the channel of England in September. Our sorry sloop was properly the occasion of much of our misfortune and retardment.

At last, at three o'clock in the afternoon of the 17th of June, we came to an anchor off New Calabar river, on five and a half fathom muddy sand, by guess north and south of Foko point, and the next morning, by day-break, we sent our longboat with three men to sail to land for intelligence and to bring some black to pilot us into Calabar, together with samples of some merchandise. We spyed a ship lying in Bandy [Bonny] river, as much as we could see it, and the next day sent one of the pilots in the pinnace to sound the bar. He returned at seven at night, with much trouble, the wind and sea being so high. Our long-boat not returning, as expected, by the 22d we began to be much concerned. The weather all the while was very cold and it blowing very hard from south-south-west. We found, as the Portuguese master had told us at Tres-Pontas, the month of June, hereabouts, to be a *Diablo*, as he expressed it.

At eleven o'clock on the morning of the 23d, we spyed a boat near the bar; but being come aboard at one, found it was a great canoo with nine black rowers, besides other blacks, and the master of our long-boat, who reported that coming out and finding it impossible to get over the bar, he dropped his grappling and a few hours afterwards the rope broke and he was so forced back into Bandy [Bonny] river, leaving his grappling on a buoy rope. The King of Bandy [Bonny], William, had sent us two or three of his pilots, in the canoo, with certificates of several English masters of ships they had piloted formerly safe in, some of them drawing thirteen foot of water. Our frigat then drew fourteen foot and a half water.

Our man reported that the ship we could see within the river was English, commanded by one Edwards, who had got his complement of slaves, being five hundred, in three weeks time, and was ready to sail for the West Indies. He reported farther, that as soon as the blacks could see our ship off at sea, they immediately went up the river to buy slaves, besides a hundred and fifty that were in the town when he left it; and that King William had assured him, he would engage to furnish five hundred slaves for our loading, all lusty and young. Upon which we consulted aboard with the officers and unanimously agreed to carry up the ship, if possible, for the greater expedition.

On the 24th, being early and the weather fair, we set all hands to get in our sheet-anchor, the only one we had; but it being so deep stuck in the mud, could not bring it up, which put us to our utmost efforts. But whether the anchor was so deep in the mud, or among rocky stones, I cannot say, the ship pitching violently, two strands of our cable gave way, tho' it was a new one, which caused us immediately to chop it off, and then to wind on the warp, on which we had fastened a buoy, being an iron-bound hogshead.

At one in the afternoon, weighing our anchor, our warp broke and with precipitation obliged us to chop off our cable, to get under sail to save the ship as well as our persons, if possible, at this time in great consternation, having thus lost all our anchors and on the bar.

Thus we sailed south-southeast better than an hour and a half, about two leagues from the place where we had lain at anchor, and then stood northwest for some time, all the while with the lead in hand to sound the depths. At three o'clock we fell on a sudden on three and a half, then came to three and finally to two and a half fathoms. All then thought the ship lost, as often touching on the ground astern, especially the third stroke was very violent; but then, by providence, happening to set all our sails, the ship passed over and got in well and received no harm. At about five o'clock we got the opening of Bandy [Bonny] river, and the sight of Captain Edward's ship, riding before the King's town. The moonshine served us to get the same tide to an anchor on fourteen fathom, before the town, on a small anchor of three hundred weight, the only one we had left; and the tide being strong, it required a long time, the ship driving, before it took hold of the ground sufficiently. Captain Edwards sent us soon after, a small anchor of six hundred weight, for that night only, until he could spare us a large anchor.

The next morning we saluted the black king of Great Bandy, with seven guns; and soon after fired as many for Captain Edwards, when he got aboard, to give us the most necessary advice concerning the trade we designed to drive there. At ten he returned ashore, being again saluted with seven guns. We also went ashore to compliment the King and make him overtures of trade, but he gave us to understand that he expected one bar of iron for each slave, more than Edwards had paid for his; and he also objected much against our basons, tankards, yellow beads, and some other merchandize, as being of little or no demand there at that time.

On the 26th we had a conference with the King and principal natives of the country, about trade, which lasted from three o'clock till night, without any result, they insisting to have thirteen bars of iron for a male and ten for a female slave; objecting that they were now scarce, because of the many ships that had exported vast quantities of late. The King treated us at supper and we took leave of him. The next morning he sent for a barrel of brandy, at two bars of iron per gallon and at ten o'clock we went ashore and renewed our conference but concluded nothing. Four days later we had a new conference at which the King's brother made us a discourse ending by saying they would be content with thirteen bars for males and nine bars and two brass rings for females, and the next day the trade was concluded on these terms; and the King promised to come aboard and be paid his duties.

There was a heavy rain all the morning, the next day, and at two o'clock in the afternoon, we fetched the King from the shore. He came attended by all his Caboceiros and officers, in three large canoos, and was saluted with seven guns. He had on an old-fashioned scarlet coat, laced with gold and silver, very rusty, with a fine hat on his head, but was bare-footed. His brother, Pepprell, came with him and was a sharp blade and a mighty talking black, always making sly objections against something or other and teasing us for this or that *Dassy* or present, as well as for drams, &c. It were to be wished that such a one as he were out of the way, to facilitate trade.

We filled them with drams of brandy and bowls of punch, till night, at such a rate that they all being about fourteen, with the King, had such loud clamorous tattling and discourses among themselves, as were hardly to be endured. With much patience, however, all our matters were at last adjusted indifferently, after their way, and the King ordered the public cryer to proclaim permission of trade with us, with the noise of his trumpets, made of elephant's teeth, we paying sixteen brass rings to the fellow for his fee. The blacks objected much against our wrought pewter and tankards, green beads, and other goods, which they would not accept of.

We gave the usual presents to the King and his officers. To the King—a hat, a firelock, and nine bunches of beads instead of a coat; to the officers—two firelocks, eight hats and nine narrow Guinea stuffs. We also advanced to the King, by way of loan, the value of 150 bars of iron, in sundry goods, in order to repair forthwith to the inland markets to buy yams.

All the regulations having been agreed upon, supper was served, and it was comical, as well as shocking, to observe the behaviour of the blacks, both King and subjects making a confused noise, and all of them talking together and emptying the dishes as soon as set down; everyone filling his pockets with meat as well as his belly, especially of hams and neat's tongues; falling on all together, without regard to rank or manners, as they could lay their hands on food, and having drank and eaten till they were ready to burst, they returned ashore receiving a salute of seven guns as they went.

Two days afterwards the King sent aboard thirty slaves, men and women, out of which we picked nineteen and returned him the rest, and so from day to day, either by means of our armed sloop making voyages to New Calabar town and to Dony, or by our contract with the King, by degrees we had aboard 648 slaves of all sexes and ages, including the sixty-five we purchased at the Gold Coast, all very fresh and sound, very few exceeding forty years of age. The King supplied us with yams and bananas, and plantains, which are a sort of banana dried, yet somewhat green, a food well liked by the natives. The yams, however, are not fit to be taken out of the ground before the month of July.

The town of Great Bandy [Bonny] is built on a little island, much as that of Calabar, it being marshy, swampy ground, and somewhat larger, but like it in buildings, and its people employ themselves in trade, and some at fishing, by means of long and large canoos, some of them sixty foot long and seven broad, rowed by sixteen, eighteen or twenty paddlers, carrying European goods and fish to the upland blacks and bringing back to the coast, by way of exchange, a vast number of slaves and some large elephant's teeth. The principal thing that passes as current money among the natives, is brass rings, for the arms and legs, which they call *bochie;* and they are so particular in the choice of them that they will often turn over a whole cask before they find two to please their fancy.

The English and Dutch trade them a great deal of copper in small bars, about three feet long and weighing about a pound and a quarter each, which the blacks of Calabar work with much art, splitting the bar into three parts, which they polish as fine as gold and twist the three pieces together very ingeniously, like cords, to make into arm rings. But the most current goods for trade are iron bars, striped Guinea clouts of many colours, horse-bells, hawks-bells, rangoes, pewter basons of one, two, three and four pounds weight; tankards of pewter, small glazed beads, yellow, green, purple and blue and purple copper armlets or arm rings, of Angola make, the latter being peculiar to the Portuguese.

Their large canoos are made of the trunks of big trees and framed much like the canoos at the Gold Coast, but much longer, sometimes being seventy feet in length. They are very sharp pointed at each end and are fitted with benches athwart, for the convenience of the paddlers who sit as near the sides of the canoos as possible. They commonly hang at the head of the canoo two shields and along the sides, bundles of spears. Every canoo also has a hearth in the head of it, on which they dress their victuals and they also have a contrivance by which they can set up an awning made of mats. Some have a sort of quarter-deck made of strong reeds, but the slaves, when they carry any, lie exposed to all weathers. Such canoos are navigated with eighteen to twenty hands and when armed for war commonly carry seventy or eighty men, with all necessary provisions, generally yams, bananas, chickens, hogs, goats or sheep and palm wine and palm oil.

Fevers, above all other distempers, destroy the greatest number of people, especially newcomers from Europe, carrying them off in less than eight days sickness. If the patient escapes, he may reasonably expect to live there several years in health, provided he is temperate as to wine and women. Cholics are frequent and so terrible as to distract the sufferer for three or four days. The cause is mostly attributed to the excessive use of women or to the evening dews. This cholic has swept away an incredible number of people since there were colonies here. The venereal distemper is very common, the blacks seeming to be little concerned at it as they have a way to cure with mercury; but few Europeans who get it escape dying miserably. I cannot therefore but seriously recommend to all such as happen to go thither, to forbear having to do with any black women as they value their own lives.

While we were by degrees taking in our complement of slaves at Great Bandy [Bonny], our mates, with the assistance of Captain Edwards and some of the more experienced native pilots, were employed several days in our pinnace and canoos, in sounding the channels and depths of the bar and banks, so that a chart could be made for the benefit of seafaring men trading thither.

On the 22d of August, 1699, we let fly our colours and fired a gun, for a signal to the blacks of our being near ready to sail and to hasten aboard with the rest of the slaves and the yams contracted for. We also traded our sloop with her masts, tack-sails, etc., to a Zealand interloper, for an anchor of about eleven hundred weight, a high extortion, if ever any was, but necessity forced us to comply to so hard a bargain, having only one small anchor left, and at six in the evening we sailed from Bandy [Bonny], with the tide of ebb, and working the ship down near the shore dropped anchor at ten o'clock in nine fathoms of water. At break of day we set sail and by following the channel discovered by our mates when exploring for soundings, we skirted the bar and soon found four and then five fathoms water.

Some captains have been faulty in not putting their ships in due order before they left the Guinea coast, a thing much to be minded. The shrouds and stays should be well set and tarred with all the running ropes and blocks. If the port or road will allow it, ships should be cleaned as low as possible and well tallowed, to give them the better way. Besides this, during the passage care should be taken, in good weather, to have the ship well caulked, without and within, as well as the decks.

As to the management of the slaves aboard, we lodged the two sexes apart, by means of a strong partition at the main-mast. The fore part was set apart for the men and behind the mast for the women. In large ships, carrying five or six hundred slaves, the deck ought to be at least five and a half or six foot high, making it the more airy and convenient and consequently far more healthy for them. We built a sort of half deck along the sides, with deals and spars brought from England, which extended no farther than the side of our scuttles, and so the slaves lay in two rows, one above the other, and as close together as they could be crowded.

The Dutch Company's ships exceed all other Europeans in their accommodations. Some have small ports or lights along the sides, well secured with iron bars, which they open from time to time for air, which much contributes to the preservation of the poor wretches who are so thickly crowded together.

The Portuguese are not to be compared with the English, Dutch or French, in point of neatness aboard their ships, but they are commendable in that they bring with them to the Coast, a quantity of coarse, thick mats, to serve as bedding for the slaves, and shift them for fresh mats every fortnight or three weeks. These mats are not only softer for the poor wretches to lie upon, than the bare deals or decks, but also must be much healthier for them, because the planks contract more or less dampness.

We were very nice in keeping the places where the slaves lay clean and neat, appointing some of the ship's crew to do that office constantly and several of the slaves themselves to be assistants to them and thrice a week we perfumed betwixt decks with a quantity of good vinegar in pails, and red-hot iron bullets in them, to expel the bad air, after the place had been well washed and scrubbed with brooms; after which the deck was cleaned with cold vinegar, and in the daytime, in good weather, we left the scuttles open and shut them again at night.

It has been observed that some slaves fancy they are being carried away to be eaten, which makes them desperate, and others are so on account of their captivity, so that if care be not taken, they will mutiny and destroy the ship's crew in hopes to get away. One day, about one in the afternoon, after dinner, according to custom we caused them, one by one, to go down between decks, to have each his pint of water. Most of them were yet above deck and many of them were provided with knives which we had indiscreetly given them two or three days before, not suspecting the least attempt of this nature from them. It afterwards appeared that others had pieces of iron which they had torn off the forecastle door, having premeditated this revolt. They had also broken off the shackles from the legs of several of their companions, which also served them. Thus armed they suddenly fell upon our men and stabbed one of the stoutest, who received fourteen or fifteen wounds from their knives so that he expired shortly. Next they assaulted our boatswain and cut one of his legs so round the bone that he could not move, the nerves being cut through.

Others cut the cook's throat to the pipe and yet others wounded three of the sailors and threw one of them overboard from the forecastle, who, however, by good providence, got hold of the bowlin of the foresail and saved himself, along the lower wale of the quarterdeck, where we stood in arms, firing on the revolted slaves, of whom we killed some and wounded many, which so terrified the rest that they gave way and dispersed themselves, some between decks and some under the fore-castle. Many of the most mutinous leaped overboard and drowned themselves with much resolution, shewing no manner of concern for life.

Thus we lost twenty-eight slaves and having mastered them, caused all to go betwixt decks, giving them good words. The next day, however, we had them all again upon deck and caused about thirty of the ringleaders to be severely whipt by all our men.

To prevent a recurrence of such misfortune we used to visit them daily, narrowly searching every corner between decks, and taking care not to leave any tools or nails or other things in the way, which, however, cannot always be so exactly observed, where so many people are in the narrow compass of a ship. We caused as many of our men as convenient to lie in the quarter-deck, and gun-room, and our principal officers in the great cabin, where we kept all our small arms in readiness with sentinels constantly at the door and avenues to it, being thus ready to disappoint any further attempts our slaves might make on a sudden. These precautions contributed much to keep them in awe and if all those who carry slaves duly observed them, we should not hear of so many revolts as have happened.

It is true, we allowed them much more liberty and used them with more tenderness than most other Europeans would think prudent, as we had them all on deck, every day in good weather. They took their meals twice a day, at ten in the morning and five at night, which being ended we made the men go down again between decks. As for the women, they were almost entirely at their own discretion to remain upon deck as long as they pleased, and many of the men enjoyed the same liberty, by turns, and few, or none, were kept fettered or in shackles. Besides, we allowed each of them, betwixt their meals, a handful of Indian wheat and mandioca and now and then short pipes and tobacco to smoke by turns; also, some cocoa-nuts, and to the women, a piece of coarse cloth to cover them.

We took care they did wash from time to time, to prevent vermin, which they are subject to. Towards evening the blacks would divert themselves on the deck, as they thought fit; some conversing together, others dancing, singing or sporting after their manner, which often made us pastime, especially the females, who, being apart from the males and on the quarter deck and many of them young sprightly maidens, full of jollity and good humour, afforded us abundance of recreation.

We messed the slaves twice a day. The first meal was of our large beans boiled, with a certain quantity of Muscovy lard, which we had from Holland, well packed up in casks. The other meal was of pease or of Indian wheat and sometimes meal of mandioca. This was obtained at Prince's Island, the Indian wheat at the Gold Coast, and was boiled with either lard or suet or grease, by turns, and sometimes with palm oil and malaguette or Guinea pepper.

I found they had better stomachs for beans than Indian wheat or yams. Horse beans are also very proper for slaves in lieu of large beans, which keep well put up in dry fats or casks.

We distributed them by ten in a mess, about a small flat tub made for that use by our coopers, in which their victuals were served, each slave having a little wooden spoon to feed himself handsomely and more cleanly than with his fingers, and they were well pleased with it. At each meal we allowed every slave a full cocoa-nut shell of water and from time to time a dram of brandy, to strengthen their stomachs. The Dutch commonly feed their slaves three times a day with indifferent good victuals, and much better than they eat in their own country. The Portuguese feed them mostly with mandioca.

As for the sick and wounded, our surgeons, in their daily visits betwixt decks, finding any indisposed, caused them to be carried to the *lazaretto* under the fore-castle, a room reserved for a sort of hospital, where proper remedies could be applied. This could not leisurely be done between decks because of the great heat that is there continually, which is sometimes so excessive that the surgeons would faint away and the candles would not burn, and besides, in such a crowd of brutish people there are many so greedy that they will snatch from the sick the fresh meat or liquor that is given them. Nor is it advisable to put sick slaves into the long-boat upon deck for being thus exposed in the open air and lying there in the cool of the nights after coming out of the excessively hot hold, they are soon taken with violent cholics and bloody fluxes and die in a few days time.

At parting from New Calabar River, we lay the head south by east, keeping as near the wind as was reasonable to weather the island of Ferdinand Po and thence ordering the navigation for St. Tome, to wood and water and for provisions. In the month of September we may very well get our passage from Bandy [Bonny] Point to St. Tome's road in fifteen or sixteen days. At that time of year we found the weather commonly so cold, though so near the line, as to be raw and pinching as on the coast of Brittany and at night every man aboard, though never so hardy, was glad to put on more clothes.

The slaves of New Calabar are a strange sort of brutish creatures, very weak and slothful, but cruel and bloody in their temper, always quarreling, biting and fighting and sometimes choking and murdering one another without mercy, and whoever carries such slaves to the West Indies, has need to pray for a quick passage, that they may arrive there alive and in health. A ship that takes in five hundred slaves, must provide above a hundred thousand yams, which is difficult because it is hard to stow them as they take up much room; and yet no less ought to be provided. Our store of yams was spent when we anchored at St. Tome after a fortnight's passage from Bandy [Bonny] Point.

From St. Tome we ran to the southward of the line three and a half or four degrees, keeping still the luff, and the farther southward we sailed, the stronger we found the gales. At four degrees south, we commonly meet with the trade wind which carries us to the northward of the equator pretty fast.

In passing the line is observed an ancient custom, common to all European sailors, which is, that those who have never been under the tropics, are obliged to give the ship's crew a piece of money or something to drink, from which no man is excused. If any man happens to be so great a miser as to refuse paying of this duty, the sailors, dressed like officers, carry him bound before a tribunal, in which a seaman in a long robe is seated, representing a judge, who examines him, hears what he has to say for himself and then pronounces sentence, which is, that he be ducked three times in the sea, after this manner. The person condemned is tied fast with a rope, the other end of which runs through a pulley at the yard arm, by which he is hoisted up and then let run amain three times under water. It is seldom that some one fails to give the company this diversion which is practiced with the utmost rigor in passing the line. This ceremony of ducking is called by the French, sea baptism, but they usually pump them into a tub of salt water instead of ducking in the sea. This custom is observed by all nations in passing the line and there are many other sports used by the sailors which afford passengers good diversion.

As soon as a slave ship arrives at port in the West Indies, the planters and other inhabitants flock aboard to buy as many slaves as they have occasion for. The price being agreed upon, they search every slave, limb by limb, to see whether they are sound and strong and it is diverting enough to see the examining even of those parts which are not to be named. This done, every buyer carries away his slaves and provides them with nourishment, clothing and health. We sold off all our slaves briskly at about seven thousand pounds weight of brown sugar, a piece, the Indian pieces, as they term it there, and set sail on our return voyage deeply laden with sugar, cotton and other goods. The frigate was very leaky but we continued our voyage without any remarkable accident, only our leaks increased very much so that we had much toil to keep up the ship to the end of our voyage, our two pumps going without intermission day and night, which extremely fatigued our crew, though numerous, and made us all very uneasy.

At length, by God's providence, we spyed land to leeward of us, being part of the English coast near Dartmouth and four days later we came to an anchor in the river Thames and so ended our voyage.

CHAPTER V

THE LIVERPOOL AND BRISTOL SLAVERS

THE growth of the English slave trade was largely based upon the development of the sugar industry in the West Indies. It was not until after Barbadoes and Antigua were colonized, about 1625, that slave labor in quantity was needed in order to raise the cane and produce the muscovado or raw sugar, to be sent to the sugar boilers in London or Bristol. Slaves were a necessary feature of this trade, which grew in importance as England gained possession of other West India islands and in time slave labor produced sugar enough to supply not only the demands of England and her colonies but also a considerable amount for exportation.

It is now difficult for us to realize that before this development came about in the West Indies, our English ancestors were only able to obtain sugar in limited quantity, principally from Spanish sources, and were dependent upon honey and other substitutes. At a later day, William Cowper, an English poet, was moved to express his longing for the products of slave labor, in the following lines:

"I own I am shocked at the purchase of slaves,
  And fear those who buy them and sell them are knaves;
  What I hear of their hardships, their tortures and groans,
  Is almost enough to draw pity from stones.
  I pity them greatly, but I must be mum,
  For how could we do without sugar and rum?"

"The Company of Royal Adventurers of England to Africa" was organized in 1662 and shortly after turned over its trading-rights to "The Royal African Company" which entered into assiento or contract, in 1689, to supply the Spanish West Indies with slaves. This lasted until 1698, when the trade was thrown open by the breaking up of the Assiento Company. In 1713, a treaty was signed between England and Spain whereby the former was granted a monopoly of the Spanish Colonial slave trade for thirty years with the provision that at least 4,800 slaves be supplied annually. The kings of Spain and England were each to receive one-fourth of the profits of the trade and the Company could import as many slaves as it wished and sell them, except in three ports, at as high a price as it was able to obtain.

How many negroes were carried to America in English ships? From 1680 to 1688 the African Company sent out 249 vessels and shipped 60,783 slaves, losing 14,387 lives in "the middle passage." In 1701, the records show that 104 ships cleared for Africa. During the twenty years between 1713 and 1733, about 15,000 slaves were annually carried to America, in English vessels. In 1771, there were 192 clearances. The Revolutionary War nearly stopped the traffic; but by 1786 the clearance had risen to 146 vessels.* In the year 1768, out of a total number of 97,000 slaves carried to America and the West Indies, English shipping took about 60,000. In 1780, there were nearly 700,000 negro slaves in the West Indies† and according to the census of 1790, there were 697,897 slaves in the United States. No one knows how many Africans were held in slavery by the Spanish and Dutch and no account has been taken of the vast number in the Portuguese possessions in Brazil and elsewhere.

During the seventeenth century the English trade with Guinea and the West Indies centered in the Port of London, but about 1701, the merchants of Bristol embarked in the slave trade and shortly were sending out over fifty vessels annually. The effect on the London trade was apparent at once. In 1701, London was employing 104 vessels in the Guinea trade. Six years later, the number was reduced to only thirty ships.

Bristol was forced into the slave trade by the successful competition of Liverpool in the exportation to the West Indies and America of provisions, and coarse checks and other Manchester manufac-

---

* *See* Bandinel, *Some Account of the Trade in Slaves from Africa*, London, 1842; and Du Bois, *Suppression of the African Slave-Trade*, Cambridge, 1896.

† Edwards, *The British Colonies in the West Indies*, London, 1798.

tures. The checks of Manchester, carried in Liverpool vessels, ousted from the American market the German, French and Scotch osnaburgs exported from Bristol, and the merchants of the latter port were forced to employ their vessels in another trade, with such success that by 1720, the year when the "South Sea Bubble" burst with so great financial disaster, London had very nearly abandoned the slave trade. Meanwhile, the Liverpool adventurers, with smaller capital, were carrying on a flourishing contraband trade in the West Indies, where Spain exacted a duty of 300 per cent on checks and osnaburgs. But this trade ceased in 1747, with the signing of the new Spanish treaty. When this contraband trade was at its height, the annual profit to the Liverpool merchants was estimated at £273,467; and this wealth laid the foundation of the fortunes of several mercantile houses in Liverpool and led them to embark in the Guinea trade, when they were cut off from profits in the West Indies.

Previous to this time, Liverpool had been competing with Bristol in the slave trade, but in a small way. Between 1709 and 1730, only one vessel of thirty tons burden sailed from the Mersey for Africa. But upon the adoption of new regulations in 1730, fifteen vessels, of an average burden of seventy-five tons each, cleared from Liverpool for the African coast. In 1751, the number had increased to fifty-three vessels with an aggregate burden of 5,334 tons, and the following year, eighty-seven slavers were owned in Liverpool,* with a carrying capacity for at least 25,000 slaves. In this trade the Liverpool merchants out-distanced all competitors and won for their town the distinction of being the chief slaving port in Europe.

"The reason the port of Liverpool could undersell the merchants of London and Bristol, was the restriction in their outfits and method of factorage. The London and Bristol Merchants not only allowed ample monthly pay to their captains, but cabin privileges, primage

---

* They traded with the following places: 5 with Benin, 11 with Angola, 3 with New Calabar, 11 with Old Calabar, 38 with the Windward and Gold Coast, 12 with Bonny, and 8 with Gambia. Williamson, *Liverpool Memorandum Book*, 1753.

and daily port charges; they also allowed their factors five per cent on the sales and five per cent on the returns, and their vessels were always manned by seamen at a monthly rate. The Liverpool merchants proceeded in a more economical but less liberal plan. The generality of their captains were on annual salaries, or, if at monthly pay, four pounds were thought great wages at that time. No cabin privileges were permitted, primage was unknown amongst them, and as to port charges, not a shilling was given, while five shillings a day was the usual pay from Bristol and seven and six from London. The captains from these ports could, therefore, occasionally eat on shore and drink their bottle of Madeira; whereas, the poor Liverpool skipper was obliged to repair on board to his piece of salt beef and biscuit, and bowl of new rum punch, sweetened with brown sugar. The factors, instead of a rate per centum, had an annual salary and were allowed the rent of their store, negro hire and other incidental charges; therefore, if the consignments were great or small, the advantages to the factor suffered no variation. Their portage was still more economical as their method was to take poor boys apprentice for long terms, who were annually increased, became good seamen, were then second mates and then first mates, then captains, and afterwards factors on the islands. This was the usual gradation at the time, whereby few men, at monthly pay, were required to navigate a Liverpool vessel."*

From this time on the Guinea trade flourished. Fast sailing vessels, especially adapted for the trade, were built on the banks of the Mersey and busts of blackamoors and elephants, emblematical of the African trade, adorned the Town Hall. Not all the negroes were disposed of in the West Indies as is shown by numerous advertisements in the current newspapers, of slaves to be sold at auction, by "inch of candle," or otherwise; and the young bloods of the town sometimes amused themselves by circulating hand bills in which young women were offered for sale.

* Williams, *History of Liverpool Privateers*, London, 1897.

VIEW OF LIVERPOOL, ENGLAND, FROM THE FORT, IN 1798

From a colored aquatint by John T. Serres, in the Macpherson Collection

View of Clarence Cove, Island of Fernando Po

Colored aquatint after a painting by W. J. Huggins, in 1833, in the Macpherson Collection

In 1756, the following articles, suitable for a Guinea voyage, were advertised to be sold at auction at the Merchant's Coffee house:

One iron furnace and copper, 27 cases with bottles, 83 pairs of shackles, 11 neck collars, 22 handcuffs for the travelling chain, 4 long chains for slaves, 54 rings, 2 travelling chains, 1 corn mill, 7 four-pound basons, 6 two-pound basons, 3 brass pans, 28 kegs of gunpowder, 12 cartouch boxes, 1 iron ladle, 1 small basket of flints. Another advertisement, the following year, lists one large negro hearth with 2 iron furnaces, 1 copper ditto for 450 slaves, 1 decoction copper kettle, ditto pan, a parcel of shackles, chains, neck collars and handcuffs, 1 iron furnace, 245 gallons, with a lead top, sufficient to boil 10 barrels of liquor.

The methods by which a slaving voyage out of Liverpool was conducted at that time, are shown in the following owner's letter of instructions printed in Gomer Williams' interesting account of the Liverpool slave trade.

Liverpool, 14 April, 1762.

Capⁿ Ambrose Lace,

Sir.—You being Master of the ship *Marquis of Granby*, and now cleard out of the Custom house, and ready to sail for Africa, America, and back to Liverpoole, the Cargoe we have shipd on Board is agreeable to the Annexed Invoice, which we consign you for sale, For which you are to have the usual Commission of 4 in 104 on the Gross Sales, and your Doctor, Mr. Lawson, 12d. per Head on all the slaves sold, and we give you these our orders to be observed in the course of your intended voyage. With the First Favourable wind you must sail and proceed in company with the *Douglas*, Capⁿ Finch, who has some Business at the Isle of Man, when you must accompany him not waiting longer for him than six days. When finished at the Isle of Man, you are to make the Best of your way in Company thro the So. Channell, and as you are Both Ships of Force, and we hope Tolerably well mannd you will be better able to Defend yourselves against the Enemy we therefore Recommend your keeping a good Look out that you may be Prepair^d against an attack, and should you be Fortunate enough to take any vessell or vessells From the Enemy, we recommend your sending them Home or to Cork whichever will be most convenient so as not to Distress your own ship, and on your arrival at Old Callebar if one or more ships be there you will observe to make an agreement with the Master or Masters so as not to advance the Price on each other and we doubt not you will use your utmost endeavours to keep down the Comeys which in Generall are to extravagant there and For which you have no Return at least not worth any thing to the Ownery and as your Cargoe is larger than we expected we hope will be able to Purchase 550 slaves, and may have to spare £400 to lay out in Ivory which we Recommend your Purchasing From the Beginning of your Trade and pray mind to be very Choice in your Slaves. Buy no Distemper^d or old Ones, But such as will answer at the Place of Sale and stand the Passage and as Callebar is Remarkable for great Mortality in Slaves we Desire you may take every Prudent Method to Prevent it, viz.—not to keep your Ship to Close in the Day time and at Night to keep the Ports shut as the night Air is very Pernicious. The Privilege we allow you is as Follows: yourself ten Slaves, your first mate Two, and your Doctor Two, which is all we allow except two or three Hundred w^t of screveloes amongst your Officers, but no Teeth, which you will take care to Observe, as we will not allow any thing more. When Finished at Callebar you are to make the Best of your way For Barbadoes, where you will Find Letters Lodged For you at the House of Messrs. Wood & Nicholas, how you are to proceed which will be to Guadaloupe or Martinico or any other of the Leeward Islands, whichever is the best Markett which you may advise with the House of Messrs Wood & Nicholas unto which place to Proceed, or any other Person you Can Confide in. We expect your Cargoe of Slaves will be taken up at £ *st^g per Head, and what more they sell For to be For the Benefitt of the Owners

* Obliterated.

and to have the Ship Loaden in the Following Manner viz: about One Hundred Casks good Mus° Sugar for the Ground Tier, the Remainder with First and Second white Sugars, and Betwixt Decks with good Cotton and Coffee, and the Remainder of the neat Proceeds in Good Bills of Exchange at as short Dates as you can. If the aforementioned Prices cannot be obtain^d For your Slaves at either Guadaloupe or Martinico, or the Leeward Islands as aforesaid we then desire as little time may be Lost as Possible, but proceed for Jamaica and on your arrivall there apply to Messrs Cuthbert & Beans, Messrs Hibberts, Messrs Gwyn and Case, or any other House you think will do best for the Concern, unto whom Deliver your Cargoe of Slaves which you think will make the Most of them, if Possible, by a Country Sale and to have your agreement in writing, and the Ship Loaden in the Following Manner; as much Broad Sound Mahogany as will serve for Dunnage, the Hold fill^d with the very Best Mus° Sugar and Ginger and Betwixt Decks with good Cotton and Pimento and about Ten Puncheons Rum, the Remainder of the neat Proceeds of your Cargoe in Bills of Exchange at as short Dates as you can get them. The House you are to sit down with must Fournish you with what money you may want for Payment of wages and other necessary Disbursements of your ship which we recommend the utmost Frugality. In annex^d you have invoice of Slops for the use of the seamen and apprentices. What the seamen have you must lay an advance on to pay Interest of Money, &c. The Apprentices only Prime cost. We recommend your keeping Good Rules and good Harmony amongst your Crew and a good watch. Particularly whilst you have any Slaves on Board, and Guard against accidents of Fire, Particularly in Time of Action. Suffer no Cartridges to be Handed out of the Magazine without Boxes, which will Prevent any Powder being sprinkled on the Deck and in Case of your Mortality (which God Forbid) your first Mate, Mr. Chapman must succeed you in command. Pray mind to embrace every opportunity that Offers advising us of your Proceedings, For our

Government as to Insurance &c. We wish you a Prosperous Voyage and Safe Return and are your assured friends.

Crosbies & Trafford	Chas Goore
Wm Rowe	Willm Boats
Robert Green	Chas Lowndes
	Thos Kelly

P.S. You and your officers' slaves
are to be equal Qy Male and Female.

And this letter may well be supplemented by the following letters to Captain Lace from "Grandy King George," King of the Old Town Tribe, at Old Calabar. They are addressed to "Mr Ambrose Lace and Company, Manchents in Liverpool," and are interesting examples of the literacy of the English trader or sea captain to whom the letter was dictated by the African King.

Ould Town, Ould Callabar, January 13, 1773.

Marchant Lace, Sr,—I take this opertunety of Wrighting to you and to acquant you of the behaveor of Sum ships Lately in my water   there was Capt Bishop of Bristol and Capt Jackson of Liverpool laying in the river when Capt Sharp arived and wanted to purchese his cargoe as I supose he ought to do but this Bishop and Jackson consulted not to let him slave with out he payed the same Coomey* that thy did   thy sent him out of the River so he went to the Camoroons and was away two munths   then he arived in my water again and thy still isisted upon his paying the Coomey   acordingly he did a Nuff to Blind them so I gave him slaves to his content and so did all my peeple, till he was full and is now ready to sail only weats for to have a fue afairs sattled and this sall be done before he sails to his sattisfection, and now he may very well Laffe at them that was so much his Enemy before, for that same day thy sent him out of the River this Jackson and Bishop and a brig that was tender to Jackson at night began to fire at my town without the least

* Coomey was the duty paid to the king for the privilege of trading.

provecation and continued it for twenty-four hours for which I gave them two cows   but it seems as after wards Jackson confirmed that Bishop and him was to cary away all our pawns as it was lickely true for Jackson did cary of his but more than that before he sailed he tould me that if I went on bord of Bishop, I shuld be stoped by him and my hed cut of and sent to the Duke at Nuetown, but I put that out of his power for to cut of my hed or cary of the pawns by stoping his boats and sum of his peeple and so I would Jackson had I known his entent when he informed me of Bishop, but he took care not to divulge his own secrets which he was much to bleam if he did so   my friend marchant Lace if You Send ship to my water again Send good man all same your Self or same marchant black. No Send ould man or man want to be grandy man, if he want to be grandy man let he stand home for marchant one time, no let him com heare or all Same Capt. Sharp he very good man, but I no tell before that time Capt. Sharp go to Camoroons he left his mate till he came back again, so they say I do bad for them but I will leave you to Judg that for if any ship fire at my town I will fire for ship again   Marchant Lace Sr there is Mr Canes Capt. Sharp and second mate a young man and a very good man he is very much Liked by me and all my peeple of Callabar, so if you plase to sand him he will make as quick a dispatch as any man you can send and I believe as much to your advantage for I want a good many ship to cum, for the more ships the more treade wee have for them for the New town peeple and has blowed abuncko for no ship to go from my water to them nor any to cum from them to me tho Bishop is now lying in Cross River   but thy only lat him stay till this pelaver is satteled for I have ofered him 10 slaves to Readeem the Pawns and let him have his white people, but he will not for I dount want to do any bad thing to him or any ship that cums to my water but there is 4 of my sons gone allredy with Jackson and I dont want any more of them caried of by any other vausell   the coomy in all for my water now is 24 thousand cop^rs besidges hats case and ship gun, Marchant Lace I did as you bob me for Lett^rs when this tend^r com I no chop for all man for you bob me No Chop to times for bionbi I back to much Cop^r for Coomy so I do all same you bob me who make my father grandy no more white man so now marchant Lace send good ship and make me grandy again for war take two much cop^r from me who man trade like me that time it be peace or break book like me so Marchant Lace if you Send Ship now and good cargo I will be bound shee no stand long before shee full for go away.

The following is another lucid passage from "Grandy King George's" correspondence:

And now war be don Wee have all the Trade true the Cuntry so that wee want nothing but ships to Incorige us and back us to cary it on so I hope you and marchant Black wount Lat ous want for that InCurigement O^r the other marchants of that Pleasce thut has a mind for to send their ships thy shall be used with Nothing but Sivellety and fare trade other Capt^{ns} may say what they Please about my doing them any bad thing for what I did was thier own faults for you may think Sr that it was vary vaxing to have my sons caried of by Capt Jackson and Robbin sons and the King of Qua son thier names is Otto Imbass Egshiom Enick Ogen Acandom Ebetham Ephiyoung Aset and to vex ous more the time that wee ware fireing at each other thy hisseted [hoisted?] on of our sons to the yard arm of Bishop and another to Jacksons yard arm and then would cary all of them away and cut of my hed if it had not been Prevented in time and yet thy say I do them bad only stoping Sum of thier peeple till I get my Pawns from them Marchant Luce when you Send a ship send drinking horns for Coomey and sum fine white mugs and sum glass tanckards with Leds to them Send Pleanty of ship guns the same as Sharp had I dount care if there was 2 or 3 on a Slave Send one Chints for me of a hundred yard ∘ 1 Neckonees of one hundred yards 1 photar of a hundred y's 1 Reamall 1 hund. yards one Cushita of a hundred yds one well baft of the same Send sum Leaced hats for trade and Licor bottles

and cases to much [to match?] for all be gon for war   Send sum
Lucking glasses at 2 Cop^rs and 4 Cop^rs for trade and Coomey to
and send Planty of hack and Bally for Trade and Coomey and
Small Bells   Let them be good ones and send sum Lango Sum
Large and sum small and sum Curl beads   Send me one Lucking
glass six foot long and six foot wide Let it have a strong wooden
freme   Send two small Scrustones that their Leds may Lift up
send Plenty of Cutlashs for Coomey of 2 Cop^rs price   Let your
Indgey goods be Right good and your ship no stand long   send
me one table and six Chears for my house and one two arm Schere
for my Salf to sat in and 12 Puter plates and 4 dishes 12 Nifes and
12 forcks and 2 Large table spoons and a trowen and one Pear of
ballonses 2 brass Juggs with their Covers to lift the same as a
tanckard and two Cop^r ones the same   two brass falagons of two
gallons each Pleanty for trade of puter ones   Send Plenty of Puter
Jugs for trade send me two Large brass beasons and puter ones for
trade   Send me one close stool and Send me one Large Red [illegi-
ble] Send me one gun for my own shuting 5 foot barill and two
pueter p*** pots.   Send me one good Case of Rezars for my Save-
ing   Send me sum Vavey brade Iron bars of 16 foot long   Send
100 of them   Send Large caps of 2 Cop^rs for Coomey &c   Please
to show this to Marchant black and shend sum Large Locks for
trade Sum chanes for my Salf two brass tea kittles and two scace-
pang a fue brass Kittles 12 or fifteen Cop^rs each Send Pleanty of
canes for Coomey and one long cane for my self gould mounted and
small Neals for Coomey and you may pay your Coomy Very Reasonable Saws or aney tools No Send Small Iron moulds for to cast
mustcats and sum small 3 pounders   Send me sum banue [brand
new?] canvess to make sails for my canows and sum large Leg mone-
lones with hendges [hinges?] to thim to lock with a Screw and two
large iron wans for two sarve in the Room of irons and Send me
one whip shaw and one cross cut shaw Send red green and white hats
for trade   Send me one red and one blue coat with gould Lace for
to fit a Large man   Send butt^r and Suger for to trade   Send sum

green sum red sum blue Velvet caps with small Leace and Send Sum files for trade, So no more at Preasent from your best friend

GRANDY KING GEORGE.

Give my Complements to the gentlemen owners of the brigg *Swift* Mr Devenport Marchant Black and Captn Black and as allso Mr Erll. Please to have my name put on Everything that you send for me.

These Liverpool slavers met with many strange adventures and misadventures.

In March, 1752, the *Clayton* snow,* Captain Patrick, of Liverpool, 200 tons burden, armed with four two-pounders and ten swivel guns, was taken off Fernando Po, by pirates, also from Liverpool. These proved to be nine men and a boy belonging to the *Three Sisters*, Captain Jenkins, who had run away with the ship's long-boat. The pirate took the opportunity of luffing up under the lee quarter of the *Clayton* when all her hands were forward, except the captain and gunner, and then boarded with sword and pistol in hand, wounded the captain in several places, captured the ship, kept the crew in irons one night, and the next morning put them on board their own long-boat and turned them adrift. The pirates had brought with them in their boat a bale of scarlet cloth and another of handkerchiefs, and told the *Clayton's* crew that if they "would go a-roving they should be clothed with scarlet." Four, unable to resist this dazzling proposal, voluntarily entered as rovers, and the chief mate and two boys were impressed into the pirate service. The rest of the crew were twelve days in getting into the river Bonny, where the king seized their long-boat, and the men had to enter on board different slavers trading there.

Captain Baille, commander of the slave ship *Carter*, writing to his owners in Liverpool, from the River Bonny, on January 31, 1757,

---

* A common type of slaver at this time was a snow, of about 140 tons, square sterned, 57 feet keel, 21 feet beam, 5 feet between decks, 9 feet in the hold—a miniature Malbolge when crammed with slaves like sardines in a box.

reveals the method sometimes resorted to by slave captains to compel the native chiefs to trade with them. He says:

"We arrived here the 6th of December, and found the *Hector*, with about 100 slaves on board, also the *Marquis of Lothian*, of Bristol, Capt. Jones (by whom I now write), who was half slaved, and then paying 50 Barrs, notwithstanding he had been there 3 months before our arrival. I have only yet purchased 15 slaves at 30 and 35 Barrs; but as soon as the bearer sails, I propose giving more; for at present there is a dozen of our people sick, besides the two mates, some of whom are very bad, and I have been for these last 8 days in a strong fever, and frequently insensible. Yesterday morning I buried Thomas Hodge, and on the 13th James Barton. Capt. Nobler of the *Phoenix* arrived here the 3d, and on the 19th our trade was stopt (as it had often been before); upon which we all marched on shore to know the reason and applied to the King thrice, though he constantly ordered himself to be denied, and wou'd not admit us. However, we heard his voice in doors, and as he used us so ill, we went on board, and determined (after having held a Council), to fire upon the town next morning, which we accordingly did, in order to bring them to reason but found that our shot had little effect from the river, upon which we agreed that the *Phoenix* and the *Hector* shou'd go into the Creek, it being nigher the town, whilst Captain Jones and I fired from the river. The *Phoenix* being the headmost vessel went in, and the *Hector* followed about a cable's length astern. The *Phoenix* had scarce entred the Creek before they received a volley of small arms from the bushes which were about 20 yards distant from the ship, and at the same time several shot from the town went through him, upon which they came to anchor, and plied their carriage guns for some time; but finding there was no possibility of standing the decks, or saving the ship, he struck his colours, but that did not avail, for they kept a continued fire upon him, both of great and small arms. His people were thrown into the utmost confusion, some went down below, whilst others jumpt into the yaul which lay under the ship's quarter, who (on seeing a number of canoes coming down to board them) desired Capt. Nobler to come down to them, which he at last did, as he found the vessel in such a shattered condition, and that it was impossible for him to get her out of the Creek before the next ebb tide, in case he cou'd keep the canoes from boarding him. With much difficulty, they got on board the *Hector*, but not without receiving a number of shot into the boat. The natives soon after boarded the *Phoenix*, cut her cables, and let her drive opposite the town, when they began to cut her up, and get out her loading, which they accomplished in a very short time. But at night in drawing off some brandy, they set her on fire, by which accident a great many of them perished in the flames. The *Phoenix's* hands are distributed amongst the other three ships, and all things are made up, and trade open, but very slow, and provisions scarce and dear."

The *Marquis of Lothian* was afterwards taken and carried into Martinico.

The following letter, dated Barbadoes, February 28, 1758, was written by Captain Joseph Harrison, commander of the slave ship *Rainbow*, to his owners, Messrs. Thomas Rumbold & Co., of Liverpool:

"We arrived here on the 25th inst. in company with Capt. Perkins from Bonny, and Capt. Forde from Angola, whom we fell in with at St. Thomas's. The packet arrived here from England the day after us. I expect to sail from hence for South Carolina in five days, having on board 225 slaves, all in good health except eight. On the 23rd of June last, I had the misfortune to fall in with a French brig privateer, of fourteen 6-pounders, to leeward of Popo. We engaged him four hours, and were so near for above four glasses, that I expected every moment we should run on board him, as he had shot away all my running rigging and the fluke of my small bow anchor. My standing rigging and sails were mostly cut to pieces, and the privateer was in a little better condition. Fifteen of his shot went through and through my sides, we being scarce the length of the ship from one another. I lost in the engagement, my boatswain—William Jackson—Robert Williams—and Henry Williams. My first and second mates, three landsmen, and one servant were wounded. The privateer being well satisfied sheered off. We were three days in repairing our rigging &c., and on the 28th got over the Bar of Benin and found only one vessel there, viz. a Portuguese sloop at Warree. I purchased eight slaves on the windward coast, and 261 at Benin, besides 5400 weight of ivory. Leaving the river, Nov. 9th, we arrived at St. Thomas's Dec. 17th, from whence our three vessels sailed, Jan. 4th. I have buried all my officers, except my first and third mates and gunner. Having lost since left Liverpool, 25 white people and 44 negroes. The negroes rose on us after we left St. Thomas's; they killed my linguister whom I got at Benin, and we then secured them without farther loss. We have an account of five privateers being to windward of Barbadoes, by a retaken vessel brought in here this day, so that we shall run a great risk when we leave Barbadoes."

The system of trade carried on by the Liverpool merchant was as follows: Ships were built and fitted to carry slaves; the out cargoes consisted of Manchester and Yorkshire goods, hatchets, cutlasses, knives, gunpowder and trinkets, pistols, muskets, etc., from Birmingham and Sheffield; these goods were bartered for slaves on the west coast of Africa; the ships then carried their cargoes of slaves to the West Indies where the slaves were sold for spice, sugar, and rum and these commodities were then carried to Liverpool and sold, thereby making three profits to the merchants in one voyage.

The following curious particulars regarding the customs paid at Whydah, when trading for slaves, were drawn up for the guidance of the captain of a Liverpool slaver.

"State of the Customs which the ships that make their whole trade at Whydah pay to ye King of Dahomey:

Eight Slaves for Permission of Trade gongon Beater and Broakers	Thes slaves paid to yᵉ Caborkees after which he gives you two small children of 7 or 8 years old which the King sends as a return for the Customs.

1 Slave for Water and washerwoman	These slaves paid to
2 Do for the Factory house	whom supplies you
7 Do for the Canoe	These to the Fort

6 Anchors Brandy is	1 Slave	
20 Cabess of Cowries is	1 Do	
40 Sililees	1 Do	
200 lb Gunpowder	1 Do	And if any other goods must be in
25 Guns	1 Do	proportion but you must observe to
10 Long Cloths	1 Do	pass the Goods Least in Demand.
10 Blue Basts	1 Do	
10 Patten Chints	1 Do	
40 Iron Barrs	1 Do	

"After the Customs are paid which should be done as soon as possable for the traders dare not trade till the Kings Customs are paid, the Vice Roy gives you the nine following Servants viz. one Conductor to take care of the goods that comes and go's to and from the waterside which you deliver him in count and he's obliged to answer for things delivred him he's paid 2 Gallinas of Cowries every time he conducts any thing whether coming or going and one flask of brandy every Sunday.

"Two Brokers which are obliged to go to the traders houses to look for slaves and stand Interpiter for the Purchas the are paid to each two Tokees of Coweres day and one flask of brandy every Sunday and at the end of your trade you give to each of them one Anchor of Brandy and one pˢ of Cloth.

"Two Boys to serve in the house the are paid each two tokees day at the end of your trade pˢ of cloth.

"One Boy to Serve at the tent water side 2 Tokees day.

"One Doorkeeper paid 2 Tokees day 1 p^s Cloth for him and ye above.

"One Waterwoman for the factory 2 Tokees day at end of trade One p^s of Cloth.

"One Washer Woman 2 Tokees day and six Tokees everytime you give her any Linnen to Wash and one p^s of Cloth at ye end of trade.

"N.B. the two last Servants are sometimes one if so you only pay one.

"To the Cannoemen for bringing the Captain on shore one Anchor Brandy and to each man a hatt and a fathom Cloth. To the Boatswain a hat ½ p^s Cloth one Cabes Cowrees a flask of brandy every Sunday and a bottle every time the cross the Barr with goods or Slaves and every time the pass a white man and at the end of trade for carring the Captn on board one anchor of Brandy and four Cabeses Cowrees.

"N.B. The above Bottles flasks &c was usely given to ye Conoemen but now the Captn gives y^m one Anchor of Brandy and one Cabese of Cowrees every Sunday for the weeks work. To the Gong Gong Beater for announcing trade 10 Gellinas of Cowrees and one flask of Brandy.

"To the Kings Messenger for Carring News of the ships Arrivell and Capt^{ns} Compliments to the King ten Gallinas.

"To the Trunk keeper a bottle brandy every Sunday and a peice of Cloth when you go away if you are satisfied with his service.

"To the Captn of the Waterside on your arrivell one anchor of brandy and at your Dep^t one p^s Cloth and one anchor of brandy.

"To the six Waterrowlers two tokees day each and two Bottles Brandy besides which you pay them 2, 3 or 4 tokees of cowrees each Cask according to the size at the end of trade two p^s Cloth and one anchor Brandy.

"To the Vice Roy who go's with his people to Compliment the Capt at his arrivell and Conduct him to the Fort one Anchor Brandy and two flasks but if Coke be their four flasks Brandy.

"To the Vice Roy for his owne Custom 1 pˢ Silk 15 yards 1 Cask of Flower one of Beef but if you are short of these you may give him some thing else in Lew of them:

"To making the Ten one Anchor Brandy 4 Cabess Cowrees.

"To the Captⁿ Gong Gong that looks after the house at night one bottle day and one pˢ Cloth if your content.

"You pay 3 Tokees of Cowrees for every load such as one Anchor 40 Sililees 10 pˢ Cloth and so in proportion for small goods but when loads are very heavy you pay more as ten Gallinas for a Chest of pipes &c.

The Tokee is	40 Cowrees
The Gallina is	200 ————
The Cabess is	4000 ————

"N.B. their go's five tokees to one Gallina and twenty Gallinas makes one Cabess."

Here is a bill of lading for slaves shipped in a Liverpool ship printed in "Liverpool as it was during the last quarter of the Eighteenth Century."

SHIPPED by the grace of God, in good order and well condition'd by James [surname illegible], in and upon the good Ship call'd the MARY BOROUGH, whereof is Master, under God, for this present voyage, Captain David Morton, and now riding at Anchor at the Barr of Senegal, and by God's grace bound for Georgey, in South Carolina, to say, twenty-four prime Slaves, six prime women Slaves, being mark'd and number'd as in the margin, and are to be deliver'd, in the like good order and well condition'd, at the aforesaid

Marked on the Right Buttock

O
O

Port of Georgia, South Carolina (the danger of the Seas and Mortality only excepted), unto Messrs. Broughton and Smith, or to their Assigns: he or they paying Freight for the said Slaves at the rate of Five pounds sterling per head at delivery, with Primage and

Avrage accustom'd. IN WITNESS whereof, the Master or Purser of the said Ship hath affirm'd to three Bills of Lading, all of this tenor and date; the one of which three bills being accomplish'd, the other two to stand void; and so God send the good ship to her desir'd port in safety, Amen.

Dated in Senegal, 1st February, 1766,

DAVID MORTON.

A voyage made in 1803-1804, by the ship *Enterprize*, may be taken as a typical example of the working of the system at that time. The owner's instructions were as follows:

Liverpool, 18 July 1803.

Cap. Caesar Lawson,

Sir.—Our ship *Enterprize*, to the command of which you are appointed, being now ready for sea, you are immediately to proceed in her, and make the best of your way to Bonny on the Coast of Africa. You will receive herewith an invoice of the Cargo on board her which you are to barter at Bonny for prime Negroes, Ivory, and Palm Oil. By Law this vessel is allowed to carry 400 Negroes, and we request that they may all be males if possible to get them, at any rate buy as few females as in your power, because we look to a Spanish market for the disposal of your cargo, where Females are a very tedious sale. In the choice of the Negroes be very particular, select those that are well formed and strong; and do not buy any above 24 years of Age, as it may happen that you will have to go to Jamaica, where you know any exceeding that age would be liable to a Duty of £10 pr head. While the slaves are on board the Ship allow them every indulgence Consistent with your own Safety, and do not suffer any of your officers or Crew to abuse or insult them in any respect. Perhaps you may be able to procure some Palm Oil on reasonable terms, which is likely to bear a great price here, we therefore wish you to purchase as much as you can with any spare cargo you may have. We have taken out Letters of Marque against the French and Batavian Republic, and if you are so fortunate as to fall in with and capture any of their vessels Send the Same direct to this Port, under the care of an active Prize Master, and a sufficient number of men out of your ship; and also put a Copy of the Commission on board her, but do not molest any neutral ship, as it would involve us in expensive Lawsuit and subject us to heavy Damages. A considerable part of our property under your care will not be insured, and we earnestly desire you will keep a particular look out to avoid the Enemy's Cruisers, which are numerous and you may hourly expect to be attacked by some of them. We request you will Keep strict and regular discipline on board the ship; do not suffer Drunkenness among any of your Officers or Crew, for it is sure to be attended with some misfortune, such as Insurrection, Mutiny and Fire. Allow to the ship's Company their regular portion of Provisions &c and take every care of such as may get sick. You must keep the ship very clean and see that no part of her Stores and Materials are embezzled, neglected, or idly wasted. As soon as you have finished your trade and laid in a sufficient quantity of Yams, wood, water, and every other necessary for the Middle Passage, proceed with a press of sail for Barbadoes, and on your arrival there call on Messrs. Barton Higginson & Co. with whom you will find Letters from us by which you are to be govern'd in prosecuting the remainder of the voyage. Do not fail to write to us by every opportunity and always inclose a copy of your preceding Letter.

You are to receive from the House in the West Indies, who may sell your cargo, your Coast Commission of £2 in £102 on the Gross Sales, and when this Sum with your Chief Mate's Privilege and your Surgeon's Privilege, Gratuity and head money are deducted, you are then to draw your Commission of £4 in £104 on the remaining amount. Your Chief Mate, Mr. James Cowill, is to receive two Slaves on an average with the Cargo, less the Island and any other duty that may be due or payable thereon at the place where you may sell your Cargo; and your Surgeon, Mr. Gilbt. Sinclair, is to receive two Slaves on an average with the Cargo less the Duty beforemen-

GEORGETOWN, DEMERARA, SHOWING THE BRITISH BARK "CAESAR" ENTERING THE HARBOR,
SEPTEMBER, 1839

From a colored aquatint, after a painting by W. J. Huggins, in the Macpherson Collection

GROUP OF NEGROES JUST LANDED TO BE SOLD FOR SLAVES
From an engraving in Stedman's *Narrative of an Expedition to Surinam*, London, 1796

tioned, and one Shilling S^{tg} head money on each slave sold. And in consideration of the aforementioned Emoluments, neither you nor your Crew, nor any of them, are directly or indirectly to carry on any private Trade on your or their accounts under a forfeiture to us of the whole of your Commissions arising on this voyage. In case of your Death, your Chief Mate, Mr. Cowill, is to succeed to the Command of the Ship, and diligently follow these and all our further orders. Any Prize that you may capture, direct the Prize Master to hoist a white flag at the fore and one at the main top Gallant Mast-heads, on his approach to this Port, which will be answered by a signal at the light House.

We hope you will have a happy and prosperous voyage, and remain

Sir, Your ob Servt

THOMAS LEYLAND & Co.

P.S. Should you capture any vessel from the Eastward of Cape of Good Hope, Send her to Falmouth and there wait for our orders. In case of your Capturing a Guineaman with Slaves on board, Send her to the address of Messrs. Bogle, Jopp & Co. of Kingston, Jamaica.

I acknowledge to have received from Messrs. Thomas Leyland & Co. the Orders of which the aforegoing is a true Copy, and I engage to execute them as well as all their further orders, the Dangers of the Seas only excepted, as witness my hand this 18 July 1803.

CAESAR LAWSON.

On the owner's account book is entered the following memoranda of the voyage:

SHIP ENTERPRIZE, 1st Voyage.
   Sailed from Liverpool, 20 July 1803
August 26th detained the Spanish Brig *St. Augustin*, Capt. Josef

Ant⁰ Ytuno, in Lat. 22, 47 North, Long. 26, 14 West; bound from Malaga to Vera Cruz, which vessel arrived at Hoylake on the 25th October.

September 10th Recaptured the *John* of Liverpool in Lat. 4, 20 North, Long. 11, 10 West with 261 Slaves on board, and on the 2nd November she arrived at Dominica.

September 23rd the *Enterprize* arrived at Bonny, and sailed from thence on the

December 6th the *St. Augustin* sailed from Liverpool.

9th January 1804 the *Enterprize* arrived at the Havanna and sold there 392 Negroes. On the 28 March she sailed from the Havannah and arrived at Liverpool 26 April 1804.

The outfit of the *Enterprize* cost £8148 18 s. 8 d.; her cargo of trading goods, £8896 3 s. 9½ d.; total £17,045 2 s. 5½ d. In January, 1804, Captain Lawson delivered to Messrs. Joaquin Perez de Urria, at Havanna, 412 Eboe slaves (viz., 194 men, 32 men-boys, 66 boys, 42 women, 36 women-girls, and 42 girls) to be sold on account of Messrs. T. Leyland & Co. Nineteen of the slaves died, and one girl, being subject to fits, could not be disposed of. The net profit on the round voyage, after selling the 392 remaining slaves, paying damages for detaining the *St. Augustine*, and crediting salvage of the *John*, profit on teeth, logwood, sugar, etc., amounted to £24,430 8 s. 11 d.

It appears from a calculation printed in Williams' work on the Liverpool slave trade, that during the eleven years from 1783 to 1793, 878 slavers owned in Liverpool, imported to the West Indies, 303,737 slaves whose estimated value amounted to the total of £15,-186,850—a brilliantly successful traffic that brought great wealth to the principal adventurers and an unhappy reputation to the busy port of Liverpool.

A tragedian, George Frederick Cooke, the predecessor of Kean, while drunk, staggered on to the stage of the Theatre Royal in Liverpool, one evening and was hissed and hooted by the audience for presenting himself in such a condition. Steadying himself, the out-raged actor shouted, "I have not come here to be insulted by a set of wretches, every brick in whose infernal town is cemented with an African's blood."

Time brings its compensations. Liverpool is now one of the great-est maritime ports in the world, a great *entrepôt* for the nations of the New World, whose development at one time demanded the labor and lives of kidnapped Africans transported overseas in the holds of ships hailing from that port.

CHAPTER VI

MUTINIES ABOARD SLAVE SHIPS IN THE EARLY DAYS

AMONG the shipmasters engaged in the Guinea trade, in the early part of the eighteenth century, was one Capt. William Snelgrave, who sailed in ships owned by London merchants. He met with many strange adventures on the African coast; had the misfortune to be captured, in 1719, by Capt. Thomas Cocklyn, the pirate, when he narrowly escaped with his life; and several times was in danger of capture at the instance of negro kings with whom he was trafficking for slaves.

In March, 1727, he arrived in the road of Whidaw, in the *Katharine Galley* of London, a short time after the king of Dahomey had fallen on the country and destroyed nearly the entire population. The fields were strewed with human bones and the populous country with which he was familiar was a dismal sight. Sailing a short distance along the coast, on the 3d of April he anchored in the road of Jaqueen and went up to the town, which is about three miles from the sea.

The following day a messenger came from the king of Dahomey with an invitation for the English captain to visit his camp, which lay about forty miles inland. The messenger, who spoke excellent English which he had learned in the factory at Whidaw, assured Captain Snelgrave that he would be quite safe while in the Dahomey country and kindly used. When the captain showed some distrust, the black messenger told him that if he didn't accept the invitation it would deeply offend the king, which might prevent him from trading on the recently conquered coast, beside other bad consequences, so Captain Snelgrave agreed to go and a Dutch shipmaster volunteered to accompany him and also two or three others.

The company set off at nine o'clock in the morning. The captain had six hammock-men who relieved each other by turn, two at a time carrying the hammock pole. When he became tired of lying in the hammock, there was a small horse, little larger than an ass, on which he rode, and traveling over good roads, at the rate of about four miles an hour, about nine the next morning they reached the camp, having spent the night on some mats spread on the ground in hovels that had not been destroyed by the army. A captain of the court, with about five hundred soldiers carrying firearms, drawn swords, shields and banners, came out to meet the company and escorted them to some chairs (taken from the Whidaws) set out beneath trees where the natives flocked about in such numbers that they were in danger of being crushed. Thousands of these people, who had come from inland kingdoms, had never before seen a white man.

At noon, a dinner of cold ham and fowls was brought, and notwithstanding the watchfulness of several servants with flappers, it was almost impossible to keep the meat free from the swarms of flies that had probably bred in the heaps of dead men's heads piled on stages not far away. These evil smelling stages were passed not long after, as they went towards the king's court, and the linguist said they comprised the heads of four thousand of the Whidaws who had been sacrificed about three weeks before.

They slept that night in hammocks and the next morning about nine o'clock were escorted to a large palisadoed area where the king of Dahomey was sitting in a gilt chair that he had recently captured from the king of Whidaw. He wore a gown flowered with gold, and behind him were a number of women, naked from the waist up, holding large umbrellas to shelter him from the hot sun. After paying their respects to his Majesty and drinking his health in palm wine, the linguist told Captain Snelgrave that "it was the King's Desire that they should stay some time with him, to see the Method of paying the Soldiers for Captives taken in War, and the Heads of the slain."

Over eighteen hundred captives had been brought into camp the evening before. They were Tuffoes, living about six days' journey distant, between the Whidaw country and Dahomey. After the wiping out of the Whidaws, the king of Dahomey had sent home twelve of his wives and a great number of slaves and quantity of loot, guarded by five hundred men. While passing through the Tuffoe country this guard was attacked and routed, the women were killed and the loot was captured. As soon as the conquest of Whidaw was completed, the king sent part of his army to the Tuffoe country and the eighteen hundred captives, that Captain Snelgrave saw brought into camp, were one of the results of that retaliatory campaign.

The captives were now brought before the king. He selected a considerable number to be kept as slaves for his own use or to be sold to Europeans; some two hundred were presented to his courtiers and court officials; and the rest of the prisoners were ordered to be sacrificed to the king's *fetiche* or guardian angel. This human sacrifice took place that afternoon, about a quarter of a mile from the camp, where small stages, about five feet high, had been erected. The first victim was a fine-looking man, about fifty years old, who showed no fear. He stood by one of the stages with his hands tied behind him. A feticheer, or priest, laid hands on the victim's head and said some words of consecration lasting about two minutes and then at a sign, a man standing behind with a broad sword, cut off the head of the victim with one blow, and threw it on the stage. The body lay on the ground for a time so that the blood might drain off and slaves then dragged it away to a place adjoining the camp.*

About four hundred captives were sacrificed in this manner. The men went to the stages, bold and unconcerned, but the cries of the

---

* Over a century later, Commander Forbes of the British Navy witnessed a similar sacrifice in the Dahomey country, when twelve victims, lashed hands and feet and tied in small baskets, were carried around the court and after a ceremony thrown from a parapet into a pit below. "The fall, upwards of twelve feet, may have stunned the victims and before sense could return, their heads were cut off and the bodies thrown to the mob, who, now armed with clubs and branches, brutally mutilated the bodies and dragged them to a distant pit." Forbes, *Dahomey and the Dahomans*, London, 1850.

women and children were most affecting and soon excited the fears of the Dutch captain that the priests might take it into their heads that white victims might be more acceptable to their *fetiche* than men of their own color. But no affront was shown the Europeans and after two hours spent standing near the stages they returned to their tent. The next morning they discovered that the bodies of the sacrificed had been taken away in the night by the people, who had boiled and feasted on them, as holy food.

At an audience with the king, the next day, an agreement was made whereby slaves, sufficient for a cargo, should be sent down to the shore at Jaqueen and that Captain Snelgrave should have three males to one female and be obliged to accept only those that he selected. The return journey was made without incident and at full speed, for the hammock-men were so much affected by the great sacrifice of Tuffoe people that they ran most of the way back to Jaqueen and arrived in an exhausted condition.

Two days later the slaves sent down by the king began to arrive in the town and one of the great captains of the king's court soon followed, to settle all matters in dispute. The day he appeared, the linguist brought to Captain Snelgrave two female slaves, saying that the king desired him to buy them, but as one was about fifty years old he told the linguist that she was past her labor and therefore declined to buy her. The young slave he purchased at the agreed price. Not long after the linguist reported that the older woman, by order of the great captain, had been sacrificed to the sea, for she had offended the king, and not having been sold, she must be destroyed. The linguist suspected this must be done because the woman had assisted some of the king's women in their love affairs and so incurred his emnity. On being questioned he related that "the Woman's Hands being tied behind her, and her Feet across, she was put into the *Cannoe*, and carried off about half a Mile from the Shore; And then he ordered the Rowers to throw her over board; which they had no sooner done but he saw some Sharks tear her to pieces in an Instant."

The next day a letter was brought ashore, from the mate of the *Katharine Galley,* which gave an account of the remarkable preservation of this slave woman. It happened that about the time the canoe of the linguist returned to the shore, one of the boats of the *Katharine Galley* left the moorings to go on board the ship and about halfway out came upon a human body lying on its back, every now and then spurting water out of its mouth. It was a woman, tied hand and foot, whom they hauled aboard, untied and rolled about to get the salt water out of her stomach. They took her on board the ship and sent word of her taking up to Captain Snelgrave.

While the preservation of the woman from sharks and her timely rescue by the boat's crew seemed quite providential, yet the captain was thereby placed in an awkward position, for should the king discover the fact he might pretend that his *fetiche* had been disappointed of this sacrifice and so desire revenge or a large present. To order the woman killed was out of the question so the captain sent orders to his mate to keep the rescue a secret and this was successfully done. The woman was exceedingly grateful for her rescue and during the voyage returned good service by helping to keep the slaves easy in their minds, especially the female negroes who usually were troublesome on account of their noise and clamor. On reaching the West Indies she was sold to Charles Dunbar, the surveyor general of Barbadoes, reputed to be a good master.

The *Katharine Galley* sailed from Jaqueen road, July 1, 1727, having on board over six hundred negroes and reached Antigua, W. I., after a tedious passage of seventeen weeks, where the cargo, having stood the voyage very well, came to a good market, and after lying there nearly three months for a return cargo of sugar, she sailed the last of February and got safe into the river Thames, on April 25, 1728, having made the round voyage in seventeen months.

Captain Snelgrave sailed in the Guinea trade for nearly thirty years and became familiar with all its details. The narrative that he wrote and which was published in London, in 1754,* may be considered a valuable contribution to our knowledge of the conduct of the trade at that time. He writes that it had been the custom, time out of mind, for negroes to make slaves of their captives taken in war, and when they had taken more than they could well employ on their plantations they were often obliged to kill many. It followed that they welcomed an opportunity to sell their surplus slaves to traders. Most crimes among the negro tribes were punished by mulcts and fines and if the offender could not pay he was sold for a slave. This was the practice of the inland people as well as those living on or near the sea shore. By this means so large a number of negroes became slaves that the trade on the Guinea coast, in the opinion of Captain Snelgrave, before the year 1730, had resulted in the exportation of at least seventy thousand natives. During the voyage to the West Indies and the American coast, the condition of the slaves in their narrow quarters on board ship was not only most uncomfortable, at the best, but usually a sickening and horrible experience that sometimes led to mutiny and wholesale death.

"These Munities," writes Captain Snelgrave, "are generally occasioned by the Sailors ill usage of these poor People, when on board the Ships wherein they are transported to our Plantations. Wherever, therefore, I have commanded, it has been my principal Care, to have the Negroes on board my Ship kindly used; and I have always strictly charged my white People to treat them with Humanity and Tenderness; In which I have usually found my Account, both in keeping them from mutinying and preserving them in health.

"And whereas it may seem strange to those that are unacquainted with the method of managing them, how we can carry so many hundreds together in a small Ship, and keep them in order; I shall just mention what is generally practised. When we purchase grown

* *A New Account of Guinea, and the Slave Trade*, by Capt. William Snelgrave, London, 1754.

People, I acquaint them by the Interpreter, 'That, now they are become my Property, I think fit to let them know what they are bought for, that they may be easy in their Minds:' (For these poor People are generally under terrible Apprehensions upon their being bought by white Men, many being afraid that we design to eat them; which, I have been told, is a story much credited by the inland Negroes;) 'So after informing them, That they are bought to till the Ground in our Country, with several other Matters; I then acquaint them, how they are to behave themselves on board, towards the white Men; that if any one abuses them, they are to complain to the Linguist, who is to inform me of it, and I will do them Justice: But if they make a Disturbance, or offer to strike a White Man, they must expect to be severely punished.'

"When we purchase the Negroes, we couple the sturdy Men together with Irons; but we suffer the Women and Children to go freely about: And soon after we have sail'd from the Coast, we undo all the Mens Irons.

"They are fed twice a day, and are allowed in fair Weather to come on Deck at seven a clock in the Morning, and to remain there, if they think proper, till Sun setting. Every Monday Morning they are served with Pipes and Tobacco, which they are very fond of. The Men Negroes lodge separate from the Women and Children; and the places where they all lye are cleaned every day, some white Men being appointed to see them do it. . . .

"The first Mutiny I saw among the Negroes, happened during my first Voyage in the Year 1704. It was on board the *Eagle Galley* of London, commanded by my Father, with whom I was Purser. We had bought our Negroes in the River of *Old Callabar* in the Bay of *Guinea*. At the time of their mutinying, we were in that River, having four hundred of them on board, and not above ten white Men who were able to do Service: For several of our Ship's Company were dead and many more sick; besides, two of our Boats were just then gone with twelve People on Shore to fetch Wood, which lay in sight of the Ship. All these Circumstances put the

Negroes on consulting how to mutiny, which they did at four a clock in the Afternoon, just as they went to Supper. But as we had always carefully examined the Mens Irons, both Morning and Evening, none had got them off, which in a great measure contributed to our Preservation. Three white Men stood on the Watch with Cutlaces in their Hands. One of them who was on the Forecastle, a stout fellow, seeing some of the Men Negroes take hold of the chief Mate, in order to throw him over board, he laid on them so heartily with the flat side of his Cutlace, that they soon quitted the Mate, who escaped from them, and run on the Quarter Deck to get Arms. I was then sick with an Ague—and lying on a Couch in the great Cabbin, the Fit being just come on. However, I no sooner heard the Outcry, *That the Slaves were mutinying,* but I took two Pistols, and run on the Deck with them; where meeting with my Father and the chief Mate, I delivered a Pistol to each of them. Whereupon they went forward on the Booms, calling to the Negroe Men that were on the Forecastle; but they did not regard their Threats, being busy with the Centry (who had disengaged the chief Mate), and they would have certainly killed him with his own Cutlace, could they have got it from him; but they could not break the Line wherewith the Handle was fastened to his Wrist. And so, tho' they had seized him, yet they could not make use of his Cutlace. Being thus disappointed, they endeavoured to throw him overboard, but he held so fast by one of them that they could not do it. My Father seeing this stout Man in so much Danger, ventured amongst the Negroes, to save him; and fired his Pistol over their Heads, thinking to frighten them. But a lusty Slave struck him with a Billet so hard, that he was almost stunned. The Slave was going to repeat the Blow, when a young Lad about seventeen years old, whom we had been kind to, interposed his Arm, and received the Blow, by which his Arm-bone was fractured. At the same instant the Mate fired his Pistol, and shot the Negroe that had struck my Father. At the sight of this the Mutiny ceased, and all the Men-negroes on the Forecastle threw themselves flat on their Faces, crying out for Mercy.

"Upon examining into the matter, we found, there were not above twenty Men Slaves concerned in this Mutiny; and the two Ringleaders were missing, having, it seems, jumped overboard as soon as they found their Project defeated, and were drowned. This was all the Loss we suffered on this occasion. For the Negroe that was shot by the Mate, the Surgeon, beyond all Expectation, cured. And I had the good Fortune to lose my Ague, by the fright and hurry I was put into. Moreover, the young Man, who had received the Blow on his Arm to save my Father, was cured by the Surgeon in our Passage to Virginia. At our Arrival in that place we gave him his Freedom; and a worthy Gentleman, one Colonel Carter, took him into his Service, till he became well enough acquainted in the Country to provide for himself.

"I have been several Voyages, when there has been no Attempt made by our Negroes to mutiny; which, I believe, was owing chiefly, to their being kindly used, and to my Officers Care in keeping a good Watch. But sometimes we meet with stout stubborn People amongst them, who are never to be made easy; and these are generally some of the Cormantines, a Nation of the Gold Coast. I went in the year 1721, in the *Henry* of London, a Voyage to that part of the Coast, and bought a good many of these People. We were obliged to secure them very well in Irons, and watch them narrowly: Yet they nevertheless mutined, tho' they had little prospect of succeeding. I lay at that time near a place called Mumfort, on the Gold Coast, having near five hundred Negroes on board, three hundred of which were Men. Our Ship's Company consisted of fifty white People, all in health: And I had very good Officers; so that I was very easy in all respects.

"This Mutiny began at Midnight (the Moon then shining very bright) in this manner. Two Men that stood Centry at the Forehatch way, where the Men Slaves came up to go to the house of Office, permitted four to go to that place; but neglected to lay the

Gratings again, as they should have done: Whereupon four more Negroes came on Deck, who had got their Irons off, and the four in the house of Office having done the same, all the eight fell on the two Centries, who immediately called out for help. The Negroes endeavoured to get their Cutlaces from them, but the Lineyards (that is the Lines by which the handles of the Cutlaces were fastened to the Mens Wrists) were so twisted in the Scuffle, that they could not get them off before we came to their Assistance. The Negroes perceiving several white Men coming towards them, with Arms in their hands, quitted the Centries, and jumped over the Ship's side into the Sea.

"I being by this time come forward on the Deck, my first care was to secure the Gratings, to prevent any more Negroes from coming up; and then I ordered People to get into the Boat, and save those that had jumped over-board, which they luckily did: For they found them all clinging to the Cables the Ship was moored by.

"After we had secured these People, I called the Linguists, and ordered them to bid the Men-Negroes between Decks be quiet (for there was a great noise amongst them). On their being silent, I asked, 'What had induced them to mutiny?' They answered, 'I was a great Rogue to buy them, in order to carry them away from their own Country; and that they were resolved to regain their Liberty if possible.' I replied, 'That they had forfeited their Freedom before I bought them, either by Crimes, or by being taken in War, according to the Custom of their Country; and they being now my Property, I was resolved to let them feel my Resentment, if they abused my Kindness: Asking at the same time, Whether they had been ill used by the white Men, or had wanted for any thing the Ship afforded?' To this they replied, 'They had nothing to complain of.' Then I observed to them, 'That if they should gain their Point and escape to the Shore, it would be no Advantage to them, because their Countrymen would catch them, and sell them to other Ships.' This served my purpose, and they seemed to be convinced of their Fault, begging, 'I would forgive them, and promising for the future to be obedient, and never mutiny again, if I would not punish them this time.' This I readily granted, and so they went to sleep. When Day-light came we called the Men-Negroes up on Deck, and examining their Irons, found them all secure. So this Affair happily ended, which I was very glad of; for these People are the stoutest and most sensible Negroes on the Coast: Neither are they so weak as to imagine as others do, that we buy them to eat them; being satisfied we carry them to work in our Plantations, as they do in their own Country.

"However, a few days after this, we discovered they were plotting again, and preparing to mutiny. For some of the Ringleaders proposed to one of our Linguists, If he could procure them an Ax, they would cut the Cables the Ship rid by in the night; and so on her driving (as they imagined) ashore, they should get out of our hands, and then would become his Servants as long as they lived.

"For the better understanding of this I must observe here, that these Linguists are Natives and Freeman of the Country, whom we hire on account of their speaking good English, during the time we remain trading on the Coast; and they are likewise Brokers between us and the black Merchants.

"This Linguist was so honest as to acquaint me with what had been proposed to him; and advised me to keep a strict Watch over the Slaves: For tho' he had represented to them the same as I had done on their mutinying, before, That they would be all catch'd again, and sold to other Ships, in case they could carry their Point, and get on Shore; yet it had no effect upon them.

"This gave me a good deal of uneasiness. For I knew several Voyages had proved unsuccessful by Mutinies; as they occasioned either the total loss of the Ship and the white Men's Lives; or at least by rendering it absolutely necessary to kill or wound a great number of the Slaves, in order to prevent a total Destruction. Moreover, I knew many of these Cormantine Negroes despised Punishment, and even Death itself: It having often happened at Barbadoes and other Islands, that on their being any ways hardly dealt with, to break them of their Stubbornness in refusing to work, twenty or more have hang'd themselves at a time in a Plantation. However, about a Month after this, a sad Accident happened, that brought our Slaves to be more orderly, and put them in a better Temper: And it was this. On our going from Mumfort to Annamaboe, which is the principal part on the Gold Coast, I met there with another of my Owner's Ships, called the *Elizabeth*. One Captain Thompson, that commanded her, was dead; as also his chief Mate: Moreover, the Ship had afterwards been taken at Cape Laboe on the windward Coast, by Roberts the Pirate, with whom several of the Sailors belonging to her had entered. However, some of the Pirates had hindered the Cargoe's being plundered, and obtained that the Ship should be restored to the second Mate: Telling him, 'They did it out of respect to the generous Character his Owner bore, in doing good to poor Sailors.'

"When I met with this Vessel I had almost disposed of my Ship's Cargoe: and the *Elizabeth* being under my Direction, I acquainted the second Mate, who then commanded her, That I thought it for our Owner's Interest, to take the Slaves from on board him, being about 120, into my Ship; and then go off the Coast; and that I would deliver him at the same time the Remains of my Cargoe, for him to dispose of with his own after I was sailed. This he readily complied with, but told me, 'He feared his Ship's Company would mutiny, and oppose my taking the Slaves from him.' And indeed, they came at that instant in a Body on the Quarter-deck; where one spoke for the rest, telling me plainly, 'that they would not allow the Slaves to be taken out by me.' I found by this they had lost all respect for their present Commander, who indeed was a weak Man. However, I calmly asked the reason, 'Why they offered to oppose my taking the Slaves?' To which they answered, 'I had no business with them.' On this I desired the Captain to send to his Scrutore, for the Book of Instructions Captain Thompson had received from our Owner; and he read to them, at my request, that Part, in which their former Captain, or his Successor (in case of Death) was to follow my Orders. Hereupon they all cried out, 'they should remain a great while longer on the Coast to purchase more Slaves, if I took these from them, which they were resolved to oppose.' I answered, 'That such of the Ship's Company as desired it, I would receive on board my own; where they should have the same Wages they had at present on board the *Elizabeth,* and I would send some of my own People to supply their Places.' This, so reasonable an Offer, was refused, one of the Men who was the Ship's Cooper telling me, that the Slaves had been on board a long time, and they had great Friendship with them: therefore they would keep them. I asked him, 'Whether he had ever been on the Coast of Guinea before?' He replied no. Then I told him, 'I supposed he had not by his way of talking, and advised him not to rely on the Friendship of the Slaves, which he might have reason to repent of when too late.' And 'Tis remarkable this very person was killed by them the next Night, as shall be presently related.

"So finding that reasoning with these Men was to no Purpose, I told them, 'When I came with my Boats to fetch the Slaves, they should find me as resolute to chastise such of them as should dare to oppose me, as I had been condescending to convince them by arguing calmly.' So I took my leave of their Captain, telling him, 'I would come next Morning to finish the Affair.'

"But that very Night, which was near a month after the Mutiny on board of us at Mumfort, the Moon shining now very bright, as it did then, we heard, about ten a Clock, two or three Musquets fired on board the *Elizabeth.* Upon that I ordered all our Boats to be manned, and having secured every thing in our Ship, to prevent our Slaves from mutinying, I went myself in our Pinnace (the other Boats following me), on board the *Elizabeth,* in our way we saw two Negroes swimming from her, but before we could reach them with our Boats, some Sharks rose from the bottom, and tore them in Pieces. We came presently along the side of the Ship, where we found two Men-Negroes holding by a Rope, with their Heads just above water; they were afraid, it seems, to swim from the Ship's

side, having seen their Companions devoured just before by the
Sharks. These two Slaves we took into our Boat, and then went into
the Ship, where we found the Negroes very quiet, and all under
Deck: but the Ship's Company was on the Quarter-Deck, in a great
Confusion, saying, 'The Cooper, who had been placed centry at the
Fore-hatch way, over the Men-Negroes, was, they believed, kill'd
by them.' I was surprised to hear this, wondering that these cow-
ardly fellows, who had so vigorously opposed my taking the Slaves
out, a few hours before, had not Courage enough to venture forward, to save their Ship-mate; but had secured themselves by shutting the Quarter-deck-door, where they all stood with Arms in their
Hands. So I went to the fore-part of the Ship with some of my
People, and there we found the Cooper lying on his back quite
dead, his Scull being cleft asunder with a Hatchet that lay by him.
At the sight of this I called for the Linguist, and bid him ask the
Negroes between Decks, 'Who had killed the white Man?' They
answered, 'They knew nothing of the matter; for there had been
no design of mutinying amongst them:' Which upon Examination
we found true; for above one hundred of the Negroes then on
board, being bought to Windward, did not understand a word of
the Gold Coast Language, and so had not been in the Plot. But this
Mutiny was contrived by a few Cormantee-Negroes, who had been
purchased about two or three days before. At last, one of the two
Men-Negroes we had taken up along the Ship side, impeached his
Companion, and he readily confessed he had kill'd the Cooper, with
no other View, but that he and his Countrymen might escape undis-
covered by swimming on Shore. For on their coming upon Deck,
they observed, that all the white Men set to watch were asleep; and
having found the Cook's Hatchet by the Fire-place, he took it up,
not designing then to do any Mischief with it; but passing by the
Cooper, who was centry, and he beginning to awake, the Negroe
rashly struck him on the head with it, and then jump'd overboard.
Upon this frank Confession, the white Men would have cut him to
Pieces; but I prevented it, and carried him to my own Ship. Early

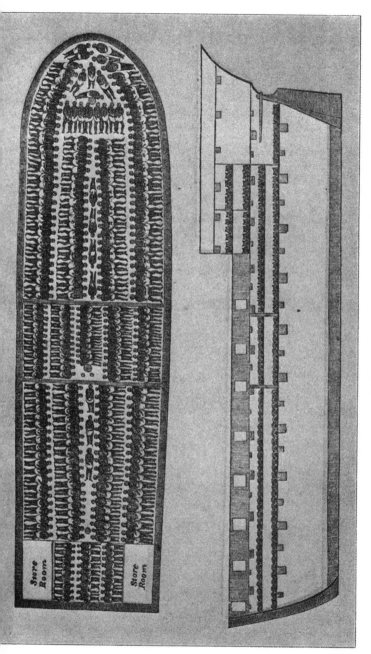

SECTION SHOWING METHOD OF STOWING SLAVES, IN 1786, ON THE SHIP "BROOKES"
OF LIVERPOOL

From Clarkson's *Abolition of the Slave Trade*, London, 1808

CARRYING SLAVES TO A PORTUGUESE SLAVE BRIG LYING IN BONNY RIVER

From a drawing by T. F. Birch, made in January, 1837, in the Macpherson Collection

the next morning, I went on board the *Elizabeth* with my Boats, and sent away all the Negroes then in her, into my own Ship: not one of the other Ship's Company offering to oppose it. Two of them, the Carpenter and Steward, desired to go with me, which I readily granted; and by way of Security for the future Success of the Voyage, I put my chief Mate, and four of my under Officers (with their own Consent), on board the *Elizabeth*; and they arrived about five Months after this, at Jamaica, having disposed of most part of the Cargoe.

"After having sent the Slaves out of the *Elizabeth*, as I have just now mentioned, I went on board my own Ship, and there being then in the Road of Anamaboe, eight sail of Ships besides us, I sent an Officer in my Boat to the Commanders of them, 'To desire their Company on board my Ship, because I had an Affair of great Consequence to communicate to them.' Soon after, most of them were pleased to come; and I having acquainted them with the whole Matter, and they having also heard the Negroe's Confession, 'That he had killed the white Man'; They unanimously advised me to put him to death; arguing, 'That Blood required Blood by all Laws both divine and human; especially as there was in this Case the clearest Proof, namely the Murderer's Confession: Moreover this would in all probability prevent future Mischiefs; for by publickly executing this Person at the Ship's Fore-yard Arm, the Negroes on board their Ships would see it; and as they were very much disposed to mutiny, it might prevent them from 'attempting it.' These Reasons, with my being in the same Circumstances, made me comply.

"Accordingly we acquainted the Negroe, that he was to die in an hour's time for murdering the white Man. He answered, 'He must confess it was a rash Action in him to kill him; but he desired me to consider, that if I put him to death, I should lose all the Money I had paid for him.' To this I bid the Interpreter reply, 'That tho' I knew it was customary in his Country to commute for Murder by a Sum of Money, yet it was not so with us; and he should find that I had no regard to my Profit in this respect: For as soon as an Hour-

Glass, just then turned, was run out, he should be put to death'; At which I observed he shewed no Concern.

"Hereupon the other Commanders went on board their respective Ships, in order to have all their Negroes upon Deck at the time of Execution, and to inform them of the occasion of it. The Hour-Glass being run out, the Murderer was carried on the Ship's Fore-castle, where he had a Rope fastened under his Arms, in order to be hoisted up to the Fore-yard Arm, to be shot to death. This some of his Countrymen observing, told him (as the Linguist informed me afterwards), 'That they would not have him be frightened; for it was plain I did not design to put him to death, otherwise the Rope would have been put about his neck, to hang him.' For it seems they had no thought of his being shot; judging he was only to be hoisted up to the Yard-arm, in order to scare him: But they immediately saw the contrary; for as soon as he was hoisted up, ten white Men who were placed behind the Barricado on the Quarter-deck, fired their Musquets, and instantly killed him. This struck a sudden Damp on our Negroe-Men, who thought, that, on account of my Profit, I would not have executed him.

"The Body being let down upon the Deck, the Head was cut off, and thrown overboard. This last part was done, to let our Negroes see, that all who offended thus, should be served in the same manner. For many of the Blacks believe, that if they are put to death and not disr_mbered, they shall return again to their own Country, after they are thrown overboard. But neither the Person that was executed, nor his Countrymen of Cormantee (as I understood afterwards), were so weak as to believe any such thing; tho' many I had on board from other Countries had that Opinion.

"When the Execution was over, I ordered the Linguist to acquaint the Men-Negroes, 'That now they might judge, no one that killed a white Man should be spared:' And I thought proper now to acquaint them once for all, 'That if they attempted to mutiny again, I should be obliged to punish the Ringleaders with death, in order to prevent further Mischief.' Upon this they all promised to be obedient, and I assured them they should be kindly used, if they kept their Promise: which they faithfully did. For we sailed, two days after, from Annamaboe for Jamaica; and tho' they were on board near four Months, from our going off the Coast, till they were sold at that Island, they never gave us the least reason to be jealous of them: which doubtless was owing to the Execution of the white Man's Murderer.

"These three Mutinies, I have here related, are all that ever happened where I was present, tho' I have gone many Voyages to the Coast of Guinea. But I have heard of several, that have ended in a very tragical manner. However, to avoid being tedious, I shall relate only one, which is very remarkable, and happen'd on board the *Ferres Galley* of London, Capt. Messervy; who, by his over-care, and too great Kindness to the Negroes on board his Ship, was destroyed by them, and the Voyage at last came to nothing. I met this Gentleman at Anamaboe on the Coast of Guinea, in January 1722. At his coming on board my Ship, he informed me of his good fortune, in that he had purchased near 300 Negroes in a few Days, at a place called Cetre-Crue, on the windward part of the Coast of Guinea, which happened in this manner.

"It seems the Inhabitants of this place, which lies near the Sea-side, had been often misused by some inland People, who for a long time had treated them in a villainous manner, whenever they went to their Towns with Salt, or any other Commodities to sell. For knowing the People of Cetre-Crue, did in a great measure depend on them for their Food, which is Rice, they took their Commodities, and gave them just what quantity of Rice they pleased, in exchange. The Cetre-Crues having long complained of this injury, without redress, resolved to bear it no longer, but to revenge themselves by Arms. And they were crowned with Success, destroying and taking all the Inhabitants of the principal Town where they used to go and buy Rice.

"Captain Messervy happened to anchor near Cetre-Crue just at that time, and had the opportunity of purchasing a great many of the

Captives at an easy rate. For the Conquerors were glad to get something for them, at that instant, since, if a Ship had not been in the Road, they would have been obliged to have killed most of the Men-Captives, for their own Security.

"After the Captain had told me this story, he desired me to spare him some Rice, having heard, I had purchased a great many Tuns to the Windward; where he had bought little, not expecting to meet with so many Slaves. This request I could not comply with, having provided no more than was necessary for my self, and for another of my Owner's Ships, which I quickly expected. And understanding from him, that he had never been on the Coast of Guinea before, I took the liberty to observe to him, 'That as he had on board so many Negroes of one Town and Language, it required the utmost Care and Management to keep them from mutinying; and that I was sorry he had so little Rice for them: For I had experienced that the Windward Slaves are always very fond of it, it being their usual Food in their own Country; and he might certainly expect dissatisfactions and Uneasiness amongst them for want of a sufficient quantity.'

"This he took kindly, and having asked my Advice about other Matters, took his leave, inviting me to come next day to see him. I went accordingly on board his Ship, about three a clock in the afternoon. At four a clock the Negroes went to Supper, and Captain Messervy desired me to excuse him for a quarter of an hour, whilst he went forward to see the Men-Negroes served with Victuals. I observed from the Quarter-Deck, that he himself put Pepper and Palm Oyl amongst the Rice they were going to eat. When he came back to me, I could not forbear observing to him, 'How imprudent it was in him to do so: For tho' it was proper for a Commander sometimes to go forward and observe how things were managed, yet he ought to take a proper time, and have a good many of his white People in Arms when he went; or else they having him so much in their Power, might encourage the Slaves to mutiny: For he might depend upon it, they always aim at the chief Person in the Ship, whom they soon distinguish by the respect shown him by the rest of the People.'

"He thanked me for this Advice, but did not seem to relish it; saying, 'He thought the old Proverb good, that *The Master's Eye makes the Horse fat.'* We then fell into other Discourse, and among other things he told me, 'He designed to go away in a few days.' Accordingly he sailed three days after for Jamaica. Some Months after I went for that place, where, at my arrival, I found his Ship, and had the following melancholy account of his Death, which happened about ten days after he left the Coast of Guinea in this manner.

"Being on the forecastle of the Ship, amongst the Men-Negroes, when they were eating their Victuals, they laid hold on him, and beat out his Brains with the little Tubs, out of which they eat their boiled Rice. This Mutiny having been plotted amongst all the grown Negroes on board, they run to the fore-part of the Ship in a body, and endeavoured to force the Barricado on the Quarter-Deck, not regarding the Musquets or Half Pikes, that were presented to their Breasts by the white Men, through the Loop-holes. So that at last the chief Mate was obliged to order one of the Quarter-deck Guns laden with Partridge-Shot, to be fired amongst them; which occasioned a terrible Destruction: For there were near eighty Negroes kill'd and drowned, many jumping overboard when the Gun was fired. This indeed put an end to the Mutiny, but most of the Slaves that remained alive grew so sullen, that several of them were starved to death, obstinately refusing to take any Sustenance; And after the Ship was arrived at Jamaica, they attempted twice to mutiny, before the Sale of them began. This, with their former Misbehaviour, coming to be publickly known, none of the Planters cared to buy them, tho' offered at a low Price. So that this proved a very unsuccessful Voyage, for the Ship was detained many Months at Jamaica on that account, and at last was lost there in a Hurricane."

CHAPTER VII

THE SHIP DOCTOR'S NARRATIVE

ON THE arrival of the ships at Bonny* and New Calabar, it is customary for them to unbend the sails, strike the yards and topmasts and begin to build what they denominate a *house*. This is effected in the following manner. The sailors first lash the booms and yards from mast to mast in order to form a *ridge-pole*. About ten feet above the deck, several spars, equal in length to the ridge-pole, are next lashed to the standing rigging and form a wall-plate. Across the ridge-pole and wall-plate, several other spars or rafters are afterwards laid and lashed at the distance of about six inches from each other. On these, other rafters or spars are laid lengthwise, equal in extent to the ridge-pole, so as to form a kind of lattice or net-work, with interstices of six inches square. The roof is then covered with mats, made of rushes of very loose texture, fastened together with rope-yarn and so placed as to lap over each other like tiles. The space between the deck and the wall-plate is likewise enclosed with a kind of lattice or net-work formed of sticks lashed across each other and leaving vacancies of about four inches square. Near the mainmast a partition is constructed of inch deal boards which reaches athwart the ship. This division is called a *barricado*. It is about eight feet in height and is made to project about two feet over the sides of the ship. In this barricado there is a door at which a sentinel is placed during the time the negroes are permitted to come upon deck. It serves also to keep the different sexes apart; and as there are small holes in it, where blunderbusses are fixed and sometimes a cannon, it is very convenient for quelling insurrections that now and then happen. Another door is made in the lattice or network at the ladder by which you enter the ship.

* This account of slaving is abstracted from Alexander Falconbridge's *Account of the Slave Trade on the Coast of Africa*, London, 1788.

This door is guarded by a sentinel during the day and is locked at night. At the head of the ship there is a third door, for the use of the sailors, which is secured in the same manner as that at the gangway. There is also in the roof a large trap-door through which the goods intended for barter, the water casks, &c., are hoisted out or in.

The design of this house is to secure those on board from the heat of the sun, which in this latitude is intense, and from the wind and rain which at particular seasons are likewise extremely violent. It answers these purposes, however, but very ineffectually. The slight texture of the mats admits both the wind and the rain, whenever it happens to be violent, and at the same time it increases the heat of the ship to a very pernicious degree, especially between decks. The increased warmth occasioned by this means, together with the smoke produced from the green mangrove (the usual firewood) which, for want of a current of air to carry it off, collects and infects every part of the ship, render a vessel during its stay here very unhealthy. The smoke also, by its acrimonious quality, often produces inflammations in the eyes which terminates sometimes in the loss of sight.

Another purpose for which these temporary houses are erected is to prevent the purchased negroes from leaping overboard. This, the horrors of their situation frequently impel them to attempt; and they now and then succeed notwithstanding all the precautions that are taken, by forcing their way through the lattice work.

The slave ships generally lie a mile below the town, in Bonny River, in seven or eight fathoms of water. Sometimes fifteen sail, English and French, but chiefly the former, meet here together. Soon after they cast anchor, the captains go on shore to make known their arrival and to inquire into the state of the trade. They likewise invite the kings of Bonny to come on board, to whom, previous to breaking bulk, they usually make presents (in that country termed *dashes*) which generally consist of pieces of cloth, cotton, chintz, silk handkerchiefs and other India goods and sometimes brandy, wine or beer.

When I was at Bonny, a few years ago, it was the residence of two kings whose names were *Norfolk* and *Peppel.* The houses of these princes were not distinguished from the cottages or huts of which the town consists, in any other manner, than by being of somewhat larger dimensions and surrounded with warehouses containing European goods designed for the purchase of slaves. These slaves, which the kings procure in the same manner as the black traders do theirs, are sold by them to the ships. And for every negro sold there by the traders, the kings receive a duty which amounts to a considerable sum in the course of a year. This duty is collected by officers, stationed on board the ships, who are termed *officer boys;* a denomination which it is thought they received from the English.

The kings of Bonny are absolute, though elective. They are assisted in the government by a small number of persons of a certain rank, who style themselves *parliament gentlemen;* an office which they generally hold for life. Every ship, on its arrival, is expected to send a present to these gentlemen, of a small quantity of bread and beef, and likewise to treat them as often as they come on board. When they do this, their approach to the ship is announced by blowing through a hollow elephant's tooth which produces a sound resembling that of a post-horn.

After the kings have been on board and have received the usual presents, permission is granted by them for trafficking with any of the black traders. When the royal guests return from the ships they are saluted by the guns.

From the time of the arrival of the ships to their departure, which is usually about three months, scarce a day passes without some negroes being purchased and carried on board; sometimes in small and sometimes in larger numbers. The whole number taken on board depends in a great measure on circumstances. In a voyage I once made, our stock of merchandise was exhausted in the purchase of about 380 negroes, when it was expected to have procured 500. The number of English and French ships then at Bonny had raised the price of negroes so much as to occasion this difference.

The reverse (and a happy reverse I think I may call it) was

known during the war of the American Revolution. When I was last at Bonny, I frequently made inquiries on this head of one of the black traders whose intelligence I believe I can depend upon. He informed me that only one ship had been there for three years during that period; and that was the *Moseley Hill*, Captain Ewing, from Liverpool, who made an extraordinary purchase, as he found negroes remarkably cheap from the dulness of trade. Upon further inquiring of my black acquaintance what was the consequence of this decay of their trade, he shrugged up his shoulders and answered, *"Only making us traders poorer and obliging us to work for our maintenance."* One of these black merchants being informed that a particular set of people, called Quakers, were for abolishing the trade, he said *it was a very bad thing, as they should then be reduced to the same state they were in during the war, when, through poverty, they were obliged to dig the ground and plant yams.*

I was once upon the coast of Angola, also, when there had not been a slave ship at the river Ambris for five years previous to our arrival, although a place to which many usually resort every year; and the failure of the trade for that period, as far as we could learn, had no other effect than to restore peace and confidence among the natives; which, upon the arrival of ships, is immediately destroyed by the inducement then held forth in the purchase of slaves. And during the suspension of trade at Bonny, as above-mentioned, none of the dreadful proceedings which are so confidently asserted to be the natural consequence of it, were known. The reduction of the price of negroes and the poverty of the black traders appear to have been the only *bad* effects of the discontinuance of trade; the *good* ones were, *most probably*, the restoration of peace and confidence among the natives and a suspension of kidnapping.

After permission has been obtained for *breaking trade*, as it is termed, the captains go ashore, from time to time, to examine the negroes that are exposed to sale and to make their purchases. The slaves are bought by the black traders at fairs, which are held for that purpose, at the distance of upwards of two hundred miles from the sea coast; and these fairs are said to be supplied from an interior part of the country. Many negroes, upon being questioned relative to the places of their nativity, have asserted that they have travelled during the revolution of several moons (their usual method of calculating time) before they have reached the places where they were purchased by the black traders. At these fairs, which are held at uncertain periods, but generally every six weeks, several thousands are frequently exposed to sale who had been collected from all parts of the country for a very considerable distance round. During one of my voyages, the black traders brought down, in different canoes, from twelve to fifteen hundred negroes which had been purchased at one fair. They consisted chiefly of men and boys, the women seldom exceeding a third of the whole number. From forty to two hundred negroes are generally purchased at a time by the black traders, according to the opulence of the buyer, and consist of all ages, from a month to sixty years and upwards. Scarcely any age or situation is deemed an exception, the price being proportionable. Women sometimes form a part of them, who happen to be so far advanced in their pregnacy as to be delivered during their journey from the fairs to the coast; and I have frequently seen instances of deliveries on board ship. The slaves purchased at these fairs are only for the supply of the markets at Bonny and Old and New Calabar.

There is great reason to believe that most of the negroes shipped from the coast of Africa are *kidnapped*. But the extreme care taken by the black traders to prevent the Europeans from gaining any intelligence of their modes of proceeding; the great distance inland from which the negroes are brought; and our ignorance of their language (with which, very frequently, the black traders themselves are equally unacquainted) prevent our obtaining such information on this head as we could wish. I have, however, by means of occasional inquiries made through interpreters, procured some intelligence relative to the point and such, as I think, puts the matter beyond a doubt.

On board one of the slave ships a negro informed me that being one evening invited to drink with some of the black traders, upon his going away they attempted to seize him. As he was very active he evaded them and got out of their hands, but was prevented from effecting his escape by a large dog which laid hold of him. These animals are kept by many of the traders for that purpose and being trained to the sport do very effective work.

I was also told by a negro woman that as she was on her return home one evening, from some neighbours to whom she had been making a visit by invitation, she was kidnapped and notwithstanding she was big with child, was sold for a slave. This transaction happened a considerable way up the country and she had passed through the hands of several purchasers before she reached the ship. A man and his son, according to their own information, were seized by professed kidnappers, while they were planting yams, and sold for slaves. This also happened in the interior parts of the country; and after passing through several hands they were purchased for the ship to which I belonged.

It frequently happens that those who kidnap others are themselves, in their turn, seized and sold. A negro in the West Indies informed me that after having been employed in kidnapping others he had experienced this reverse. And he assured me that it was a common incident among his countrymen.

Continual enmity is thus fostered among the negroes of Africa and all social intercourse between them destroyed; which most assuredly would not be the case had they not these opportunities of finding a ready sale for each other.

During my stay on the coast of Africa, I was an eyewitness of the following transaction:—A black trader invited a negro who resided a little way up the country, to come and see him. After the entertainment was over the trader proposed to his guest to treat him with a sight of one of the ships lying in the river. The unsuspicious countryman readily consented and accompanied the trader in a canoe to the side of the ship, which he viewed with pleasure and astonishment. While there, some black traders on board, who appeared to be in the secret, leaped into the canoe, seized the unfortunate man and dragging him into the ship immediately sold him.

Previous to my being in this employ I entertained a belief, as many others have done, that the kings and principal men bred negroes for sale as we do cattle. During the different times I was in the country, I took no little pains to satisfy myself in this particular; but notwithstanding I made many inquiries, I was not able to obtain the least intelligence of this being the case. All the information I could procure, confirmed me in the belief that to kidnapping and to crimes (and many of these were fabricated as a pretext) the slave trade owes its chief support.

Here is an instance that tends to prove that artifice is often made use of. Several black traders, one of whom was a person of consequence and exercised an authority somewhat similar to that of our magistrates, being in want of some particular kind of merchandise and not having a slave to barter for it, they accused a fisherman at the river Ambris, with extortion in the sale of his fish; and as they were interested in the decision they immediately adjudged the poor fellow guilty and condemned him to be sold. He was accordingly purchased by the ship to which I belonged and brought on board.

As an additional proof that kidnapping is not only the general but almost the sole mode by which slaves are procured, the black traders in purchasing them, choose those which are the roughest and most hardy; alleging that the smooth negroes have been *gentlemen*. From which we may conclude they mean that nothing but fraud or force could have reduced these smooth-skinned gentlemen to a state of slavery.

In order to prove that the wars among the Africans do not furnish the number of slaves they are supposed to do, I may say that I never saw any negroes with recent wounds; which must have been the consequence, at least with some of them, had they been taken in battle. And it being my particular province, as the surgeon, to examine the slaves when they are purchased, such a circumstance could not have escaped my observation. As a farther corroboration it might be remarked, that on the Gold and Windward Coasts, where fairs are not held, the number of slaves procured at a time are usually very small.

The preparations made at Bonny by the black traders, upon setting out for the fairs which are held up the country, are very considerable. From twenty to thirty canoes, capable of containing thirty to forty negroes each, are assembled for this purpose; and such goods put on board as they expect will be wanted for the purchase of the number of slaves they intend to buy. When their loading is completed they commence their voyage with colors flying and music playing and in about ten or eleven days generally return to Bonny with full cargoes. As soon as the canoes arrive at the trader's landing-place, the purchased negroes are cleaned and oiled with palm oil and on the following day they are exposed for sale to the captains.

The black traders do not always purchase their slaves at the same rate. The speed with which the information of the arrival of ships upon the coast is conveyed to the fairs, considering that it is the interest of the traders to keep them ignorant, is really surprising. In a very short time after any ships arrive upon the coast, especially if several make their appearance together, those who dispose of the negroes at the fairs are frequently known to increase their prices; and these fairs are not the only means, though they are the chief, by which the black traders on the coast are supplied with negroes. Small parties of from five to ten are frequently brought to the houses of the traders, by those who make a practice of kidnapping and who are constantly employed in procuring a supply while purchasers are to be found.

When the negroes that the black traders have to dispose of, are shown to the European purchasers, they first examine them relative to their age. They then minutely inspect their persons and inquire into the state of their health; if they are afflicted with any disease or are deformed or have bad eyes or teeth; if they are lame or weak in the joints or distorted in the back or of a slender make or are narrow in the chest; in short, if they have been or are afflicted in any manner so as to render them incapable of much labor. If any of the foregoing defects are discovered in them they are rejected. But if approved of, they are generally taken on board the ship the same evening. The purchaser has liberty to return on the following morning, but not afterwards, such as upon re-examination are found exceptionable.

The traders frequently beat the negroes which are objected to by the captains and use them with great severity. It matters not whether they are refused on account of age, illness, deformity or for any other reason. At New Calabar, in particular, the traders have frequently been known to put them to death. Instances have happened at that place, when negroes have been objected to, that the traders have dropped their canoes under the stern of the vessel and instantly beheaded them in sight of the captain.

On the Windward Coast another mode of procuring slaves is pursued; that is, by *boating,* a mode that is very destructive to the crews of the ships. The sailors who are employed upon this trade go in boats up the rivers, seeking for negroes among the villages situated on the banks of these streams. But this method is very slow and not always effectual. After being absent from the ship during a fortnight or three weeks, they sometimes return with only from eight to twelve negroes.

I have good reason to believe that of the one hundred and twenty negroes purchased for the ship to which I then belonged, then lying at the river Ambris, by far the greater part, if not the whole, were kidnapped. This, with various other instances, confirms me in the belief that it is kidnapping that supplies the thousands of negroes annually sold off the Windward and other Coasts where boating prevails.

As soon as the wretched negroes fall into the hands of the black traders, they experience an earnest of the sufferings which they are doomed in future to undergo. And there is not the least doubt that even before they can reach the fairs, great numbers perish from cruel usage. They are brought from the places where they are purchased, to Bonny, &c., in canoes, at the bottom of which they lie, having their hands tied with a kind of willow twigs and a strict watch is kept over them. Their usage in other respects, during the time of the passage, which generally lasts several days, is equally cruel. Their allowance of food is so scanty that it is barely sufficient to support nature and they are also much exposed to the violent rains which frequently fall, being covered only with mats that afford but a slight defence; and as there is usually water in the bottom of the canoes they are scarcely ever dry.

And after they become the property of Europeans their treatment is no less severe. The men, on being brought aboard ship, are immediately fastened together, two and two, by handcuffs on their wrists and by irons rivetted on their legs. They are then sent down between the decks and placed in a space partitioned off for that purpose. The women also are placed in a separate space between decks, but without being ironed. An adjoining room, on the same deck, is set apart for the boys.

At the same time, however, they are frequently stowed so close as to admit of no other position than lying on their sides. Nor will the height between decks, unless directly under the grating, allow them to stand; especially where there are platforms on either side, which is generally the case. These platforms are a kind of shelf, about eight or nine feet in width, extending from the side of the ship towards the centre. They are placed nearly midway between the decks, at the distance of two or three feet from each deck. Upon these the negroes are stowed in the same manner as they are on the deck underneath.

In each of the apartments are placed three or four large buckets, of a conical form, nearly two feet in diameter at the bottom and only one foot at the top and in depth about twenty-eight inches, to which, when necessary, the negroes have recourse. It often happens that those who are placed at a distance from the buckets, in endeavouring to get to them, tumble over their companions, in consequence of their being shackled. These accidents, although unavoidable, are productive of continual quarrels in which some of them are always bruised. In this situation, unable to proceed and prevented from getting to the tubs, they desist from the attempt; and as the necessities of nature are not to be resisted, they ease themselves as they lie. This becomes a fresh source of broils and disturbances and tends to render the condition of the poor wretches still more uncomfortable. The nuisance arising from these circumstances is not unfrequently increased by the tubs being much too small for the purpose intended and their being usually emptied but once every day. The rule for doing so, however, varies in different ships according to the attention paid to the health and convenience of the slaves by the captain.

When the ships have disposed of all their merchandize in the purchase of negroes and have laid in their stock of wood, water and yams, they prepare for sailing by getting up the yards and topmasts, reeving the running rigging, bending the sails, and by taking down the temporary house. They then drop down the river to wait for a favorable opportunity to pass over the bar which is formed by a number of sandbanks lying across the mouth of the river, with navigable channels between them. It is not uncommon for ships to get upon the bar and sometimes they are lost.

About eight o'clock in the morning the negroes are generally brought upon deck. Their irons being examined, a long chain, which is locked to a ring-bolt fixed in the deck, is run through the rings of the shackles of the men and then locked to another ring-bolt fixed in the deck. By this means fifty or sixty and sometimes more are fastened to one chain in order to prevent them from rising or endeavoring to escape. If the weather proves favorable they are permitted to remain in that situation till four or five in the afternoon when they are disengaged from the chain and sent below.

The diet of the negroes while on board, consists chiefly of horse-beans boiled to the consistence of a pulp; of boiled yams and rice and sometimes of a small quantity of beef or pork. The latter are frequently taken from the provisions laid in for the sailors. They sometimes make use of a sauce composed of palm-oil mixed with flour, water and pepper, which the sailors call *slabber-sauce*. Yams are the favorite food of the Eboe or Bight negroes, and rice or corn of those from the Gold and Windward Coasts; each preferring the produce of their native soil.

In their own country the negroes in general live on animal food and fish, with roots, yams and Indian corn. The horse-beans and rice, with which they are fed aboard ship, are chiefly brought from Europe. The latter, however, is sometimes purchased on the coast where it is superior to any other.

The Gold Coast negroes scarcely ever refuse any food that is offered them and they generally eat larger quantities of whatever is placed before them than any other species of negroes, whom they also excel in strength of body and mind. Most of the slaves have such an aversion to the horse-beans that unless they are narrowly watched, when fed upon deck, they will throw them overboard or in each other's faces when they quarrel.

They are commonly fed twice a day; about eight o'clock in the morning and four in the afternoon. In most ships they are only fed with their *own food* once a day. Their food is served up to them in tubs about the size of a small water bucket. They are placed round these tubs, in companies of ten to each tub, out of which they feed themselves with wooden spoons. These they soon lose and when they are not allowed others they feed themselves with their hands. In favorable weather they are fed upon deck but in bad weather their food is given them below. Numberless quarrels take place among them during their meals; more especially when they are put upon short allowance, which frequently happens if the passage from the coast of Guinea to the West India Islands proves of unusual length. In that case, the weak are obliged to be content with a very scanty portion. Their allowance of water is about half a pint each at every meal. It is handed round in a bucket and given to each negro in a pannekin, a small utensil with a straight handle, somewhat similar to

A View of Charleston, South Carolina

From a line engraving after a painting by T. Mellish, published about 1750, by John Bowles, London, in the Macpherson Collection

THE VOYAGE OF THE SABLE VENUS, FROM ANGOLA TO THE WEST INDIES

From a painting by T. Stothard, engraved for Edwards' *History of the West Indies*, London, 1818

This picture inspired the muse of a member of the British Parliament, as follows:

"Her skin excell'd the raven's plume,
Her breath the fragrant orange bloom,
Her eye the tropic beam:
Soft was her lip of silken down,
And mild her look as evening sun
That gilds the Cobre stream."

a sauce-boat. However, when the ships approach the islands with a favorable breeze, the slaves are no longer restricted.

Upon the negroes refusing to take food, I have seen coals of fire, glowing hot, put on a shovel and placed so near their lips as to scorch and burn them. And this has been accompanied with threats of forcing them to swallow the coals if they persisted in refusing to eat. This generally had the desired effect. I have also been credibly informed that a certain captain in the slave-trade, poured melted lead on such of his negroes as obstinately refused their food.

Exercise being considered necessary for the preservation of their health they are sometimes obliged to dance when the weather will permit their coming on deck. If they go about it reluctantly or do not move with agility, they are flogged; a person standing by them all the time with a cat-o'-nine-tails in his hand for that purpose. Their music, upon these occasions, consists of a drum, sometimes with only one head; and when that is worn out they make use of the bottom of one of the tubs before described. The poor wretches are frequently compelled to sing also; but when they do so, their songs are generally, as may naturally be expected, melancholy lamentations of their exile from their native country.

The women are furnished with beads for the purpose of affording them some amusement. But this end is generally defeated by the squabbles which are occasioned in consequence of their stealing from each other.

On board some ships the common sailors are allowed to have intercourse with such of the black women whose consent they can procure. And some of them have been known to take the inconstancy of their paramours so much to heart as to leap overboard and drown themselves. The officers are permitted to indulge their passions among them at pleasure and sometimes are guilty of such brutal excesses as disgrace human nature.

The hardships suffered by the negroes during the passage are scarcely to be conceived. They are far more violently affected by seasickness than Europeans and it frequently terminates in death, especially among the women. But the exclusion of fresh air is the most intolerable. For the purpose of admitting fresh air, most of the ships in the slave-trade are provided, between the decks, with five or six air-ports on each side of the ship, of about six inches in length and four in breadth; in addition to which, some few ships, but not one in twenty, have what they denominate *wind-sails*. But whenever the sea is rough and the rain heavy it becomes necessary to shut these and every other conveyance by which the air is admitted. The fresh air being thus excluded, the negroes' rooms very soon grow intolerably hot. The confined air, rendered noxious by the effuvia exhaled from their bodies and by being repeatedly breathed, soon produces fevers and fluxes which generally carry off great numbers of them.

During the voyages I made, I was frequently a witness to the fatal effects of this exclusion of the fresh air. One instance will serve to convey some idea, though a very faint one, of their terrible sufferings. Some wet and blowing weather having occasioned the port-holes to be shut and the grating to be covered, fluxes and fevers among the negroes ensued. While they were in this situation, I frequently went down among them till at length their rooms became so extremely hot as to be only bearable for a very short time. But the excessive heat was not the only thing that rendered their situation intolerable. The deck, that is, the floor of their rooms, was so covered with the blood and mucus which had proceeded from them in consequence of the flux, that it resembled a slaughter-house. It is not in the power of the human imagination to picture a situation more dreadful or disgusting. Numbers of the slaves having fainted they were carried upon deck where several of them died and the rest with great difficulty were restored. It had nearly proved fatal to me also. The climate was too warm to admit the wearing of any clothing but a shirt and that I had pulled off before I went down; notwithstanding which, by only continuing among them for about a quarter of an hour, I was so overcome with the heat, stench and foul air that I nearly fainted; and it was only with assistance that I could get on deck. The consequence was that I soon after fell sick of the same disorder from which I did not recover for several months.

A circumstance of this kind sometimes repeatedly happens in the course of a voyage; and often to a greater degree than that which has just been described, particularly when the slaves are much crowded, which was not the case at that time, the ship being more than a hundred short of the number she was to have taken.

A certain Liverpool ship once took on board at Bonny, at least seven hundred negroes. By shipping so large a number, the slaves were so crowded that they were obliged to lie one upon another. This occasioned such a mortality among them that without meeting with unusual bad weather or having a longer voyage than common, nearly one half of them died before the ship arrived in the West Indies.

That it may be possible to form some idea of the almost incredible small space into which so large a number of negroes were crammed, the following particulars of this ship are given. According to Liverpool custom she measured 235 tons. Her width across the beam was 25 feet. Length between the decks, 92 feet, which was divided into four rooms, thus:

Store room, in which no negroes were placed	15 feet
Negroe's rooms—men's rooms—about	45 feet
women's ditto—about	10 feet
boy's ditto—about	22 feet
Total room for negroes	77 feet

Exclusive of the platform before described, from 8 to 9 feet in breadth and equal in length to that of the rooms.

The ships in this trade are usually fitted out to receive only one third women negroes, or perhaps a smaller number, which the dimensions of the room allotted for them, above given, plainly show but in a greater disproportion.

One would naturally suppose that an attention to their own interest would prompt the owners of the Guinea ships not to permit their captains to take on board a greater number of negroes than the ship would allow room sufficient for them to lie with ease to themselves or, at least, without rubbing against each other. However that may be, a more striking instance than the above, of avarice, completely and deservedly disappointed, was surely never displayed; for there is little room to doubt but that in consequence of the expected premium usually allowed to the captains, of £6. per cent. sterling on the produce of the negroes, this vessel was so crowded as to occasion such a heavy loss.

The place allotted for the sick negroes is under the half deck, where they lie on the bare planks. By this means those who are emaciated frequently have their skin and even their flesh entirely rubbed off, by the motion of the ship, from the prominent parts of the shoulders, elbows and hips so as to render the bones quite bare. And some of them, by constantly lying in the blood and mucus that had flowed from those afflicted with the flux and which is generally so violent as to prevent their being kept clean, have their flesh much sooner rubbed off than those who have only to contend with the mere friction of the ship. The excruciating pain which the poor sufferers feel from being obliged to continue in such a dreadful situation, frequently for several weeks, in case they happen to live so long, is not to be conceived or described. Few, indeed, are ever able to withstand the fatal effects of it. The utmost skill of the surgeon is here ineffectual. If plasters are applied they are very soon displaced by the friction of the ship; and when bandages are used the negroes very soon take them off and appropriate them to other purposes.

The surgeon, upon going between decks in the morning to examine the condition of the slaves, frequently finds several dead; and among the men, sometimes a dead and living negro fastened by their irons together. When this is the case they are brought upon the deck and laid on the grating when the living negro is disengaged and the dead one thrown overboard. We should here remark that the surgeons employed in the Guinea trade are generally driven to engage in so disagreeable an employment by the confined state of their finances. An exertion of the greatest skill and attention could afford the diseased negroes little relief so long as the causes of their diseases, namely, the breathing of a putrid atmosphere and wallowing in their own excrements, remain. When once the fever and dysentery get to any height at sea, a cure is scarcely ever effected.

Almost the only means by which the surgeon can render himself useful to the slaves is by seeing that their food is properly cooked and distributed among them. It is true, when they arrive near the markets for which they are destined, care is taken to polish them for sale by an application of the lunar caustic to such as are afflicted with the yaws. This, however, affords but a temporary relief as the disease most assuredly breaks out whenever the negro is put upon a vegetable diet.

It has been asserted in favor of the captains in this trade, that the sick slaves are usually fed from their tables. The great number generally ill at a time, proves the falsity of such an assertion. Were a captain even disposed to do this, how could he feed half the slaves in the ship from his own table? For it is well known that more than half are often sick at a time. Two or three perhaps might be fed.

The loss of slaves, through mortality, arising from the causes just mentioned, is frequently very considerable. One half, sometimes two thirds and even beyond that have been known to perish. On one voyage, before we left Bonny River no less than fifteen died of fevers and dysenteries occasioned by their confinement. On the Windward Coasts, where slaves are procured more slowly, very few die in proportion to the numbers which die at Bonny and at Old and New Calabar where they are obtained much faster; the latter being of a more delicate make and habit.

As very few of the negroes can bear the loss of their liberty and the hardships they endure, they are ever on the watch to take advantage of the least negligence. Insurrections are frequently the consequence; which are seldom suppressed without much bloodshed. Sometimes these are successful and the whole ship's company is cut off.

One evening while a ship to which I belonged lay in Bonny River, a number of negroes were brought on board and shortly after one of them forced his way through the network on the larboard side of the vessel, jumped overboard and was devoured by the sharks. During the time we were there, fifteen negroes belonging to a vessel from Liverpool found means to throw themselves into the river and very few were saved; the rest fell a sacrifice to the sharks.

Circumstances of this kind are very frequent. On the coast of Angola, at the River Ambris, the following incident happened:—During the time of our living on shore we erected a tent to shelter ourselves from the weather. After having been there several weeks and being unable to purchase the number of slaves we wanted, through the opposition of another English slave vessel, we determined to leave the place. The night before our departure the tent was struck, which was no sooner seen by some of the negro women on board than it was considered as a prelude to our sailing and about eighteen of them, when they were sent between decks, threw themselves into the sea through one of the gun ports, the ship carrying guns between decks. They were all of them, however, excepting one, soon picked up; the negress missing was at last found about a mile from the shore.

A young female negro, falling into a desponding way, it was judged necessary in order to attempt her recovery to send her on shore to the hut of one of the black traders. Elated at the prospect of regaining her liberty she soon recovered her usual cheerfulness, but hearing, by accident, that it was intended to take her on board the ship again, the young woman hung herself.

It frequently happens that the negroes on being purchased by Europeans, become raving mad and many of them die in that state, particularly the women. One day at Bonny, I saw a middle-aged, stout woman, who had been brought down from a fair the preceding day, chained to the post of a black trader's door, in a state of furious insanity. On board the ship was a young negro woman chained to the deck, who had lost her senses soon after she was purchased and taken on board. In a former voyage we were obliged to confine a female negro of about twenty-three years of age, on her becoming a lunatic. She was afterwards sold during one of her lucid intervals. One morning upon examining the place allotted for the sick negroes, I noticed that one of them, who was so emaciated as scarcely to be able to walk, was missing and was convinced that he must have gone overboard in the night, probably to put a more expeditious end to his sufferings.

The first place the slave ships touch at in their passage to the West Indies, is either the Island of St. Thomas, or Princes Island, where they usually carry their sick on shore for the benefit of the air and also replenish their stock of water. The former of these islands is nearly circular, being one hundred and twenty miles round, and lies exactly under the equator, about forty-five leagues from the African continent. It abounds with wood and water and produces Indian corn, rice, fruits, sugar and some cinnamon. The air is rather prejudicial to an European constitution; nevertheless it is well peopled by the Portuguese. Princes Island, which is much smaller, lies in 1° 30′ North, and likewise produces Indian corn and a variety of fruits and roots, besides sugar cane. Black cattle, hogs and goats are numerous there; but it is infested with a mischievous and dangerous species of monkeys.

During one of the voyages I made, I was landed upon the Island of St. Thomas with nearly one hundred sick negroes who were placed in an old house taken on purpose for their reception. Little benefit, however, accrued from their going on shore, as several of them died there and the remainder continued nearly in the same situation as when they were landed, though our continuance was prolonged for about twelve days and the island is deemed upon the whole healthy.

When the ships arrive in the West Indies the slaves are disposed of by different methods. Sometimes the mode of disposal is that of selling them by what is termed a *scramble* and a day is soon fixed for that purpose. But previously the sick or refuse slaves, of which there are frequently many, are usually taken on shore and sold at a tavern, by vendue or public auction. These, in general, are purchased by the Jews and surgeons, but chiefly the former, upon speculation, at so low a price as five or six dollars a head. I was informed by a mulatto woman that she purchased a sick slave at Grenada, upon speculation, for the small sum of one dollar, as the poor wretch was apparently dying of the flux. It seldom happens that any who are carried ashore in the emaciated state to which they are generally reduced by that disorder, long survive their landing. I once saw sixteen taken on shore and sold in the foregoing manner, the whole of whom died before I left the island. Sometimes the captains march their slaves through the town at which they intend to dispose of them and then place them in rows where they are examined and purchased.

The mode of selling them by *scramble* is most common. Here, all the negroes scrambled for bear an equal price; which is agreed upon between the captains and the purchasers before the sale begins. On a day appointed, the negroes are landed and placed altogether in a large yard belonging to the merchants to whom the ship is consigned. As soon as the hour agreed on arrives, the doors of the yard are suddenly thrown open and in rushes a considerable number of purchasers, with all the ferocity of brutes. Some instantly seize such of the negroes as they can conveniently lay hold of with their hands. Others, being prepared with several handkerchiefs tied together, encircle with these as many as they are able; while others, by means of a rope, effect the same purpose. It is scarcely possible to describe the confusion of which this mode of selling is productive. It likewise causes much animosity among the purchasers who not unfrequently fall out and quarrel with each other. The poor astonished negroes are so much terrified by these proceedings, that several of them, on one occasion, climbed over the walls of the courtyard and ran wild about the town but were soon hunted down and retaken.

While on a former voyage from Africa to Kingston in Jamaica, I saw a sale there by *scramble*, on board a snow. The negroes were collected together upon the main and quarter decks and the ship was darkened by sails suspended over them in order to prevent the purchasers from being able to see, so as to pick or choose. The signal being given the buyers rushed in, as usual, to seize their prey, when the negroes became so terrified that nearly thirty of them jumped into the sea, but they were soon retaken, chiefly by boats from other ships.

On board a ship lying at Port Maria, in Jamaica, I saw another *scramble* in which, as usual, the negroes were greatly terrified. The women, in particular, clung to each other, shrieking in terror at the savage manner in which their brutal purchasers rushed upon and seized them.

Various are the deceptions made use of in the disposal of the sick slaves and many of these must excite the liveliest sensations of horror. A Liverpool captain boasted of his having cheated some Jews by the following stratagem:—A lot of slaves afflicted with the flux, being landed for sale, he directed the surgeon to stop the anus of each of them with oakum. Thus prepared they were taken to the place of sale, where, being unable to stand but for a very short time, they were usually permitted to sit. The Jews, when they examine them, oblige them to stand up in order that they may see if there be any discharge; and when there is no appearance they consider it as a symptom of recovery. In the present instance, such an appearance being prevented, the bargain was struck and the slaves were accordingly sold. But it was not long before discovery of the cheat followed, for the excruciating pain which the prevention of a discharge of such an acrimonious nature occasioned, not being to be borne by the poor wretches, the temporary obstruction was removed and the deluded Jews were speedily convinced of the imposition.

So severely are the negroes sometimes afflicted with this troublesome and painful disorder that I have seen large numbers of them, after being landed, obliged by the virulence of the complaint to stop almost every minute as they passed on.

The whole of their cargoes being disposed of the ships are immediately made ready to proceed to sea. It is very seldom, however, that they are not detained for want of a sufficient number of sailors to navigate the ship, as the slave trade may justly be denominated the grave of seamen. Though the crews of the ships, upon their leaving England, generally amount to between forty and fifty men, scarcely three-fourths and sometimes not one-third of the complement, ever return to the port from whence they sailed, through mortality and desertion.

The time during which the slave ships are absent from England, varies according to the destination of the voyage and the number of ships they happen to meet on the coast. To Bonny, or Old and New Calabar, a voyage is usually performed in about ten months. Those to the Windward and Gold Coasts are rather more uncertain, but last in general from fifteen to eighteen months.

CHAPTER VIII

THE GUINEA VOYAGE AND THE SAILOR

IT HAS been asserted that the English slave trade was a desirable employment and a nursery for seamen. What follows should supply ample information upon which to base a judgment on that question. The slaving crews were principally collected through the agency of public houses under the influence and in the pay of the merchants. There was always plenty of good liquor to be had and painted girls enough to go round. The main idea was to get the sailor into debt to the house and there were plenty of opportunities for the unthinking man. Sometimes it was the landlady who made it necessary for the seaman to make a will in her favor, but usually it was the crimp who persuaded the drunken man to sign articles the very night when he cunningly had boasted that he would cheat the merchant out of a night's entertainment. When a man signed articles he was given a note for his advance money, not payable until he was safely at sea and the crew list was brought back by the pilot. In order to pay off debts, buy some clothes and a little more liquor, a man must make a will and sign a power of attorney, and there is where the landlady came in.

Until a vessel got clear of the Channel and there was little probability that contrary winds or bad weather might drive her back into an English port, the seamen were well used and the allowance of provisions was sufficient. But as soon as they were fairly out at sea and there was no chance for desertion, the provision ration was shortened and the allowance of water was cut very nearly to the limit. There was the chance that bad weather might force the ship to bear away for Lisbon, but with the Bay of Biscay safely astern it was common to flog the men upon the slightest pretext. Of course there were captains and captains. Some were more humane than others. But the slave trade as conducted showed little humanity to the blacks from Africa, and it was but a step to treat with equal indifference the rights of the white slaves kidnapped in the slums of Liverpool and Bristol.

The allowance of water during the first part of the passage was usually three pints per day; this amount, however, was reduced as the African coast drew near, to one quart, wine measure. In a hot climate, with much calm weather and a blazing sun, this pittance soon disappeared. Many a man could not restrain his thirst and drinking up his entire allowance the moment it was served, the rest of the day and night, was nothing other than a living hell for him. One seaman relates* that he hit upon the experiment of licking the heavy dew off the hen coops, early in the morning, until his delicious secret was discovered and he no longer had a monopoly of this form of refreshment.

The short allowance of water was due in part to the natural cause of a shortage on board, for the hold of every slaver was stowed as full as possible with goods for trade and necessaries for sailors were but a secondary consideration. The captains, however, never suffered from thirst and besides plenty of beer and wine, had a large tea-kettle of water every morning and another every evening. Stanfield was certain there was no want of water in the cabin, for the third mate, who was his friend, frequently gave him a little out of his own portion.

As for grog—it was only served on some special occasion and when on the coast, as opportunity offered, this frequently led the men to barter their clothes with the natives for brandy, so that sometimes men reduced themselves almost to a state of nakedness in order to obtain a little spirit. This condition shortly brought on pains in the head and body, a fever, and in a few days, death, as the men must lie on deck at night exposed to the heavy and unwholesome dews.

The temporary house, that was always built over the deck after reaching the coast, supplied but an indifferent shelter from the weather and also prevented a good circulation of air. The stench

* James F. Stanfield, *The Guinea Voyage*, Edinburgh, 1807.

that came from the crowded blacks was very offensive to the crew and the smoke from the mangrove wood, which was burned aboard, inflamed their eyes and sometimes brought on temporary blindness.

The construction of the temporary house over the deck was, in itself, a severe test of physical endurance for the men, who were obliged to cut the bambo and thatch by the riverside, oftentimes while standing in muddy slime, up to the waist; pestered by snakes, worms and clouds of mosquitoes; their feet frequently slipping from under them and the ship's officers allowing little rest until the disagreeable work was completed, and afterwards, when the slaves began to come aboard, there was the daily task of cleaning up the filth and blood from where the blacks lay at night, an indescribably repulsive piece of work, offensive to every sense and frequently reeking with contagion leading to disease and death.

Nor were the seamen better off during the "middle passage," after sailing from the slave coast, a voyage usually lasting from six to eight weeks, as they were obliged to sleep on deck, the slaves occupying all space below; and this exposure to all weathers could not help but be injurious to bodily health and frequently brought on fevers which proved fatal. The only shelter from the wind and frequent rains would be an old tarpaulin, full of holes, thrown over a boom.

On reaching the West Indies, as soon as the men could get ashore, they would at once flock to the grog shops and proceed to get drunk; and because they had been kept from grog and all liquors for so long a time, their debauch would become more beastly and in such a climate their debilitated constitutions soon gave way and death followed. Scurvy also added its toll, brought on by a scanty diet of salted food and an exposure to all weathers.

It was ghastly business, this sailing of British slave ships, and there is plenty of evidence as to the cruel neglect of the seamen and the devilish brutality of many of the slaving captains. Alexander Falconbridge, a surgeon on several slavers, not only testified before the Parliamentary Commission, but also wrote a small book on the subject, from which the following account is taken.*

"In one of these voyages, I was witness to the following instance of cruel usage. Most of the sailors were treated with brutal severity; but one in particular, a man advanced in years, experienced it in an uncommon degree. Having made some complaint relative to his allowance of water, and this being construed into an insult, one of the officers seized him, and with the blows he bestowed upon him, beat out several of his teeth. Not content with this, while the poor old man was yet bleeding, one of the iron pump-bolts was fixed in his mouth, and kept there by a piece of rope-yarn tied round his head. Being unable to spit out the blood which flowed from the wound, the man was almost choked, and obliged to swallow it. He was then tied to the rail of the quarter-deck, having declared, upon being gagged, that he would jump overboard and drown himself. About two hours after he was taken from the quarter-deck rail, and fastened to the grating companion of the steerage, under the half deck, where he remained all night with a sentinel placed over him.

"A young man on board one of the ships, was frequently beaten in a very severe manner, for very trifling faults. This was done sometimes with what is termed *a cat* (an instrument of correction which consists of a handle or stem, made of a rope three inches and a half in circumference, and about eighteen inches long, at one end of which are fastened nine branches, or tails, composed of log line, with three or more knots upon each branch) and sometimes he was beaten with a bamboo. Being one day cruelly beaten with the latter, the poor lad, unable to endure the severe usage, leaped out of one of the gun ports on the larboard side of the cabin, into the river. He, however, providentially escaped being devoured by the sharks, and was taken up by a canoe belonging to one of the black traders then

* Falconbridge, *An Account of the Slave Trade on the Coast of Africa*, London, 1788.

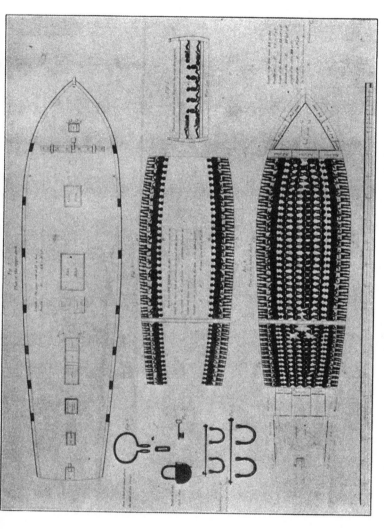

Method of Stowing Slaves on the French Brig "Vigilanti" of Nantes, Captured in the River Bonny, April 15, 1822

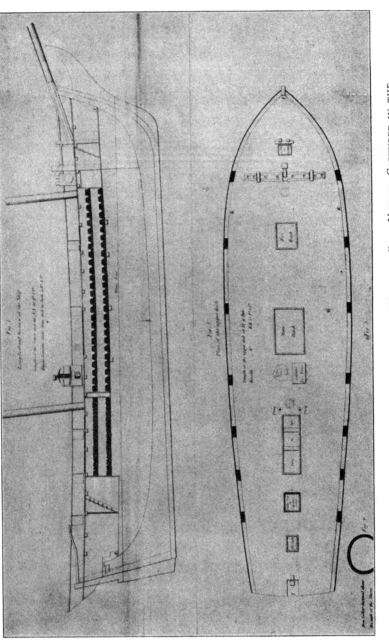

SECTION AND DECK PLAN OF THE FRENCH BRIG "VIGILANTI," OF NANTES, CAPTURED IN THE
RIVER BONNY, APRIL 15, 1822

lying alongside the vessel. As soon as he was brought on board, he was dragged to the quarter-deck, and his head forced into a tub of water, which had been left there for the negro women to wash their hands in. In this situation he was kept till he was nearly suffocated; the person who held him, exclaiming, with the malignity of a demon, 'If you want drowning, I will drown you myself.' Upon my inquiring of the young man, if he knew the danger to which he exposed himself by jumping overboard, he replied, 'that he expected to be devoured by the sharks, but he preferred even that, to being treated daily with so much cruelty.'

"Another seaman having been in some degree negligent, had a long chain fixed round his neck, at the end of which was fastened a log of wood. In this situation he performed his duty (from which he was not in the least spared) for several weeks, till at length he was nearly exhausted by fatigue; and after his release from the log, he was frequently beaten for trivial faults. Once, in particular, when an accident happened, through the carelessness of another seaman, he was tied up, although the fault was not in the least imputable to him, along with the other person, and they were both flogged till their backs were raw. Chian pepper was then mixed in a bucket, with salt water, and with this the harrowed parts of the backs of the unoffending seamen were washed, as an addition to their torture.

"The same seaman having on another time accidentally broken a plate, a fish-gig was thrown at him with great violence. The fish-gig is an instrument used for striking fish, and consists of several strong barbed points fixed on a pole, about six feet long, loaded at the end with lead. The man escaped the threatening danger, by stooping his head, and the missile weapon struck in the barricado. Knives and forks were at other times thrown at him; and a large Newfoundland dog was frequently set at him, which, thus encouraged, would not only tear his clothes, but wound him. At length, after several severe floggings, and other ill treatment, the poor fellow appeared to be totally insensible to beating and careless of the event.

"I must here add, that whenever any of the crew were beaten, the Newfoundland dog, just mentioned, from the encouragement he met with, would generally leap upon them, tear their clothes, and bite them. He was particularly inveterate against one of the seamen, who, from being often knocked down, and severely beaten, appeared quite stupid and incapable of doing his duty. In this state, he was taken on board another ship and returned to England.

"In one of my voyages, a seaman came on board the ship I belonged to, while on the coast, as a passenger to the West Indies. He was just recovered from a fever and notwithstanding this he was very unmercifully beaten during the passage, which, together with the feeble state he was in at the time, rendered him nearly incapable of walking, and it was but by stealth that any medical assistance could be given to him.

"A young man was likewise beaten and kicked almost daily, for trifling, and even imaginary faults. The poor youth happening to have a very bad toe, through a hurt, he was placed as a sentry over the sick slaves, a station which required much walking. This, in addition to the pain it occasioned, increased a fever he already had. Soon after he was compelled, although so ill, to sit on the gratings, and being there overcome with illness and fatigue, he chanced to fall asleep; which being observed from the quarter-deck, he was soon awakened and with many oaths upbraided for neglect of duty. He was then kicked from the gratings, and so cruelly beaten, that it was with great difficulty he crawled to one of the officers who was more humane, and complaining of the cruel treatment he had just received, petitioned for a little barley-water (which was kept for the sick slaves) to quench the intolerable thirst he experienced.

"Another seaman was knocked down several times a day, for faults of no deep dye. It being observed at one time, that the hen coops had not been removed by the sailors who were then washing the deck, nor washed under, which it was his duty to see done, one of the officers immediately knocked him down, then seized and dragged him to the stern of the vessel, where he threw him violently against the deck. By this treatment, various parts of his body was much bruised, his face swelled, and he had a bad eye for a fortnight. He was afterwards severely beaten for a very trifling fault and kicked till he fell down. When he got on shore in the West Indies, he carried his shirt, stained with the blood which had flowed from his wounds, to one of the magistrates of the island, and applied to him for redress; but the ship being consigned to one of them, all the redress he could procure, was his discharge.

"Many other instances of similar severity might be produced; but the foregoing will suffice, to give some idea of the treatment seamen are liable to, and generally experience, in this employ; the consequence of which usually is desertion or death.

"Of the former, I will give one instance. While a ship I belonged to lay at Bonny, early one morning near a dozen of the crew deserted in one of the long boats. They were driven to this desperate measure, as one of them afterwards informed me, by the cruel treatment they had experienced on board. Two of them, in particular, had been severely beaten and flogged the preceding day. One of these having neglected to see that the arms of the ship were kept fit for use, was tied up to the mizen shrouds, and after being stripped, very severely flogged on the back; his trowsers were then pulled down, and the flogging was repeated. The other seaman, who was esteemed a careful, cleanly, sober fellow, had been punished little less severely, though it did not appear that he had been guilty at that time of any fault.

"It is customary for most of the captains of the slave ships to go on shore every evening to do business with the black traders. Upon these occasions many of them get intoxicated and when they return on board, give proofs of their inebriation by beating and ill using some or other of the crew. This was the present case; the seaman here spoken of, was beaten, without any reason being assigned, with a knotted bamboo, for a considerable time; by which he was very much bruised, and being before in an ill state of health, suffered considerably.

"Irritated by the ill usage which all of them, in their turn, had experienced, they resolved to attempt an escape, and effected it early in the morning. The person on the watch discovered, that the net-work on the main deck had been cut, and that one of the long-boats was gone; and, upon farther examination it was found, that near a dozen of the seamen were missing. A few hours after, the captain went in the cutter in pursuit of the deserters, but without success.

"On my return to England, I received from one of them, the following account of their adventures during this undertaking.

"When they left the vessel, they proposed going to Old Calabar, being determined to perish, rather than return to the ship. All the provisions they took with them was, a bag containing about half a hundred weight of bread, half a small cheese, and a cask of water of about 38 gallons. They made a sail of a hammock, and erected one of the boat's oars for a mast. Thus slenderly provided, they dropped down the river of Bonny, and kept along the coast; but mistaking one river for another, they were seized by the natives, who stripped them, and marched them across the country, for a considerable distance, to the place to which they themselves intended going. During the march, several were taken ill, and some of them died. Those who survived, were sold to an English ship which lay there. Every one of these deserters, except three, died on the coast, or during their passage to the West Indies; and one of the remaining three died soon after his arrival there. So that only two out of the whole number, lived to arrive in England, and those in a very infirm state of health.

"While I am upon the subject of the desertions among the sailors, I must add, that the captains in this trade generally take out with them tobacco and slops, which they sell at an exorbitant price to the sailors. And in case of their desertion or decease, they have it in their power to charge to the seamens' accounts, whatever quantity they please, without contradiction. This proves an additional reason for cruel usage. In case of desertion, the sailors forfeit their wages, by which the expenses of the voyage are lessened, and consequently the merchants reap benefits from it."

Another surgeon, on board a Bristol slaver, the brig *Little Pearl*, testified before the Parliamentary Commission concerning the barbarities wantonly inflicted upon the helpless sailors, giving the following account of the treatment of a black Portuguese sailor who had shipped at Bristol as cook of the vessel.

"This unhappy man was the common butt on which the captain and mates daily exercised their cruelty. The former, indeed, appeared to enjoy a particular pleasure in flogging and tormenting him. Among other instances of wanton and unnecessary barbarity, he often amused himself with making the man swallow cockroaches alive, on pain of being most severely flogged, and having beef brine rubbed into his wounds. This last severe and humiliating alternative the man sometimes preferred to the swallowing the nauseous vermin, and when this was the case, he was under the necessity of applying poultices to the wounds afterwards given him to prevent a mortification. For the greater part of our stay upon the coast, this man was fastened by the neck to the copper (or caboose) with a chain of such a length as to permit him to draw water at the ship's side. In this situation he remained upon deck night and day, exposed to the weather, and was compelled to dress victuals not only for the crew, but for all the slaves, without any assistance whatever. The body of this poor wretch, from the crown of his head to the soles of his feet, was covered with scars and lacerations, intersecting each other in all directions, so that he was a most miserable object to behold.

"On the second day after their arrival in St. Vincent's, the mate ordered the men aloft to hand the sails, which had been loosed to dry. This they positively refused to do, till they received some refreshment. They had been in a starving condition for about three days, though, as they observed, there was plenty of provisions on board; and if there had not, a supply might have been easily gotten from the merchants to whom the vessel was consigned. The captain hearing of this behaviour of the seamen, carried the whole crew before a magistrate, who advised them to return to their duty on board, adding, that he was sure the captain would take care that they should have a plentiful supply of provisions. This advice they instantly complied with, and accompanied the captain on board; where they had no sooner come, than he ordered them aloft to hand the sails. This they refused to do, with the same firmness as before, saying that they could not work without victuals. In consequence of this the captain went on shore, and returned with warrants and a constable, whom he ordered to apprehend three of the best men.

"In company with the captain he carried them on shore, and committed them to gaol. The remainder of the crew, during the captain's absence, hailed a vessel which lay at no great distance, and begged them to send a boat. With this request the crew of the ship, who probably had heard of what had passed on board the *Little Pearl*, immediately complied; and in this boat the discontented seamen rowed on shore, forfeiting their wages, and leaving part of their clothes behind; nor has he ever heard what became of them since.

"The cooper, who was a very hard-working man, and advanced in years, having shortly after this received his half-pay with the rest of the officers, went on shore to buy some necessaries, and returned on board in the evening, rather overcome with liquor. He was immediately seized by the captain and mate, both of whom beat him so very unmercifully, that he lay almost in a state of insensibility on the bare deck for twelve or fourteen hours. The next morning he found several large contusions on his head, one of his eyes was entirely closed and violently inflamed, his mouth was much cut and swelled, and he had lost a quantity of blood, which he saw upon the deck.

"After this nothing material occurred till they were about to sail; when the three men, who were imprisoned, were brought on board by the captain. Finding that their wages had been expended by the captain in paying the gaol fees, &c., two of them remonstrated with him on the subject; on which he immediately knocked them down, kicked them, and beat them most cruelly, and confined all the three in the men's room. The boatswain, enraged at this piece of injustice, and being a little in liquor, could not help speaking of it in terms which the latter so much disliked, that he treated him worse, if possible, than the two seamen; he was dragged in a state of insensibility to the fore grating, and was thrown down headlong into the room where the three seamen were confined, and where they all remained till the vessel got out to sea. They were then released, and performed their duty till they arrived in Bristol. He has since been informed by the three seamen who were imprisoned, that the balance of their wages for the whole voyage, when paid them in England, did not exceed five shillings each."

One other narrative of brutality and this chapter is ended. The boatswain on the slaver in which Stanfield sailed,* was a hearty man when they left the Guinea coast. Not long after he was seized with the flux, but no remission of work was allowed him.

"He grew so bad at last that the mucus, blood and whole strings of intestines came from him without intermission. In this deplorable condition, when he could hardly stand, he was forced to the wheel, to steer the vessel, a task that under ordinary conditions might have required two men had there been sailors enough for the purpose. The poor man was placed on one of the mess tubs, not being able to stand and also so that he might not dirty the deck and here he remained as long as he was able to move his hands. He died that night and the body was thrown overboard, as usual, without any covering but a shirt. It grew calm during the night and continued so for the greater part of the next day and in the morning the corpse of the boatswain lay floating alongside and kept close to the ship for

* James F. Stanfield, *The Guinea Voyage*, Edinburgh, 1807.

some hours,—a horrid spectacle that seemed to give us the idea of the body of a victim calling out to Heaven for vengence on our barbarity!

"As the crew fell off, a greater weight of labour pressed upon the few survivors and towards the end of the middle passage all idea of keeping the slaves in chains was given up; for there was not strength left among the white men, to pull a single rope with effect. The slaves (at least a number of them) were therefore freed from their irons, and *they* pulled and hauled as they were directed by the inefficient sailors. We were fortunate in having favourable weather; a smart gale of wind, such as with an able crew would not have given us more trouble than to reef our sails, must have inevitably sent us to destruction.

"In this state of weakness but little attention could be paid to those whose misery made them helpless and in want of aid. I remember that a man who was sick, one night crawled out of his hammock and was so weak that he was unable to get back and so laid himself down on the gratings. There was no one to assist him and in the morning, when I came on deck, he was still alive, but covered with blood, for the hogs had picked his toes to the bone and his body was otherwise mangled by them in a manner too shocking to relate."

CHAPTER IX

THE BRIG *RUBY* OF BRISTOL, AFRICAN SLAVER

A SURGEON'S berth on board ship never filled my purse or kept me long on shore.* I served five years in His Majesty's Navy, but quit the King's service at the peace with the American States and with no better opening offering was obliged to ship as surgeon's mate for a voyage to the river Bonny, on board the *Alexander*, Captain MacTaggart. When we reached Bristol, on the return voyage from Jamaica, I was offered a surgeon's berth for an African voyage in the brig *Little Pearl*, commanded by Capt. Joseph Williams, and made two rounds in her. It is the story of the second voyage that I am to relate, after her name had been changed to the *Ruby*, why, I never knew. Much red blood was spilled in her, however, and the name was good enough. Certainly those of us on board didn't care.

The brig was low and small and when we sailed from King's Road, the steerage and nearly all the space between decks was filled with goods taken out to be bartered for slaves. In the small unoccupied space forward it was impossible for the sailors to live without being continually wet from the head seas or the rain; and this was their situation during the entire passage to the coast. When the *Pearl* came to anchor at Bimbe, this space forward was made over into a storehouse for glass and pot-ware for trade, so the poor devils of sailors then had no place on which they could lay their heads. After that all, except four, slept on the bare decks and as the decks were washed every night and there was no sun to dry them, as we arrived at the edge of the rainy season, it was a wet berth for poor Jack. For a short time four hammocks were allowed to be slung from the booms, but these were soon ordered down.

* The material for this chapter is taken from James Arnold's testimony before the Parliamentary Committee as printed in the *Report to the House of Lords on the Abolition of the Slave Trade*, 2 vols., London, 1789.

We sailed from King's Road early on the morning of the 8th of August, 1787, having on board nineteen persons, including the captain, mates, men and boys. When the vessel was getting under weigh, all hands were called up to sign articles and when my turn came I asked permission to read them first, not wishing to put my name to the unknown, but Captain Williams roughly refused, saying if I didn't sign them I might go ashore. As I had less than five pounds that I could call my own, it was practically a case of Hobson's choice and so I signed my name and walked forward. It was the same with the rest. No one was permitted to read the clauses in the articles.

For the first five weeks we had plenty of provisions. The sailors were served with pease, flour, pork, beef and suet a plenty; but it was a different story when we reached the Coast. Not only was their allowance reduced but they were deprived of the common necessaries of life. Every Sunday morning each man was served with three pounds of bread and this must last him for the entire week following. Each morning he was served out three-quarters of a pound of wretched pork or beef, that shrunk to about four ounces and a half when it was boiled. It was impossible for a man to have more than one meal a day with this ration and the bread usually lasted only three days. Much of the time yams and plantains were not to be had and to make their situation more wretched still very little spirit was given out. Once or twice a month a pint of brandy was served amongst eight people and three months once elapsed without their tasting a drop of spirit notwithstanding the fact that in wooding the ship they sometimes stood in water up to their armpits.

While slavers lay on the Coast it was usual for the captains to visit each other, and the seamen who rowed them from ship to ship were often absent for twelve hours without eating. My lot on board, as surgeon, was but little better in the matter of food than the men before the mast and the only time while we were at Bimbe, when I had all I wanted to eat, was once when I was a prisoner on shore and the natives gave me four meals a day.

The *Ruby* reached Bimbe, on the 25th of September. It is a small island and lies south of Old Calabar, off the high lands of the Cameroons. In those parts it was usual to trust the principal traders with goods from the ships and those we had dealings with were King George, King Peter, and Quon, a clever trader, all from the Cameroons; and King Mason and his son Captain Dick, Peter, Bimbe Tom, Bimbe Jack and Great and Little Tim, from the island of Bimbe. But though we trusted the traders with goods with which they went to the fairs to buy slaves on our account, yet it was customary for them to leave with us a pledge for their return. This pledge took the form of their children or relations, known as "pawns." As the traders brought us slaves and so paid off their indebtedness the pawns were released; but if they were unable to discharge them at the appointed day—the day fixed for sailing—the pawns were to be taken to the West Indies and sold and while this was agreed upon and was wholly regular, it sometimes led to violent reactions.

While we were lying at the island of Bimbe, Captain Bibby of the *Molly*, of Liverpool, came out of the river Cameroons with several pawns on board belonging to King George, King Peter and the trader Quon. Captain Bibby had given them notice that he should sail for the Cape on a certain day and would wait there for three days before he went to sea and if the pawns were not redeemed by that time, he should carry them to the West Indies and sell them. It chanced that King George and the other traders were not able at that time to redeem their pawns and so in great haste they came to Captain Williams of the *Ruby*, asking him to spare them some slaves and ivory so they might redeem the pawns which Captain Bibby had threatened to take away.

Captain Williams let them have eleven slaves and five teeth which were carried to the *Molly* and six or seven pawns were released and brought to the *Ruby* to be held as security. The next day, however, the *Molly* sailed for the West Indies having on board about thirty pawns, which so enraged the traders that they immedi-

ately left us and returned to the Cameroons. Here, they put a stop
to all trade with the captains, five of whom were seized and carried
away into the country where they were kept chained to trees, as we
afterwards learned. It was an awkward situation and after conference, a schooner, with slaves aboard, was dispatched to overtake the
Molly and bring back the pawns that had been carried off by Captain
Bibby.

On the island of Bimbe the largest trader and man of greatest
consequence, was called Bimbe Jack. One morning he came on board
with ivory to trade. The captain had reserved his best trading guns
for the purchase of slaves and when an inferior sort were offered
Bimbe Jack refused to take them, saying that he couldn't work them
off on the other traders. This enraged Captain Williams who immediately laid hands on him and ordered him put in chains. An iron
collar was put round his neck to which was fastened a large chain,
the end of which was put through ring bolts on the deck and then
padlocked. Black Tim, another trader who was on board at that time,
seeing what was done, quickly jumped into his canoe, alongside the
brig, and his canoe-boys pulled away at once. As it was impossible
to stop him, Captain Williams ordered two topsails to be bent and
the brig was got over the bar so that she couldn't be cut off by
negroes from the island.

The *Ruby* lay outside the bar for three or four days, during which
there was much heavy weather and then, because of want of water
for the middle passage, she came in again and a boat was sent ashore
with water casks and a well-armed crew. The third day after, when
the watering had been nearly completed, a trader from Bimbe came
on board and demanded a debt of salt. One or two people came
with him, but his canoe-men remained in the canoe, which was lying
by the bows of the vessel. The chief mate and some of the crew
were soon busy measuring and keeping a reckoning of the salt. There
were then but ten white persons aboard, the rest being ashore employed in watering.

In a short time, a second canoe was discovered coming to the brig, with a slave aboard, and a third, with two slaves. The mate then began to be suspicious and went to the captain, expressing his alarm and for his pains was told to mind his own business and get about the measuring of the salt. The two traders, with their slaves, were then permitted to come aboard and went down to the captain's cabin. While they were there, bargaining, another canoe came along-side, with fish and while the captain came on deck to trade, the two traders in his cabin got possession of the key to Bimbe Jack's shackles and going to where he sat on the deck attempted to unlock the chain. The carpenter happened to see this and as he called out to the cap-tain, was seized by Bimbe Jack with the assistance of another negro. Captain Williams was quickly overpowered by the two traders and at the same time the negroes who were overlooking the measuring of the salt, standing by the chief mate, the cooper and others, pushed them all into the canoe that was lying at the bow of the brig. Some of the other canoe-men came aboard and a considerable number of natives who were fishing in canoes at no great distance, soon joined them and in no time the rest of us were secured and the vessel was completely in their power.

We were put into their canoes and Bimbe Jack was released and also three Cameroon traders who had been detained in much the same manner. The negroes also released all the Cameroons and Bimbe pawns on board and eight men-boy slaves that were on deck, and prisoners, pawns and slaves were then carried ashore.

On reaching the landing, the blacks, particularly the women, be-gan to pelt us with stones, fish, sand and whatever else they could lay hands on and not content with that we were hardly on land be-fore they began to tear our clothes from off our backs. The captain was stripped stark-naked and the same iron collar that he had or-dered about Bimbe Jack's neck was clasped about his own and he was soon chained to a tree. The carpenter and chief mate were also fastened to the same tree where they were kept during the entire night, several natives standing guard all the while, armed with lances and muskets. The rest of us were taken to different trader's houses and treated well.

Bimbe Jack, although he had been so ill-used by the captain, took compassion on him and brought a coat to shelter him and also brought some rum and water. The next morning he was released from the tree, but he continued to wear the collar and chain and was well guarded. As for the mate and the carpenter, they still remained at the tree.

It had been determined, at a palaver, that the captain, because of his ill-treatment of Bimbe Jack, should give up to the natives all the articles of trade that remained on board (amounting to the equivalent in the value of thirty-six slaves); that the pawns and slaves that had been released should be forfeited to them; and that every debt then due to the ship should be cancelled. Upon no other terms should we be released. There was no choice and the captain consenting, the goods were brought ashore and we were then released and permitted to go aboard the *Ruby*.

This narrow escape made Captain Williams more cautious but he afterwards frequently threatened that he would some day return with a ship of sufficient force, lay seige to the island and take away all he was able. The *Comet*, of Liverpool, was not so fortunate, for about the same time she was cut off by natives at Ferdinand Po, while trading for yams, and but one person was saved.

The first slave that was traded for, after the brig anchored at the island of Bimbe, was a girl of about fifteen who was promptly named Eve, for it was usual on slave ships to give the names of Adam and Eve to the first man and woman brought on board. This girl was clever and intelligent and afterwards told me that a goat had been found in her father's garden which she believed had been purposely put there and that one of the great men of the village had come in the morning, and finding the goat in the garden, had charged her father with stealing it. Nothing would satisfy the great man, as a penalty for the offence, except the giving up of one of his daughters to be sold as a slave. The poor man had three girls and the great man selected Eve and sold her to the traders who brought her to our brig. Three months afterwards, a young girl of about eight was brought on board, who proved to be a younger sister of Eve.

The slaves that were brought to the *Ruby*, reached there from various causes. Most of them were bought at fairs, by traders, who brought them to the coast, but many were kidnapped as opportunity offered, and others were sold for debt or for adultery, either real or falsely charged. Others were inticed to the vessel and there seized and confined. Three weeks after the *Ruby* arrived at Bimbe, a black trader brought a native aboard. They were taken down into the captain's cabin and given something to drink and were sociable and merry; but when the two came on deck, the trader's companion, on a signal from the captain, was seized by sailors and put in irons. The poor devil was afterwards carried to the West Indies and sold as a slave. At least five of our cargo were obtained in this manner.

One day a woman was brought out to us to be sold. As she had a child in her arms, the captain refused to take her and she was taken back to the shore; but the next morning she was brought out again, this time without the child which had been killed the night before by the black trader in order to accommodate a sale of the mother.

Not infrequently, after slaves were brought on board, they would refuse to eat and Captain Williams would order them flogged unmercifully until they obeyed, in fact, he usually plied the cat on the naked backs of the blacks and seemed to find a pleasant sensation in the sight of blood and the sound of their moans. One slave was repeatedly flogged, for two or three days, by both the captain and the chief mate, until his body was so lacerated that it was a gory mass of raw flesh. While the man was in this deplorable condition, a trader came on board with a slave and the captain, in his usual arbitrary way, insisted that the trader give up his own slave in exchange for the man who had refused to eat. The trader was obliged to agree to the unfair exchange, and the quite helpless slave was dragged along the deck, like a corpse, to the trader's canoe. In this manner we got rid of him.

Among those brought on board was a woman who was in a very dejected state of mind. Before long she was seized with convulsions and on recovering she began to laugh excessively and then cried and made a dreadful noise that greatly disturbed the ship so that the captain got rid of her the next day.

It was his general practice on the receipt of a woman slave—especially a young one—to send for her to come to his cabin so that he might lie with her. Sometimes they would refuse to comply with his desires and would be severely beaten by him and sent below. There was one young girl that he retained for some time as his favorite and kept her in his cabin, until one day when she was playing with his son, she accidentally tore his shirt. When the captain learned of it, he whipped her unmercifully with the cat and beat her up with his fists until she threw herself from him against the pumps and in doing so injured her head so severely that she died three days after. She had then been living with him as his mistress for five or six months.

The captain had a frightful temper and seemed to delight in cruelty. In October, 1787, while the *Ruby* was lying at Bimbe, the cook was bringing some billets of wood from the main hatchway to his galley and carrying too great a load, left one on the main deck, which the captain happened to see. When the cook returned from the galley the captain knocked him flat on the deck and beat him up so badly that he was obliged to come to me to dress his cuts. On a previous voyage this poor fellow had been terribly beaten by the captain, because he had chanced to say; "It is hard that the hogs should be served with pease before the white people."

There was always a great deal of sickness among the seamen while the slave ships lay on the Coast and the treatment of the sick by Captain Williams was shocking. A sick man was not allowed to go between the decks nor to have any more shelter than when he was well. No herb tea or wine, nor any additional nourishment was allowed and frequently a little rice was substituted for the regular ration and the captain would say "No work, no victuals." He was a heartless brute. In December, 1787, one of the seamen, William Bullson, was very sick with inflammatory fever. One day the captain asked me how he was and when I replied that he was nearly gone, he said "Let him die and be damned." A few days later when the chief mate became sick and went to the steerage, among the women, for shelter, the captain missing him asked where he was and when told said, "He can't be sick enough to go to hell yet."

The principal causes of the deaths of seamen while on a slaving voyage, were fevers—inflammatory or putrid—and dysentery. These were usually caused by the manner of wooding the ships, by exposure during the middle passage, by a want of the common necessaries of life and by ill-usage; and when they once became sick it was very difficult to save them for want of proper and nourishing food. There were nineteen who went out in the *Ruby* and four of them died during the voyage.

It was usually difficult to ascertain a seaman's real name. He was generally called by the name of a "red or blue villain" according to the color of his jacket and low and vulgar names were commonly used as a means of concealing a man's real name.

The chief mate, John Smith, was accustomed to use the cat on the men slaves with the slightest provocation, usually bringing blood. While we lay at Bimbe, not long before sailing for the West Indies, an insurrection broke out among the slaves largely because of his brutality. Hearing some noise below he went down to quiet them. It was night and he carried a lanthorn in his hand. Thinking that he had come down to flog them some of the slaves watched an opportunity and snatched the lanthorn from his hand and seizing him were soon in a fair way for killing him. Smith was a powerful man and by main strength he succeeded in getting to the gratings and so was dragged upon deck by some of the crew, fortunate in escaping with only a small wound in the back from a shackle bolt. The men slaves disappointed in not revenging themselves upon the mate and finding that they had created an alarm attempted to force the gratings which were with great difficulty kept down and secured. They next attempted to reach the deck through a small scuttle which served as an entrance to a sick berth partitioned off in the fore part of the men's quarters, but were forced below. The insurrection now seemed serious and the captain ordered the slaves fired upon through the gratings and other seamen armed with muskets and blunderbusses got into the boat and fired through the air ports in the bows of the brig. This was kept up for some time until the slaves yielded and quiet was restored.

At daylight, the next morning, the slaves were ordered on deck, two at a time and their arms were pinioned as they came up. Here they were placed under a strong guard on the quarter deck and seamen were then sent below to search for missing men. Among the articles of trade which the small size of the brig made it necessary to keep in the men's room was a cask of knives which the slaves had seen opened in the course of trade. Three men who were out of irons had armed themselves from this cask and as the seamen entered the men's room they slipped through the scuttle into the hold. By the persuasion of a black trader on board one of the men surrendered himself quietly and the second was coming up to surrender, but having a knife in each hand, one of the crew, thinking that he was advancing to attack him, fired his musket and killed him on the spot. The third man told the trader that he would sooner die than surrender as he had entered into an oath which they call sangaree (an oath to stick to each other and made by sucking a few drops of another's blood).

The fellow remained in the hold about eight hours, though severely scalded with a mixture of water and fat, which was repeatedly thrown down upon him, until the black trader at last persuaded him that the whites would do him no injury if he came up but certainly would kill in the end if he held out. A rope was then let down but when he raised himself as far as the lower deck he saw an armed sailor waiting for him, as he supposed to kill him, and so attempted to slip down into the hold again but was seized by the sailor and dragged on deck. In the scuffle a seaman struck him over the head with his pistol and fractured his skull. He was also wounded in many places by the cutlasses of the seamen who had followed him into the hold and pricked him as opportunity offered, while he was skulking among the casks. A great part of his skin had also peeled off where the hot fat and water had been thrown over him so that all in all he was a most miserable looking object. When the captain came forward to inspect the man he ordered the mate to put an iron collar around his neck and chain him to the foremast at the same time ordering me not to give the black devil any medical assistance and telling the men at their peril not to give the fellow any food. He lived for three days in a state of stupefaction and his body was then thrown overboard in the sight of all the slaves aboard.

Meanwhile, the head of the man who had been shot was cut off and the poor devil who had come up on the promises of the black trader, was treated in the same way and the two gory heads were successively handed to the slaves, chained on deck, and they were obliged to kiss the lips of the bloody heads. Some men who refused to obey were unmercifully flogged by the captain and had the bloody part of a head rubbed against their faces.

While the musket fire was going on the slaves had crowded into a corner so that only one boy of about fifteen years was injured. The thigh bone of this boy was shattered and when the captain discovered his condition and that the boy would be of little value when he reached the West Indies, if he ever did get there, he ordered bricks tied to his neck and then had him thrown overboard alive.

The *Ruby* remained at Bimbe for nearly eight months before she completed her cargo. While on the middle passage the slaves were allowed to come on deck about eight o'clock every morning in good weather. The women were not confined but the men were always in irons, during the entire voyage. The slaves had two meals a day consisting of plantains and yams and while on the middle passage, rice, horse beans and sometimes a bit of bread was given them. One pint of water per day was served to each of them in a pannikin.

In order to keep them in good health it was usual to make them dance. It was the business of the chief mate to make the men dance and the second mate danced the women; but this was only done by means of a frequent use of the cat. The men could only jump up and rattle their chains but the women were driven in one among another all the while singing or saying words that had been taught them:—"Messe, messe, mackarida," that is:—"Good living or messing well among white men," thereby praising us for letting them live so well. But there was another time when the women were sitting by themselves, below, when I heard them singing other words and then always in tears. Their songs then always told the story of their lives and their grief at leaving their friends and country.

After the slaves received their last meal for the day they were driven below. If the sea was rough the slaves were unable to dance and whenever it rained hard they were kept below, and the gratings were covered with tarpaulins which made it very hot below and nearly suffocated the slaves. At such times I have found women in a fainting condition or insensible. Dysentery usually followed a spell of bad weather and the mucus and filth among the slaves below made the slave deck a horrible place.

We sailed with a cargo of one hundred and five slaves and only lost eight during the passage. In this we were fortunate and at no time on the voyage or while we were at Bimbe was there danger of smallpox. An acquaintance of mine who sailed in the *Britannia,* with 450 slaves aboard, lost 230 on the middle passage, mostly by smallpox. A small girl brought the infection into the vessel. When the captain discovered the situation he ordered her placed in an empty water puncheon in the hold. The disorder soon began to spread, notwithstanding a general inoculation, and the sick berths were soon insufficient to hold all the sick. Only those who were so bad as to be incapable of moving were admitted. There they lay in one mass of scab and corruption, frequently sticking to each other and to the deck till they were separated to be thrown overboard.

The *Ruby* reached the Barbadoes on June 27th, 1788, after a passage of nearly seven weeks, and from there went to St. Vincent's to sell the slaves, where she found that none were wanted as the market was overstocked. This was also the case at Grenada, where we found two Liverpool slavers, the *Kitty* and the *Viper*, that had been there for some time. At last a Dutchman from Demerara, happened in port and took our slaves through Messrs. Campbell, Baillie & Company. They sold at £35.5.0 per head and after spending three weeks in port we sailed and reached King's Road on Saturday evening, August 23d, 1788.

CHAPTER X

CAPTAIN CROW, THE LAST SLAVER OUT OF LIVERPOOL

THE English slave trade was abolished by Act of Parliament on May 1, 1807. For many years Liverpool had been a great center for the African slave trade and when the end seemed in sight, Henry Clarke, the owner of the ship *Kitty's Amelia*, of three hundred tons burden and mounting eighteen guns, cleared her for a last voyage just previous to the passing of the Abolition Bill. Her master was Capt. Hugh Crow, a Manxman, who had been in the Guinea trade for sixteen years and who, in after years, wrote that it had been his opinion "that the traffic in negroes was permitted by that Providence that rules over all, as a necessary evil, and that it ought not to have been done away with to humour the folly or the fancy of a set of people who knew little or nothing about the subject." He believed that the pretended philanthropists, through the abolition of slavery, had become indirectly responsible for the death of thousands of slaves, because they had caused the trade to be transferred to the ships of other nations where cruelty and a disregard for human life was shown "to which Englishmen could never bring themselves to resort."

The *Kitty's Amelia* did not actually sail for the African coast until July 27th, but her technical clearance before May 1st protected her while outfitting was being completed and insurance effected with the underwriters at fifteen guineas per cent which was five per cent lower than the usual premium. Her crew was composed of nearly sixty men and while making a course down St. George's Channel, four of the best of the crew, in spite of their protections, were impressed by H.M. frigate *Princess Charlotte*. The ship had been commissioned as a letter of marque and during the voyage several vessels were chased and boarded but no prizes were taken.

She arrived at Bonny after a passage of about seven weeks and was immediately boarded by King Holiday who anxiously inquired if it was true that the *Kitty's Amelia* was to be the last ship that would come to Bonny for negroes. Captain Crow in his memoirs* gives a curious account of what was said at that long palaver. The king's sentiments on abolition were expressed as follows:

"Crow," he remarked, "you and me sabby each other long time, and me know you tell me true mouth (speak truth); for all captains come to river tell me you King and you big mans stop we trade, and s'pose dat true, what we do? For you sabby me have too much wife, it be we country fash, and have too much child, and some may turn big rogue man, all same time we see some bad white man for some you ship, and we hear too much white man grow big rogue for you country. But God make you sabby book and make big ship—den you sen you bad people much far for other country, and we hear you hang much people, and too much man go dead for you warm (war). But God make we black and we no sabby book, and we no havy head for make ship for sen we bad mans for more country, and we law is, s'pose some of we child go bad and we no can sell 'em, we father must kill dem own child; and s'pose trade be done we force kill too much child same way. But we tink trade no stop, for all we Ju-Ju-man (the priests) tell we so, for dem say you country no can niber pass God A'mighty."

And Crow thought that the king's remarks were not lacking in sense and shrewdness.

There were ten or twelve vessels at Bonny waiting for slaves and Captain Crow was obliged to lie there a long time for his turn. During this period of waiting malignant fever and dysentery broke out among the crew. It was supposed that the sickness originated in some goods aboard returned on the ship from a former voyage when the ship was sickly. The rotten goods were thrown overboard, but

---

* *Memoirs of the late Captain H. Crow of Liverpool, . . . with descriptive sketches of the Western Coast of Africa,* London, 1830.

VIEW OF THE TOWN AND HARBOR OF LIVERPOOL, ENGLAND

From a colored aquatint by W. J. Bennett, engraved in 1811, in the Macpherson Collection

VIEW OF THE CITY OF RIO DE JANEIRO

From a colored lithograph published by Lemercier, Paris, in the Macpherson Collection

the sickness delayed the slaving. Terrible storms came up as the ship lay at her anchorage and she dragged her anchors and narrowly escaped going ashore.

In time the complement of slaves was made up and the ship sailed from Bonny for the last time with "as fine a cargo of blacks, as ever had been taken from Africa"; but disease lingered aboard and baffled the skill of the two doctors and as both whites and blacks were dying at an alarming rate, Captain Crow put in to the island of St. Thomas, in the gulf of Guinea, to recruit. Before long the sick seemed to have recovered and the ship resumed her voyage, but they had not been long at sea before the sickness broke out afresh and attacked both whites and blacks. The chief mate died and Captain Crow began to fear a great disaster, for if anything happened to him there would be no one left on board capable of navigating the ship. To add to the terror of the situation, about that time, fire broke out in the hold. The captain relates:

"One afternoon, when we were ten or twelve hundred miles from any land, and were sailing at the rate of seven or eight knots, the alarm was given that the ship was on fire in the afterhold. I was in the cabin at the time and springing upon deck, the first persons that I saw were two young men with their flannel shirts blazing on their backs; at the same time I perceived a dense cloud of smoke issuing from below, and looking round me I found the people in the act of cutting away the stern and quarter boats that they might abandon the vessel. At this critical juncture I had the presence of mind to exclaim in an animating tone, 'Is it possible, my lads, that you can desert me at a moment when it is your bounden duty, as men, to assist me.' And observing them to hesitate, I added, 'Follow me, my brave fellows, and we shall soon save the ship.' These few words had the desired effect, for they immediately rallied and came forward to assist me. To show them a proper example I was the first man to venture below, for I thought of the poor blacks entrusted to my care and who could not be saved in the boats, and I was determined, rather than desert them, to extinguish the fire or perish in the attempt.

"When we got below we found the fire blazing with great fury on the starboard side, and as it was known to the crew that there were forty-five barrels of gunpowder in the magazine, within about three feet only of the fire, it required every possible encouragement on my part to lead them on to endeavour to extinguish the rapidly increasing flames. When I first saw the extent of the conflagration, and thought of its proximity to the powder, a thrill of despair ran through my whole frame; but by a strong mental effort I suppressed my disheartening feelings, and only thought of active exertion, unconnected with the thought of imminent danger. We paused for a moment, struggling, as it were, to determine how to proceed. Very fortunately for us our spare sails were stowed close at hand. These we dragged out and by extraordinary activity we succeeded in throwing them over the flames which they so far checked that we gained time to obtain a good supply of water down the hatchway and in the course of ten or fifteen minutes, by favour of Almighty God, we extinguished the flames. . . . The accident, I found, was occasioned by the ignorance and carelessness of the two young men whose clothes I had seen burning on their backs. Through the want of regular officers, they had been entrusted to draw off some rum from the store cask and not knowing the danger to which they exposed themselves and the ship, had taken down a lighted candle, a spark from which had ignited the spirit." . . .

"It may not be uninteresting to learn with what kind of provisions the negroes were supplied. We frequently bought from the natives considerable quantities of dried shrimps to make broth; and a very excellent dish they made, when mixed with flour and palm oil and seasoned with pepper and salt. Both whites and blacks were fond of this mess. In addition to yams we gave them for a change, fine shelled beans and rice cooked together, and this was served up to each individual with a plentiful proportion of the soup. On other days their soup was mixed with peeled yams, cut up thin and boiled, with a proportion of pounded biscuit. For the sick we provided strong soups and middle messes, prepared from mutton, goats' flesh, fowls, etc., to which were added sago and lilipees, the whole mixed with port wine and sugar. I am thus particular in describing the ingredients which composed the food of the blacks, to show that no attention to their health was spared in this respect. Their personal comfort was also carefully studied. On their coming on deck, about eight o'clock in the morning, water was provided to wash their hands and faces, a mixture of lime juice to cleanse their mouths, towels to wipe with and chew sticks to clean their teeth. These were generally pieces of young branches of the common lime or of the citron of sweet lime tree, the skin of which is smooth, green and pleasantly aromatic. They are used about the thickness of a quill and the end being chewed, the white, fine fibre of the wood soon forms a brush with which the teeth may be effectually cleaned by rubbing them up and down. These sticks impart an agreeable flavor to the mouth and are sold in little bundles, for a mere trifle, in the public markets of the West Indies. A draw of brandy bitters was given to each of the men and clean spoons being served out, they breakfasted about nine o'clock. About eleven, if the day were fine, they washed their bodies all over, and after wiping themselves dry, were allowed to use palm oil, their favorite cosmetic. Pipes and tobacco were then supplied to the men and beads and other articles were distributed among the women to amuse them, after which they were permitted to dance and run about on deck to keep them in good spirits. A middle mess of bread and cocoa-nuts was given them about mid-day. The third meal was served out about three o'clock and after everything was cleaned out and arranged below, they were generally sent down about four or five o'clock in the evening. I always took great pains to promote the health and comfort of all on board, by proper diet, regularity, exercise, and cleanliness, for I considered that on keeping the ship clean and orderly, which was always my hobby, the success of our voyage mainly depended."

Such ideal and humane conditions on board a slaver were by no means general as will be discovered elsewhere in the present volume.

The sickness on board the *Kitty's Amelia* abated as they neared the West Indies, but by the time she arrived at Kingston, after a passage of eight weeks from St. Thomas, the two doctors had died and the deaths on the voyage amounted to eighty, of which thirty were whites. Captain Crow found that the mortality on board his ship was only half that on other ships in the harbor, where he found sixteen slavers at anchor, some of which had been there for several months, their cargoes unsold, due to a glutting of the market, and slaves and crews were dying daily. His cargo, however, being in better condition than the others, he was able to sell at a profit and return to Liverpool where he retired with a comfortable fortune.

Captain Crow lost his right eye when very young and was known, far and wide, as "Mind your eye Crow." His first voyage to the Guinea Coast was in the Liverpool slave ship *Prince,* sailing in 1790. His brother, William Crow, was also employed in the same trade and was chief mate of the *Othello* when she caught fire one night at Bonny and blew up, causing the death of several whites and about 120 blacks, among them a brother of King Pepple.

In October, 1796, he sailed from Liverpool as mate on the slaver *James,* and after taking in a cargo of negroes at Bonny, she weighed anchor and 'had made barely five leagues when she grounded at half-ebb on a bank and with six feet of water in her hold was carried over the tail of the bank by the tide and came to anchor in deep water. The captain went off in a boat to get assistance from Bonny, leaving Crow in charge of the ship with four hundred blacks aboard. The pumps were kept going and Crow went down into the hold with the carpenter, found the leak, and crammed it with pieces of beef. Eventually the ship was stranded in Bonny Creek and the slaves put aboard other vessels.

A night or two after, a horde of negroes came aboard and began to plunder the ship. Crow, who had been left to guard the vessel, had stowed his own belongings on the booms and supplied himself with plenty of six-pound shot, with which he defended himself stoutly against all attempts to dislodge him until King Pepple came alongside and commanded the people to withdraw, and rescued Crow, who afterwards took passage to Kingston and thence reached Liverpool.

CHAPTER XI

THE RECOLLECTIONS OF A SLAVE TRADER

I NEVER saw my father.* He was a seafaring man, sailing as mate of a coaster and was lost in a gale four months after his marriage with my mother, the daughter of a spinner in one of the cotton mills at Stockford, England. I can just remember her and also a room full of strange people, a red box and a man standing beside it, talking in a loud voice; then a dismal walk through the rain, to a field where some men had just finished digging a hole in the ground. My home after that was in the Stockford workhouse until one day the work-master came in company with a swarthy-featured stranger and said: "Look sharp, my lad, and you'll see your uncle!" I did "look sharp" and saw a man about thirty years old, dressed in a jaunty suit of sailor's store clothes, with a broad palm-leaf hat on his head, round gold rings in his ears and heavy gold watch seals hanging from his fob. This grand-looking personage spoke kindly to me, gave me a few half-pence, told me to cheer up and try to be a man and then walked away with Mr. Crump, the master. He never came to the workhouse again but I was told that he had left some money for me with the parish overseers and promised to look after me as I grew older.

One day, when I was twelve years old, there came a summons to go before the overseers, three stout, red-faced men, in powdered wigs, who sat at a green-covered table, with snuff boxes before them. After the master had pulled me roughly by the arm into their awful presence, the oldest one said: "Philip Drake, how would you like to go to your uncle?" Of course I joyfully said—I should like to go to him and a few days later I was hustled away at daybreak, to ride ten miles to the seaport from which a collier was to start for the

* The following narrative is abstracted from *Revelations of a Slave Smuggler: being the Autobiography of Capt. Richard Drake, an African Trader for Fifty Years—from 1807 to 1857*, New York, 1860.

Welsh coast, to intercept the Irish emigrant ship as it left Holyhead. I wore a pair of new leather brogans, corduroy breeches and a real leather hat and carried a bundle of patched clothing tied up in an old Spitalfields handkerchief. Safely tucked away in a pocket was a letter, made formidable by a stamp in green wax, addressed to "Maurice Halter, Boston, United States." This was my future passport.

It was a cold, drizzly morning when I tumbled over the wet side of the coal-lighter, on a deck crowded with shivering men, women and children like myself, where I was knocked about by sailors and nearly swept overboard by a swing of the sloop's boom, before I managed to creep under shelter behind a huge pile of corded boxes and clothes bags. The rain soaked through my brown stuff frock and the tossing of the sloop sickened me long before we made Anglesley light and hove-to under the lee of a weather-beaten packet ship, from the Irish coast, bound for Boston in the United States. The sea was rough, causing confusion and difficulty in transferring the collier's freight; but at last it was effected and with some forty other English paupers, I found myself dumped among four hundred Irish emigrants, in the steerage of the ship *Polly*, of Waterford, Captain Herring.

Since that day I have experienced many hardships and seen bad voyages but my first taste of the ocean, on board the *Polly*, was a thing to be remembered. Child as I was, I did not know what arrangement had been made for my keeping and for two days I was totally neglected by everybody. I crawled to a dark corner of the bulkhead and lay coiled up with my head on my little bundle. The ship's motion renewed my sickness and through the long, dark night I strained and gasped for breath, thinking to die any moment. In the morning I was unable to move. Around me were the emigrants, some lying still, some sick, others talking, laughing or quarreling. Women were cooking food, old men were smoking pipes and the air was close and stifling. Cursing and groaning was heard on every side. After the second morning I lost consciousness and before long was raving with fever. Had it not been for the charity of a poor family whose bed was stretched near my nook in the bulkhead there would have been one less poor English orphan.

The packet ship *Polly*, of Waterford, must have been as bad as any slaver that ever skulked the "Middle Passage" with battened-down hatches. She was 202 tons burden and carried 450 odd steerage passengers. They were so thick between decks that the air became putrid and whenever her sick squads were ordered up the gangways, one or more was sure to die with the first gulp of fresh air. The steerage became pestilential before our voyage was half over, for the emigrants' beds were never cleaned and whole families literally wallowed in poisonous filth. The bodies of men and women, and their tattered garments, were incrusted and impregnated with the most offensive matter. Typhus fever and dysentery soon broke out and then the mortality raged fearfully.

The *Polly's* crew, when she left Ireland, consisted of but ten men and four died of dysentery before we were half way across the Atlantic. One day when I had crawled to the deck and lay on a coil of chain near the capstan, I counted thirty corpses that were hauled up during the morning and thrown overboard. Most of the bodies were women with their long hair tangled in their filthy garments.

The ship's provisions began to run short after a time and were doled out in the most niggardly way until the dysentery thinned out the passengers, when there was enough and to spare of oatmeal and damaged rice. But water grew scantier every day. Foul weather set in and the *Polly* was driven from her course into the hot latitudes and when we made the first light, off Cape Ann, we had 186 left out of 450 odd passengers and some of these died before landing.

The *Polly* reached Boston in April 1802 and her passengers were placed in quarantine on one of the islands in the harbor, and there I remained until one day when a little old man in a snuff-colored coat and rusty hat, came enquiring for Tommy Driscoll. During the voyage Tommy had fallen overboard and could not be saved and when the old man heard the story he befriended me and took me to his home in Sun Court, near Ann Street now North Street, in the North End of Boston.

Thaddeus Mooney was an apothecary and in his shop I was taught to pound drugs in a big mortar and to run errands for my new master. As for the unsealed letter to Maurice Halter, Doctor Mooney made many inquiries but without result. No one seemed to know of a Mr. Halter.

One September afternoon, two years later, as I was passing the Moon Tavern, a noted starting post for the Eastern coaches, I caught sight of a man sitting in one of its large bow windows which projected into the street. There was something familiar about the swarthy face, glittering eyes and gold earrings and suddenly it came to me that this must be my uncle. And so it was, but Capt. Richard Willing and not Maurice Halter, which accounted for the unsuccessful inquiries that had been made. After a long conversation during which the captain asked many searching questions as to what I knew about books, figures and even shop matters, I was told that I should sail with him on his next voyage, the ship being then at New York.

It was nearly dusk when we were rowed off to a vessel lying at anchor in the Sound near New Rochelle, and a storm was coming up, but that night saw us well on a southerly course which soon gave plenty of sea-room.

The next morning the captain said to me, "I want you to understand that you've got no uncle on board this vessel; I'm captain of all on board; you are to help the surgeon, as his mate, and keep your mouth shut. If you do your duty, we shan't quarrel—if you don't, then look out, my lad!"

The crew consisted of thirty men, including the captain, mates and surgeon whose name was Maxwell. He was a Scotchman, about thirty years old, stout and thick, with a pock-marked face and yellow, bilious eyes. Thanks to my experience with Doctor Mooney, I was quite as much at home with the surgeon's bottles and boxes as was Maxwell. The two of us slept in berths on deck, midships, where the medicine chest was kept, and messed with the mates. Captain Willing had his meals in the cabin.

The brig was a sharply-built craft of about three hundred tons, and a swift sailor. She was named the *Coralline* and was well defended with an ample magazine and a dozen heavy carronades, as it was a time of war when French cruisers swarmed the seas. After passing through a hurricane off the coast of Brazil, during which the bowsprit was sprung and the foretopmast carried away, the brig came to anchor in the wonderful harbor at Rio, where repairs were made and all hands kept busy stowing a mixed cargo of colored cottons, kegs of powder and rum, trinkets, tobacco and other goods suitable for a trading voyage. The surgeon ordered a new supply of medical stores—calomel, sulphur, Peruvian bark and other drugs and after a month's stay, the anchor was weighed early one morning and a course set for the coast of Africa.

On August 22, 1805, the *Coralline* anchored at a trading station at the mouth of the river Volta, which enters the Bight of Benin between the Gold Coast and the Dahomy country. Here a schooner was chartered from the trader at the post and Captain Willing began working up the river. Along the banks the natives could be seen working in their cornfields; herds of cattle were browsing in the grass and towards night some negroes in a canoe brought milk and bartered for trinkets. The next day rice fields were seen with dozens of canals crossing in all directions. On August 29th, the schooner anchored in front of Malee, a town of about three thousand inhabitants, with a market place in the center, the huts forming a semi-circle on the hillside overlooking the river. Here, Captain Willing organized an expedition to the Kong Mountains, lying to the northeast, to trade with the gold mines. There was a war going on at the time, between the King of Ashantee, who ruled over Malee, and the Dahomy nation, and many prisoners had been taken which were being shipped down the river to be sold as slaves or sent to the mountains to wash out gold.

We set out with a long procession of black traders and soldiers, as a guard for the white men, and soon after leaving the town entered a dense forest. The head man of the Ashantee soldiers was a ferocious-looking negro, as black as jet, with wool braided in stiff hanks. His teeth were filed sharp and his cheeks slashed with two deep cuts, colored by some red earth, which gave him an unearthly appearance. Quobah was a giant in height. He carried a spear and had a powder horn and pouch strapped to his neck. Three slaves bore his arms—one carrying a heavy, curved broadsword, another his club and a third his musket. We had nothing to do but walk as there were plenty of blacks to carry all luggage. There must have been one hundred and fifty in the company. The day's journeys were short and at night we halted in some beautiful valley and were served like lords with African delicacies. The women ground corn, cooked rice cakes, and milked the cows that were driven along with the party as pack-beasts. After supper the blacks beat their tomtoms or wooden drums and kept up singing and dancing until it was time to camp down. Then the Ashantee soldiers set a watch; the white men swung their hammocks under the trees and the night passed well enough except for the crying of wild animals.

One evening we encamped on the bank of a smooth river shaded by immense trees. The sun was setting splendidly as we ate our supper. Some of the blacks were lounging about, smoking their pipes and others lay on the grass while their wives fed them with butter-rolls and nice bits of a kid that had been killed and stewed since we halted. Suddenly we were attacked and the air seemed filled with arrows. The forest appeared alive with savages. I was seated under a tree drinking water from a calabash, when the attack began and almost immediately I saw a negro making for me, armed with a huge club. Quobah, our Ashantee chief, jumped before him, but a dozen enemies darted in from all sides and I was beaten down before I could lift an arm.

When I came to my senses I found myself lying at the foot of a tree, tied hand and foot. The forest seemed on fire from hundreds of torches that had been stuck in the ground or were waved up and down in the hands of the negroes who were running to and fro, singing and yelling like maniacs. Their bodies were smeared with white in bars and streaks so that they looked like skeletons as they leaped back and forth. One of them spied me as I turned my face and suddenly jumped toward me, screeching horribly, and dashed close to my face the thing he was holding. It was a human head—the head of a white man—dripping with blood. A short distance from where I lay was a log on the river bank and every now and then a victim was dragged to this log, to be held by the legs, with his head on the log, when a dull blow from a heavy war club would end his life immediately.

Before sunrise the black camp was in motion. I saw our cows driven past and behind them about fifty of the Malee soldiers and their attendants, tied together, in couples. In the company of hideous savages that followed were a number of female warriors with bows and arrows slung across their naked breasts, each carrying aloft on the point of a spear, a head or leg of one of the massacred prisoners. I had heard of the women-warriors—the Amazons—of the Dahomey King and these led me to imagine who were my captors.

It was a week's march, along a well-beaten track through the forest, before we reached our destination, the walled town of Yallaba which fronted on a sluggish river and was rendered nearly inaccessible on three sides by a wide swamp. Quobah and I were led before an old black man, fat and greasy, dressed in a shirt of red muslin, such as curtains are made of, and wearing a tarpaulin hat on his grey wool. He was seated on a pile of soft sheepskins and I was made to kneel before this old fellow who turned out to be the King of Yallaba. I was entirely naked as my clothes had been stolen on the march by the chattering women. The King pinched my flesh, rubbing it with his black hand and muttering something in his lingo. The women then gave me milk in a gourd and led me away.

Such was my reception at Yallaba. I soon found that my youth and white skin had made a favorable impression on the fat King, who was called Mammee. My fetters were removed and I was permitted to roam about the courtyard of the square house or palace. It was not a very grand mansion, but it extended over an acre or more and was guarded by fifty female soldiers. I was taken in charge by the King's women and treated liberally with milk, curds, fruit and rice cakes, and afterwards kept among the house slaves and helped the women to pound corn between two flat stones and prepare fagots for fires.

It was about the middle of September, 1805, when I began my captivity in the Yallaba valley and it was not long before I began to understand and speak many words of the Dahomey language. The King's youngest daughter, a handsome girl in spite of her tawny skin, took quite a fancy to me and was my constant teacher. Her name was Soolah and when I first saw her she was about twelve years old.

Quobah, the Ashantee chief, was considered quite a prize and about three months after our arrival I was told by Soolah that he was to be sacrificed at a grand feast in honor of the King's fetish. But in this affair events took a strange turn. For some time a lion had been ravaging the country about the King's town and one morning Soolah came to tell me that the beast had attacked the slaves who were gathering corn and killed a dozen the night before. The King was in great trouble and a consultation with the priests was to be held and the fetish consulted about the alarming visitor. As a result it was decided to sacrifice Quobah at once. Accordingly the Ashantee captive was led into the public square and all the people gathered about to witness his massacre. King Mammee sat on his throne of sheepskins and the priests were all armed with immense clubs and swords.

Quobah stood with his arms folded until he heard all that his enemies had to say and then he addressed the King and priests abruptly. He proposed that, as he was to be sacrificed in any event, he should be allowed to choose his own method by volunteering to go out alone and fight the lion. The priests decided this to be lawful, the King was satisfied and the field people of Yallaba were glad to find a champion to attack the lion. No time was to be lost as the sun was declining and the lion was expected to visit the valley again that evening.

Before long Quobah was brought out from his hut. He was armed with a long spear, his own huge sword, and with my carbine, the only really serviceable firearm in the town. He alone appeared to be unmoved as he marched to the south gate. Scarcely had he got beyond the heavy stone that secured the log door, before a terrific roar sounded from the fields and an enormous lion came cantering toward the approaching man. The priests and women began to howl and the men pounded their war drums to frighten the lion, but he only lashed his tail the fiercer and crouched for a spring. Quobah sunk on one knee and the next moment the lion leaped and came down on the sharp point of Quobah's spear which the crafty warrior had suddenly raised, the butt resting on the ground. The Ashantee jumped aside and left the brute floundering with the lance through his shoulder.

At this instant another loud roar was heard from the forest and soon a lioness came crashing through the corn followed by two half-grown cubs. Then, indeed, it seemed that all was over with the Ashantee, for the wounded lion had broken the spear to fragments in his struggle and was crouching for another spring, though evidently severely wounded. Quobah lifted the carbine and then as the lion made his second leap, the Ashantee sprang nimbly aside and as the beast fell heavily on its wounded shoulder he ran close to him and fired the carbine into his jaws. When the smoke cleared we could see the lion writhing in his death agony and the lioness snuffing the ground about a dozen feet from Quobah. An instant later she gave a frightful roar and rose with a flying leap, directly for the warrior, who awaited her attack and as she fell, with all his giant strength drove his sword-blade straight into the animal's mouth. We heard a stifled roar but every movement was shrouded in the cloud of dust that whirled around the man and the beasts; then, as the dust settled, we could see the lion and the lioness stretched side by side and Quobah lying across them, covered with blood. The cubs sat on their haunches, a little way off. The Ashantee was still living, but his left arm had been mangled and his breast was torn by the lioness' claw. He recovered in a few weeks and was solemnly set free and allowed to go to his own country with the skins of the lion and the lioness as his trophy.

When Quobah took his departure I ventured to ask King Mammee if I, too, might return to my people, but the old man promptly refused, telling me that he had other plans for my future. I continued to grow in his favor and as I better understood the Dahoman language it seemed that I was in a fair way to become a person of consideration and after the season of rains this was, in a way, confirmed for I was allowed to accompany an expedition organized to capture slaves for the great Dahoman market held yearly at Abomey, the capital town.

The preparations for this expedition had been going on for some months and when we set off from Yallaba there were three hundred men in the party. We travelled easterly for two days before we joined the main body of about twelve hundred. Four hundred of these were women soldiers. Besides warriors there were gangs of slaves to carry provisions and luggage and women to prepare food for the soldiers. On the seventh morning of the march we reached the enemy's borders and came in sight of a peaceful village. Here our hunting began. The Abomey chief fired off his gun and gave a shrill yell and immediately our whole army rushed upon the village. The resistance was not very great as our approach was unexpected and the inhabitants soon tried to escape but found themselves completely surrounded. In less than an hour we had secured about three hundred prisoners. The old people and infants were not considered of value and were knocked on the head or stuck with spears as fast as they were brought in. The captives were yoked together in couples with bamboo collars, a long ox-hide band connecting a half dozen collars together. Besides this, their hands were bound behind and a

SLAVE HUNTERS ATTACKING A NEGRO TOWN

From a wood engraving in Canot's *Twenty Years of an African Slaver*, New York, 1854

BRANDING A NEGRESS AT THE RIO PONGO
From a wood engraving in Canot's *Twenty Years of an African Slaver,*
New York, 1854

tall Dahoman marched beside every couple, beating them with a heavy whip whenever they appeared to lag.

Two days later we arrived near a larger town than the one we had surprised. It was in a valley and I had a fine view of it from the top of a wooded hill where we camped. Here our captives were made to lie down and stakes were driven in the earth, fastening them securely. When the night was somewhat advanced the main portion of our force set off in small parties to creep on the unsuspecting town and in about an hour a bright flame shot up followed by a chorus of yells, cries and groans. In a few minutes the whole valley seemed in flames. From the brow of the hill I could see the Dahoman warriors running about whirling their weapons. The naked women and children were flying in all directions and in the light from the blazing huts I could see the wretched people rushing from the flames to be received on the spear points of their enemies. It was nearly morning when the work of capture and massacre was finished. More than four hundred choice slaves had been taken and after they had been shackled we pushed on, without rest, for fear of pursuit, as we had heard that the enemy were assembling in our rear. On the homeward march we surprised three other small villages so that our hunt resulted in the capture of nearly a thousand slaves. When we reached our valley there was a great feast and old King Mammee sat on his pile of sheepskins and distributed feathers to the principal men and the priests made a solemn sacrifice of two young boys to the King's fetish. The poor lads were cut to pieces with knives by the women soldiers and afterwards burned before the idol.

I had now been among the Yallabas nearly a year and could talk their lingo quite glibly. Soolah, the youngest daughter of King Mammee, had been a sort of playmate of mine from the first and during the year had grown into quite a little woman. My associates were among the princes and young chiefs and I shared in all the feastings of the King, who led an indulgent life with his score of wives. My full dress consisted of a piece of calico wrapped about the loins and a sort of cloak which Soolah wove of mango leaves, split fine and fringed with colored threads of unravelled cotton.

One day King Mammee sent for me and after a long harangue said that he intended that I should become his son by marrying Soolah. He told me that his fetish and mine would then become very powerful. My vanity was touched by this mark of royal favor and I was not averse to the princess who was the handsomest young negress I had ever seen and so I consented at once. Soolah was sent for and she came, dressed in her white cotton shift and attended by her sisters and a train of maids and the ceremony of marriage was performed by the women leading her to my hut. After a special feast, with singing and dancing, I became a husband at the age of seventeen years.

I had not been living with Soolah very long before another great slave hunt was announced which I was to accompany as doctor. This turned out to be my last expedition with the Yallabas, for before we reached the rendezvous of the other Dahoman war parties, we were set upon by a superior force of hostile negroes and nearly all of our party taken prisoners. I was stripped and tied and then marched a twenty day's journey through a dense forest, till we reached a negro settlement on a large river. This was Fandee, a town of the Foulah tribe, located on the Gambia river. The Yallaba warriors were sent off in gangs to work in the rice fields and I was taken before the Foulah prince, a man fully six feet and a half in height, who wore gold rings in his ears, which reminded me of my uncle. I could understand his language with my knowledge of the Dahoman tongue and soon he had my story with the result that I was released from strict confinement and permitted to go about the town. The women of Fandee were quite free and attractive and very curious about the white stranger, but though I saw many handsome forms among them, I couldn't help thinking with regret of my Yallaba wife Soolah.

A month later I was taken in charge by a company of Foulahs and carried down the river in a canoe, until we reached a trading station and slave market where I was greeted for the first time in two years by the sound of a white man's voice, in my own language. Captain Fraley was a British trader, engaged in the African trade, and had half a dozen sloops at different stations on the Gambia, taking in cargoes of negroes to ship from the coast. The place where I had been brought by the Foulahs was one of these stations, called Wadee. It was merely a depot for slaves with a few sheds built for their shelter. Captain Fraley had heard from one of his negro agents that a white man was at Fandee and had bought me from the Foulah prince for half a dozen muskets, a keg of rum and a piece of Manchester cotton. "You see, my boy," said the Bristol trader, laughing as he shook my hand, "you're a regularly purchased slave, but I'm ready to bargain for your ransom on favorable terms." I soon learned that my uncle had escaped the Dahoman massacre, for Captain Fraley was acquainted with him and had seen him within a year.

The captain took me on board his sloop which was to sail down the river the next morning. She was more like a pleasure yacht than a trading vessel, being about twenty-five tons burden, with four comfortable lockers in her snug little cabin. I was given a cot in one of them and during the night was awakened by a noise of groaning which startled me so that I went on deck, though the air was chill and a thick mist covered the river. Captain Fraley heard me and asked what was the matter and when I inquired about the groaning noise he replied that was only the "darkies." Next morning all was explained. The sloop's hold was crowded with a cargo of eighty slaves stowed in a space of hardly thirty feet, as the hold was only ten feet long. The blacks were placed in a sitting position, one within another's legs, so that each did not occupy more than three feet of space.

We dropped down the Gambia and were joined next day by a smaller sloop of ten tons, with forty slaves aboard, in a hold about nine by four feet, length and width. Our own craft was afterward made to accommodate a deck-load, as there was quite a stock of slaves waiting at all the stations.

I found Captain Fraley a pleasant man in the cabin, but he had no feeling where negroes were concerned as a matter of traffic. He was engaged in extensive operations on the river Gambia and owned quite a fleet of Bristol and Liverpool craft, which he supplied with cargoes from his factories on the African coast. His mode of obtaining slaves was generally by fair barter, but he also organized hunting parties on his private account, to operate with various negro kings. It was customary for parties of sailors and coast blacks to lie in wait near the streams and little villages and seize the stragglers by twos and threes, when they were fishing or cultivating their patches of corn. Sometimes an attack was made on the huts by night and as many seized as could be conveniently managed in the boats.

Captain Fraley had heard that my uncle was at a slave station near the Congo river and agreed to give me a passage in one of his coasters, just starting southward,—a Bristol brig carrying supplies to a factory on the Angola coast from which she would bring back a cargo of slaves to the Gambia stations where his chief depots were located. She was a heavy sailer and when we reached Embomma, about a hundred miles from the Congo, we found that Captain Willing had left the settlement a week before, so there was nothing for me to do but to stay on the brig and go to Angola and thence back to the river Gambia.

The brig was named the *Friendship* and her captain was a Londoner—one Thorley—a rough but honest seaman who treated me very well. The mate was an Irishman and there were eight Portuguese and Danish sailors on board, an English cabin-boy and two Guinea negroes. We had hardly cleared the Congo river outward, when the Portuguese and Danes mutinied and took the vessel. I was below talking with Captain Thorley, when we heard a noise on deck and he ran up to see what it was about. I waited a few moments before I followed and, to my horror, stumbled over the little cabin-boy, lying by the companion rail, with his head split open. The crew were just then throwing Captain Thorley overboard after having knocked him in the head with the cook's axe. At the same time I heard a faint cry of "Boat! Boat!" and saw our Irish mate drifting astern. One of the Portuguese sailors ran toward me, brandishing a handspike, but I called out in Spanish, begging my life, and he turned away. The two Guinea men were called from below, where they were asleep, and the Portuguese cook brought them each a tin cup full of rum. While they were drinking it, two of the mutineers shot them with musket balls through the stomach and they were then thrown overboard.

I thought my turn was now sure to come, but the fellows, after talking together a few minutes, held up a cross before me and demanded that I should swear never to divulge what they had done, which I was glad enough to do, though with small faith in their goodwill to me. They then began to overhaul the brig and after plundering the officer's chests, filled two boats with provisions and whatever articles they thought most valuable. I was allowed to get into one of the boats and after scuttling the brig, they pushed off and steered for the coast which was reached on the third day after the murders. Both boats were swamped in making a landing, but some of the provisions and rum-kegs were washed ashore.

About noon we started for the bush, but had not walked far before a gang of blacks appeared, armed with clubs and spears, and in a few minutes we were all stripped and bound and I was once more a captive among the negroes. We had fallen into the hands of a tribe of Kroomen, as the coast negroes are called, and my ability to talk a little of their lingo was of service. They marched us inland to their village and our rum was distributed and a bullock killed for a feast. Here we stayed for two days and then were taken back to the beach where we found a boat belonging to an English ship, then in the offing, and soon were safely on board *The Brothers*, a Liverpool slaver. I told her captain the story of the loss of the *Friendship* and the mutineers were at once put in irons.

The Brothers was a ship of five hundred tons, with a crew of forty,—English, Scotch and Portuguese. She was coasting for a cargo of slaves and had a small schooner on deck to run up the rivers. Captain Baker, her commander, told me that my uncle was at Calabar and promised to take me there. When we arrived at the outlet of Calabar river, I learned that Captain Willing was on the Qua, a smaller stream about eight miles inland and as Captain Baker hoisted out his schooner here I went on board of her to ascend the river. When we reached the Qua river, I found that my uncle had gone still farther inland, on a negro hunt, but on one of his schooners, lying before the negro depot, I found my old friend Doctor Maxwell.

The surgeon was hardly able to believe the evidence of his eyes. Instead of the pale-faced, undersized lad of fifteen, he saw a stout, manly fellow, tanned like a Moor. I related my adventures and a Fishman messenger was sent off to my uncle with the news of my resurrection, as Doctor Maxwell called it. He told me that he had been to Brazil and the West Indies twice, since their escape from the massacre on the night of the attack by the Dahomen. Only one white had been killed on that occasion, a sailor, whose head I had seen. The *Coralline* was then at a place called Cameroons, a couple of hundred miles down the coast from Calabar, and Captain Willing was in partnership with a rich Spaniard at Rio and was shipping cargoes of slaves every month from various stations on the Guinea coast. The fifth day after my arrival, a message came from my uncle that I should join him at once and in company with a couple of Fishmen I set off for the tramp inland.

My uncle was at a large negro town, called Gambo, and he welcomed me most cordially and told me that my knowledge of negro tongues would make me very useful to him as an interpreter. Next day I was presented to the negro king of Gambo, who was called Ephraim. There was some difference between the languages of the Dahomans and Foulahs and the Gambo natives, but I soon contrived to pick up a stock of new words.

Captain Willing was making up a kaffle of slaves from the several lots brought in by the hunting parties. A kaffle is the common name for a train of slaves to be driven to the rivers or seacoast. He had a standing bargain for supplies so there was no chaffering. He bought in lots of twenty, allowing a thirty-gallon keg of brandy, a half dozen pieces of colored cottons or twenty-five pounds of gunpowder for any prime lot. Iron spearheads, coral beads, tobacco and gilt trinkets were exchanged proportionately for other lots.

The business of examination and choice of stock was done in a shady wood near the center of the town where my uncle's quarters were. In shirt and duck trowsers with palm-leaf hat, he would walk up and down the fettered line of slaves. Shakoe, the mulatto overseer, was a sort of negro doctor as well and could tell an unsound slave almost at a glance. He handled the naked blacks from head to foot, squeezing their joints and muscles, twisting their arms and legs, examining teeth, eyes and chest, and pinching breasts and groins without mercy. The slaves stood in couples, stark naked, and were made to jump, cry out, lie down and roll and hold their breath for a long time. The women and girls were used no more gently than the men by this mulatto inspector.

The day before we were to start from Gambo, the branding was done and a good deal of flogging had to be done also to keep the frightened negroes quiet. Shakoe's lash and the heavy whips of his assistant negroes were not idle for a moment. The slaves were fetched up singly, made to lie down on their faces where they were held by a big negro while another kept the branding irons hot in a fire close by and a third applied them between the shoulders of the shrieking wretches. At first there was horrible yelling, for the poor negroes expected to be tortured to death and I was called upon to talk to them in their own lingo, though my assurances didn't have much effect. Shakoe plied his leather until it became actually encrusted with blood.

After the scourgings and brandings were through with for that day, the negroes were allowed double rations of rice, yams and beans and then coupled for the march. That night King Ephraim gave a feast to my uncle and a slave sacrifice was made to the fetish for good luck. The sick, maimed and feeble negroes, discarded in making up the kaffle, supplied victims enough for the occasion and several of them were cut to pieces before we started from Gambo.

Our march to the river was a painful one. Shakoe and his assistant "devils," as the slaves, no doubt, considered them, marked their way with blood. When we reached the Qua and marched along its banks to the Calabar depot, I let the whole kaffle pass me and the slaves presented a deplorable appearance as they moved along, scarred and bleeding.

Doctor Maxwell and the two skippers of the vessels were at the station to receive us. Here the kaffle was overhauled and the barber's work done. The heads of all slaves, without distinction of age or sex, were shaved and they were then scrubbed with sand while standing in the water. The schooners were fitted with bulkheads, in the fashion of regular slavers, and the sexes divided on each side. The largest males were packed first in the hold, sitting cross-legged in rows, back to back. They faced each other closely and a hundred were crammed into each schooner under decks. The women and girls were all stowed in one hold. After securing these below, about fifty were tied around the masts and rails of both vessels, so that every available foot of space was covered with black flesh. As it was impossible to shift them while we were in the river, they were served their rations from wooden buckets let down by bamboo poles to each row. We made good progress down the Calabar and arrived at the Cameroons in five days losing only three boys and two girls who were suffocated in the hold and thrown overboard at sea. At Cameroons we found the *Coralline*, waiting for her freight, and I soon trod her familiar decks.

The barracoon, where the slaves were collected, was a large building near the landing place and the next morning after we arrived the loading of the ship commenced early. The blacks were all stripped naked and shipped by twos and threes, in canoes, through the surf. They were shackled down in tiers, on the deck of the

Coralline, sitting between each other's legs, fore and aft. One slave deck rested on stanchions, over the water stowage and the blacks were strung across in gangs of six or eight, according to size, and their ankle-bolts were secured by two iron rods running amidships and padlocked in the center. When the rods were drawn out the shackles would drop and a gang could take its turn to go on deck for air.

We sailed on May 11th, 1808, bound for Dutch Guiana. There was a fine breeze and everything was in order. The slaves were given two meals a day, of boiled beans or rice and each had a light wooden dish and spoon tied about the neck. The ninth day out we had an exciting time as there was an attempted revolt. It was all due to Shakoe. The mulatto was hated by every slave on board and that morning one of them struck him with his shackle and then jumped overboard. Shakoe became furious and rushed down into the hold cutting right and left with his whip. By some means a gang got loose and broke off the iron rod that fastened their ring bolts. They at once attacked Shakoe and beat his brains out and succeeded in liberating half a dozen other gangs and got on deck all together. Our watch and the negro sentinels immediately fired their muskets into the crowd of naked blacks who had begun to arm themselves with handspikes, buckets and any other loose missiles. Doctor Maxwell and I were on deck at the time and Captain Willing came up in a hurry with a pistol in each hand. Our white crew rushed aft and the mate served out arms with which the blacks were driven back but not before two sailors were killed and one wounded. It was a terrible affair while it lasted. The negroes fought like wild beasts and had they succeeded in releasing all below, we should have been overpowered and everyone slaughtered. Thirteen blacks were shot on the deck and seven seriously wounded. All these were flung into the sea. It was a narrow escape for the brig. Slaving is a dangerous business at sea as well as ashore. Shakoe deserved his fate as he abused the blacks shamefully. His head was beaten to pieces,—a ghastly sight, and the negroes tore his whip into bits no larger than my finger.

On July 14th the *Coralline* anchored at Berbice, Dutch Guiana. The blacks were landed at once and two days later were placed on sale in the market. There was a scarcity of hands on the sugar plantations and good prices were paid for the slaves. The Dutch maids, in short green jackets and scarlet petticoats, walked around inspecting the naked Africans as if it was a common thing. The auctioneer sat on a high chair at one end of the large room and the slaves stood on a stool in front of him. He made them turn round about, as they stood in their breech-cloths before the people, and the purchasers walked up and felt of them to try their flesh and soundness. The darkies were obliged to go through every sort of motion. It seemed at times as if their arms would be pulled out of joint or their jaws cracked by some of the Dutch boors. One dame was not satisfied until she forced a wench to screech by squeezing her breast cruelly. In two days the vendue was over. The grown men fetched as high as a thousand guilders and the boys and girls and women from seven to eight hundred, which were considered good prices.

Leaving Berbice, the *Coralline* made a quick run to Rio de Janeiro where I met my uncle's partner, Don Juan de Cobral, a Portuguese trader of great wealth, who lived in style at a country house in the mountains, a few miles out from Rio. He had a dozen illegitimate children, whom he was educating, and lived with their mothers on his large estate. Donna Maria, a quadroon girl, sixteen years old, was at her father's house when I first went there with my uncle, and entertained us with playing on the harp and singing. She was the handsomest young woman, with negro blood in her veins, that I ever saw. This girl, with several of her brothers and sisters, was sold in 1813 to help pay her father's creditors.

A few days after our arrival at Rio, my uncle took me for a walk on the promenade overlooking the wonderful bay, during which he told me that he had withdrawn from his partnership with Don Juan. I also learned that the English government had abolished the slave

A Dutch Planter in Surinam in his Morning Dress
From an engraving in Stedman's *Narrative of an Expedition to Surinam*, London, 1796

CAPTURE OF THE SLAVER "HENNA," OCT. 26, 1843, OFF MERCURY ISLAND, S. W. COAST OF
AFRICA, BY H.M. SCHOONER "ARIEL"

From a water color in the Macpherson Collection

trade with her colonies and that henceforth no slaver could sail under the British flag. "Captain Fraley," said my uncle, "has broken up his coast stations and left the field clear for us. The *Coralline* is now a Spanish vessel and you and I, Phil, must sink our English birth-rights and resign all claims to our larger estates in Stockford."

I laughed at my uncle's joke and said I was as ready to sail under the Spanish flag as any other. Shortly after this the *Coralline* shipped a new crew of Portuguese and Spaniards and we sailed from Rio, bound for the Guinea coast. Cape Palmas, on the Ivory Coast, was reached on Nov. 3, 1808, where we shipped forty Kroo fishermen with their canoes and three days later reached a place called Assinam, on the Windward Coast, about two miles from a river said to be populous. The country thereabout was ruled by a king known as Prince Vinegar who reminded me of my old father-in-law, King Mammee. Here we set up covered sheds surrounded by a picket fence and in time the settlement grew to be one of the most thriving on the Coast and was the means of saving scores of British merchants from ruin if it did no good otherwise. The river made a bend near us creating a little harbor. By means of our fast schooners, together with the *Coralline* and her mate, an American-built brig named the *Florida,* we kept up a constant tapping of the coast between Cape Palmas and the Rio Gambia, where Captain Fraley's stations were still supplied with negroes. My uncle Richard called himself Don Ricardo and my name was transmogrified into Felipe. Our settle-ment we christened Rio Basso where we soon had extensive barra-coons erected on the mainland and on several small islands in the river. My uncle made several voyages in the *Corraline,* with full cargoes, and before long became noted in Africa and the West Indies as a shrewd and successful trader who never lost a cargo, though privateers were swarming in every sea.

CHAPTER XII

FACTORY LIFE ON THE GUINEA COAST

FACTORY life in Africa is no desirable lot for a civilized being, but I passed five years at Rio Basso without much tediousness. My uncle made a liberal contract for my services and allowed me three negroes per month to ship on my own account. I made myself familiar with King Vinegar's people on the river and visited many black nations further inland. Don Miguel Barca, the factor, was a hasty tempered man but on the whole we got on very well together. Under his management we had a couple of hundred darkies constantly at work cutting down trees and assisting our white force which numbered twenty—Spaniards, Portuguese and Dutchmen. Besides being surgeon, I was accountant and paymaster and had to settle with King Vinegar and the other chiefs for the provisions they sent in. All this time we were loading and trans-shipping cargoes of slaves from various parts of the coast. As soon as our barracoons were ready they were filled with stock and no vessel had to wait an extra day for lack of negroes.

Our first accomodations were poor enough, tents and hovels being the only shelter; but before the rains we got under a commodious roof and in the course of a year I had a house to myself. The factor, Don Miguel, had a larger house than mine, for his family was extensive in the female line. He had two quarteroon wives from the Verds and I don't know how many favorites, of mulatto and even darker hues.

Our barracoons, as the slave pens were called, were located close to the river. They were built of cane, matted with vine and plastered with mud, the whole strengthened by uprights and picket barriers. Here the slaves were driven, on arrival, and placed in charge of gangsmen of their own color. The gangsmen superintended the head-shaving, washing and branding and saw that the blacks were duly secured every night to posts driven in the ground. There was a gangsman to every twenty slaves and they took turns through the night standing guard, with whips, to keep order.

We had a quarantine hospital built on a little island further down the river, for treatment of sick stock, and a burial place in the sand behind. I instructed a dozen of the more intelligent blacks in the mysteries of simple drugging, cupping and blistering and in a short time could boast of quite a medical board. We were generally lucky and lost only a small average among the slaves. Out of seventy-two thousand slaves received and transshipped from Rio Basso, in five years, we lost only eight thousand and this included deaths by accidental drowning, suicides, and a smallpox epidemic in 1811, when our barracoons were crowded and when we shipped 30,000 blacks to Brazil and the West Indies. My uncle always gave reasonable care to his slaves but some of the traders that came to our factory for water and supplies were ruthless. The *Pongas*, owned by an American trader, came in one day for water and I went aboard. She was loaded on the Gambia and the poor blacks were packed like herrings on the sitting plan instead of the horizontal stowage adopted by the French captains from the Senegal settlements. She was crammed with a thousand blacks, wedged in her three-foot between-decks. In one partition of her bulkhead, sixteen by eighteen feet, two hundred and fifty women were squeezed and many of the wenches were big with child. The men were stowed in each other's laps, without an inch to move right or left. The vessel stank horribly and Don Miguel predicted that she would lose half her cargo.

The French slavers were fitted up at that time with more regard to the comfort of their living freight. They were amply supplied with bread, salt and allspice, for slave diet, and each black was provided with a pewter plate and spoon and a tobacco pipe. The slaves slept horizontally on the decks and in fine weather were made to exercise and were kept employed in making ropes, hats and baskets for which they received rations of brandy and tobacco.

In August, 1814, I was at a trading station on the Kambia trying to make life tolerable during a dismal rainy season, with no society but the overseer, a Brazilian Portuguese, and a few Foulah girls, our household handmaidens. One day news arrived of a vessel at the river's mouth, and shortly after my worthy uncle appeared. "Phil," he said, very abruptly, "I have a love affair on hand." "A love affair!" I repeated, in great astonishment, and when he related the details, I found that Don Ricardo, instead of being a mere money-getting, callous-hearted slave trader, was quite a chevalier in the way of romantic amours. He wanted my assistance on a short expedition having for its purpose the possession of a Spanish beauty as a companion to make his life in Africa more agreeable. Of course I agreed to go with him and when I reached the brig and saw his cabin fitted up luxuriously for a lady's occupancy, I began to realize how a "love affair" can polish a slave trader into something very tender and make a slave brig's cabin fit for other purposes than packing negro women for the middle passage.

Our destination was the island of Teneriffe and we cast anchor in the harbor of Oritava. The next day my uncle took me to a convent where he had an interview with his young lady, a splendid specimen of Spanish beauty. That she was in love with him I hadn't the least doubt, though our interview took place in the public parlor. He told me that she had been devoted by her parents to take the veil and was then in her novitiate, but there was nothing of the nun about her, it was plain to see. The convent was a gloomy prison-house, with iron-grated windows and gates strong enough for a fort.

That night we went ashore in the yawl with a dozen of the crew. Eight of them stayed on the shore and the rest followed us to the convent. My uncle climbed the wall and soon after a fire broke out in the building. A bell began to ring and immediately we heard shrieking of women. Then my uncle appeared with Donna Emelia in his arms. We all hurried back to the boat and with his lady and two men to row he went out to the brig. He directed me to return with the crew to the convent and assist the people. It was a frightful scene. The nuns were flying in all directions, most of them completely naked as they slept without clothing. Some in the upper cells could be seen through the windows, unable to escape and tearing about in their despair. I heard, before I left, that seven had been burned to death and also the rumor that the fire was caused by coals spilled out of an earthen stove, but I have always had other suspicions. At any rate, my uncle secured his sweetheart, who seemed to be about seventeen, a queenly type with something of the look of a sorceress. Donna Emelia appeared on deck the next day, as merry as a cricket and as splendid as a bird of paradise and all on board soon heard that she was the captain's wife. My uncle appeared to be the happiest of men.

When we arrived at the Kambia, I found Diego Ramos ready to sail for Cuba in our American ship *Miranda*. He had taken advantage of the first week of dry weather to bargain for a kaffle brought in by one of the neighboring kings and had got the slaves stowed aboard during the last days of our absence. We said nothing to him about the result of our trip and as I had been thinking of taking a run to the West Indies, it was soon arranged that I should go with Ramos. Don Ricardo wished to use my bachelor house as a place in which to spend his honeymoon, as he laughingly expressed it. "Its the only place on the coast not yet run down by negro traders and I want Emelia to get accustomed to this life before she meets with Don Miguel and his rough companions." So Diego Ramos and I took possession of our shed on the *Miranda's* quarterdeck—all between decks being packed with her cargo—and soon were off, with a flowing sheet, for the isles of profitable speculation.

Our blacks were a good-natured lot and jumped to the lash so promptly that there was not much occasion for scoring their naked flanks. We had tamborines aboard, which some of the younger darkies fought for regularly, and every evening we enjoyed the novelty of African war songs and ring dances, fore and aft, with the satisfaction of knowing that these pleasant exercises were keeping our stock in good condition and of course enhancing our prospects of making a profitable voyage. It was after one of these musical evenings, when the tired performers had been stowed again between decks, to sweat

through another stifling night, that our hopes were dashed to nothing. I had turned in and was sound asleep when there was a sudden
cry of "fire." When I came on deck the sailors were throwing buckets
of water down the forecastle gratings and the air was soon full of
the shrieks and half-stifled groans of the suffocating blacks. In spite
of every effort the flames increased and soon broke out by the main
gratings.

"All is lost," said Diego, to me, and then raising his voice
he shouted, "Bear away, lads! lashings and spars for a raft, my
hearties!" The men at once sprang to the work of cutting away the
masts and bowsprit and hoisting out the boats. Regardless of the
yells and shrieks of the doomed blacks, Diego ordered wet tarpau-
lines to be thrown over the gratings to keep down the fire. The men
worked for their lives and in a very short time we had a well-secured
raft, with two casks of water on it and a supply of provisions. Our
more valuable possessions were placed in the two boats. Fortunately
the sea was calm and we got away from the burning brig without
difficulty, having first shifted the hatch gratings and flung down
the shackle-keys to the slave gangs below. I shall never forget the
dreadful screech that rung in our ears as the panic-stricken blacks
scrambled on deck and discovered that we were leaving the vessel.
Some of them jumped overboard and began to swim towards us.
The shouts of the men and the screams of the women rose in horrible discord.

The raft was large enough to accommodate nearly a hundred of
the blacks and we took on about that number after which sailors,
stationed on each side, kept off the rest with handspikes. Morning
came at last with a grey fog covering the ocean. It was then found
that one of the water casks was only half full and the other leaked.
A rum keg was emptied and filled with the precious water and then
transferred to one of the boats.

In a few hours the fog dispersed and the hot sun began to beat
down on us. We had no protection from it and could only obtain a
measure of relief by wrapping wet clothing around our heads. Be-

fore night came every white man was wild with the torture of the heat. The negroes seemed to suffer but little, but every now and then the overseers drenched their naked backs with buckets of salt water. The next day was a repetition of the first and when the third began to brighten with sickening heat, Ramos called a council of his officers and myself. Not a sail had been seen and our men were becoming as feeble as children. It was determined that we should abandon the raft which anchored us, as it were, in the ocean and by taking to the boats, endeavor to reach land. Accordingly another round of a few drops of water and a stout dram of rum was served to each of the eager blacks, under cover of which our bread bag and the few gallons of water left were transferred to the boats and we then quietly shoved off, letting the raft fall astern.

The negroes were evidently bewildered, at first, on finding themselves free of their white masters, but soon the idea that they were being deserted seemed to penetrate their black heads and they jumped to their feet with loud cries and frantic motions of their arms, tearing their wool and beating their heads. Diego Ramos looked at me and showed his white teeth. "It's a hard case," said he; "but the poor devils must go! and that breaks up our year's profits, amigo!"

Just at this moment, a joyful cry broke from one of our seamen. "Sail ho!" he screamed at the top of his lungs. "Sail ho! on the weather quarter!" Sure enough, there was a square-rigged vessel looming up with every bit of canvas set and bearing right down on us. Every man stood up in the boats and began to wave jackets and hands and it was not long before we saw a signal run up in token that we had been seen and a little later we were safely on board H.B.M. transport ship *Indus*. Diego Ramos and I were received by her commander very politely and we at once made confession of our business, the raft of negroes, still in sight making all evasion useless. Nothing was said, of course, in reference to our abandonment of the negroes and so we obtained considerable credit from the

Briton, for our humanity in constructing a raft for the negroes and keeping their company so long.

As plain Philip Drake of Stockford, I should have fared hard on the royal transport and taken the place of one of my own blacks, as far as shackles were concerned; but as Don Felipe Drax, a Brazilian merchant and passenger on board the lost brig of Don Diego Ramos, I was allowed a seat at the cabin table, with my partner, and treated with every forbearance that a British officer could exhibit towards foreigners rescued from shipwreck. Captain Simmons shook his grey little head at Don Diego's arguments, but laughed at his jokes and altogether we had a pleasant mess daily till the *Indus* cast anchor in Cape Coast harbor, at the Sierra Leone settlement, where our negroes were to be adjudicated by the resident commissioners. The darkies were landed in canoes and placed in the Royal Yard and in a few days the commissioners decided they should be apprenticed among the settlers for a term of a dozen years, by which time Don Diego said they would be christianized and worn out. Captain Simmons and his officers were ordered salvage and my partner and I pocketed our losses with as good grace as possible. Ramos looked up a coaster for our passage to New Tyre, my Kambia settlement, and not long after we sailed. This was the end of our speculation in the *Miranda*. The firm of Ramos and Drax remained extant, but the profits of its last venture were mostly divided between fire, water, and British philanthropy.

On reaching the Kambia settlement I found that my uncle's honeymoon had changed the appearance of my thatched house. Handsome additions had been made; verandas, balconies and lattice-work, after the Spanish style, making the rough outside look like a palace. Great alterations had also been made in our barracoons and a number of negro gangs were still at work bringing timber from the forest. Piles had been driven in the shore making an outer support for a pier. We soon learned the reason for my uncle's efforts toward the establishment of a regular trading factory on the Kambia. During our absence a noted Foulah king, named Moussy, had made overtures for a regular alliance for the purposes of traffic, and as New Tyre was a capital location for a depot for caravans from all the Kambia country, my shrewd uncle had lost no time, during our absence, in enlarging the capacities of the settlement. He had also made arrangements for the speedy delivery of a large kaffle at our barracoons, so that, if the *Miranda's* voyage had turned out well, on our return we would have been surprised by a freight that would have sent her back to the West Indies in short order. After learning these facts I consulted with Diego and the result was a partnership between Don Ricardo Villeno and ourselves under the firm name of Villeno and Co., which in time became widely known in Africa and the West Indies.

I took up my quarters in the house of Pablo Crux, our Brazilian overseer, leaving Don Ricardo and his creole wife in possession of my old residence. Preparations for the reception of King Moussy's caravan went on actively. By January 1816, our large barracoon was nearly complete and I had opened new accounts in the name of the firm.

Before long I learned that Donna Emelia was not my good uncle's first lady love,—by several. It appeared there had been a Fayal girl who had died on the Congo, a few years before, and that a light quadroon, now with Don Miguel, was formerly the favorite of Don Ricardo. As for Donna Emelia, she was a splendid creature. When we dined at the "residency," as he called his house, she would play on the harp and sing for us. Her voice was like a nightingale's. Booby that I was, I felt my eyes pipe, and the young lady, I thought, enjoyed my emotion. Diego pretended that he believed her to be only a school girl, but I though her a deep one. My uncle was certainly infatuated with his new love and ran her errands, picked up her handkerchief and watched her as a cat does a mouse. They seemed to be exceedingly happy together.

About the middle of the month we had news of the caravan, coming on the direct trail from King Moussy's chief town. It was said to consist of about twelve hundred picked slaves, Mandingoes,

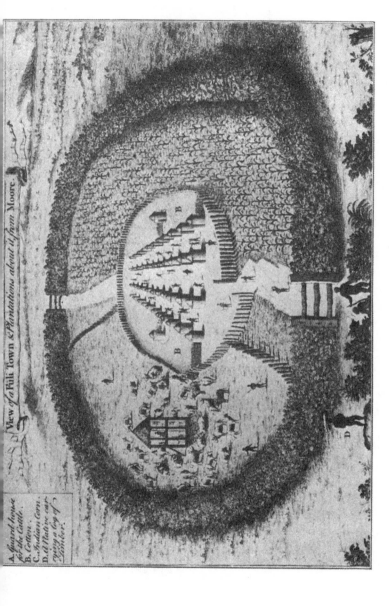

A. *Guard house for the Cattle.*
B. *Cotton.*
C. *Indian Corn.*
D. *A Native carrying a log of Timber.*

View of a Fulli Town & Plantations about it, from Moore.

VIEW OF A TOWN OF THE FOULAH TRIBE OF NEGROES

From an engraving by Basire, in Astley's *Collection of Voyages*, London, 1745

CAPTURE OF THE SLAVER "BORBOLETA," MAY 26, 1845, BY THE BOATS OF H.M. BRIG
"PANTALOON," AFTER A TWO DAYS' CHASE OFF LAGOS, WEST AFRICA

From a colored lithograph, after a drawing by H. John Vernon, in the Macpherson Collection

Soosoos and condemned Foulahs. The entire caravan numbered about two thousand persons and my uncle and Diego went out to meet it leaving me in charge of the residency. No one was to go near his lady's apartments, on any pretence. The donna was a nun again and I was to guard her convent door, by swinging my cot in the saloon. During the first night of their absence, I was suddenly awakened by Yunga, the Foulah girl, with a message from her mistress who was very ill with cramps. I looked up my hot drops and hurried to the Donna's apartment. She appeared to be in great pain and I administered the medicine which seemed to give no relief. The Foulah girls were sent flying in all directions for new remedies and I found myself alone with the Donna. She flung her arms around my neck, kissed my lips and passionately begged me to save her. I tried to calm her but she clung to me till the returning girls nearly discovered us. Twice during the next day I had to attend her summons and for the life of me I couldn't make out if she was really in pain or danger. The next day, however, she was rational enough and insisted that I had saved her life. She patted my check and seemed simplicity itself.

The caravan arrived on the 18th with much noise and rattle, cracking of guns and beating of tomtoms and drums. The Foulah king was a noble specimen of his nation; over six feet tall and dressed in a white *tobe*, with scarf and head dress of dyed cotton cloth mixed with silk. I was the principal interpreter at the *palabra* and a grand kickup it was. Some seven hundred Foulah warriors armed with clubs, swords and bows and arrows, many also having guns, were drawn up on our plaza and negro traders, from the interior, numbering about a score, squatted in front and around the king and his officers. Our retainers fired a grand salute which was followed by an opening chorus by a band of black singers, with cymbal-strikers to accompany them. Then came the grand feast. Our slaughtered bullock, rum, and pipes kept the savages in admiration all day long and King Moussy became our fast friend. Donna Emelia was in high glee at the strange sight and the Foulahs thought her a white fetish.

The day after the grand *palabra*, the ship *Cabenda* arrived at our moorings, bringing a heavy cargo of goods for trade—just in time. She was my uncle's best vessel, a ship of 300 tons burden. We also had three other vessels anchored off the factory, one of them named *La Senora Emelia*, in compliment to our lady of the residency. King Moussy and his troops were camped in a fine palm valley, about a mile from the residency, and the slaves, in gangs, under their various owners, were fastened by cords of twisted bamboo fibres to stakes in the ground. Donna Emelia accompanied my uncle and Pablo Crux on a tour of inspection and was not at all put out of face at the spectacle. I thought at the time that the sight of over a thousand stark naked blacks was hardly the most delicate amusement for a young "school girl," as Diego called her.

The cargo of the *Cabenda* was landed as rapidly as possible and two days after her arrival our great market was in full operation. It reminded me of the square in Fandu. In addition to the thousand or more slaves, several tons of African merchandise was displayed,—ivory, gold dust, rice, cattle, skins, bees-wax, black wood, honey and many other articles of inland production. In exchange we had cotton cloth, powder, rum, tobacco, cheap muskets and a variety of pinchbeck trinkets, corals and the like, to please the taste of savages. This barter was only on the side as the main business was slave buying. We allowed for a stout negro of twenty, a value of about fourteen English shillings or three Spanish dollars, in merchandise. Women and boys brought less. Our powder was coarse and the guns were roughly made in England for this market. The spirits, cotton, powder and guns came in my uncle's coasters from English trading stations on the Congo. We bought on the coast and paid higher prices for these goods, in order to prevent the old factories from breaking up as sometimes they were very convenient as a temporary slave depot.

King Moussy and I became great cronies. It quite won the old fellow's heart because I could understand his lingo. He owned about two hundred of the slaves in the caravan. The rest were ventures of smaller caravans that paid him a tribute for the escort of his warriors. He got a percentage on all the sales, whether slaves or goods and we paid him a bonus of one hundred muskets, twenty kegs of powder, two pieces of cotton and a soldier's red coat, as his dasch or present, in consideration of the treaty made with my uncle. He was not a bad fellow, but cunning as a fox, and moreover he had decidedly good taste for a savage, as he hinted to me that he would be willing to give up the dasch, and throw in a hundred darkies, if the *Moneego*, Don Ricardo, would sell him his wife, Donna Emelia. Our market was over by the 25th of January and we were well rid of the negro king and his army of cormorants who threatened to eat us out of house and home. As a result we had bought eleven hundred first-class slaves, enough to freight two vessels to the Brazils.

New Tyre continued to thrive. With the assistance of King Moussy we were able to dispatch a full dozen cargoes from the Kambia alone and including my uncle's settlement at Rio Basso, we sent to Cuba and the Brazils, during the year 1816, a total of 43,000 slaves, and Villeno & Company soon became equally well known to native kings, West India traders and European brokers. If one of our coast schooners poked her nose up the Gambia, the Congo, the Calabra, or Bonny, almost immediately negroes were in motion to the shore in gangs of all sizes.

Donna Emelia remained charming. She seemed never to tire of my accounts of African life as I had seen it during my captivity with the Dahomans and Foulahs. Diego Ramos was away most of the time, as captain of one of our vessels, and Don Ricardo remained with his lodestone—Donna Emelia. He built a cottage for her in Palm valley, about two miles from the river, in a natural garden of tropical flowers and fruits. Quite an extensive area was inclosed with high pickets and gates, like a stockade, which was watched by several black sentinels armed with loaded muskets.

Toward the close of 1816, my uncle went to Rio Basso and took Donna Emelia with him. When they returned, in a few weeks, the

Spanish favorite was accompanied by a quadroon girl and her mother, a good featured mulattress. The girl was about twenty years old and had one of the rich, rosy faces that are sometimes seen on the coast. Her figure was superb. My uncle introduced her to me, laughingly, as my housekeeper, and as I was no novice to the customs of Africa, I accepted both her and the mulattress as acquisitions to my household. But to my surprise, that same day the quadroon made a most eloquent appeal to my generosity, accompanied by a protestation of her love for Don Ricardo. This opened my eyes and I called to mind what Diego Ramos had told me concerning some of my uncle's former favorites and of a quadroon that had been transferred to Don Miguel, at Rio Basso. On questioning the mulattress, I learned that her daughter had lived with Don Ricardo for three years and borne him a child which survived but a short time. Marina, the quadroon, was passionately attached to him and had attempted to drown herself at Rio Basso, which caused Don Miguel to interest himself and prevail on my uncle to allow her to return with him to New Tyre, as a companion of Donna Emelia. But Don Ricardo. always jealous in everything that had to do with his creole, thought best to transfer the cast-off quadroon to his twenty-six year old nephew. On learning the facts about her, I permitted the grateful woman to take charge of my quarters, much to my apparent gain in point of comfort and attentive service.

When I next dined with my uncle in Palm valley, it was to be joked considerably by Donna Emelia, concerning my "handsome wife," all of which I took in good part and laughed with Don Ricardo, over our wine, as if I was very well satisfied with his Rio Basso present.

A short time after this, Diego Ramos arrived from the Verds for a cargo. He reported a fleet of British vessels bound for Cape Castle and a voyage of survey up and down the coast and rivers. They had been empowered to make descents upon all places suspected to be dependent, to any extent, upon English men or English capital and to break up slave factories wherever British complicity could be proven against the managers. This was serious news for Don Ricardo and myself for we were both British subjects, though time and change of name had made us able to pass for Spaniards, Brazilians or creoles, as we had chosen to appear. My uncle was well fitted to sustain either character and to deceive the closest scrutiny, but I was not so sure of my own versatility and neither was he. After reflection it was decided that I must go with Diego Ramos, on his next voyage, and so be out of the way in case the British vessels should appear before New Tyre.

We sailed Feb. 13th, 1817, in the *Cabenda,* our largest ship, loaded with 850 slaves, a quantity of ivory and gold dust, and bound direct for Rio de Janeiro. Nothing of importance occurred during the voyage and we landed our slaves on April 6th, with only a small loss during the passage. Soon after our arrival I met with my old friend Doctor Maxwell and had a chat with him over old times. He was as grey as a badger and portly as a porpoise. The next day we went out to the estate of Mr. Floss, to whom our slaves were consigned, and were entertained by him. He lived in grand style and gave concerts and balls to the neighboring gentry. That evening there was a sumptuous entertainment, the dons and donnas wearing their richest clothing. The men shone in all colors and the ladies' taffeta petticoats were fringed with gold lace and their tight velvet jackets were laced and buttoned with pearl tassels.

The next day the very deuce was to pay and we found ourselves barricaded in Doctor Maxwell's house with the negroes collected in a state of insurrection. All communication with the mansion was cut off and risings on neighboring plantations were expected. The negroes began by setting fire to the cane fields, devastating crops and smashing machinery in the *ingenios.* Troops were ordered out and a battle was fought, and the blacks dispersed to the hills from which they made sallies and burned several country houses—including the mansion of Mr. Floss. We had been shut up in the doctor's house for two days when Mr. Floss reached us pursued by a gang of negroes. He had been skulking in the fields since his mansion was destroyed and barely succeeded in reaching our house. Hardly had he been admitted before we were surrounded by hundreds of yelling blacks. It was near night and they had lighted torches and numerous weapons. We tried to parley with them but they demanded the delivery of Floss alive into their hands, something that could not be thought of and so we prepared for defence hoping that troops might arrive to our assistance. We had half a dozen faithful blacks in the house, with two Brazilian overseers, Doctor Maxwell, the superintendent, Mr. Floss, Ramos and myself, to oppose the enraged slaves whose numbers were constantly increasing.

Finding us resolved to defend the house, the blacks tried to set it afire. We shot several of them but at last they succeeded in piling up loads of dry cane and we were compelled to retreat from doors and windows to the central court. The house was built like a hollow square, with the *corral* or yard in its center and there we stood at bay when the blacks entered. I gave up all for lost when I saw the yelling devils jumping through the fire to get at us. They were led by a gigantic negro who sprang upon Floss. Poor Maxwell was seized by another and Ramos and I would have shared their fate if I had not suddenly recognized the leading savage. It was my old acquaintance, the Ashantee Quobah, whom I had last seen after his fight with the lions at Yallaba. I knew him at once and called out to him in the negro tongue just as he had dashed Floss to the ground and placed his foot on him. The negroes heard what I said and hesitated, when I quickly asked for an armistice.

Quobah flourished an enormous club, motioning the savages back, and then turned to me. I spoke rapidly as I saw that it was a matter of life and death and fortunately the Ashantee remembered me and ordered his furious followers not to molest us. Ramos and I were bound with cords and dragged out of the burning building and Floss and Maxwell were roped about the neck and cruelly beaten with clubs and whips. The insurgents hurried us in front of the burning house and then began a dreadful torture and massacre. The Brazilian overseers and their negroes were cut to pieces. Floss and

Maxwell were stripped, fastened to stakes, and sugar sap was poured over their naked bodies. The blacks then piled cane around them and tortured them with slow fire. It was a horrible sight. The wretched victims begged in vain for mercy until they fainted under their agony. Then Quobah struck the Doctor a blow with his club, which dashed his skull open, and this was a signal to the blacks to finish their work. They scattered the burning cane and tore the charred bodies of their victims into a thousand pieces, as they danced and trampled on the embers. Quobah then came and cut the cords from Ramos and me and told us to escape. His voice was hoarse and his eyes were like two balls of fire. "Go and tell the white King how Quobah has avenged himself on these dead brutes," he said to me. "Quobah is ready to die, but he will be a slave no more." We lost no time in getting away from the scene of the massacre and wandered about the woods until morning when we fell in with a troop of soldiers from the presidency barracks.

The insurrection lasted for three days and Quobah, the Ashantee, it afterwards turned out, was the head of the conspiracy. He had lately been brought from Africa and sold to Mr. Floss and by his order, flogged several times, to break him in. This had been Floss's usual custom with high-strung darkies. Poor fellow! it cost him his life. Doctor Maxwell had also been unpopular with the blacks and I recalled some of his former opinions. "Niggers must be treated like niggers," was one of the unfortunate surgeon's maxims which I remembered.

The year 1817-1818 was marked by many other negro insurrections. In Barbadoes, Trinidad and St. Thomas, the whites lived in constant fear of massacre. This was said to be due to the numbers of savage Africans that were smuggled into the British colonies from Spanish and Portuguese islands. Laws were passed for registering all slaves, but were enforced in only a few islands.

Quobah, the Ashantee, was never taken by the Brazilians. He fled to the wild plains, with a few followers, and was either killed or adopted by the Indians. It was noticed at the time, that both Brazilian and West Indian insurgents adopted flags and were apparently organized and there was little doubt that some plan had been concocted for a general rising of the slaves. I afterwards heard that a negro flag was found in Barbadoes, divided into three colors, one bearing the figure of a white man hanging by the neck; the second, a black chief standing over a white woman; and the third, a negro with a crown on his head and a beautiful white woman seated by his side. It was thought at the time that some negro agents from Hayti had stirred up the slaves both on the continent and the islands. The Barbadoan rebels burned whole parishes and similar devastation was done on other islands. The result was that thousands of slaves were shot, hanged, or starved in their retreats and many sugar estates were left without laborers. All this enhanced the price of negroes and improved the market and Diego Ramos predicted more than average luck for us during the next twelve months. Fortunately, the *Cabenda's* freight had been settled for before the death of Mr. Floss. His drafts were on Paris houses and were as good as gold at the French factories on the Senegal river. France had before this abolished the slave traffic—on paper, but her citizens were not so scrupulous or timid as H.B.M. subjects.

We cast anchor again in the Rio Pongo about the middle of the rainy season. All things were as before, though the settlement had been honored by two visits from the British squadron, then very active along the coast. My uncle, however, had passed muster. Our barracoons were empty; the storehouses full. Don Ricardo had exhibited his Portuguese permits which allowed him liberty to engage in such African trade as he pleased. The Don had, moreover, exercised diplomacy in another way. He had dispatched one of his negro agents to the Congo river, where a British expedition of discovery was in trouble, and there contrived to negotiate some favors from the native kings which were of special importance to the English explorers. This had gone a great way with our bamboozled countrymen and the house of Villeno & Company instead of suffering spoliation, became of greater importance than ever on the African coast.

We had accounts of British severities on the Calabar, the Congo and Gambia rivers, as well as near Cape Palmas. Captain Fraley's old Bangara factory on the Congo, had been destroyed and its manager, an American factor named Curtis, had been summarily ejected. Another American, named Cooke, had been carried to Sierra Leone and then sent in irons to Portsmouth. Another factory, near the town of a native king, Mungo Cattee, had been destroyed and nearly twenty tons of elephant's teeth had been seized. Other depredations had been committed by the British but thus far both New Tyre and Rio Basso had escaped scot free.

My private establishment seemed like home again, after shipboard life, but I noticed a change in the quarteroon girl, Marina, as soon as I set eyes on her. The bright flush was gone from her cheeks and her black eyes, which had been as brilliant as stars, were heavy and half closed under their long lashes. She smiled faintly in welcoming us but soon appeared to grow stupid and forgetful. Donna Emelia, at Palm Valley, gave me a warm greeting and my uncle was in the best of spirits with her, himself, and everybody.

We met two strangers at my uncle's table,—Pedro Blanco, a Malaga sailor, and Blas Covado, a Mexican. The first, afterwards amassed a million and a half of silver dollars in the African trade and made a position for himself much more important than was my uncle's at that time, and this was accomplished during a time when nearly every government was in arms to suppress the traffic. As for Covada, he was obsequious to everybody and seemed a white-livered dog. He was an accountant or factotum to my uncle and appeared to have his confidence.

Marina's condition puzzled me more and more. I could get little out of the old woman save that the white lady in Palm Valley had an evil fetish that had bewitched Marina. I also learned that the girl had passed all the time of my absence in the cottage of Donna Emelia, as her personal attendant. I had heard before that time, of a strange African distemper, commonly known as the "sleepy disease," and Marina's appearance answered to some of its symptoms; but her old mother, who knew of this malady, would not believe her daughter was its subject and I soon found that she was right. The old woman insisted that Marina always came home "bewitched" after a visit to the Donna's house. This startled me and I made a search among the quarteroon's little articles of toilet and soon discovered evidence of what I had begun to fear. There was a small vial, half full of a fluid; some pills; some mango pickle; all of which I found to be impregnated with *strychnine*.

The matter of a slave girl dying, even by slow poison, was not of much rarity in Africa, and had Marina been one of our marketable blacks, it would have been only a consideration of our loss in dollars and cents. The "witchcraft," as the mulattress believed it, would have been attributed to some malevolent fellow slave and the case forgotten in a day or two. But my interest in the quarteroon, as my uncle's former favorite, coupled with her passion for him and her late residence at Palm Valley, furnished me with grounds for conjecture and I resolved to closely question Marina. The next day, however, her spasms returned and in spite of all my remedies, increased in violence and in three days she was dead. The mulattress was crazy with grief and survived her "bewitched" daughter only a few weeks. My uncle expressed astonishment and apparent grief and Donna Emelia was profuse with expression of sympathy for what she called *my* bereavement. After Marina was buried, the Donna insisted that I should live at Palm Valley, an invitation that Don Ricardo seconded and from that date my misfortunes in after life commenced.

As I became better acquainted with the Donna I found that her mind was well cultivated. She had a choice library and fascinated me with her conversation and pretty manners. Palm Valley soon became a little paradise for me, notwithstanding Ramos' remark that there was an angel and a devil in it. And this I found to be true, within a week of the day when I went to live there. She could tempt an angel, I believe, and I became a fool and a villain. She swore that she had loved me from the day when we first met, but there was something in her eyes that made me feel uneasy. She seemed at times as artless as a child and at others, artful beyond all scrutiny. Though not twenty years of age, her head was older than mine or my uncle's and it was no wonder we were both fascinated and both deceived.

The fine weather brought activity to New Tyre as to all the coast. Diego Ramos went coasting to the Congo and Pedro Blanco with our good-natured Dutchman, sailed for the Senegal, in a French trader. Toward the end of the year it became advisable to send to Rio Basso for a vessel or two to relieve us of our large stock of negroes, waiting in the Kambia barracoons for shipment. My uncle was unwilling to leave the attractions of Palm Valley and the Mexican, Blas Covado, was dispatched with confidential instructions. He left New Tyre in a small sloop and returned in due time, but instead of bringing a slave vessel he made his appearance on the deck of a British cruiser which cast anchor opposite our factory, landed a hundred men, and took possession of the station in the name of the Governor of Sierra Leone.

The blow was like a thunderclap and Don Ricardo could hardly believe his senses when he found himself with me and our three other white men, summoned before the captain of H.B.M. sloop-of-war *Princess Caroline*, charged with maintaining a slave establishment "contrary to the peace and dignity of H.M. Government." He protested his innocence, of course, and demanded under what plea they invaded a station over which the Portuguese flag was flying.

"Because," the English officer replied, "you are no Portuguese, but a cursed English renegade and slaving vagabond!"

My uncle started back and his eye flashed mischief, as I had often seen it before, but he controlled his temper wonderfully.

"May I ask what you intend to do in my house and under *that* flag?" he asked, pointing to the colors on our flag-staff in front of the piazza where we were standing.

"Burn one and pull down the other," answered the British captain savagely. "But first, we shall send you and your under-devils aboard ship! Here, Mr. Bayley," he continued, addressing a midshipman, "give these outlaws ribbons on their wrists and take 'em to the boats."

The young officer touched his hat and a movement was made among the marines and sailors drawn up on the grass before the large piazza of the residency, when suddenly my uncle thrust his hands in the bosom of his loose marino shirt and drew out two pistols.

"Captain," he said, speaking through his set teeth, "I demand your authority for this, and if a man of you attempts to handcuff one of us, I'll blow his brains out if I die the next minute!"

The Englishman's blue face lost some of its color for a moment, as he saw his breast covered by one pistol-barrel while the other was levelled at his subaltern. With an oath, he pointed to the Mexican, Blas Covado, who had just come up between two sailors.

"There's the King's evidence to hang you!" he blustered. "He'll tell you there's not a stone left of your Rio Basso slave-pens, as there wont be of these by tomorrow morning, by the Lord Harry! Men, do your duty!"

We saw at once how matters stood and no sooner had the British officer given his last order, than Don Ricardo's pistol exploded and he sprang into the open door of the residency, crying, "Follow me, Philip!" It was a desperate chance, but we made it, with the British yelling like bloodhounds close at our heels. We had the advantage of a knowledge of the paths and had nearly reached Palm Valley, when we saw a dozen soldiers emerging from a cross-path only forty rods behind us. They were led by the treacherous Mexican, Covado. By that time, however, we were close to our shelter and could hail our black sentinels, but we didn't reach the gate before we received the sailors' fire. I felt a bullet graze my cheek and rushed head-

CAPTURE OF THE SPANISH SLAVER "FORMIDABLE," DEC. 7, 1834, OFF SIERRA LEONE,
BY H.M. BRIG "BUZZARD"

From a colored aquatint, after the painting by W. J. Huggins, in the Macpherson Collection

FEMALE SAMBOE SLAVE GIVEN TWO HUNDRED LASHES
From an engraving in Stedman's *Narrative of an Expedition to Surinam*, London, 1796

long through the open gateway expecting my uncle to follow. Just then one of our negro watchmen gave a loud screech and I heard a musket shot. Turning quickly I saw Don Ricardo stagger in with the sentinel's gun in his hand. He had snatched it, as he reached our gate, and fired at our pursuers, shooting the Mexican traitor through the head. In another moment we had closed and barred the gate and were as secure as our stockade defences could make us. Then I discovered that my uncle was wounded. He had been struck by a bullet in the right breast and I had hardly time to extend my arms before he fell into them like a log.

Don Ricardo's wound was dangerous, I saw at once, and I staunched and dressed it as well as I was able. He grew weaker, but about midnight was able to speak and told the Donna and me that he was bleeding internally and couldn't survive. He spoke with great earnestness and asked me to promise to protect Emelia, if necessary, with my life. She became frantic and it was necessary for me to call the Foulah wenches and have her taken away. My uncle then gave me the keys of his chest and told me to take the money and papers which it contained. Soon after his mind began to wander. I called Pablo to take my place and went to Donna Emelia, to tell her what my uncle had said. She threw herself into my arms, kissing and fondling and swearing that she would never leave me and that we should live and die together. She had never appeared more beautiful than on that night, with her dishevelled but glossy ringlets flowing over her heaving breasts and her large black eyes sparkling with tears. But she was far more practical than I was and soon began to speak of escaping from Palm Valley.

I was loath to abandon my uncle, but the creole persuaded me there was no help for it and that we should only sacrifice ourselves by remaining. With Pablo's assistance I packed up a few valuables and necessaries, including all my uncle's papers, and such ready money as I had, and then loaded a couple of our kroos with provisions and Donna Emelia's clothing and went to a pleasure boat that lay in a little cove about a quarter of a mile away in a sheltered part of the river some two miles above the factory. Here I left the Brazilian with four kroomen and one of the Foulah girls, while I returned for the Donna. I didn't dare go into the room where my uncle lay raving, in charge of the other women, but carried Emelia in my arms, out by our rear pickets, and followed by two blacks with more of the creole's goods, we reached the boat which was a pinnace that had been fitted up for short excursions on the river.

It was after midnight when we got under way with half a dozen kroos to row, and pushed up the river under a brilliant starlight. It was not until we were pushing off that the Brazilian became aware that Don Ricardo had been left behind; but I satisfied him, as best I could, of the necessity of the case. At daybreak we ran into a small creek and lay concealed among the dense growth of sedges until night when we rowed up the stream to a small negro village where Pablo expected to find a friendly chief of King Moussy's nation. We found the town deserted, except for a few old men and children, the warriors having been called to a great slave hunt inland. Here, in vacant bamboo huts, we found accommodations and the creole was obliged to content herself with quarters much less luxurious than those which my poor uncle had furnished.

One of our faithful kroos was dispatched in a canoe to reconnoitre. The next day he came back and reported that our storehouses, barracoons and dwellings were in ashes. The cottage in Palm Valley had not been spared and New Tyre was again a wilderness. But the British sloop-of-war had gone and we soon followed in a coasting schooner belonging to our house, which arrived just in time.

After leaving the Kambia we ran along the coast for a hundred miles, till we spoke a French brig bound for the Senegal. By this time the creole had made me promise to leave Africa at once. I found among my uncle's papers ready cash, in Bank of England notes, to the amount of £8000, and accepted drafts of the Villeno partnership, on Spanish and French houses, to the amount of nearly £8000, which, added to my own cash in gold, gave me over $80,-000. I directed Pablo to take the schooner to the Congo station and await the arrival of Diego Ramos and took passage in the French brig and shortly after reached the Senegal. There we succeeded in finding a Bordeaux brig, the *Elisée*, bound to her owners, with a general cargo of African products, and I engaged a cabin for Donna Emelia, who passed as my wife, under our assumed name of Morillo. On arriving at Bordeaux we obtained passports, as Spanish travellers, and ten days afterward found ourselves in Paris.

My first business in Paris was to negotiate my uncle's securities and in a week I had turned everything into cash and in another began to spend it. Our money was a passport better than rank or title. Before we had had six weeks of fashionable life, we had had fully as many quarrels, and the creole developed a temper that I had not expected. In six months, we had spent nearly £7000, and the greater part of it on Donna Emelia's extravagant fancies. Nearly half of our fortune had been squandered, but when I spoke to my wife about it she laughed. I then insisted that we should leave Paris and at last she consented. Six months later found us settled on a handsome *ranche*, in the neighborhood of Matanzas, Cuba, which I had purchased for twenty thousand Spanish dollars.

The business of sugar-growing was new to me, but I had an experienced overseer and for a few months everything worked to my satisfaction. But the restless disposition of Donna Emelia demanded change. We made occasional trips to Havana but she always returned dissatisfied until, at last, she discovered a new amusement at home. One day when I returned from Matanzas I was met by my groom with a frightened look and when I demanded the reason was told that my lady had been flogging his wife, a good-looking house servant who had charge of the laundry. The girl had offended Donna Emelia three days before and had been flogged every day since, always in my absence. She was now in prison. The word "prison" startled me and I went to my wife. The Donna was in good humor and laughed and said the girl had carelessly torn a costly lace vandyke and so had been punished and shut up, but should be released and go to her husband that evening. I smoked my cigar and forgot about the matter until three days afterward my groom threw himself on his knees and told me his wife was dead or dying. This shocked me and I asked where the wench was and he led me to an out house where I pried open the locked door and found the negress lying absolutely naked, her back completely flayed and covered with flies. She was fastened by an iron chain to a post. Near by was hanging a slave whip stiff with blood. The chain had eaten into the girl's flesh, ulcerating her hips and stomach. She was past relief and died that evening.

I was bewildered on learning that the slave had been beaten by Donna Emelia's *own hand,* to the condition in which I found her. My wife had been in the habit of shutting herself up alone with her victim and beating her until she became insensible. At least a score of floggings had been administered. At once I taxed her warmly with the affair, telling her of the girl's death, and she wept and swore the wench had insulted and greatly provoked her and that she had no idea of punishing her until greatly aggravated. Her tears and seeming sorrow at last disarmed resentment and I agreed to say no more.

Our visitors were numerous. The Donna arranged concerts, dances, serenades and boating parties. Among other amusements, gaming was not forgotten, and I was initiated into its mysteries by heavy losses in which my guests profited. Among them was a youth named Da Souza, who claimed to be a Brazilian officer of the Imperial Guard of Dom Pedro, but I believed him to be a mulatto. He was Donna Emelia's constant attendant and tried to ingratiate himself with me in every way and in time I began to tolerate him so that we came to be partners in gaming bouts.

One day I was asked to see a Congo girl who was sick and found her in spasms that reminded me of the strange disease of my quadroon Marina. When I asked what the girl had eaten, she showed me some candied limes which her mistress had given her. This fruit I took away to analyze and soon found it to be impregnated with strychnine, like the mangoes that Marina had eaten before her death.

There could be no doubt concerning Donna Emelia's devilish character. It was evident that she delighted in cruelty and crime. Unable to think or act, I resorted to my usual stimulus of spirits until I lost all control of myself.

What I next did I never knew, but I came to myself to realize that I was at a gaming table with Da Souza and other of my wife's companions. They told me afterwards that I had been playing all night and my swindling companions showed my signature to more than twenty notes of hand amounting to nearly $40,000. or more than the value of my plantation and everything else that I could call my own. It was then that my wife showed her true character and taunted me with being a drunkard and with gambling away my all. I retorted by accusing her of murder and she became quite beside herself with rage and fright. We had a fearful quarrel. She even confessed that the child with which she was pregnant was Da Souza's and not mine, and then I cursed the brazen woman and fled from the house in search of the mulatto. Fortunately for him, he was not to be found.

Three weeks after this I recovered from a miserable round of dissipation in Havana, with less than a hundred dollars in my possession and just then I suddenly came upon my uncle Ricardo, haggard in face and thin in body like one in the last stage of consumption. "A word with you," he said, and I followed him, shaking like a leaf, to a room in a public house on the Mole, where he faced me and asked what I deserved at his hands. "Death!—a dog's death!" I answered recklessly and as he had a knife in his grasp I expected to feel its point; but he seemed suddenly to change his purpose and covering his face with his hands he burst into a flood of tears. I threw myself on my knees and tried to take his hand. At first he spurned me but when I chanced to mention Emelia's name he listened. I made a clean breast; told him every circumstance to the last wretched scene at our Matanzas plantation.

Don Ricardo heard me out and then asked that I swear to the truth of all I had told him and this I did. Then he asked if I would go with him to Donna Emelia and in a short time we were driving at post-haste for my late *ranche*. We rode all night.

On entering the plantation grounds I met a slave who conducted us quietly to the house which was ablaze with candles. The rooms were crowded with men and women, the new guests of my late home. I remained under the orange trees but Don Ricardo went forward and stepping through the casement crossed the saloon to a sofa where Donna Emelia sat with the mulatto, Da Souza, beside her. I saw her eyes flash and heard her scream, which was followed by the sudden report of a pistol. My uncle had shot himself through the heart.

CHAPTER XIII

SLAVE SMUGGLING A HUNDRED YEARS AGO

RUINED and desperate, with the last dollar of my ill-gotten wealth squandered, I looked to Africa as the place in which to mend my fortunes. Havana had nothing to offer and I seized the first opportunity that presented itself,—a berth as *medico* or surgeon, in a Spanish schooner called the *Diana,* bound for the river Bonny. At the Bight we joined company with four other craft and were engaged in getting out our complement, at Bonny settlement, when we were attacked by a British man-of-war. Having plenty of pluck and powder, we boldly defended ourselves until compelled to strike. Many of our slaves jumped overboard, into the jaws of sharks, and I succeeded, with a number of the crew, in seizing one of the boats and escaping to the woods behind the town. Here we were assisted by a Calabar chief, whom I had formerly known, till the cruiser hauled off with her prizes and a Spanish brig arrived and took us aboard. This was the *Boa Morte,* formerly an American trader, commanded by Capt. Pierre Leclerc, a creole of St. Domingo. Ten days after the departure of the cruiser, the *Boa Morte* completed her cargo and sailed for Pensacola, in the Floridas, with nine hundred slaves aboard. I shipped in her as a supernumerary doctor.

Captain Leclerc was a peppery little fellow, an old slaver, who had an interest in the freight. I had my berth in the round house as every inch of space was occupied by blacks. The cabin and hold were knocked into slave decks and packed tight at that. Leclerc reckoned up his anticipated profits and made a good showing. He had a hundred prime blacks—only twenty females—all branded in good Spanish, with his name, and he estimated that his venture ought to bring him a net of $8000.—a tolerable set-up.

For the first few days everything went well, with only three cases of sickness,—a low fever. Quinine made them right again although the sharks followed us as if they smelt sickness. The sixth day out, Pedro, my assistant, reported one of our patients blind. We had half the gangs on deck for exercise and they danced and sang, under the driver's whip, but were far from sprightly. Captain Leclerc said he never knew such a sluggish lot, yet they all appeared healthy. The next day the ophthalmia appeared to be spreading among the slaves as eight were reported blind and the following day the number had increased to nineteen. The captain also was ailing and took to his berth.

The captain's illness turned out to be smallpox, that scourge of destruction, and two of the crew soon came down with it. It was impossible to keep the disease from the slaves and the ship turned out to be well named. We soon began to feed corpses to the following sharks and one day hauled sixty bodies out of the hold. The crew revolted at this work and we had to rely on gangs of slaves to drag the dead heaps from among the living. Captain Leclerc before long was out of danger but remained blind from ophthalmia.

During the first week I got only about a dozen hours' sleep and the mate had only six able-bodied men in his crew. We were obliged to stimulate the blacks with rum in order to get their help in removing corpses and I, too, found it necessary to excite myself with laudanum and liquor in order to keep at work in my horrible surroundings. The mate said if we had only known it in time we might have saved our cargo by poisoning the first cases; but no one could have forseen the rapid spread of the pest. Some of the blacks went mad and screeched like wild beasts and then those we had made drunk almost controlled the ship. The mate was obliged to shoot one of them or the fellow might have strangled him.

On November 17th we had a violent storm and the hatches had to be closed while the work of death went on unseen below; but Captain Leclerc improved and could see a little. It was a frightful hurricane. Our ship was whirled about like a top and driven before the gale all night, without a rag of canvas. Three days later we anchored safely in Pensacola Bay. Our surviving negroes were landed on one of the shallow beaches near the mouth of the Escambia river and here, with the assistance of laborers from the neighboring town, we rigged sheds for our sick and took measures for lime-washing and fumigating the ship. Strange as it may seem we saved five hundred and nineteen out of our nine hundred slaves.

After the accounts had been closed I was offered a chance to accompany one of the consignees on a land trip during which our negroes were to be sold. The kaffle, in charge of negro drivers, was to strike up the Escambia river and thence across the boundary line into Georgia, where some of our wild Africans were mixed with various squads of native blacks and driven inland till sold off, singly or by couples, on the road. At that time the United States had enacted laws declaring the African slave trade illegal, but the Spanish possessions were thriving on the inland exchange of negroes and mulattoes. Florida was a nursery for slave-breeders and many American citizens grew rich by trafficking in Guinea negroes and regularly smuggled them, in small parties, throughout the Southern States.

Through the influence of my associate I became a guest at many plantations on our line of travel, which gave me an opportunity to study the practical working of slavery in a civilized and democratic country and compare it with Cuba and the Brazilian empire. I also was enabled to estimate the influence of civilization on the Congo and Ashantee stock after a generation or two of American contact and compare their condition on American plantations with their native life in African forests.

We spent one night at a plantation on the Ockmulgee river, in Georgia, and our host, Mr. Olds, spoke very frankly on the subject of slaveholding and particularly of the local treatment of "black boys," as they were termed by his neighbors. A case had lately occurred of a "boy" being hung up by the wrists, to a tree, with a wooden rail tied to his feet, and beaten by his master until he died under the torture. This was done on suspicion of a petty theft which had been committed by the master's young son who afterward confessed. A slave's testimony was not taken against a white man.

In Carolina, slave merchants drove their kaffles over the highways in gangs of ten and had pens in the principal villages where they held vendues. The number of mulattoes was astonishing. I saw some really handsome quadroons on the auction block. The slaves seemed to be well treated and fat, though ragged and sometimes nearly naked. The men wore linsey woolsey shirts and trowsers and the women a petticoat of coarse ducking and all went barefoot. There was much waste of labor in all operations. I saw a gang of blacks, with two oxen, engaged a whole morning in drawing a log of timber from the river, to be used in the building of a house not far distant. In Rio Basso we should have a dozen trees cut down and shifted by such a force in the same time.

In Virginia were the oldest plantations and they were well stocked. A respectable citizen at Fredericksburg on the Rappahannock river, told me that slave-breeding was the most profitable business in that quarter. Whole farms were used as nurseries to supply the market with young mulattoes. Irish and Scotch overseers usually had charge of the gangs. The fertility of the negroes in Virginia seemed to be about the same as in Africa. On a farm near Alexandria I counted thirty about to become mothers and the huts swarmed with pickaninies of different shades.

At Philadelphia we found a brig about ready to sail for the Cape de Verdes on a trading voyage. She was the *Adelaide*, owned by an old skipper named Blackmore, and our business being settled I took passage in this vessel. We made a short run to Santa Cruz, Island of Teneriffe, and a few days after spoke an English vessel in want of water which we supplied. This vessel was bound to the African coast and as I had no bulky baggage was able to bargain for a berth on board and thereby secure a direct passage to the coast. This unlucky brig was the *Charles* and her commander was named Graham.

As we neared the African coast the weather became squally and

VIEW OF CHARLESTON, SOUTH CAROLINA

From a colored aquatint, published in 1841, after a painting by William J. Bennett, in the
Macpherson Collection

British Prize Brigantine "Netuna," Beating off the Spanish Slaver "Caroline," Mar. 20, 1826, in the Bight of Benin

The *Netuna* carried 1 gun and 5 men; the *Caroline*, 10 guns and 90 men. From a colored aquatint,

finally increased to a violent gale. We lost our topmasts and the old brig began to leak so that I was obliged to take my turn at the pump. Late at night, with a tremendous shock, we ran on a reef and the heavy seas soon drove us into the rigging. Fortunately she didn't break up and when morning came we found the brig had beaten over a line of reefs and was fast on the inner edge in a shallow lagoon. Not long after the sun rose a number of canoes filled with Mandingoes put off from the shore and boarded us. While they were looting the wreck a number of us on board launched the long boat and pushed off. When we reached shore my knowledge of negro dialects was turned to good service and we were permitted to send a messenger to Goree, not far distant, and three days later a sloop, with British soldiers, arrived off the reef and a boat was sent ashore for us. On reaching Goree, I found a coasting schooner bound for Bonny and secured passage in her.

Among the slavers sailing out of old Calabar, at that time, was the Brazilian brig *Gloria* and in her I now made half a dozen trips, occupying nearly two years, with "soldiering" time between voyages. I never knew who owned her. She was a staunch, handsome clipper craft and deserved better masters. On the first voyage out of Calabar we had not been out a week before I found that the captain and crew were desperadoes of the worst kind. Once off the coast the ship became half bedlam and half brothel. Ruiz, our captain, and his two mates set an example of reckless wickedness. They stripped themselves and danced with black wenches while our crazy mulatto cook played the fiddle. There was little attempt at discipline and rum and lewdness reigned supreme. At first I was frightened at this state of things but my appetite for liquor, contracted since that unfortunate intimacy with Donna Emelia, soon brought me to the level of the rest.

Meanwhile our slaves crammed in hold, cabin and peak and packed like herrings on shelves around our vessel's sides, were kept down by gratings fully half the time. The shrieks and groans of the stifling wretches below echoed our orgies above. On the eighth day out I made my rounds of the half deck, holding a camphor bag in my teeth for the stench was hideous. The sick and dying were chained together. I saw pregnant women give birth to babies while chained to corpses which our drunken overseers had not removed. The younger women fared best at first as they were allowed to come on deck as companions for our crew. Of this part of their devilish practices I kept clear but drank as hard as the rest. Toward the end of the run, which lasted nearly six weeks, the mortality thinned out the main hold and some scores of women were driven below as company for the males. The quarrelling and bestiality that followed was sickening. They tore and gnawed each other in fights over the rum rations which our captain ordered and for possession of the miserable wenches.

At last we arrived at Bahia and landed our cargo. Nearly a third of the slaves had died during the voyage. From Bahia we ran down to Rio for a cargo and sailed for Africa with the same officers and crew.

This trip we cast anchor in a small river not far from the American colony of Liberia and our captain took me ashore with his first mate and a dozen of the crew, all of us well armed and sober. We had several breakers of rum with us, as a "dash" for the negro chief, King Boatswain, a half-Christian black, and spent the day feasting in his village. When night came he summoned several hundred of his warriors and we sallied out against a tribe of blacks called Queahs. We came upon them while all were asleep and burnt their bamboo huts and made a general slaughter. The men and women were massacred and the boys and girls driven to the river where they were soon transferred to the *Gloria's* bowels.

The next day Captain Ruiz invited King Boatswain to a big banquet on board the brig. The old fellow was sick but his son came with over two hundred of his principal men. We had abundance of rum and tobacco, the former, thanks to my medical skill, heavily drugged with laudanum. Before night we had every darkey under hatches and were off with a flying jib. Our entire cargo cost no more than the "dash" given to the savage chief.

The last voyage of the *Gloria* was a climax of horror. We sailed from the Verdes and were making southerly, in ballast, when we overhauled a Portuguese schooner and ran alongside. She had a full cargo of slaves and Captain Ruiz proposed we attack her. The crew were ready and inspired by rum soon mastered the schooner's hands. Our captain blew out the brains of the only passenger aboard who we discovered had with him a large quantity of gold dust. The Portuguese were knocked in the head with axes and the slaves and gold dust quickly transferred to the *Gloria*. The schooner was then scuttled and we kept on our way with 190 ill-gotten slaves in our hold. The next day we ran into a storm which almost capsized the brig and set the negroes frantic, so that they tried to break through the gratings. Ruiz was half drunk, as usual, and suspecting a rising, ordered the crew to fire their muskets through the gratings until the negroes became quiet. By this foolish freak forty were killed and wounded and had to be thrown overboard. We ran for Accoa and landed at Papoe, a town belonging to a Dahoman chief, where we found six hundred blacks waiting for a Spanish slaver and four hundred of these were purchased and paid for with the gold dust taken from the murdered Portuguese passenger.

Hardly were we out a fortnight when it was discovered that our roystering crew had neglected to change the sea-water in the lower casks, which had served as ballast and which ought to have been replaced with fresh water in Africa. We were drawing from the last casks before the discovery was made and the horror of the situation sobered Captain Ruiz. He gave orders to hoist the precious remnant abaft the main grating and made me calculate how long it would sustain the crew and cargo. I found that a half-gill a day would hold out to the Spanish Main and it was decided, in order to save our cargo, that we should allow the slaves a half-gill and the crew a gill each day.

Then began a torture worse than death for the blacks. They

suffered continual torment. Instead of lowering buckets of water to them, as was customary, it became necessary to pour the water in half-pint measures. Those farthest from the grating never got a drop and soon became raving mad for drink. Fevers and fluxs soon added to their misery and deaths followed so fast that in a short time at least a hundred slaves were shackled to dead partners. Our captain and crew as well as I, drank hard, but thirst and disease kept down all licentiousness. Matters grew worse daily and at last Captain Ruiz ordered the hatches down and swore he would make the run on our regular rations and take the chances with his stock. That night we caroused and satisfied our thirst while the negroes suffocated below. Next morning came on a storm which drove us on our course a hundred knots and two days later Ruiz and four of the crew were taken suddenly ill. Their tongues swelled and grew black, their flesh turned yellow and in six hours they were dead. The first mate went next and then three more of the crew and a black driver whose body became leprous with yellow spots. I began to notice a strange, fetid smell pervading the vessel and a low, heavy fog on deck, almost like steam, and then the horrid truth became apparent. Our rotting negroes under hatches had generated the plague and it was the death-mist that I saw rising.

By this time all of our men but three, and myself, had been attacked and we abandoned the *Gloria,* taking in the long boat the remnant of water, a sack of biscuit, a beaker of rum and what gold dust and other valuables we could hastily gather together. Nine of our late comrades lay dead on the *Gloria's* deck and five were dying. After running for two days we struck a current and in three more reached Tortola, one of the Leeward Islands. We made a landing on the reefs and were picked up by some fishermen.

Falling sick at Tortola, I parted from my comrades of the *Gloria.* We had divided our ill-gotten gold dust and my share amounted to £130, with which, after my recovery, I took a vessel for Rio de Janeiro and there obtained a berth as surgeon once more and kept sober for nearly eighteen months during which I made about three thousand dollars by private ventures. But ill-luck came again to dog me when I shipped in a Spanish schooner from Porto Rico and encountered new disasters.

She was the *Ponchecta*, a fast schooner designed to make quick passages and smuggle her cargoes ashore on the coast of Brazil and thereby escape an import duty of $10, per head. We had Brazilian papers and our arrangement was to run cargoes into different rivers and creeks and then make for Bahia and report "in ballast" or "coasting." The *Ponchecta* was rated by imperial license as a vessel of one hundred tons but actually measured but eighty. This was to provide for emergencies, the law allowing only *five* slaves to be carried for every *two* tons. By getting a permit on fraudulent measurement, we could cram twenty-five per cent. more cargo without appearing to break regulations.

The *Ponchecta* was commanded by a Porto Rico Spaniard named Antonio Mendez, an old slave smuggler. We shaped our course for Badagry, in the Bight of Benin, which at that time (1828-9) was doing a thriving business in slaves as the market was generally well stocked by kaffles arriving through the kingdom of Dahomey. From the Rio Volta, south to the Niger and north to the Gambia, the intervening country was then engaged in internal slave wars of the fiercest kind. Dahomans, Ashantees, Foulahs, Mandingoes, Sherbross, Fellatahs and Bambarras were preying on each other like wild beasts and kept the slave market constantly supplied. We soon had seven hundred slaves on board, in our eighty ton vessel and while packing was going on I visited one of the baccaroons where eight hundred sick or old slaves were confined for want of buyers. They were considered useless stock and before we sailed were all taken out in canoes by the Badagran negroes and knocked in the head and thrown overboard.

Our schooner was loaded beyond capacity and the deck had to be fitted with temporary platforms or shelves, as high as the taffrail, above which stiff netting was drawn to prevent the shackled slaves from leaping overboard. In walking the deck we frequently trod on a hand or foot sticking out from the lower tier.

About a week out we encountered a severe storm and the second night after, I was awakened by a crash, as if the skies were falling, and springing from my bunk, near the after gangway, I ran into Captain Mendez. "Save yourself, doctor!" he yelled, "the brig's sinking. We've been run down." The negroes were screeching on both sides and the sailors were running to and fro like mad. How I got into the stern boat I never knew, but I found myself there with the captain and about half of the crew. It was raining hard and we rowed about until daylight. The gale had lulled but the heavy rain was like a waterspout. All this time we could hear the screeching slaves.

When morning broke we saw the *Ponchecta* a-lee, her decks almost awash, and we lay by until she went down, about an hour later, full of manacled slaves. She had been struck on the beam by the *Mersey*, an armed East Indiaman, bound for Zanzibar, which lay by after the collision and eventually picked us up and landed us at Kahenda on the Guinea coast.

The loss of the *Ponchecta* left me penniless again as all I possessed went down in her. At Kahenda we found several slavers under Brazilian colors and Captain Mendez found a passage for himself and me in a brig bound for Angola, the Portuguese settlement, whose Governor he knew and there he was lucky enough to receive the command of a slaving schooner which the Governor was dispatching to the Brazils. I resumed my place with him, as surgeon, and made the voyage out and back without incident.

In March 1830 we arrived at the river Gallinas, not far from my old station at Rio Basso, and on landing found that its thriving factories were controlled by my old acquaintance Don Pedro Blanco, who was particular in his regrets at the death of my uncle. He knew nothing of Diego Ramos nor of my elopement with the Donna Emelia, my change of name having baffled all trace of us. I was glad to accept his offer of a situation at Gallinas and settled down as half-clerk, half doctor for Don Pedro Blanco. When I formerly knew him on the Kambia, I had been in possession of influence and wealth and he was an adventurer seeking a location. Since that time I had squandered a fortune and he had accumulated one.

Gallinas was a depot and market for slaves brought from all stations that penetrated the Guinea coast as well as territory farther south and my knowledge of negro dialects was of considerable value to my employer. The river from which the town took its name was full of small islands and on several of those near the sea, as well as on the banks, were located factories, barracoons, dwelling-houses and store houses. The success of Blanco had attracted a dozen other traders and agents who had located there and the Don was something of a prince among them. In African fashion he supported a harem and had quite a retinue of house servants, guards, etc., besides the clerks and overseers of his barracoons. I kept my place with him for six years and during that time made one voyage as clerk and one as captain of a slaver.

The schooner *Napoleon* was a ninety-ton Baltimore clipper, a model for symmetry and speed. She came out from Cuba, in ballast, as a new craft, and made two successful trips before, at Don Pedro's request, I filled the place of mate and surgeon on a voyage when she sailed with 250 full-grown men and a hundred boys and girls, for the Cuban market. The cargo was consigned to my old friend Gomez and rated A-1. By actual calculation the average cost per head of the 350 blacks was $16, and in Havana the market average was $360, yielding a net profit, if safely delivered, of $120,400. for the cargo, from which should be deducted about $20,000. as the average cost of the clipper's round trip, including commissions. This would mark her earnings for the voyage, as about $100,000. Such were the enormous profits of the slave trade in 1835. After that, with greater risks, the average of successful voyages ran higher still.

The *Napoleon* had trouble before her departure. The men slaves composing her freight were some of the fiercest warriors of the Kassaos, the Fi nation, and the Sherbroo Buttom people, who had

been provoked into a cruel war by the traders. It was only with difficulty that they were got on board the clipper, though secured by
one foot chains round the neck as well as their ankle irons. On
reaching the boats a rush was made by several for the purpose of
leaping into the sea and thumb screws had to be clapped on them
before they would be quiet. These warriors were finely built negroes
and the boys and girls were handsome and spirited.

We had a splendid run and expected to make the Moro the next
day, when our dreaded enemy, a British cruiser, hove in sight and all
sail was crowded on the clipper. It was near sunset and we were
sure that we could slip away easily. But the cruiser proved to be a
crack sailer and overhauled us rapidly. Captain Mina was in despair
as we had a stiff breeze and a few hours more would bring us to a
point of the island where our cargo could be landed safely. Just then
the wind fell off abruptly and the moaning sea warned us of an approaching tropical tempest. Everything was clewed up to meet the
expected tornado and very soon we had a heavy sultry squall of
rain. The sky and sea turning the color of ink; the deluge of rain
stopped in about an hour but the darkness continued. We could just
see the lights of Matanzas harbor gleaming through the mist and
an idea suddenly came to me and in ten minutes our crew were in
the boats, with sweeps, towing the clipper landward. I took my station in the leading boat and steered for the reefs and a point of land
which I well remembered enclosed my former plantation and before
the moon broke out our clipper with her topmasts shipped was safely
anchored behind some trees.

Whether the officers of the British cruiser thought the schooner
had foundered or was "the Flying Dutchman," we never knew, but
a few days later we entered the harbor, with Porto Rico papers, and
Gomez, our consignee, placed a hundred thousand dollars credit to
Blanco's account. Five thousand dollars of that sum I received as a
douceur, when we returned to Gallinas to relate the story, and the
Don promised that I should command his next vessel.

There were some half a dozen vessels then lying at anchor at

Gallinas, among them two handsome American craft, the *Fanny Butler* and the *Venus* from Philadelphia, and a Brazilian bark which I liked the looks of on account of her capacity and serviceable appearance. I proposed to the Don that we should risk the landing of a cargo at a place called Ponta Negra, between Bahia and Cape Frio, and he took to the project as it promised large returns. We loaded the Brazilian bark *Aguila* with 520 prime slaves and I hauled out of Gallinas flats, on September 6th, 1836, and set sail for the Brazils, on my first voyage as captain, in high hopes of a fortune.

The *Aguila* was two hundred tons burden and I had taken particular care to have her well fumigated and amply supplied with provisions and water. All things promised well. I had the gangs up every day, in rotation, under their overseers, to exercise and sing. I made them dash buckets of cold water over each other regularly and fed them well with rice and yams. The mid-passage was safely accomplished and on sighting the Brazilian coast I stood in for Ponta Negra to make a landing. I knew the place well having visited it with Captain Mendez, and finding good anchorage off the cliffs, my mate and I went ashore and leaving our boat in a sheltered creek, we walked about half a league to the handsome cottage and lookout of Don Felix, a noted smuggler whom I had met once before. He received us with Brazilian hospitality, gave us a sumptuous dinner after which we walked to his observatory to smoke our cigars. The prospect from this elevation, of the moonlit ocean and coast, was magnificent, but the most interesting object within sight to me was the *Aguila*, at anchor with a cargo that was to make me a wealthy man once more.

Don Felix puffed his cigar and sipped his wine for half an hour before we rose for business and I was looking at my vessel, when suddenly I saw a bright flash and the next moment an explosion rent the air while a volume of smoke and flame shot up from the water and hung like a black cloud before its contents descended. When this cleared away my vessel was no longer in sight. Her magazine had blown up and every soul on board had perished save one poor maimed sailor who managed to make the shore.

Three months passed away before I was able to leave my bed in the hospitable house of Don Felix. The disappointing blow left me a mere wreck and it was a year before I felt able to undertake the shortest voyage. It was necessary, however, for me to make a struggle for existence and in 1838 once more I reached the African coast, acting in the capacity of interpreter for a party of slave-traders who designed to visit some of the interior African kings, at their capital towns. There were three, beside myself, and we sailed from Rio and landed at Cape Appolonia on the Gold Coast. Here we hired guides and carriers and started across the Fantu country for Ashantee, falling in with several black slave-traders on the way.

When we reached Coomassie, the King of Ashantee, Quacoe Dooah, was not be seen until the third day after our arrival, but he gave orders for our good treatment and set a guard over our goods. There must have been over 25,000 persons collected in the great market place when we arrived. Hundreds of well-dressed black officers were strutting about, each wearing gold bracelets and anklets larger than slave shackles. When the royal interpreter called on us I astonished him with my knowledge of Ashantee.

Early the next morning we were awakened by the war drum announcing an Ashantee human sacrifice and were told that five hundred men, girls and boys were to be offered. A procession of the victims passed our huts soon after. One poor wretch had a knife passed through both cheeks and his two ears had been cut off and dangled from the knife blade and handle. A long spear was thrust under his shoulder blades, through the tendons, and he was led along by this, bleeding like a bullock. Then followed a young woman, stark naked, with both breasts cut smoothly off and her hips and belly stuck full of arrows. Another girl walked behind with her two breasts skewered by a knife and a cord passed through her nostrils by which to conduct her. There was no end to the horrible ingenuity of torture displayed.

A Slaver Driven Ashore on the Brazilian Coast by H.M. Brig "Frolic"

From a colored lithograph by H. John Vernon, published about 1840, in the Macpherson Collection

Capture of the American Slaver "Mary Adeline," off the Congo, in 1852,
by H.M. Brigantine "Dolphin"

From a colored lithograph by H. John Vernon, in the Macpherson Collection

The next day we were present at the bloody sacrifice and saw the King of Ashantee. He sat in a gilded wooden chair, in the midst of his chief men. Velvet umbrellas, with immense brass-mounted handles, covered them like a canopy. A long retinue of guards and household attendants stood around, carrying gold swords, silver and gold dishes, tobacco pipes and silk flags. The display of barbarian riches was dazzling and all this wealth of the Ashantee King was derived from the enormous profits of his slave sales. The interpreter told me that the King had sold over ten thousand slaves since the last rainy season, a little over five months' time, besides killing as many more in slave-hunts and sacrifices.

After an interview with the King, we followed the grand procession to the palace. Before reaching it a great musket firing commenced, the big drum was beaten and there was a rush of the blacks. The orgie began when a gigantic savage dashed out the brains of a victim with his club. A gourd was held to catch the blood, and the victim's heart was cut out with knives and held up to the King. I had heard that it was usual for each chief to sink his teeth in the bloody heart, but that time this feature of the ceremony was dispensed with. Some of the soldiers, however, actually drank of the wretched victim's blood, from the gourd in which it was caught. I will not attempt to describe the rest of this unnatural sacrifice. It was a confused massacre. Heads and limbs were severed or sawed off by dull knives and tossed about on poles. The bodies of men and women were disembowelled and dragged about and at last left to the dogs to devour. Such was the sacrifice at Coomassie.

We remained there ten months bargaining for slaves and then travelled farther inland through a beautiful country. The rainy season was spent at the Portuguese settlement on the Rio Cacheo and in September, 1839, we set out for Dahomey. At the capital, Abomey, the King collected his fetish men and gave a great feast. Four thousand slaves were sold to the traders, of which our party bought and branded seven hundred and dispatched them in kaffles to the great slaving depot at Whydah. A hundred of our purchase

were Amazons or women soldiers of the King's guard who had engaged in a revolt and were punished by being sold off. They were
fine-limbed, robust females, made healthy by their exercise in military service.

When we reached Ayudah, or Whydah, I met with a surprise.
The great slave trader who had built up the enterprise at this station was usually spoken of as Cha-Chu, but when I met him I
recognized him at once as my old friend and Cuban enemy, De
Souza, the Brazilian creole. He instantly recalled me and after some
conversation invited me to dine with him. I accepted and the dinner
turned out to be an orgie. His house was like a palace and he had a
harem filled with women from all parts of the world. He offered to
lend me a wife while I stayed at Whydah. "You shall have French,
Spanish, Greek, Caucasian, English, Dutch, Italian, African or
American," he said, laughing; "or, if you prefer an old flame, there
is Donna Emelia." I started and repeated the name. "Yes," said
Cha-Chu, "She's here, though, I confess, rather *abattu*. I've not
seen her for a year or two. I advise you to select a younger one."
This ended our confab. So Emelia, the brilliant, unprincipaled
woman was an inmate of the seraglio of Cha-Chu, mingling with
blacks, whites and browns. A cast off, half-forgotten concubine. It
was a wonder she had not poisoned him long before that.

I left Whydah and returned to Brazil with the company of
traders in a large ship that carried a thousand blacks. We lost only
eighty on the voyage. After arrival I was glad to be offered a per-
manent position with the trading company. My specialty was to
superintend the slave nursery or fattening farm for negroes who
were not merchantable on arrival. They were brought to the farm
in feluccas to be "doctored" for the market. The greater part, on
arrival, were living skeletons and they often dropped dead in the
corrals or yards. Some were ophthalmic, others scrofulous and many
were insane. The majority were reduced by dysentery and required
delicate handling in order to save them. We lost about forty per
cent. on the average of all that came to the farm. The joint stock

company that owned the fattening farm had established agencies along the coast, at intervals, for a distance of 2600 miles and controlled an immense smuggling traffic in negroes. Its headquarters were at Pernambuco.

I remained in the service of this company for seven years until I became sick of a fever and nearly died. On recovering I obtained a transfer to another establishment on one of the Bay Islands near the coast of Honduras in the Gulf of Mexico. Here a slave depot and farm were located to which cargoes were brought in American clippers from slave settlements near Cape Mesurado, Africa. The negroes were landed under the name of colonists and the company had permits from Central American authorities. They also had a branch farm on the Rio Grande, in Texas, which was broken up and its stock disposed at the breaking out of the war between the United States and Mexico.

Our island depot was admirably suited for its purpose, being near the mainland with good anchorage on the ocean side. Our farm and nursery were in the center of the island, on a navigable creek. Here we received Bozal blacks and set them at work in agricultural operations and in making goods for the African market, to exchange for their fellow-countrymen. They were taught to gabble broken Spanish and English, accustomed to discipline and well fed and well treated. I saw no misery among these negroes as it was our company's object to get them into prime marketable condition.

This joint-stock company was connected with leading American and Spanish mercantile houses and our island was visited almost weekly by agents from Cuba, New York, Baltimore, Philadelphia or New Orleans. During the Mexican war we had about 1600 slaves in good condition and were receiving and shipping constantly. The seasoned and instructed slaves were taken to Texas, overland, and to Cuba, in sailing boats. As no squad contained more than half a dozen, no difficulty was found in posting them to the United States without discovery and generally without suspicion. A single negro, sent by special agent as far as Savannah, would pay all his costs and fifty per cent. profit in the market. The Bay Island plantation sent ventures weekly to the Florida Keys. Slaves were taken into the great American swamps and kept there till wanted for the market and hundreds were also sold as runaways captured in the Florida wilderness. We had agents in every slave State and our coasters were built in Maine and came out loaded with lumber.

My connection with the island ended in 1853 when I came to Baltimore, on business connected with the depot. I had with me a considerable sum of money for a firm in New York City, on account of goods for the African trade, and while in Baltimore went on a drunken spree that lasted a week. When I came to myself I was in a low lodging-house, at Fell's Point, without a dollar in my pockets. I was helpless and soon after was committed to the city workhouse as a vagrant. From there I begged my way to Philadelphia and later to New York City and there I shall end my miserable life. May God forgive me for my crimes and have mercy on me hereafter.

CHAPTER XIV

SLAVING VOYAGES BY RHODE ISLAND VESSELS

NEWPORT, Rhode Island, was a well-known slaving port during the eighteenth century and Bristol was not far behind. The trade in negroes and rum was then considered entirely respectable and legitimate and although the voyage to the coast of Africa was one of the most hazardous that could be made, the profits from a successful venture were very great and the trade was continued until long after the time of the American Revolution. The owners of vessels and the distillers of rum, oftentimes one and the same person, found in this trade an outlet for their industry and the preacher and the philanthropist fancied that they saw in it a means of Christianizing a race plunged in heathen darkness. One highly respected elder, whose "ventures" in slaving had usually turned out well, always returned thanks, on the Sunday following the arrival of a slaver in the harbor of Newport, "that an overruling Providence has been pleased to bring to this land of freedom another cargo of benighted heathen, to enjoy the blessing of a Gospel dispensation."*

In the early days, some of the most respectable and wealthy merchants of Newport, Bristol and Providence were actively engaged in the slave trade which was usually carried on in small craft of not more than fifty to seventy tons burden, as it was found that the smaller vessels were the more profitable. The first leg of the voyage was from the home port with a cargo of New England rum, not long distilled, and a small stock of iron, cloth and trinkets to be used in barter on the Guinea coast. When the cargo of slaves had been secured, the "middle passage" to the West Indies was made and the live freight was exchanged for hogsheads of molasses which were

* George C. Mason, "The African Slave Trade in Colonial Times," in *The American Historical Record*, vol. I, Philadelphia, 1872.

brought to Rhode Island to be distilled into rum, and so the round continued for many years.

Sloops, brigantines and schooners were generally employed in this trade—rarely a ship—and the fitting out of these vessels required the services of tradesmen, carpenters, joiners, painters, caulkers, sailmakers and riggers—the folk who, with the sailors, made up the populace of the northern seaport towns, ruled socially and commercially by the wealthier merchant-shipowners.* There was also a larger number of small craft voyaging to and from the West Indies, bringing molasses, cocoa, indigo and coffee; and from the Carolinas, the necessary naval stores.

Molasses was the all-important feature of the slaving trade, which required rum as a means of barter for slaves, for without molasses there could be no New England rum and at times molasses was in great demand with an insufficient supply on hand. In the summer of 1752, a Newport merchant wrote to a shipowner:

"We are sorry to find you are ordering your sloop here in expectation of having her loaded with rum in about five weeks. We cannot give you encouragement of getting that quantity of rum these three months, for there are so many vessels lading for Guinea, we can't get one hogshead of rum for cash. . . . We have lately been to New London and all along the sea port towns, in order to purchase the molasses, but can't get one hogshead."†

The cost of distilling, about that time, was 5½ pence per gallon and good distillers were expected to turn out gallon for gallon. The number of still houses in operation was almost beyond belief. In Newport, there were no less than twenty-two. In 1750, rum was the "chief manufacture" in New England and about that time fifteen thousand hogsheads of molasses were annually converted into rum in Massachusetts alone. With rum, New England carried on a lucrative trade with the Indians and rum also served to keep the

* Verner W. Crane, *A Rhode Island Slaver*, Providence, 1922.
† Mason, *The African Slave Trade in Colonial Times*, 1872.

fisheries alive. There was no article that could take the place of rum in the Guinea trade. Here is what Capt. George Scott wrote to his Newport owners in 1740 on this point:

"We left Anamaboe ye 8th of May, with most of our people and slaves sick. We have lost 29 slaves. Our purchase was 129. We have five that swell'd and how it will be with them I can't tell. We have one-third of dry cargo left and two hhds. rum. . . . I have repented a hundred times ye buying of them dry goods. Had we laid out two thousand pound in rum, bread and flour, it would purchased more in value than all our dry goods."

Let us take one of these Newport slavers, the brigantine *Sanderson*, Capt. David Lindsay, master, William Johnston, owner, and follow her voyage out and back. She was a square-sterned vessel of only forty tons burden, built at Portsmouth, R. I., in 1745, and her portledge bill listed the captain, two mates and six men. She carried no surgeon. Her cargo consisted of 8,220 gallons of rum, 79 bars of iron, flour, rice, snuff, iron pots, tar, loaf and brown sugar, wine, vinegar, butter, pork, beef, tobacco, a trunk of shirts, 3,000 staves, and the usual supply of shackles, handcuffs, etc. Insurance to the amount of £100 was effected in New York at 18 per cent.

On Feb. 28, 1753, Captain Lindsay wrote to his owner from Anamaboe:

"I have Gott 13 or 14 hhds. of Rum yet Left a bord & God noes when I shall Gett clear of it. Ye Traid is so dull it is actualy a noof to make a man Creasey. My cheefe mate after making four or five Trips in the boat was taken sick & Remains very bad yett: then I sent Mr. Taylor & he Gott not well and three more of my men has sick. I should be glad I cood come Rite home with my slaves, for my vessiel will not last to proceed farr. We can see Day Lite al round her bow under Deck. Heare lyes Captain Hamlet, James Jep-

son, Carpenter, Butler and Lindsay. Gardner is dun. All these are
rum ships. I've sent a Small boye to my wife."

Captain Lindsay turned up at last at the Barbadoes, notwithstanding his leaky craft, and on June 17th he wrote to his owner that he
had arrived safely in ten weeks from Anamaboe, with fifty-six
slaves aboard, "all in helth and fatt. I lost one small gall." His
slaves sold at better than £30 each, and after deducting duties and
commissions the net proceeds amounted to £1324.0.3. The brigantine
took aboard at the Barbadoes fifty-five hogsheads of rum, three hogsheads and twenty-seven barrels of sugar and Captain Lindsay received bills on Liverpool for the balance due the owner. Newport
was reached safely and June 19, 1754, he sailed again, bound for
the coast of Africa, this time in the newly built schooner, *Sierre
Leone*, forty tons burden, in which he made a round voyage in ten
months, concerning which his owners wrote, "Lindsay's arrival is
very agreeable to us and we wish we may never make a worse voyage."

Guinea coast captains were not all as fortunate as Lindsay. Capt.
George Scott wrote from Anamaboe, in April, 1740, to his Newport
owner, as follows:

"I have been not very well for five weeks past, which is made our
voyage very backward, and am now very well recovered, Blessed
be God. We have now five people sick and bonner* so bad he will
not recover. I am heartily tired of ye voyage, everything runs so
cross that I undertake to make a voyage. I being not very well,
kept my cheif mate aboard and sent ye second mate in ye Long
Boat to Leward a trading. He had not been gone above four days
before he hired a canoue and sends her up with his gold taken to me
for goods, without any orders from me; i sent ye canoue immediately back without goods. Going down they overset the canoue, the
blacks came of from ye shore and took them up and put them in
irons. The blacks where ye boat lay detained ye Mate ashore, in

* A common negro name at that time.

which time a man slave he had bought, got out of ye boat with two ounces of gold and has gott clean off. I was obliged to go down with ye sloop and pay thirty-two pounds in ye best of goods before they would let ye Mate come off. Upon the hole I've lost nigh three hundred pounds with that trip, in money, by the mate's folly. I am sure he will never be able to make satisfaction.

"I bought sume slaves and Goods from a Dutchman for gold, which I thought to sell to ye French. In a few little time after my slaves was all taken with the flucks, so that I could not sell them; lost three with it and have three more very bad; ye rest all well and good slaves. We have now about one hundred and no gold. I think to purchase about twenty and go off ye coast; ye time of year don't doe to tarry much longer. Every-thing of provision is very dear and scarce; it costs for water Tenn shillings for one day. I shall go to Shama and water our vessell and sail of ye coast with what I can purchase. Every man slave that we pay all goods for here, costs twelve pounds ster⁸ prime. Our slaves is mostly large. 60 men and men boys, 20 women, the rest boys and girls, but three under four foot high."*

The sloop *Adventure*, Capt. Robert Champlin, owned by Christopher Champlin of Newport, cleared from Newport, Oct. 25, 1773, bound for Sierra Leone and the Gold Coast on a slaving voyage. She carried ten men besides the master, including two mates, a cooper, a cook, a boy and five sailors. Among the items of her outfitting were a pair of swivel guns and 100 grape shot; double-warded secret padlocks; "12 pr. Hand Cufs and Shackles"; a twenty-one-foot boat; twenty-six gallons of vinegar to wash down the slave quarters between decks; and a medicine chest well stocked with Peruvian bark. Rum made in Newport comprised the larger part of the cargo.

The owner's instructions directed the master to trade so far as possible at the "castles" instead of with the natives. "To lay a long

* Mason, *The African Slave Trade in Colonial Times*, 1872.

time on the Coast to piddle with the blacks must be against the voyage." It turned out that the tribes were at war and no black trade was running. At the "castles," the price for slaves was 140 to 160 gallons of rum per head. Rice was bought on the Windward Coast, but no slaves. It was only after four months' cruising and trading that a full cargo was obtained, which found a market at Grenada, at £35 to £39 per head. The return voyage was molasses and the owners reckoned a net profit of about 23 per cent on the voyage, or £400, sterling.*

A typical voyage of a Rhode Island slaver, at a later date, is that of the ship *Ann*, Jonathan Dennison, master, which sailed from Bristol, on July 24, 1806, bound for Cape Coast Castle, on the Gold Coast, with a cargo of rum, brandy, gin, wine and English goods. This cargo was to be traded for slaves to be taken to Montevideo and there sold and with the proceeds a return cargo of ox hides, dried beef, tallow and other produce was to be purchased. The owner of the *Ann* was James De Wolf of Bristol and his instructions to the captain were carried out to the letter until the ship reached the river La Plata, where she was captured, on Nov. 15, 1806, by the British ship-of-war *Leda*, the port of Montevideo then being under blockade. She was taken to the Cape of Good Hope where a Vice Admiralty Court, on Sept. 7, 1807, decreed that she be restored upon payment of costs; but the King's proctor entered an appeal and the following January, the Lords Commissioners, sitting in the Council Chamber, at Whitehall, in London, reversed the sentence and condemned the ship and cargo as a lawful prize.†

The ship *Ann* was built at Dighton, Mass., in 1804; she had two decks; her width was 27 feet, depth 13 feet 6 inches and she measured 309 tons. She was square-sterned, had neither galleries

---

* Crane, *A Rhode Island Slaver*, Providence, 1922.

† The briefs in this case were printed in London, for the benefit of the Lords Commissioners, sitting as a Court of Appeal, and from one of these rare originals owned by the Marine Research Society, the accompanying account of the voyage has been abstracted.

or figurehead, mounted four guns, and carried a crew of twenty-two men. The owner's instructions were as follows:

Bristol, R. I. 18th July 1806.

Capt. Jonathan Dennison
 Sir,

 Your having engaged to go a Voyage to Africa in my ship *Ann*, my Instructions are that you proceed with all possible Dispatch direct to Cape Coast, and make Trade at that Place and its Vicinity, and purchase as many good, healthy young Slaves as may be in your power to purchase, by bartering away your present Cargo with the Natives; and after compleating your Business in Africa, you will proceed to Monte Video in South America, and there dispose of your Slaves, and purchase a Return Cargo of Ox Hides and dried Beef, and some Tallow and other Produce of that Country, such as you may judge will pay a handsome Profit, and after compleating your Business there, you will return home to this Port with all possible Dispatch.

I am, Sir,
Your Friend and Owner,
JAS. DE WOLF.*

 The cargo of the *Ann* consisted of the following: "184 Hogsheads, 26 Tierces, 29 Barrels and 4 Half Barrels new Rum, 16 Boxes Claret Wine, 6 Pipes Molasses, 3 Boxes Hats, 1 Case Cambricks, 6 Hogsheads Cod-Fish, 10 Bbls. Oil, 2 Pipes Gin, 4 Regr. Casks, 3 Hogsheads Tobacco, 20 Firkins Butter, 28 Dozen Silk Hats, 6½ Dozen Cotton ditto, 2 Children's Samplers, 20 Pots and Kettles, 110, 2, 20, Bar Iron, 10 0, 23, American Steel, 2043 lbs. Hams, 8 Pipes Brandy, 80 Hogsheads Salt, 5 Chaldrons Coal, 3 Casks Porter, 6 Chases Bales India Goods, 2 Boxes Callicoes, 1

---

 * James De Wolf, a considerable shipowner, had served his time in the slave trade. He afterwards engaged in other trade and in privateering and accumulated a considerable fortune. He represented his town in the Rhode Island Legislature for nearly thirty years, and was a member of the United States Senate.

Trunk, 30 M. Boards, 1118 feet Oars, 17000 Staves 1200 Ps Nan-keens, 1 cask Claret Wine, 1 Bale Muslins, and Ship Stores for the Voyage."

The *Ann* sailed from Bristol on July 24, 1806, and reached the coast early in September. From the ship's log we learn that she was off Frisco, a small trading town, on Sept. 8th, forty-six days out. The weather was thick for the first part, but came off calm and flattering the latter part of the day. Cast the lead every hour and found from twenty-six to thirty-two fathoms of water. At 11 A.M. King Peter came off in a canoe.

At four o'clock the next morning, a small breeze sprung up and studding sails were set. The ship was then about four leagues from the land. King Peter again came off and told the captain that he was off Spisko. He was given a bottle of rum and sent over the side. In the morning saw two ships at anchor at Lahoe, probably buying ivory. Saw many canoes off fishing.

The next morning, Sept. 10th, there were light winds and a current set against them, so all sails were set. In the afternoon saw a schooner-rigged boat standing up along shore, under English colors; supposed that she belonged to one of the ships that lay at Jack Lahoe. At three o'clock a canoe came aboard from Jacques, a small town, and the captain "gave him a Bottle of Rum, and sent him ashore." There was a fine breeze all the afternoon but it died away at sunset. Soundings from thirty to forty fathoms.

The following morning, Sept. 11th, the ship was abreast of Little Batsam and saw a ship and brig at anchor. The ship got under way and stretched off and in the afternoon tacked in shore to speak the *Ann*. She was under Spanish colors, but soon fired a shot across the bow of the *Ann* and hoisted English colors. When within hailing distance she ordered Captain Dennison to send his papers for examination and later an officer came aboard to search the ship, but found nothing. When the *Ann's* boat was discharged she brought back an English cheese, a present from the captain of the English ship, and Captain Dennison returned the compliment by sending back some onions and three tumblers. The English officer said that an officer of his ship and six men had deserted in their whale boat, having stolen a quantity of guns and trading goods. At 4 P.M. they parted, good friends, and an hour later passed Great Batsam River. Saw a lugger boat standing down. Smoky weather all day.

"Friday, Sept. 12th. At 3 P.M. saw Appallona Fort by the English Colours; we past Axim Fort in the Night; about 12 o'clock we passed Cape 3 Points, as we supposed; in the morning hauled in for the Land: saw Dicks Cove Castle; at 9 passed by Secondu; at 12 passed by Commenda; at 2 o'clock came to in Elmina Road; as no Vessel lying there, I was in great hopes of making good Trade, as no Vessel was there; the next Morning I went on shore, but found they was full of all Sorts of Goods and Rum in abundance, they wanted nothing; to anchor in Elmina Roads is to bring the Two Flag Staffes in one in 7 Fathoms water. Kept 4 hands in a Watch."

Notwithstanding the state of trade at Elmina, Captain Dennison was able to dispose of a part of his cargo there and the long boat was hoisted out and a derrick was rigged. On the 14th, some slaves were brought out to the ship. The top-gallant yards were sent down and the best bower bent to a cable. The next morning two boat-loads of water were brought off and trade continued mainly in rum and dry goods. On the seventeenth, Mr. Willard went down to Cape Coast Castle to see what trade could be made there, but found no chance. The next day the mate enters in his log: "Pike has been deficient of his Duty 5 days, the Cook 3 days drunk, and deficient of his Duty. So ends this Day with pleasant Weather." On the 20th, Pike had been drunk for seven days and the cook, five.

On Sunday, Sept. 21st, "all Hands were employed in clearing up the tween Decks, and backing out the fore Peake, and sundry other Jobs." On Monday, "broke out Part of the Lower Hold; the Second Mate went on shore and got upset and very near drowned." During the rest of the week more rum and other goods were landed and sickness began to make its appearance. The captain also had a bad fall but was able to be about.

On Sunday, Sept. 28th, a caboose and a little house were built on deck and the heavy swell parted the small bower cable. Early the next morning they hove up the best bower "and got a Warp to the Buoy of the small Bower, and hove till we parted the Buoy Rope. After that got the Hawser and swept the Anchor, the Swell being so bad we dar'nt heave a Point." Pike got drunk and was very "wranglesome." Two days afterwards, while sweeping for their lost anchor, they found and brought up an old one. Three more slaves were brought on board.

Day after day they continued to sweep for their small bower but without success and on Oct. 6th, sail was made for Anamaboe, where Captains Drown and Brooks lay at anchor. Ill luck followed, for when the anchor was hove short the next morning, they capsized the windlass and broke the pawls, but got on a stopper and repaired the windlass. That night a tornado came up and it blew "more fresh." On the 8th the ship ran down to Leggo and came to anchor in eight fathoms. Spoke the ship *Union* of Newport, without any anchor. The next day ran down to Acra, where the windlass was again capsized and the pawls broken. The captain still remained very lame.

At Acra there was considerable trade in rum and all hands were kept busy discharging cargo and building a bulkhead to keep the slaves apart. This continued until the 18th, when sail was made to beat up the coast to Leggo, which was reached three days later and after a stay there of two days the ship was got under way bound to Elmina, beating up against the wind all the while.

The *Ann* remained at anchor at Elmina until November 6th, all hands being employed in getting water, building the barricade, hogging the inside of the ship and other sundry jobs. Three hands were on the sick list and also the mate, Daniel Shaw. On Nov. 7th, thirty-five slaves were brought aboard, and two days later, at 5 A.M., they got under way and ran down to Anamaboe and, after

Capture of American Slave Ship "Martha," June 6, 1850, off Ambriz, by U.S. Brig "Perry"

From a lithograph in Foote's *Africa and the American Flag*, New York, 1854

Capture of the American Slaver "Orion," Nov. 30, 1859, with 888 Slaves, by
H.M. Sloop-of-War "Pluto"

From a water color by J. Taylor (1876) in the Macpherson Collection

taking in some corn and wood, "sail was made for Leggo, where we spoke Captain Drown and left letters with him. On the 12th we got all our corn aboard and at 5 P.M. made the slaves dance. Charles Ryal came aft and knocked down one of the slaves and when the mate told him to go forward and struck him in the face he told the mate he would have three hundred dollars to spend in Gorges Street or have his life." "So ends the day," reads the log.

Acra was reached, a second time, on the thirteenth, where the captain settled his accounts with Whitehead, the merchant, while all hands were employed in getting ready for sea. Two days later, at sunset, everything was got aboard and at midnight they weighed anchor bound for Rio del Plata, "with the Help of God," having 163 prime slaves aboard; all hands employed unbending the cables, getting the anchor secure, and clearing the decks. Most of the slaves aboard were of the Fanteen tribe.

No record has been preserved of what may have happened during the voyage to Montevideo. We only know that the island of Lobus was sighted on Jan. 5, 1807, and the next day the ship spoke the British sloop of war *Medusa*, whose commander ordered the *Ann* to proceed to Maldeno, where the British fleet was. This Captain Dennison endeavored to do but the wind blew so fresh and the current ran so strong that after eight hours' struggle the crew became exhausted and the ship was put about and stood before the wind for Montevideo. At 9 A.M. she was fired on and captured by the British ship-of-war *Leda* and afterwards a prize-master and crew were placed aboard and the *Ann* was ordered to the Cape of Good Hope, where she was released by the Admiralty Court, but upon an appeal was eventually condemned in London, as a lawful prize. What became of the slaves does not appear, but as Parliament did not outlaw the slave trade until May 1, 1807, undoubtedly the cargo went the same way as the ship—"to the sole use of His Majesty, his Heirs and Successors."

CHAPTER XV

SOME AMERICAN SLAVE SHIPS

THE first American-built slaver seems to have been a small ship, the *Desire*, built at Marblehead, Massachusetts, in 1636. In the summer of 1637, she went on a trading voyage to the West Indies and part of her cargo was two women and fifteen boys, members of the Pequot tribe of Indians, who had been taken captive after the swamp fight at Fairfield, Connecticut. The *Desire* came to anchor at "Providence Isle" and there the unfortunate Indians were sold into slavery. The return cargo was cotton, tobacco and negro slaves, and when the ship reached Boston, on Feb. 26, 1638, three of these negroes were sold to Samuel Maverick, who lived on the island in the harbor now known as East Boston. How many were brought to Boston at that time is not known, but it was not long before negro and Indian slaves were owned in all of the New England settlements, though in limited numbers.

Edward Randolph, the government agent, in a report made in 1676, states that a few slaves had been brought into New England from Guinea, Madagascar and the West Indies, and Governor Bradstreet, writing in 1680, said that "no company of slaves have been brought since the establishment of the Colony fifty years ago, except about two years ago, after a twenty months' voyage to Madagascar, a vessel brought forty or fifty negroes."*

This seems to refer to a considerable importation,—a vessel whose principal cargo was slaves, for the frequent appearance of negroes in New England, in the latter part of the seventeenth century and in still greater numbers in the following century, shows that there must have been a constant influx, though never in large numbers. In 1742 there were 1,514 slaves owned in Boston and twelve years later the number had increased to 4,489. When the census was taken in 1764, there were 5,779 negro slaves and free blacks living in the town.

* *Massachusetts Historical Society Collections*, VIII, 337.

In 1708, Governor Cranston of Rhode Island reported that one hundred and three vessels had been built in that province between 1698 and 1708, all of which were trading with the West Indies and the Southern Colonies. They took out lumber and fish and brought back molasses in the direct trade, but "in most cases made a slave voyage in between." Not infrequently these Rhode Island slavers, after having sold their prime slaves in the West Indies, brought home to New England the less salable remnants of their cargoes.

Here is the advertisement of one of these Rhode Islanders, taken from the July 3, 1758, issue of the *Boston Gazette:*

> Just imported from Africa, and to be sold on board the brig *Jenney,* William Ellery, Commander, now lying at New-Boston [*i.e.,* West End of Boston], A Number of likely Negro Boys and Girls, from 12 to 24 years of Age; Inquire of said Ellery on board said Brig, where constant attendance is given.
>
> *Note.* The above Slaves have all had the Small-Pox.—Treasurer's Notes, and New England Rum will be as Pay.—

This trade in Indians and Africans and in the ownership of slaves was a universally recognized economic condition until the latter part of the eighteenth century. It was like the belief in witchcraft or that the world was flat. It was accepted by all.

In 1641, Massachusetts adopted its first code of laws in which it was provided "There shall never be any Bond Slavery, Villinage, or Captivity amongst us, unless it be lawful Captives taken in just Wars, and such strangers as willingly sell themselves, or are sold to us. . . . This exempts none from servitude who shall be judged thereto by authority." It was under this authority that the Court at Salem directed that Daniel and Provided Southwick, the children of Quakers, should be sold to the English in Virginia or Barbadoes. But the ship masters at that time (1659) were more humane than the judges and no one would have anything to do with the proposed transportation and sale of white children and they eventually were released. Seven years earlier, in 1652, two hundred and seventy

Scotchmen, taken prisoners at the battle of Dunbar, were sent to Boston and sold for a term of years, into servitude comparable with negro slavery. In London, the capital city of the realm, there were 20,000 negro slaves, as late as 1764, and these blacks were openly bought and sold on "Change." It was then the swagger thing for a gentleman to put a silver collar about the neck of his body servant, and Matthew Dyer, working goldsmith at the Crown in Duck Lane, Orchard Street, Westminster, advertised that he made "silver padlocks and collars for Blacks or Dogs."

There formerly was considerable noise and vituperation on both sides of Mason and Dixon's line concerning "the Divine institution" of slavery and the trade in human flesh. As late as Mar. 26, 1884, a congressman from North Carolina, during a speech in Congress, saw fit to remark that "Massachusetts is a State more responsible under heaven than any other community in this land for the introduction of slavery into this Continent, with all the curses that have followed it; that it is the nursing mother of the horrors of the middle passage, and that after slavery in Massachusetts was found not to pay, her slaves were sold down South for a consideration, and then their former owners thanked God and sang the long metre Doxology through their noses, that they were responsible no longer for the sin of human slavery."*

It is as silly and futile to talk through one's nose as it is inharmonious and unpleasant to sing through that organ. Slavery was largely a question of economic conditions and excluding the saints, the philosophers and the fanatics, men placed under similar conditions usually think and act very much alike.

American slave ships made their voyages to and from the African coast until the very outbreak of the Civil War brought on by that trade. During the three years ending December 31, 1807, two hundred and two slave ships entered the port of Charleston, South Carolina. Seventy of these were owned in Great Britain, three in France, one in Sweden, sixty-one in Charleston, fifty-nine in Rhode

* *Congressional Record*, Mar. 26, 1884, p. 2284.

Island and eight in other American ports. Altogether, 39,075 slaves were brought in. Of the fifty-nine ships hailing from Rhode Island, Bristol vessels brought 3,914; Newport, 3,488; Providence, 556, and Warren, 280, mostly in brigs and schooners of two hundred tons or less.*

In this chapter it is proposed to narrate the adventures of certain of these ships concerning which exact information is now obtainable.

Among the vessels sailing from Charleston, during this period, was the brig *Tartar*, James Taylor, master, owned by Frederick Tavell of Charleston, a native of Switzerland. She cleared Nov. 22, 1806, bound for Pongo River, just north of Sierra Leone, for a cargo of slaves, and the owner instructed Francis Roux, the supercargo, to make his trade as much as possible at the Rio Pongo and not to trade at other places on the coast. The underwriters not allowing a stay on the coast of more than four months, any cargo not disposed of must be brought back to Charleston, and in case slaves were found to be scarce, he was authorized to trade for beeswax to the amount of one-third of the return cargo. All slaves taken aboard must be marked or stamped. "Those belonging to the Cargo must be marked F T, and those that may be shipped on board by James Taylor, Captain, for Returns of his Four Hogsheads Tobacco, shall bear his Marks, in order to have Mortality, if any, supported by property concerned."

The brig measured 160 tons burden and mounted no guns. Her master, James Taylor, was born in Boston, but lived in Charleston, as did most of the crew. The ship's doctor was a Frenchman. The cargo, for trade on the coast, consisted of tobacco, brandy, claret, tar, flour, five bales of dry goods, ten dozen of negro low pipes and a box of white hats.

The brig arrived at the Rio Pongo, Jan. 24, 1807, and slaves being scarce, the lading was not completed until Jan. 9, 1808, notwithstanding the limitation of the underwriters. The slaves were all natives of the Windward Coast and bore various marks in ac-

* Munro, *Tales of an Old Sea Port* (Bristol, R. I.), Princeton, 1917.

cordance with their ownership, viz., an O on the right thigh; an O on the right shoulder; a pipe bowl on the left hip; an O on the left arm.

The *Tartar* made the passage toward the American coast without any unusual event until Feb. 2, 1808, when near Martinique, she was overhauled and captured by H.M. ship of war *Ulysses* and taken to Barbadoes, where she was condemned as a lawful prize because (1) she was proceeding from Africa to a colony of the enemy (*i.e.*, France), under a false designation, *i.e.*, to Charleston: and (2) because trade in slaves was contrary to the laws of America after Jan. 1, 1808. Captain Taylor deposed that he had laid a course for Martinique because he was likely to be in need of provisions, and had he received an advantageous offer he should have sold his slaves while there.*

The schooner *Nancy* of Charleston, South Carolina, sailed from that port on June 1, 1807, bound for Africa, on a slaving voyage. She was built at Great Egg Harbor, New Jersey, and was owned by John Gardner and John C. Phillips, merchants of Charleston. She carried a cargo of lumber and provisions, a small supply of trading goods, such as handkerchiefs and beads, and $6,000 in money. Her master, Joshua Viall, was a native of Warren, Rhode Island, and his crew consisted of six Americans and three Portuguese, one of whom died of the African disease, or slow fever, on the return voyage.

The *Nancy* arrived at Senegal about the first of August, and there Captain Viall sold his lumber and provisions and with the proceeds and the cash he had brought with him, purchased eighty slaves at an average cost of $125 each. The *Nancy* was only 67 feet long, 20 feet 6 inches wide and 9 feet deep, which did not allow much spare room for either crew or cargo, or for Thomas Bartholomew, a pas-

---

* The briefs in this case were printed in London for the benefit of the Lords Commissioners, sitting as a Court of Appeal, and from one of these rare originals, owned by the Marine Research Society, this account of the voyage has been abstracted.

senger. Four or five days out from Senegal, as the slaves were messing together one afternoon, the males and females apart, one of the males seized the master as he was pouring molasses into his victuals, whereupon the rest of the males rose and tried to seize Captain Viall, but he escaped from their clutches and with the aid of the crew drove the blacks below after small arms had been given out. One negro jumped overboard during the mêlée and a few were slightly wounded. This outbreak left the crew in a very nervous state, especially when the two mates and two of the seamen soon after fell sick of fevers, and not long after one of the seamen, in a night watch, imagining that the slaves were about to rise, shot and killed one of the slaves and the next night stabbed another.

Finding himself short-handed, Captain Viall decided to make for a neutral port in the West Indies—St. Thomas or St. Bartholomew— to obtain hands to navigate the schooner. About five leagues northward of St. Thomas he fell in with H.M. schooner *Venus,* and notwithstanding that he was in distress and asked for assistance, a prize crew was put aboard and the *Nancy* was ordered to Tortola, where she was condemned for prosecuting a voyage from a French colony and actually intending for the Havana or some other port in the West Indies, hostile to Great Britain, instead of for Charleston, the port named in her papers.

From time to time, after the abolition of the slave trade in 1808, sporadic efforts were made by the United States Navy to suppress the "smuggling" trade in slaves, but it was not until 1819 that a squadron was sent to the African coast charged with the duty of suppressing the trade carried on in American vessels. A number of the officers in command were Southerners and the effectiveness of the work done by them may be judged from the fact that Captain M. C. Perry reported, "I could not even hear of an American slaving vessel; and I am fully impressed with the belief that there is not one at present afloat"; while Captain Trenchard reported that there were three hundred slave ships on the coast and backed up his opinion by capturing five American slavers. Beggarly appropriations by Congress made it impossible to keep American naval vessels on the African coast until the Ashburton Treaty with Great Britain, in 1842, made it compulsory that the United States should maintain a "sufficient and adequate" naval force for the "suppression" of the slave trade and the following year Commodore Perry was sent to the African coast with four vessels under his command.

The slave coast was three thousand miles long and in playing the game of "hide and seek" the odds were always with the slaver, for he had only to run up a Spanish or Portuguese flag to be secure from attack or injury. Moreover, in following the orders issued by the Navy Department, only slavers with slaves actually on board could be seized. Consequently, fully equipped slavers would sail past the American fleet, deliberately make all preparations for shipping a cargo and then, when the English were not near, "sell" the ship to a Spaniard, hoist the Spanish flag, and again sail gaily past the American fleet with a full cargo of slaves.*

In 1845, the U.S. brig *Truxton*, captured, in the Rio Pongo, the schooner *Spitfire* of New Orleans, that had already run several cargoes. She only measured about one hundred tons but when captured had stowed 346 negroes, and the previous year had landed 339 near Matanzas, Cuba. "Between her decks, where the slaves were packed, there was not room enough for a man to sit, unless inclining his head forward; their food was half a pint of rice per day, with one pint of water. No one can imagine the sufferings of slaves on their passage across, unless the conveyances in which they are taken are examined. A good hearty negro costs but twenty dollars, or thereabouts, and brings from three to four hundred dollars in Cuba."†

From this time on, United States war vessels were kept on the African coast and slaving vessels were taken at intervals. One of the most important captures was the ship *Martha* of New York, taken by the U.S. brig *Perry*, in June, 1850. The *Martha* was a large ship with two tiers of painted ports and was standing in for the land

---

* DuBois, *The Suppression of the African Slave Trade*, Cambridge, 1896.
† Foote, *Africa and the American Flag*, New York, 1854.

towards Ambriz when overhauled. When within range of the guns
of the *Perry*, she hoisted the American ensign, shortened sail and
backed her main topsail. An officer was sent to board her and as his
boat was rounding her stern, the people on board, recognized his
uniform, and for the first time became aware that the brig was an
American vessel. The American colors were at once hauled down
and Brazilian colors hoisted in place. When the officer reached the
deck, the captain of the *Martha* denied having papers, log, or anything else; but it had been noted on the *Perry*, that something had
been thrown overboard, and another boat was sent which picked up
the writing desk of the captain, containing papers identifying him
as an American citizen. When confronted with this evidence, he admitted that his ship was equipped for the slave trade. A slave deck
was found already laid below, with ample supplies of farina and
beans, four hundred wooden spoons, and necessary iron bars and
woodwork for securing slaves. The captain had expected to ship
eighteen hundred slaves during the following night and before daylight to have been clear of the coast. The *Martha* was condemned
at New York and the captain was admitted to bail for $5,000, which
was afterwards reduced to $3,000, which he forfeited and eventually
escaped justice.

As the clipper ship trade with California and China became less
profitable in the late '50's, it is not strange that some of these fast
vessels should have been used in the slave trade. One of the best
known was the *Nightingale*, a beautiful ship built at Portsmouth,
New Hampshire, in 1851. She was lavishly decorated and her first
voyage was to accommodate a trans-Atlantic excursion to the World's
Fair in London; but her builder got into financial difficulties and
the intended voyage never was made. After making several quick
passages in the Australian and China trade she was sold in New
York, in 1860, to unknown parties, and her history during the
next eight months is veiled in mystery. It has been stated that she at
once sailed for Rio and went under the Brazilian flag, but Commo-

dore Perkins, while acting master of U.S.S. *Sumter*, on the African coast, wrote home on April 15, 1860:

"The clipper ship *Nightingale* of Salem, shipped a cargo of 2000 negroes and has gone clear with them. . . . She is a powerful clipper and is the property of the captain, Bowen, who is called the 'Prince of Slavers.' "

The *Nightingale* returned to New York in the late summer of 1860 and loaded with grain for Liverpool. On Nov. 24, 1860, she sailed for St. Thomas, on the West Coast of Africa, and the *London Times* remarked at the time, "It was well known in certain circles before she sailed that she was a slaver." She was reported at St. Thomas, Jan. 14, 1861, and continued to dodge about the African coast until April 21st, when she was seized by the U.S. sloop-of-war *Saratoga*, Captain Taylor, who described her capture as follows:

"For some time the American ship *Nightingale* of Boston, Francis Bowen, master, has been watched on this coast under the suspicion of being engaged in the slave trade. Several times we have fallen in with her and although fully assured that she was about to engage in this illicit trade she has had the benefit of the doubt. A few days ago observing her at anchor at Kabenda, I came in and boarded her and was induced to believe she was then preparing to receive slaves. Under this impression the ship was got under way and went some distance off but with the intention of returning under the cover of the night; which was done and at 10 P. M. we anchored and sent two boats under Lieutenant Guthrie to surprise her and it was found that she had 961 slaves on board and was expecting more. Lieut. Guthrie took possession of her as a prize and I have directed him to take her to New York. She is a clipper of 1000 tons and has *Nightingale* of Boston on her stern and flies American colors."

The slaves were landed at Liberia, but not before one hundred and sixty of them had died from African fever, which also attacked the crew. On reaching Monrovia, little surplus food was found and the mortality among the fever-stricken negroes must have been appalling.

The *Nightingale* arrived at New York, June 13, 1861, where Lieutenant Guthrie reported that Francis Bowen and a Spaniard named Valentino Cortino, had made their escape while the ship lay at anchor at St. Thomas. John J. Guthrie was a North Carolinian and Bowen afterwards related that Guthrie had allowed him to get away. The *Nightingale* was condemned and purchased for the government and afterwards used as a supply and store ship with the Gulf blockading squadron. She was abandoned at sea April 17, 1893, in the North Atlantic, at the time flying the Norwegian flag.*

The *Sunny South*, another fast clipper ship, built at Williamsburg, New York, in 1854, was sold in 1859, at Havana, for $18,000 and renamed the *Emanuela* and afterwards used in the slave trade. On Oct. 10, 1860, she was captured in the doldrums of the Mozambique Channel, with over eight hundred slaves aboard, by the *Brisk*, British screw sloop-of-war. When first sighted in a haze, her occupation was not suspected on account of her size and the unusually large number of staysails and studding-sails set, and when she hove to, she did so under full sail, without clewing anything up. She was sent in to Mauritius, condemned as a prize and sold to be used as a British cruiser.

One of the last of the slave-smuggling fleet was the yacht *Wanderer*, built at Port Jefferson, Long Island, for a wealthy member of the New York Yacht Club. She was launched in June, 1857, and measured 260 tons burden. The next year she was sold to Capt. W. C. Corrie. Her sailing master, Semmes, was a brother of the man who afterwards commanded the Confederate cruiser *Alabama*. The *Wanderer* cleared from Charleston for Trinidad, as if on a pleasure voyage, but made St. Helena and then went to the Congo. All the while she was flying the flag of the New York Yacht Club and when Captain Corrie fell in with the British warship *Medusa*,

* Howe and Matthews, *American Clipper Ships*, Salem, 1926.

"NIGHTINGALE," 1060 TONS, BUILT AT PORTSMOUTH, N. H., IN 1851

From a lithograph by N. Currier, after the drawing by C. Parsons made in 1854.

Chase of the Slaver "Gabriel," July 6, 1841, by H.M. Brig "Acorn"

From a colored lithograph, after a drawing by N. M. Condy, in the Macpherson Collection

cruising on the Congo coast in search of slaves, he ran alongside and entertained the British officers with the best on board.

The supercargo afterwards told newspaper reporters that after a sufficient number of bottles had been emptied, the British officers were facetiously invited to inspect the *Wanderer*, to see if she was not a slaver—a good joke that was appreciated by everybody. After the *Medusa* had proceeded up the coast, the *Wanderer* quietly slipped into the Congo, to the crowded barracoons, where 750 young negroes from thirteen to eighteen years of age were taken aboard. She got clear of the coast with her cargo, which she safely landed on the Georgia coast about the 1st of December, 1858.

One of the owners of the *Wanderer*, Capt. A. C. McGhee of Columbus, Georgia, was aboard and many years after he told the story of the voyage.

"The most difficult part of the voyage was to get into port. The only way to enter the mouth of the Savannah river was under the black muzzles of the guns of the fort and it would have been madness to attempt to enter with the contraband cargo, in open daylight. Instead, Captain Semmes crept into the mouth of the Great Ogeechee, by night, and ascended the river to the big swamp and there lay concealed while he communicated with Charles L. A. Lamar, his Savannah owner.

"Lamar thereupon announced that he was going to give a grand ball in honor of the officers and garrison of the fort, and insisted that the soldiers, as well as their superiors, should partake of the good cheer. When the gayety was at its height, the *Wanderer* stole into the river and passed the guns of the fort unchallenged in the darkness and made her way to Lamar's plantations, some distance up the river. The human cargo was soon disembarked and placed in charge of the old rice-field negroes, who were nearly as savage as the new importations."*

This venture was conducted on such a scale and so many were

* John R. Spears, *The American Slave Trade*, New York, 1900.

concerned in it, that it was impossible to keep the story a secret for long and before the month was over the United States District Attorney was on the trail and Lamar wrote to an associate that "hell is to pay." Arrests followed, there were hearings and Congress heard of it; but the smugglers eventually escaped. The *Wanderer* was condemned and sold at auction, when she was bid in by her former owners at a fourth of her value. It was afterwards said by one of the owners that the "slaves that had been purchased for a few beads and bandanna handkerchiefs [of course an exaggeration] were sold in the market for from $600 to $700 apiece. The owners of the vessel paid Captain Semmes $3500 for his services and cleared upward of $10,000 apiece on the venture for themselves."

Not long after this the case of the *Wanderer* was brought to the attention of the New York Yacht Club and on Feb. 2, 1859, Captain Corrie was expelled from membership and the *Wanderer* no longer had the right to fly the flag of the club.

As slave trading at that time must be done "under cover," it is not strange that exact information of the succeeding movements of the vessel is now difficult to obtain. One story relates that she sailed for the West Coast of Africa in the spring of 1859, under Captain Semmes, and again brought to the Georgia coast a cargo of slaves, many of whom were sent to New Orleans and there sold. In October, 1859, she went to sea, without papers, under command of a "Captain Martin," and on Nov. 22d, when off the Canaries, the captain hailed a French vessel and went aboard to obtain a supply of provisions. The rest of the crew, having shipped without knowing the nature of the proposed voyage, seized the *Wanderer* and setting all sail steered for Boston, where they arrived Dec. 24th and at once surrendered to the United States authorities. On board were two Portuguese women whom "Captain Martin" had carried off from one of the Azores with the intention of trading them on the African coast for negroes.

On learning of the arrival of the *Wanderer*, Lamar came to Boston, and entered a formal demand for the vessel, claiming that

Martin had piratically seized her, and after a long hearing and appeal she was restored to him.* Early in March, 1860, she cleared from Boston and after reaching Savannah is said to have again made a voyage to the West Coast. After the war broke out she was seized by the Federal authorities and used as a revenue cutter. Later, she was in the Central American trade and eventually was driven ashore on Cape Henry, where her bones found a last resting place.

It was the fate of a New England sea captain, a native of Portland, Maine, to pay the extreme penalty for slave trading, as late as Feb. 21, 1862. In the summer of 1860, Capt. Nathaniel Gordon, master of the ship *Erie*, of 500 tons burden, and an experienced slaver, sailed from New York, via Havana, for the Congo River, where he took aboard 890 negroes, 600 of whom were boys and girls, and "thrust them, densely crowded, between the decks and immediately set sail for Cuba." So reads the indictment. When only fifty miles from the African coast, the *Erie* was taken by the U.S. warship *Mohican,* the negroes were carried to Liberia and released and Gordon and his ship were sent to New York. Gordon was brought to trial as a pirate, under the May 15, 1820, law, which made slave trading an act of piracy, and the outcome was a mistrial. The following November, he was again brought to trial and in two days a verdict of "guilty" was returned. He was hanged on Feb. 21, 1862, after attempting to commit suicide by poison,—a fate richly deserved but not attained by thousands of others who had traded in human flesh.

* Bradlee, "The Last of the American Slavers," in the *Marine Journal*, May 22, 1926.

CHAPTER XVI

SIX MONTHS ON A SLAVER IN 1860

THE ship *Thomas Watson*, a smart looking vessel of about four hundred tons burden, lay at anchor off the Battery, New York harbor, one day in June, 1860, having just arrived from New London, Connecticut, where she had been fitted out and received her crew, who had shipped for a three years' whaling cruise. Some of the sailors, when they came aboard, were a bit mystified by the clean and neat appearance of her decks and bulwarks—for whalers usually are dirtier than a "lime-juicer" and the smell of oil pervades every part of the vessel. About an hour before sunset the wind freshened to a smart breeze and the mate came on deck and ordered the windlass manned and hove the anchor to a short stay, after which a signal was made for a tug and soon the ship was on the way to Sandy Hook. Meantime the wind had increased and the tug casting loose from the ship's side took the tow-line, out ahead. Sail was then made and the wind was in such a quarter that soon the tug could not keep the tow-line out of water more than half the time and when the Hook was reached and the line was cast off, the ship ran over it and the crew could not haul it in without checking headway. This the captain would not permit and so gave the order to cut the line.

After the ship had been at sea nine or ten days, all hands were kept on deck in the afternoon to practice making and shortening sail, for most of the crew were landsmen and never had smelled salt water before this voyage. As soon as this was thoroughly learned, the men were assigned their stations in the boats and great pains taken to teach them the proper handling of the oars. When the latitude of the Azores was reached a lookout was stationed aloft and directed to keep his "weather-eye open for blows," and this humbug of looking out for "blows" was persisted in until the ship ar-

rived off the coast of Africa and the farce of whaling could no longer
answer any purpose.

Among the crew was a young sailor named Edward Manning,
who had signed articles under the fictitious name of Edward Mel-
ville. He afterwards wrote an account of his experiences during
this voyage, which was published in 1879* and from this narrative
the following account has been condensed, as it preserves an excellent description of life on board a slaver during the last days of
slaving, with intimate details not to be found elsewhere.

It was not until after we had done with cruising off the Azores
Islands and had taken our departure for other parts, that our suspicions were aroused that the whaling business was merely a blind.
The first evidence came to light after the crew had been set to
work breaking out the hold, and it appeared in the shape of huge
quantities of rice, hard-tack, salt beef, pork, etc., in quantities large
enough to feed a regiment for a long time. We also found a great
amount of light pine flooring. For what purpose it was intended we
could not then imagine, but it will be seen, later on, that this was a
very useful part of our outfit. The ship had no regular "between-
decks." A small deck had been built directly under the main-hatch
and it was called the "blubber-room." The blubber was supposed
to be sent there for "mincing."

For weeks the sham of whaling was carried on and, whenever a
blow was cried out from aloft, all boats were called away. The
master of a *bona fide* whaler could not have been more anxious to
secure his fish than our captain appeared to be. The strict discipline
of a whaler was also kept up and no favors had been shown in the
way of grub. We still had only our allowance of salt beef, pork,
hard-tack, and beans.

Up to this time, however, we had not achieved much as a whaler,
two or three porpoises being the net catch of fish, and they were har-
pooned from the bow. The blubber that we stripped from them,

* *Six Months on a Slaver*, by Edward Manning, New York, 1879.

after being minced and tried out, yielded but an insignificant quantity of oil—not enough to make the try-pots even smell oily.

When not in the boats the work of breaking out the hold still went on with vigor. After a large quantity of rice and hard-bread had been shifted to the lazaret, the other stores were stowed up even with the deck of the blubber-room. This was about five feet below the main-deck. The pine flooring, which aroused our curiosity when it first came to light, was now laid smoothly down on top of the stores, thereby making a fair-looking floor. When we commenced breaking out the forward part of the hold it was found to contain chiefly large oil casks filled with fresh water. After stowing them in like manner as we had done the stores, namely, even with the blubber-room, we laid the pine flooring on top of them, and then had a smooth floor, fore and aft. This was the second tangible piece of evidence that our "whales" would not be taken out of the "mighty ocean."

The crew generally seemed to be well pleased at the new phase the voyage had taken and were anxious for the time to come when the ship would be well filled with "blackfish" oil, as they termed the negroes, and her bow pointed toward the States. I did not share in their satisfaction at the changed aspect of affairs, for I had scruples about being made an outlaw in this summary manner and I foolishly expressed my sentiments openly. I thus brought on myself the ill-will of the captain. Later on, after the voyage was ended and while I was waiting for a passage in a Mexican schooner from Campeachy, Yucatan, to New Orleans, he swore that I should never leave the beach alive. This, however, was all brag. I knew him to be a coward and it did not intimidate me in the least.

Nearly three months had passed since we took our departure from Sandy Hook and during all that time, with the exception of breaking out the hold, there had been nothing unusual to change the monotonous routine of daily work. But I judged now, by the whitish appearance of the water and the orders given to the lookout to "keep his eyes wide open," that we must be approaching land. The captain also passed a large part of the time on deck, night and day, and whenever a sail was reported from aloft, he would jump into the rigging, spy-glass in hand, and intently watch the approach of the stranger. If the course she was sailing would bring her within hailing distance, we at once avoided her by changing our course. Two or three times the skippers of different vessels manifested a desire to communicate with us by following in our wake, but, our ship being a smart sailer, they were soon convinced that there was no chance of overhauling us.

One night we had received orders from the captain that the whole watch should keep a sharp lookout for land ahead and just at daybreak the cry of "land-ho" was heard from a man stationed on the foretop-sail yard. The captain and mate at once went up to the maintop-sail yard, where they remained nearly an hour, scanning the horizon in the direction where land had been reported. When they returned to the deck it was noticed that the captain's demeanor to the mate had taken a decided change for the better. Perhaps he had plainly told the latter what he intended to do, after which he no doubt thought it prudent to treat his subordinate with a little more respect, considering that he had taken the responsibility of making him an outlaw without his consent.

At three o'clock or thereabouts, that afternoon, a small boat was descried by the lookout. It appeared to be about two or three miles distant and, as near as could be made out, her crew were pulling toward our ship. When this was reported to the captain he directed the man at the wheel to steer for her. We soon overhauled the boat and found her full of negroes, whom I afterward learned were kroomen. These kroomen were black as coal tar and perfectly naked. They were sitting on the gunwales of their boat and propelling her with paddles. Standing up in the bow was a powerfully built negro holding in his right hand a bright-red rag which he kept waving to and fro. The crew kept time with their paddles to the motion of this rag and at every stroke they gave utterance to curious sounds which much resembled the noise made by a flock of crows. Right amidships of the boat we could see a white man, of dark complexion, whom we afterward knew as "the Spaniard." He was straddling a cask and by his vehement gesticulation seemed to be urging the kroomen to do their best.

The maintop-sail was now braced aback and a ladder was put over the ship's side. As soon as the boat had reached us our friend of the cask mounted the ladder. Upon gaining the deck he rushed toward our skipper and threw his arms around his neck, shook his hand again and again and kept up such a constant fire of words that no opportunity was given the latter to open his mouth. The Spaniard finally recovered somewhat from the excitement of the meeting, after which the captain invited him into the cabin.

As they went below orders were given to the kroomen to come on board and to make the boat fast astern, giving her plenty of scope by using a line from the ship. After this we were directed to "fill away and stand in closer to the beach." We ran toward land as far as was safe, when the ship was again hove-to. The boat's crew consisted of nineteen or twenty kroomen, all large and muscular fellows. They were all naked, not even having on a hat to protect their heads from the rays of a sun that would have melted the skulls of us white men, had we not had them well covered. Each one had a string of cowries tied round his ankles and wrists. These, as I supposed, were used in lieu of money for bartering. Two or three of them could speak a little broken English. This they had probably learned from the sailors of the English men-of-war frequenting the coast.

After a brief consultation our visitors selected one of their number to act as spokesman. He at once made good use of his knowledge of the English language by begging for something to eat. This we supplied. After their hunger was appeased they commenced begging, through their interpreter, for old shirts, hats, tobacco, and everything else they could see or think of. Some of our men went below and brought up a lot of old hats, shirts, etc., which they offered to exchange for the cowries worn by the negroes on their ankles and wrists. The kroomen seemed loath to part with these at first, but the sight of a red flannel shirt was too tempting an object for the leader (the knight of the red rag in the boat) to resist and he soon succumbed. After this it was an easy thing to strike up a trade with them. For an old shirt I secured a small string of cowries, which are still in my possession. It was a ludicrous sight to behold them strutting up and down the deck in their new attire. None was completely clad. One fellow had on a sou'wester and a short shirt; another, only a pair of overalls; and another, a pair of old seaboots and a straw hat. This last was the most extraordinary toilet I had ever seen.

The captain and his Spanish friend now came on deck and on beholding the fantastic appearance of the kroomen, gave vent to a tremendous roar. The boat was hauled to the gangway and her funny looking crew ordered into her and after giving our skipper another affectionate embrace the Spaniard took his departure. The maintop-sail was once more filled away and we stood out to sea, braced up sharp on the wind.

About this time our grub began to improve. The salt-horse kid was now accompanied with pickled onions, canned meats and other luxuries. Meanwhile "Bungs," the ship's cooper, was kept busy making small kids and as fast as he finished a lot we spliced rope handles in them. Away down in the run, with many things piled on top of them, we had some time before brought to light about forty of the same suspicous-looking kids. Later on it will be seen the use they were put to.

After our departure from the African coast we cruised about for a period of two weeks and during that time not a word was spoken by our captain which would even lead us to infer that the vessel was there for the purpose of carrying off a cargo of negroes. Of course there could be no doubt of it—that we felt sure of; but what his reasons were for not imparting some information on the subject at this stage of affairs, was a mystery we could not solve. Even if the men had the will to remonstrate, they were powerless to do anything. There was not another person on board who had sufficient knowledge of navigation to take charge of the ship and he knew it. The mate of a merchantman is supposed to be a competent navigator, but in this instance the rule did not hold good. Our mate knew less of navigation than I did, for I could figure out a day's work by dead-reckoning and that was more than he could do.

The whaling humbug was played out now. The reporting of "blows" was still carried on, but no boats were ever after lowered for this purpose. During this whole two weeks I doubt if we were at any time more than ninety or a hundred miles distant from the coast, for the distance run off was generally recovered at the end of every forty-eight hours, by sailing the other way.

The cooper finished making his kids and with those found in the hold he mustered about sixty. All our provisions and water were handy but the hold was very much lumbered up with a large quantity of shooks and staves. These were finally hoisted to the deck and lashed along the bulwarks.

One night, shortly after this work had been done, the yards were squared and the course altered. The man at the wheel was cautioned to very careful with his steering and the captain remained on deck all night. Sleep was out of the question in the forecastle and the watch below lay down on their sea-chests. Those who were able to think were no doubt wondering what the next day would bring forth; for, ignorant as they were of navigation, they had sense enough to know that, with a fair wind, the ship could not be more than a few hours in reaching the coast. I could see that they were anxious and perhaps a little frightened, for they all knew there was a gloomy outlook ahead should the ship be taken with a load of negroes on board. Confinement for several weeks in a prison on this sickly coast was not a pleasant thing to contemplate.

At last the long, dreary night came to an end and, as I expected, at the break of day the cry of "land-ho" was heard from aloft. At that cry the captain exhibited openly his nervousness or cowardice. Calling to the mate in a very shaky voice he directed him to take the spy-glass, go aloft to the main-royal yard as quickly as he could, and take a look all around inshore, and if he saw anything that had the least appearance of a vessel to report it immediately. He then directed the second mate to see that all hands were on deck and to have them ready for quick work. As it happened, we were already there, and as anxious as he, no doubt, for a few hours would decide our fate.

The wind being light, the ship's progress was slow, and it was fully two hours before the land opened out sufficiently to tell how it looked. The part of the coast we were approaching appeared to be uninhabited, with a dense thicket two or three hundred yards back of the beach. As we came nearer I could see a long, low shed, just on the outskirts of the thicket facing the water. During all this time the captain had been nervously moving about and every five or ten minutes hailing the mate to inquire if he saw anything yet. On receiving a negative answer, he would mutter audibly: "It's strange. She ought to be there."

After the mate had been aloft nearly three hours, he suddenly cried out,

"Sail-ho!"

"Where away?" said the captain.

"Right ahead, and close to the beach, sir," responded the mate.

Orders were now given to the second mate to get both anchors ready to let go, with a range of twenty fathoms on each chain. All hands went at it with a will and the business was soon despatched.

"Can you make out her rig and has she any flag or signal set?" yelled out the captain to the mate.

"She is schooner-rigged and has something flying at the main, but I can't make it out," was the reply.

I now went aloft to the foretop and, looking toward the beach, I saw the vessel reported by the mate apparently lying at anchor. While I was aloft my chum passed me with a white signal flung over

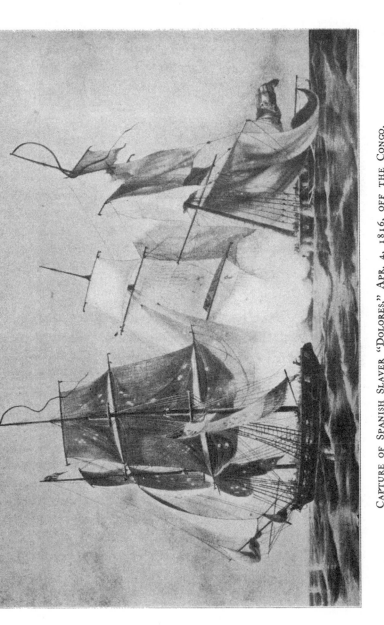

CAPTURE OF SPANISH SLAVER "DOLORES," APR. 4, 1816, OFF THE CONGO,
BY H.M. BRIG "FERRET"

From a colored lithograph, after the painting by W. J. Huggins, in the Macpherson Collection

THE CAPTURE OF THE SLAVER "BOLODORA," BY H.M. SCHOONER "PICKLE," JUNE 6, 1829
From the colored aquatint, after the painting by W. J. Huggins, in the Macpherson Collection

his shoulder and as he started up the topmast rigging I asked him what he was going to do with it.

"Bend her on to the signal halyards and stand by to run her up."

The signal halyards had been rove but a short time previously and the ends made fast in the cross-trees.

"I think that signal is plain white, sir, and there is a boat pulling off from the beach," sung out the mate.

"All right," replied the captain: "run up the signal."

"Ay, ay, sir," answered Frank, and a moment later, the white signal waved from the fore-truck.

The land opened out rapidly and I could now see the long, low shed quite plainly. It looked as if it had been constructed by sticking poles in the ground and using brush from the surrounding thicket for the roof. This shed, I afterward learned, was called a "barracoon."

When the boat reported by the mate was some four or five hundred yards from the beach, her crew ceased paddling and awaited our approach. The captain hailed the mate and told him to come down from aloft and after he had reached the deck we commenced taking in light sails, preparatory to coming to anchor.

We soon overhauled the small boat and our friend, the "palm-oil trader," stepped on board and gave our captain another affectionate kiss. He was very much excited and I inferred from his actions that he desired the ship brought at once to anchor. The captain seemed to think differently, for he continued to run her in and did not anchor until we were dangerously near the breakers. The sails were allowed to hang in the buntlines, not half hauled up, and even the royals did not have the turn of a gasket around them. It was surprising that the ship did not drag her anchor, with so much sail for the wind to act on. She lay hard aback and kept the small scope of chain out as taut as a harp-string.

"Let everything hang as it is," sung out the captain to the mate, "and send all hands into the hold to put down the flooring. Don't be particular, but bear a hand."

We went below and commenced to execute this order. The "palm-oil merchant" danced up and down the deck like a lunatic and every minute or two poked his head down the main-hatch and ordered us to "hurree uppe." No such driving was necessary, however, for we had sense enough to realize that our anchor was down in a dangerous place and we worked with a will. We soon had the flooring laid; not very smoothly, it is true, but well enough to answer the purpose for the present.

"Man the boats, men! Step smart now, my lads!" was the next order.

We tumbled into our boats and shoved clear of the ship. We had pulled but a short distance when a large surf-boat passed us, crammed full of naked negroes—men, women, and children. She was manned by kroomen and they were using paddles to propel her. They were all jabbering at once in their monkeyish lingo and every few minutes I could see a paddle raised and brought down on the head of some unlucky negro.

When they had reached the ship I cast my eye ahead to see where we were going. I found that we had arrived within fifty or sixty yards of the beach. Five or six strokes more would have put us in the breakers, when the order was given to lie on our oars. Looking toward the barracoon, I saw a long line of negroes walking in single file, toward the beach, where a surf-boat was ready for launching. After a number of them had gathered around the boat she was shoved out far enough to float, the crew standing in the water up to their waists and holding fast to the gunwales on each side, in order to keep her bow to the breakers. The negroes were then seized, one by one, and tumbled in promiscously. After loading her full, the crew jumped in and seized the paddles.

This manoeuvre had to be executed quickly and it required experienced hands to make it successful. The least sheer of the boat would have brought the breakers quartering on the bow, when there would have been danger of her being knocked broadside to them. Once in that position, nothing could have saved her from being rolled over by the heavy surf then running and the negroes precipitated into the sea where possibly more than half of them would have perished. She was, however, brought safely out of the surf and her course directed toward our boat. The mate now gave us orders to receive the negroes and carry them to the ship. He cautioned us to take in our oars the moment the surf-boat reached us and then to seize the paddles and stand ready to knock the negroes over the head if they should all attempt to jump into our boat at once.

This warning was timely, for no sooner had she gained our side than the rush began. We did our best to keep them back by using the only argument they could understand, namely, hard knocks over the head. We were nearly swamped, nevertheless, by a number of them getting on one side of our boat as they piled into her. After they were all in we shipped the oars and started for our vessel, the surf-boat returning to the beach for another load. We made slow progress, the boat being so overloaded that it was impossible to take a fair stroke without chafing the backs of the negroes or striking them in the face with the oars.

When we finally reached the ship they were passed up the ladder until they came within the grasp of two swarthy Portuguese, stationed in the gangway. These men, who had come from the shore in the first boat, hauled the negroes up on deck. The poor creatures were much scratched and bruised by this rough handling.

At the same time we had constantly to watch the simple blacks, to prevent them from putting their hands on the outside of the gunwales where there was great danger of getting them smashed against the ship's side at every roll of the boat.

After discharging our freight we started for another load, which we obtained in the same manner and we landed them safely on board. In this way we went back and forth until the last negro was put aboard the ship, when the boats were hoisted. During the time we had been thus engaged, the large surf-boats from the beach, although loaded to their utmost capacity with negroes, had, strange to say, made their way, in every case, through the breakers without losing a man.

When we arrived on board everything was in confusion. The negroes had been put into the hold without the least regard for stowage. Consequently, they were literally piled on one another; and the unsteady motion of the ship, combined with the foul air and great heat, made the place simply horrible. Naturally, they were nearly all dreadfully sick at the stomach. The women had been put in the steerage. The ship had what sailors call a high poop-deck— that is, the cabin had been built on the maindeck. The forward part had been partitioned off and the staterooms removed as far as practicable, leaving almost a clear deck to the dividing line. This we called the steerage. The wind circulated freely through it; therefore, it could be called a Paradise compared with the hold. Hence, the women fared much better than the men.

Now that our cargo was secured, we hove short the anchor and made sail, the ship lying in the wind at the time. Then, after hauling the head-sheets to windward and bracing up the head-yards on the opposite tack to the one we intended to cast, the anchor was hove up. But the ship would not fall off, and commenced drifting astern. This would not do for we were already too close to the beach and our captain gave the order to let go the anchor—the only safe thing to do under the circumstances. The Spaniard, however, opposed it and when he heard the chain rattle out through the hawsehole he flew up and down the quarterdeck like a wild man, crying out, "Oh, no, no, captain! English! English!" Then seizing a rope's end he made unpleasant motions with it about his neck—meaning, no doubt, that there was danger of getting their guzzles squeezed should the anchor be let go. We now took the end of a six-inch hawser through the after-chock and, carrying it forward, made it fast to the chain close to the water, after which the hawser was bowsed taut aft. In the meantime, the second mate had unshackled the chain at the thirty-fathom shackle and, leading the end out clear for running, he stood by to let it slip.

Everything being ready, the order was given to slip the cable and as the chain went out the hawse-pipe the hawser was bowsed in aft. As the strain increased on the hawser the ship's head fell off and as soon as the canvas would draw we put it on the ship. We soon had the pleasure of seeing the vessel go ahead instead of making sternway; and we could consider ourselves fortunate in escaping with only the loss of an anchor and hawser. The remainder of the day we devoted to feeding and watering the negroes. We also threw overboard all the shooks and staves lashed on the maindeck, after which we had more room. It was now time to set the watch for the night; so nothing more could be done for the comfort of the negroes until morning.

I omitted to state that the two Portuguese, who had assisted in hauling the negroes over the side, returned to the beach in one of the surf-boats after the cargo had all been taken on board.

Early next morning preparations were made to get a meal ready for the negroes. One of the try-pots was filled about three-quarters full of rice and two of the most intelligent of the blacks were appointed cooks, the cooper acting as superintendent. While this was being done we went down into the hold to see how they had fared during the dreadful night that had just passed. Their haggard looks bore evidence of the misery they had undergone. Pent up in such close quarters and inhaling such a terrible stench, it was miraculous that one-half of them had not perished. We found five or six dead bodies which were at once hoisted to the deck and consigned to the deep. There was no pretence of any religious ceremony. Just as they were, naked and forlorn, they were tossed overboard and for a long time we could see the bodies floating in the wake of the ship. I could not stay below long for the stench almost suffocated me. On reaching the deck I heard the captain say that at eight bells the negroes must all be ordered up on deck to mess and while they were thus employed we should thoroughly cleanse the hold.

Just before seven bells the captain notified the crew that there would be no more forenoon watches below, for we were so short-handed that no one could be spared from duty during the day. We were also told that, purely as a matter of safety, all hands ought to remain on deck in the daytime, lest the negroes might feel their power when they saw how weak in numbers we were. We could say nothing against this arrangement, for it looked reasonable enough. We must be satisfied with eight hours' rest every other night, or perhaps even with less; for, should it be necessary to shorten sail, all hands would certainly be required on deck.

The crew breakfasted at seven o'clock and at half-past seven we turned to and commenced operations by sending the negroes on deck. After the deck was filled so completely that there was scarcely room enough to give us a chance to feed them, we found that a great number would have to remain below and mess there. They were now divided off into messes and the kids were filled by the cooper and his cooks with the rice, which they had all ready, and smoking hot, by this time. The kids were passed around to the messes and, in addition to the rice, each man was allowed two sea-biscuits. Very few of them had any inclination to eat, but the Spaniard, who took exclusive charge of them, seized a rope's end and raised their appetites by showering blows on their bare shoulders. The poor negroes, being thus forcibly compelled to eat, quickly stuck their two forefingers into the hot rice and, taking up some, put it into their mouths. It being very hot they rolled it about with their tongues and their eyes looked as if they would burst from their sockets before it was cool enough to swallow. After two or three meals they learned to cool it before putting it into their mouths.

This feeding consumed nearly three hours; the hard usage they had received, combined with the nausea caused by seasickness, mak-ing·it difficult for them to swallow or to retain any food on their stomachs. After the kids were removed, a tin pot, containing about a quart of fresh water, was passed to each one of them.

Before proceeding farther it would, perhaps, be well to describe the negroes. The kroomen were in every respect superior to the others. Large and well-built, with every appearance of robust health, they would undoubtedly bring the highest price in the market. They could all understand the Portuguese language and hence were invaluable to the Spaniard as interpreters. On the plantation where our cargo had been confined, prior to the time when they had been sent to the barracoon, the kroomen acted as bosses over the others. On board the ship they were armed with whips and given authority to abuse and beat the common negroes whenever they felt like it. It seemed to me that they felt like it much oftener than was necessary and took an actual pleasure in doing it.

On the backs of all the kroomen a letter had been branded and some also had their front teeth filed to a sharp point. Their complexions varied, some being very black and some a bright bronze color. Those whose teeth were not filed had beautiful sets. They were as white and lustrous as pearl and as regular and perfect in every respect as if they had been artificial. The kroomen were much better proportioned than the other negroes; their noses were not so flat nor the lips so thick. I suppose they all had names in their own dialect, but the effort required to pronounce them was too much for us, so we picked out our favorites and dubbed them "Main-stay," "Cat-head," "Bull's-eye," "Rope-yarn," and various other sea phrases. These men did certain parts of the work and at night kept order and silence in the hold. The business of feeding the negroes was entrusted to them. We merely superintended the operation and saw that each received the proper allowance and no more. We never had occasion to punish them, as they faithfully performed the work allotted to them. They even formed quite an attachment to certain members of the crew, who furnished them with clothes and tobacco. Give them a pipe and tobacco and the measure of their happiness was full. No apprehension of trouble in the future seemed to interfere with their present comfort.

The other negroes numbered about eight hundred and included all sizes and ages—from infants at the breast to men and women of forty. Many of them were branded with curious devices. In some cases the whole body was covered with marks—not even the face being excepted. A large number, also, had the front teeth filed, like the kroomen, and when they opened their big thick lips they looked hideous. They were devoid of all intelligence, not even having as much sagacity as a Newfoundland dog. They were also arrant cowards; one white man being sufficient to intimidate and manage a hundred of them. The women were the pluckiest and had they all been of that sex we should probably have had a mutiny on board before the ship had been at sea two weeks. They numbered about two hundred and were stowed in the poop, as I said before. They were, with a few exceptions, all fine specimens of their race, physically. Five or six of the younger ones were hopelessly sick— consumption was, I believe, the complaint. They made more noise at night than all the males together. While on watch I often saw the Spaniard, whip in hand, bounce in among them and fiercely cut out right and left. This treatment would have the desired effect, for that night at least.

We had about fifty or sixty negro boys on board, ranging from six to fourteen years of age. They were all sound in body and enjoyed excellent health. The little fellows made no trouble at night, the awful looks of the kroomen acting like magic in suppressing any such tendency.

Before sending the negroes below, the hold had to be thoroughly cleaned and a system devised for keeping it so. The Spanish captain, as he finally came to be called—no other name having transpired among the seamen—divided most of the kroomen into gangs and partitioned off the hold, each gang having a part of it to keep clean and a number of negroes to attend to. Those that remained were stationed on deck, to do whatever was required of them.

After these preliminaries were all arranged the work was commenced. In a short time the hold was thoroughly scrubbed out and the flooring laid down evenly, which made it much more comfortable to lie upon. Just forward of the fore-hatch, two spare try-pots had been lashed. They took up a great deal of room that was needed for other purposes and as they were a superfluous luxury for this kind of whaling, we got the captain's permission to try our strength on them with a top-maul. After a great many blows had been given, we finally broke them into pieces small enough to handle and then tossed them overboard. The hold was now greatly improved and the negroes were sent below with a better prospect of being able to live there. Windsails were set at each hatchway and kept trimmed, and when there was any wind a refreshing air was distributed throughout the hold.

The Spanish captain, who was our mainstay in regulating the negroes, was an exceedingly ferocious man among them. Our own captain said of him that he had run eight cargoes to the Island of Cuba and had never once met with an accident. Having had such an extensive experience in the business, he must have thoroughly understood the best and safest way of handling them. When the number of negroes on board is compared with that of the crew (there were only eighteen of us), it will be seen that orders in regard to them, whether for punishment or anything else, had to be promptly executed and without the least appearance of fear. So great was their terror of the Spaniard that I verily believe he could have controlled the whole of them single-handed. Yet I never saw him practice any deliberate cruelty with the exception of two or three instances to be mentioned hereafter.

Among the little girls he was a great favorite and I cannot recall a single instance when he punished them or caused it to be done by the kroomen. During many a hot, sultry day, when the awning was spread across the main-deck, he would permit the little ones to gambol and play under it, often exerting his fancy to assist their childish amusements. He would frequently take small strips of calico, eighteen or twenty inches in length, tie them in the rigging, and then start a race, giving each an equal chance, to see who could secure one of the pieces. This was a prize to the lucky one, and she was regarded with envy by those who failed to secure a strip. The calico was afterward put to a practical use in the way of aprons. The Spaniard was also well skilled in medicine and by his intelligent treatment of the sick saved a number of lives.

As soon as the negroes were sent below after their first meal, he arranged for feeding them in the future at regular intervals. At eight o'clock in the morning breakfast was to be served. Then the kids were to be rinsed out, filled with salt-water and one passed to each mess, the members of which should be made to wash their hands and faces. After this, every man, woman, and child was to be allowed one quart of water each. The same programme was to be enforced at the afternoon meal, which was to commence at three o'clock. At first it required nearly three hours for each meal, but after a week's practice the time was reduced to about two hours.

On the first day, when we had finished feeding them in the afternoon, it was six o'clock, the time appointed for all the negroes to be stowed away for the night. After the deck was cleared we went below to see that the kroomen arranged them properly. Commencing forward, we made the first man lie down, head to windward, facing toward the bow, and the knees slightly drawn toward the chin. Another one was then placed alongside, with his breast touching the back of the first and his knees bent at a similar angle. In this manner we stowed them, in tiers, the length and width of the hold. The kroomen were allowed the privilege of reclining as they chose, but it was their duty to keep the others in their proper places. When daylight came the negroes could change their positions to suit themselves.

At five o'clock every morning we commenced to wash down the maindeck, which was also the signal for the cooper to call his cooks and prepare the food for the negroes. After scrubbing and scraping until seven o'clock, the watch on deck would call the watch below and all hands go to breakfast. We were allowed half an hour for breakfast, after which the negroes had to be sent on deck and arranged in their proper messes for the meal. In the course of a week's time we had them nicely regulated and after that there was no further trouble.

The Spanish captain now selected from among the kroomen his medical assistant. This negro went by the name of "shikko"—signifying, in their dialect, doctor—and he was very useful in helping his master. The shikko having found a great many sick below, the Spanish captain immediately held a consultation with the captain of the ship which resulted in a hospital being extemporized under the top-gallant forecastle. All the invalids were conveyed there and received prompt treatment. Dysentery, caused largely, no doubt, by the change of diet and water, was the principal and most fatal disease that attacked them. After lingering a long time, and suffering greatly, the first patients all died. Two or three cases of small-pox broke out, which received prompt treatment; but these also were fatal. It was providential that this loathsome disease did not spread. Had it done so, God only knows what would have been our fate. There occurred one remarkable case which the captain called the coast scurvy. The man sick with it swelled until his whole skin was transparent. No medicine gave him any relief and his sufferings were terrible to witness. He lived fully two weeks in dreadful agony before death relieved him. There was a case of palsy among the males and that the Spanish captain could do nothing for. When the poor victim took the water-cup in his hand it would shake very much and this pleased the negroes so that they would shout and laugh at an immoderate rate. Sometimes an application of the whip was necessary to quiet them.

Only one birth occurred on the passage. A woman was delivered of twins—one dead and the other living but a few hours after birth.

When the negroes were all below and stowed for the night, one of the watch was stationed at each hatch to guard it for two hours. At the expiration of this time he was relieved by another and so on until daylight. While on this duty the men were armed with native African swords or knives which the Spanish captain supplied. They looked like large rusty cheese-knives and, in my opinion, the only thing they were good for was to bang against the combings of the hatch. When the negroes were noisy the watch would yell out something which sounded like "Yock ho!" This always acted like magic for on hearing it they would quiet down instantly.

The crew expressed a wish for revolvers, to protect themselves in case of a sudden attack in force, but the Spanish captain said the sight of these rusty old knives would have inspired more fear than a dozen revolvers, the bulk of the negroes not even knowing the use of a pistol and hence having no fear of it. I thought that story would do to "tell to the marines." The crew, fully armed with revolvers, would have been a formidable force and in case of a misunderstanding with the after-guards, would have held the balance of power. We carried our sheath-knives belted around the waist, which is customary with sailors, until our captain gave us a sensible hint to put them out of sight when among the negroes or the latter might take a notion to grab them.

The hatches had never been put on, the hold being open night and day. After we had been out four weeks some of them became so bold at night that they would disregard the orders of the kroomen and come to the hatchway. A slap over the head with the flat side of the sword, given by the man on watch, was something they could better understand and it never failed to be followed by an instant disappearance on the part of the offender.

One morning a krooman reported to the Spanish captain a negro who had resisted his authority during the night. The offender was hustled upon deck, stretched out at full length, face downward, and tied to the ring-bolts. One of the kroomen now commenced lashing the poor creature over the back and when he flagged another took his place and renewed the beating. The negro was grit to the bone and made not the slightest outcry. Not until life was almost extinct did the Spaniard order him released. It was the latter's wish to draw blood, but the negro's hide was so tough it could not be done by thrashing.

There was a large and corpulent woman in the steerage whom the sailors called "Miss Porpoise" and, judging by the grin that was always on her countenance, she seemed to be happy and contented with her present quarters. One day she appeared anxious to look over the rail and to gratify her desire some one gave her permission to do so. I was suddenly startled by the shrill cries of a female and on looking aft I saw the Spaniard lambasting "Miss Porpoise." He was holding her by the wool with his left hand and she was bawling at a tremendous rate. After he had given her a sound thrashing a nail was driven into one of the beams in the steerage, when a piece of ordinary twine was tied around Miss Porpoise's arm and secured to the nail. He called to an interpreter and told him something which, on being translated, had a pacifying effect on "Miss Porpoise's" nerves, for her bawling at once ceased and she tried to avoid his eye.

It afterward transpired that this excitement was caused by "Miss Porpoise" trying to jump overboard. She nearly succeeded, as her body was half-way over the rail before the Spaniard saw her, and he was just in time to seize her legs and haul her back. We watched her after this, but she never broke the twine by which her arm was held. It was not a very secure way of putting her in irons but it nevertheless answered the purpose.

For several weeks after leaving the African coast, in consequence of light winds and calms, the vessel made but a poor run, so that there was every prospect of a long passage. About this time the allowance of water was reduced. There was no change made in the allowance of food, for we had an ample stock on board. On the contrary, the negroes were fed better, a certain quantity of pork and beef being given them twice a week. Good care and plenty to eat made a marked improvement in their appearance, at which the Spanish captain was proportionately pleased. A fine healthy negro would bring a much higher price than a puny, sickly one; therefore, to feed them well and take good care of them meant an increase of doubloons to the owners. Up to this period we had lost but about twenty and this mortality was caused principally by dysentery. When the wind was light during the day the maindeck awning was spread and the negroes in the hold were allowed to come up and stretch their limbs. This was a great relief from the intense heat and foul air of the hold and was no doubt the cause of saving a number of lives.

One afternoon the weather clouded up and by six o'clock it rained hard. We had made preparations to catch all the water we could by spreading the awning, leaving the crowfoot-halyards slack so it would settle down in the centre. The rain continued off and on until midnight by which time some eight or nine large casks had been filled. This stroke of good luck was thoroughly appreciated.

Among the ship's stores, stowed aft in the lazaret, were five or six barrels of New England rum. The sailors all knew of its being there; for, at the time we were breaking out the stores, two or three barrels had been unearthed and some of them had got a taste by sucking it through a straw when the officers' backs were turned. When the negroes were taken on board, the crew supposed an allowance of grog would be a sure thing for the balance of the voyage. In this they were mistaken for not a smell did they get except what they had stolen. The old man appropriated it all to himself and managed to get dead drunk every day by 4 P.M., after which he would retire to one of the spare boats on the poopdeck and sleep off the effects. He made this a regular business, leaving the ship in charge of the officers. The Spanish captain remonstrated with him and pointed out the bad example he was setting the crew. Arguments had no effect, however, for he continued to drink until the cargo was disposed of.

One afternoon an occurrence took place which came near resulting seriously. Just before arriving at the sleepy-drunk stage he always manifested a very ugly temper and usually relieved himself by cursing the men. During the earlier part of the afternoon mentioned the wind had died out and the ship was becalmed. The yards were squared and the courses hauled up to prevent chafing. The captain came on deck and gave orders to set the studding-sails. This was useless, as there was no wind and the officers told him so. He then began to swear at the officer of the deck and told him to go below, after which he bawled out to the men to reeve the gear. Having had plenty of work all the forenoon and scarcely any rest during the previous night, they were not in the humor for such unnecessary labor and, as they took the gear in hand to reeve, there was much audible growling. The captain had just rum enough in him to forget the kind of a voyage the ship was on and he cursed and threatened to trice up the first man he heard growl.

This was too much to take from him and the men threw the gear on deck and made a move toward him. Very opportunely for the old man the Spanish captain came on deck and took in the situation at a glance. Placing himself between the ladder that led to the poop and the men, he vehemently gesticulated and said, "No, no! Bad—very bad!" He called the officers and told them to tell the men not to do anything rash, for the captain was drunk and did not know what he was doing. It was some time before the men could be pacified and induced to go forward. I think the captain must have been sensible of his danger, for, drunk as he was, he had the prudence to go below instead of lying down in the boat as he had done on former occasions. This was a good lesson for him. He never again threatened to trice us up and his orders were not embellished with so many disgusting oaths as heretofore.

About this time the negroes were given their first bath. They were hustled upon deck and arranged in tiers, standing. The hose was now attached to the head-pump and a lively stream squirted over them. They laughed and chattered good-naturedly while receiving this ducking. After being confined in the hold all night the cool sea-water must have been very refreshing.

Nothing else of consequence transpired during this part of the voyage unless it was the appearance of a sail which was sighted from aloft one afternoon about five o'clock. As soon as the stranger could be made out from the deck the captain was anxious to determine the course she was steering. On a nearer approach it was evident that she was heading toward our ship. We did not, however, alter our course until we were absolutely certain that she would come close to us, for this running off caused too much loss of ground. But we had finally to do it or the stranger would soon have been within hailing distance.

About the seventh week of the voyage from the coast there was a fine breeze blowing and the ship was making splendid time. I began to soliloquize as follows: If this glorious wind holds on ten or twelve days longer we must make land somewhere. It is nearly time, too, that the negroes were disposed of, for it does not require a very bright pair of eyes to see that they have not quite so much fear of the white man as they had when brought on board. Latterly it has been a difficult matter to keep them quiet during the night and many a rap on the hatch has now to be given before they will pay attention and cease their noise. The kroomen, also, have become bolder and sometimes an order given to them has to be accompanied with a crack of the whip, so little inclination do they show to move.

On Monday afternoon the negroes were sent on deck, as orders had been given to fumigate the hold. We took small tin pots filled with tar and marline-spikes heated nearly red-hot and, spreading ourselves throughout the hold, we commenced operations by sticking the hot irons into the tar, when a dense smoke followed. This we continued to do until the smoke became suffocating and we had to return to the deck for air. The hatches were put on and not taken off for two hours. This tar-smoke sweetened and purified the atmosphere below completely. After the smoke was let out we found that the sickening odor, which had before been so strong, was completely eradicated.

It was a dangerous way to fumigate, I thought, for had the tar ignited when it boiled over the tin pots and was running down be-

Capture of the Slaver "El Almirante," Feb. 1, 1829, in the Bight of Benin, by H.M. Brig "Black Joke"

From a colored aquatint, after the painting by W. J. Huggins, in the Macpherson Collection

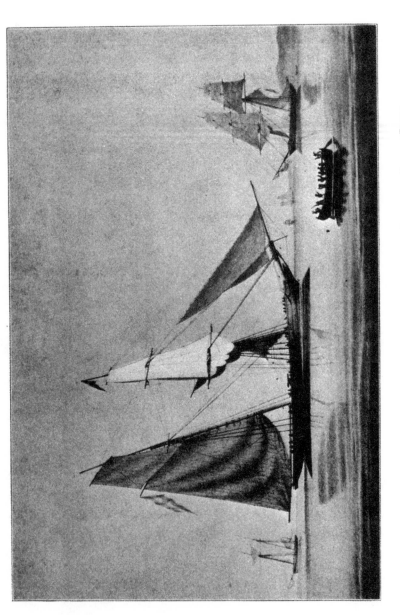

THE SLAVER "L'ANTONIO," WITH OTHER BLACK CRAFT, LYING IN BONNY RIVER

From a colored lithograph published in London, in 1841, in the Macpherson Collection

tween the casks and dunnage, it would have been difficult to save
the ship from destruction by fire. In that case the loss of life would
have been appalling; all the negroes would certainly have perished,
either by fire or water. No accident happened, however, and I think
all felt relieved when this necessary but dangerous duty was over.

On Wednesday morning of this same week one of the crew,
while on guard-duty, discovered that a part of the flooring, just
abaft the fore-hatch, had been taken out. Thinking that the negroes
were up to some mischief, he secreted himself forward of the hatch,
and, elevating his head enough to peer over the combing, awaited
developments. In a short time he saw a large negro crawl up to a
water-cask and try to get the bung out. He hammered around it
with his fist, in the same way we usually did with a mallet or
marline-spike, to loosen the bung and after getting it started removed it with his fingers. He then ran into the cask a thin stick, about
three feet in length and drawing it quickly out, caught the water
in the palm of his hand as it ran down. This he continued to do
until he became satisfied, when the stick was passed to another who
quenched his thirst in the same manner. Finally, the man watching
at the hatch concluded that this had been carried on long enough
and marking the fellow who had removed the bung, so as to be able
to identify him when the gratings were removed in the morning,
struck the hatch with his sword and frightened the negroes off. Before they were sent on deck he went below to find the culprit and
the stick. The man was easily found but the stick was not. It had,
no doubt, been hidden under the flooring, and it would have been a
big job to find it. The board over the cask had been returned to its
proper place and if they had not been caught in the act it would
never have been discovered.

After breakfast the affair was reported to the Spanish captain.
He caused all the kroomen stationed in the forward part of the
hold to be brought before him at the mast and by the use of his
interpreter endeavored to find out if they knew anything about it.
They were ignorant of the whole affair, not having seen or heard

anything of it. The Spaniard believed they lied and flew into a great passion and threatened to do all sorts of terrible things to them if they did not expose the guilty ones. No threats could intimidate any one of them sufficiently to make him turn informer; they were obdurate and he finally dismissed them by slashing out right and left with his whip.

The culprit was now brought before him when he gave orders to the kroomen to lash him to the ring-bolts in the deck. After securing the poor wretch so that it would be impossible for him to move a limb, the order was given to the kroomen to proceed to business. This they did by beating him with their whips, putting forth all their strength in delivering the blows. The punishment continued so long that I thought the man would have died under it; but his endurance was wonderful and he only uttered a few groans. When the beating was finally discontinued the Spaniard stooped down alongside of him and taking a razor out of his pocket, opened it and cut long, straight gashes in the flesh. Afterward he took a flat piece of wood, resembling a ruler, and beat gently all around the wounds which had the effect of making them bleed freely. Having accomplished this he ordered the "shikko" to get a pot full of brine out of the harness cask and apply it to the bleeding wounds. When this was done the poor negro could suppress his anguish no longer and groaned aloud. After being kept in this awful agony for ten minutes he was released from the ring-bolts and put in double irons.

The captain of the ship and all the crew witnessed this inhuman punishment and I will give our own commander credit for having more heart than the Spaniard for he told him he was too severe on the negro. The crew were all bitterly incensed against the "d— Dago," as they called him, and gave vent to their feelings by calling him "a bloody cannibal" and expressing a desire to serve him the same way to see how he would like it.

This was the only negro punished in this manner. I think if it had been attempted again the captain would have interfered and if he had not the men would have prevented it. The unfortunate victim of the Spaniard's cruelty did not recover while on board and was still very sick when landed.

When the negroes were again watered we received orders to give them a full allowance—about a quart. Perhaps the captains were afraid thirst would make them desperate at night and thought it would be better to allow them a little more water than to have them steal it.

One afternoon the captain called for "Chips" and me and instructed us to rig a stage over the stern and scrape off the ship's name, adding that we were "now bloody pirates and should sail without a name."

Although the wind had been light during the day and the sea was smooth, yet, after getting on the stage, we found we had a difficult and dangerous task to perform. The swell was quite heavy and as it struck the vessel's stern it lifted it high out of the water. When the wave reached the bow the motion was reversed. This is what sailors call "kicking."

The stage was let down too far, which nearly cost us our lives; for at the first moment the vessel lifted it swung in under the counter and we had barely time to give it a swing out when the stern dropped. Had we lost one second's time in doing this we should have been smashed as flat as a pancake. As it was we received a ducking and it required all our strength to hold on and save ourselves from being washed away. After raising the stage we finally succeeded in scraping off the name. We were now outlaws and would be a prize for any vessel strong enough to capture us. The ship might be taken but the captain swore that the negroes never should. In case of such an emergency he would "walk them all overboard and send them to hell!"

The voyage, however, was soon to be ended, for the fine winds we had experienced during the past two weeks had brought us near to the Island of Cuba. Every thread of canvas that the ship could carry had been spread, which made her jump through the water like a racehorse. My whole thoughts were centered on this breeze and if it moderated a little, down went my spirits; but if it increased, up they would go.

Many a day when the negroes were on deck I have thought how easy a matter it would be for them to overpower us and send all hands to Davy Jones. What a great difference between them and the Chinese coolies! One-third as many coolies would have long since despatched us all had they been allowed on deck without being ironed as the negroes were. The racks in the steerage were full of spare harpoons and lances and they would have been formidable weapons in the hands of an enemy. Ordinary common sense on the captain's part should have taught him the necessity of having them removed, in the first place, to some part of the ship less accessible to the blacks. This was not done, however, until after they had stared the negroes in the face for five weeks and the kroomen were noticing them more than was thought good for our safety.

Sunday morning dawned bright and clear with the wind still fair and blowing fresh. It was time that the ship was made to look more like a merchantman for we were now getting in the track of West Indian vessels. It was by no means improbable that the unusual appearance of a whaler in these waters would arouse suspicion and the commander of some man-of-war might be notified of the fact and have a desire to investigate us. The ship was painted black with the exception of a narrow yellow ribbon running around the hull. This was painted out but the appearance of the vessel was not much altered. Two of the whale-boats were taken in on deck and the davits unshipped and hove overboard. We had now four boats on deck, taking up considerable room; if the ship had been supplied with gallows or bearers, two of them could have been put out of the way. As they were a nuisance on deck and interfered with the working of the ship, the captain ordered them to be scuttled and thrown overboard. A large number of harpoons and lances, a fine chest of carpenter's and cooper's tools and a great many other things were also sent after them. The captain gave no reason for this wholesale destruction of the ship's property, probably considering it no one's business.

On Monday there was a strong breeze and the royals had to be furled. The ship being so crank, on account of insufficient ballast, the quantity of canvas that was carried careened her to such extent that on leaning over the weather-side one could almost see the keel. This made it very uncomfortable for the negroes in the hold and at every heavy lurch they would fly to leeward faster than was safe or pleasant. The stiff breeze had also raised quite a heavy sea which made a large number sick. This diminished their appetites and when the food was served out in the afternoon very few of them would touch it. The Spanish captain swore that they should eat, anyhow, since the trouble had been taken to cook the food; and he made the poor darkies swallow it or take a lambasting.

The captain expected to make land late this afternoon or the next morning. The lookouts were doubled and instructions given to watch for high land and a small craft. I think it was about noon, or a little later, when the man on the lookout forward suddenly sung out—"Land-ho!" The captain happened to be on deck and he at once went aloft where he remained for some time. On his return he engaged the Spaniard in conversation. The ship's course was not altered and we rapidly lessened our distance from the shore.

Shortly after this the cry of "Sail-ho!" from aloft startled us. We anxiously watched the approach of the stranger, which we soon made out to be a small sloop standing for us. Both of the captains watched her movements intently. The strong breeze soon brought her close to us, when our fore-royal halyards were let go. As the yard settled down it was answered by the slacking down of her peak. This seemed to dispel all doubt in the minds of the two captains and the ship was hove to immediately. The peak of the sloop's mainsail was hoisted when she came within hailing distance and luffed up in the wind. The Spanish captain now hailed her in his own language and after a short conversation with the sloop's skipper we were ordered to man the starboard boat. This was promptly done and we lowered her and pulled alongside of the sloop. Her skipper jumped in and we brought him to the ship. He remained some time in conversation with our captain, the Spaniard in the meantime writing a letter. This he gave to his visitor, together with some verbal instructions, after which we carried the latter back to his sloop. As soon as we had shoved clear of his vessel's side he at once made sail and stood in for the land.

After the boat was hoisted we filled away the main-topsail and stood off shore. This disappointed all hands for we expected that the negroes were to be landed and to now see her head turned seaward was a great disappointment. It afterwards transpired that the skipper of the sloop had been on the lookout for us for some time, to deliver instructions. We also learned that arrangements had to be made to send out a couple of small craft to receive our cargo. These vessels were to lay outside of the cruising ground of the men-of-war that patrolled this part of the coast. We were to lay off shore, as much out of danger as possible, until Saturday morning, by which time we must come back to the position we had left.

Word had been passed to feed the negroes in the hold for it was too late to have them sent on deck; besides, it would not be prudent to have too many of them in sight while the ship was on such dangerous ground. Fortunately the cook had not neglected to have their food prepared so there was no delay on that score.

I had the wheel at this time and there was not another person on deck with me except the ship's cook. The wind continued to increase and gradually hauled to the northward so far that I could not keep the ship on her compass-course without the sails lifting. I bawled out three or four times to the cook, but he must have been making such a noise with his pots and kettles that no human voice from aft could reach him. I had her off three or four points when the wind, in a sudden squall, veered nearly north and knocked her sails almost aback. I quickly hove up the helm and the ship, not having had time to lose all way, slowly fell off and the sails filled. The wind was so strong that she careened until the lee-rail was under

water. The waves now rushed down the hatchways, washing the
negroes, flooring, and everything movable down to leeward and
creating an intense excitement among all hands. A few minutes afterward the captain and crew crawled upon deck, when the ship was
at once put under close-reef and hove-to. It now blew a strong
"norther."

The gale lasted until sundown the next day, after which it moderated enough to set the top-gallant sails. I was glad to see it subside
for the sake of the poor negroes, who suffered greatly from the
pitching and rolling of the vessel and the want of pure air. The
hatch-hoods had to be kept on during the gale to prevent the water
from going below and this materially interfered with the ventilation
of the hold. The following day we had pleasant weather and when
the ship was on her course the wind was about abeam. As we had
been driven off shore a long distance, it was necessary to set all sail
to enable us to reach the rendezvous by the appointed time, which
was the next morning.

The crew joked among themselves about the ludicrous condition
of things generally in the hold when the gale first struck the ship.
It seems that they had finished the feeding and the water-tubs had
been filled and placed in convenient locations for serving out, when
suddenly, and without any warning, they were pitched head-over-
heels to leeward and nearly mashed by the piles of negroes that
tumbled on top of them. The water-tubs, too, went flying in the
same direction, spilling out their contents and barking a good many
shins. It was some time before the sailors could extricate themselves
from under the negroes, fright so completely paralyzing the darkies
that they were incapable of moving a limb.

Frank, my chum, told me that the "niggers turned as white as
chalk." I make a little allowance, however, for his excited imagination. The captain fared no better than the common sailors, for
he was knocked down and a score of negroes tumbled on top of
him. He afterward observed that they smelled "worse than rotten
codfish" and the effluvia was harder to stand than all their weight.

During the afternoon the last porker, out of a dozen taken on board before we left America, was slaughtered and a "whack" sent forward in the shape of a sea-pie. We had quite an affection for this little pig and felt sorry when he was so cruelly slain. After the cargo was shipped he was released from his pen and allowed to roam about the main-deck. Being thus brought in contact with so many men he became very tame and had "acquired considerable knowledge," as the cook expressed it. Some of the sailors taught him a number of tricks the best of which was jumping through a hoop. This the porker became expert at and could accomplish his feat without touching a leg to the hoop. They also taught him to come when whistled for. He was considered a member of the starboard watch for when that watch was called he was sure to turn out from under the windlass and snoop around on deck until they went below again, at eight bells. When the sea-pie came forward we did justice to his remains thus proving that our love for him was strong, —even in death.

All hands voluntarily remained on deck all night and took lookouts below and aloft, for we were again getting close to the island and in the track of vessels. No light was allowed in the cabin and the binnacle was covered over with a canvas hood—a small hole only being left open through which the man at the wheel could see the compass.

For some reason the negroes became very much excited and made a great deal of noise and all the threats of the Spaniard had no effect in quieting them. Had any vessel passed near us I think the people on board would have been astonished at hearing such a bedlam of sounds. Two or three lights were reported by the men on lookout but we easily avoided them.

The night finally came to an end as even the longest one must and we prepared to give the negroes the last breakfast they would ever take on board. Orders were given to consume as little time as possible in feeding them and in obedience to these instructions we were not over-particular and hurried matters all that we could. In consideration of its being the last meal we gave them a blow-out on water by allowing every one all he could drink. This meal was served in the hold, not a negro being allowed to put his head on deck, the kroomen not excepted. We then swallowed a hasty breakfast ourselves, after which a stage was rigged to put over the side. This was afterward used in transferring the negroes. During all this time the lookouts had continued their vigilance but no sign of any small vessels could be seen on any part of the horizon. At four bells (ten o'clock) land was made out from the foretop-gallant yard. The captain now considered the ship close enough in and had her hove-to.

A little before twelve o'clock a sail was reported inshore and to the westward of our ship and a few minutes later another one was made out in about the same position. The captain now took the spyglass and went aloft where he remained fully an hour watching the strangers. During the time we made out the two vessels to be schooners.

When the captain returned to the deck the Spaniard accosted him, and advised that the ship should be filled-away at once and her course shaped for the schooners as near as the wind would permit. The captain was inclined to keep the ship where she was until a nearer approach of the strangers would enable him to see that everything was all right but the Spaniard scouted his fears and said even if they were not the vessels we expected we would have ample time to get out of their way. The captain then yielded the point and had the yards braced up sharp and the vessel hauled to the wind. When sharp on the wind we were only a point to leeward of the schooners. The wind was slowly moderating and it was necessary that we should make our ship do her best to lessen the distance from the schooners before it died out and left us becalmed in a dangerous place.

By two o'clock they were near enough to signal, when the fore-royal yard was settled down and a few minutes later we hauled down the flying-jib. Every eye was now intently watching them and if our signals should not be answered, adieu to our hopes for to-day. After being kept in suspense for ten or fifteen minutes the welcome answer was made. It was received with three rousing cheers which fairly made the old ship tremble.

It being now certain that schooners were our expected allies, orders were given to clear up the decks and get everything ready for transferring the negroes. I was glad there was something to do for it was a relief to have my thoughts diverted from the schooners for, while watching them, it did seem that an eternity of time must elapse before they could reach us. Lines were placed on both sides of the ship, fore and aft, to be in readiness for heaving when they approached near enough.

After an hour and a half had passed the schooners were quite close to us and the order was given to take in all light sails and clew-up the foresail and mainsail, after which the main-topsail was braced aback. By this time one of them had come within hailing distance, when the Spaniard challenged her and received a satisfactory response.

"Stand by the lines to lu'ard!" sung out the captain.

She now rounded-to on our lee, when a line was thrown to her. It fell short but this blunder was repaired by one of the schooner's crew throwing a line to us which was caught and the end passed forward to be made fast so she could be hauled up to the waist. Before it could be secured the other schooner luffed-to under our stern and hove a line to her consort which was caught and made fast. "Dick of the Mizzen" had now secured the first line and we sung out to the schooner's men to haul in. Hardly had a fair strain been put on it, and the men were lying back for another good pull, when, to our great disgust, Dick's granny-knot slipped and the end went overboard. Before another line could be thrown to them the schooner dropped astern.

Dick now got a cursing from all hands and the mate was so exasperated that he gave him three or four vigorous kicks and warned the poor fellow to keep his thick head out of his sight or he would be the death of him.

"Better luck next time!" sung out the captain. "Five or six men stand by the lines and the rest get the stage over the side."

This was promptly done and ladders were also put down the hatchways for the negroes to mount when the order should be given. We lost considerable time before we again had the schooners alongside. This time a more competent person made fast the line. One of them was then hauled under the stage when word was passed for three or four of the men to go below and start the negroes up the ladders. Others were stationed in the waist to assist them over on to the stage. A large valise was now passed from the schooner to the ship and taken charge of by our captain. It was filled with doubloons, I afterward learned.

As fast as the negroes reached the deck they were given a crack with the whip to make them move more quickly and then shoved over the side on the stage, from which they had to jump to the schooner's deck. It took an hour to clear out the hold and then came the women's turn. I thought it would be difficult to make them jump from the stage; but they did not seem to mind it and succeeded very well.

"Good-bye, Miss Plum Duff," said George, giving that lady a slap as she went over the side. "I'll never see your like again."

"Good-bye, Desdemony," said "Dick of the Mizzen." "Won't you leave me a lock of your hair?" Dick had not strictly obeyed the mate's order to keep his thick head out of sight.

Many such remarks were made by the men as the women passed over the side and as they were successfully landed on the schooner's deck a loud "well-done" saluted them. The kroomen were the last to leave and as they passed over they were given tobacco and old clothes. Every negro being reported out of the ship, the order was given to cast off the lines and fill-away.

While we had been engaged unloading the negroes, the other schooner had hauled alongside her mate and taken on board about one-half of them. Both vessels were filled with negroes and the problem how to prevent their woolly heads from being seen by a passing vessel, should one get near enough, I left for the Spaniard to solve.

Just as we braced up, the Spaniard sung out from the schooner's deck for us to send him some hardtack. The captain ordered four barrels thrown overboard, taking an oath that he wouldn't lower a boat for the devil himself! He perhaps thought hardtack soaked in salt-water would do the darkies no harm.

Sail was made on the schooners and their bows pointed toward the land. We also put every rag of canvas that would draw on our ship. Our progress was slow, however, the wind being hardly strong enough to keep the sails full. The captain gave orders to throw the kids overboard and after this job was done he wanted the pine flooring in the hold taken up and piled aft. The mate said it was getting too dark below to work and it had better be left until morning. This was decided on and I went forward to the top-gallant forecastle and watched the receding schooners until the shadows of night enveloped them. Sometime later, looking in on deck, I saw the men seated around the try-pots eating their supper.

"Well, boys," said George, the cook, who had come forward to pick up some chips the cooper had left after preparing the last breakfast for the negroes, "we have been nearly six months on a slaver."

"We ain't out of the slaver yet," said someone.

"It don't make any difference. We are now on a legal merchant-man or a whaler," replied George.

"That's so, George," spoke up Frank; "but it would puzzle the devil to tell which one of the two."

The ship was run to Campeachy, Yucatan, and anchored on the banks off that port. Prior to this we had thrown overboard all the pine flooring that had been used during the passage from Africa, after which chloride of lime was generously sprinkled throughout the hold. No amount of this disinfectant had the effect of totally eradicating the peculiar odor that infected the hold and we finally decided that nothing but fire could purify it perfectly.

The crew would no longer remain by the ship, although the captain was urgent for them to do so, but went on shore and secured board in the city of Campeachy. They behaved as most sailors do when they have any cash in their pockets and as they had been liberally paid in Spanish doubloons, they fairly "took the roof off the town."

After being in Campeachy about three weeks we embarked in a Mexican schooner for New Orleans, where we arrived in January, 1861. The most intense excitement prevailed in New Orleans at the time, and I had doubts of being able to get north, should my departure be delayed. I therefore came at once, by rail, to New York. Shortly after I made a voyage to China and on my return to America I entered the navy as a volunteer officer, where I remained until after the close of the Rebellion.

NOTE.—The ship *Thomas Watson* was built at Baltimore, Maryland, in 1848, and measured 348 tons. In 1858 she carried a New York registry with J. A. Machado, owner or consignor, and Captain Elliott, master. In 1861 she was recorded as owned in Russia and Captains Higginson and Allen, were masters. She is said to have been the first American vessel on which Confederate colors were hoisted in England and this was reported to have occurred while the ship lay in the dock at Liverpool. After a short career as a blockade runner, she met her fate on Stony Reef, near Charleston, South Carolina. While attempting to get into the harbor she was chased by the blockading cruisers and ran on the reef. Her cargo was made up of salt, blankets, flannels and a few other things and on the 15th of October, 1861, she was burned to the water's edge while lying aground on the reef.

CHAPTER XVII

THE LAST VOYAGE OF AN AMERICAN SLAVER

IN THE year 1850 there died in New Orleans, a slave owner, John McDonogh, who, after making bequests to the cities of New Orleans and Baltimore for educational purposes, provided that his slaves should be given their freedom after a certain number of years, conditional upon their emigration to Liberia. The period having elapsed in the spring of 1859, the commissioners in charge of the estate began to look about for some vessel in which the freed slaves might be sent to the negro republic on the African coast. At first it was proposed to ship them on board the sailing-packet that left Baltimore each spring, with emigrants and supplies, returning later in the year with a cargo of the products of the colony: but about that time it was learned that the ship *Rebecca,* then lying at the government wharf in New Orleans, proposed sailing for the West Coast of Africa about the first of May and could supply suitable accommodations for the freed slaves and their baggage, and negotiations were soon concluded. At the last moment it was decided by the commissioners to send a doctor with them and application was hurriedly made to Dr. Howard Smith, a professor at the medical school, who recommended a young student, George Howe of Natchez, Mississippi, who had just completed his course of lectures.

It was nine o'clock on the morning of the day the *Rebecca* was to sail, when Doctor Smith found the young student at the gates of the Charity Hospital and without replying to his greeting, said: "George, how would you like to go to the coast of Africa?" Howe at once replied, "First rate, doctor." "How soon can you get ready?" Believing him to be joking, Howe said: "I am ready now." Taking him at his word, the doctor then explained the situation and the necessity for haste and when he had finished the young man jumped into the doctor's buggy and was soon in the office of the McDonogh commissioners, where he signed an agreement to make the voyage as medical officer in charge of the freed slaves.*

In the office some of the gentlemen indulged in pleasant jokes about "wool and ivory," and one of them wrote a letter to the surgeon of the United States man-of-war *Vincennes*, stationed on the coast of Africa, saying, "This is a letter of introduction and may be of use to you." Howe was so engrossed with the idea of going to Africa that he did not attach any special significance to the jokes and going to his lodgings packed his books and clothing.

He was on board the ship at twelve o'clock and on presenting himself to the captain, found that he appeared annoyed, but soon asked him to the cabin and ordered the steward to prepare a room. Going upon deck, Howe saw a motley group of negroes, mulattoes, quadroons, men, women, and children of all ages, numbering forty-three, busily engaged in getting their baggage on board. Many of them were not anxious to go, and seemed much disheartened at the idea of leaving home. Just then several of the commissioners arrived with their wives, who were known to the negroes, and after a while, they were successful in imparting new courage and cheerful faces to the immigrants.

The ship left the wharf at four o'clock in the evening. Early next morning, they were at the mouth of the river and in another hour on the open sea. A pleasant southerly breeze drove the ship along at about eight miles an hour and dinner being called, Howe found at the captain's table, Captain C——, a naturalized Scotch-Englishman, the first mate, Mr. T——, a Long Islander, and two Spanish gentlemen speaking very little English. An introduction followed, one Spanish gentleman explaining that they were on their way to a trading point on the African coast, representing a commercial house in Havana, and that having waited a long while unsuccessfully for an opportunity to get there, he had taken passage on this vessel as far as its voyage extended.

---

* For a full account of this voyage, *see* "The Last Slave-Ship," by George Howe, M.D., in *Scribner's Magazine*, July, 1890.

VIEW OF NEW ORLEANS, LOUISIANA, FROM ABOVE THE MIDDLE FERRY

From a colored aquatint, published in 1841, after a painting by William J. Bennett, in the Macpherson Collection

A VIEW OF FREETOWN, SIERRA LEONE

From a colored aquatint, published Sept. 14, 1837, after the painting by W. J. Huggins, in the Macpherson Collection

Dinner over, the mate remained in the cabin and the other officers came to the table, and were introduced. "This is Doctor Saw-
bones; I am mate; here is the second mate; there is the carpenter.
Now, how is it that you were engaged at the last moment to come
with us?" After Howe had explained all he knew about it, the
mate said: "It would have been better for you to have known something about the ship and her destination before you accepted." This
recalled the jokes of the commissioners and set the young doctor
thinking and that night during the mate's watch, he approached him
and, after a few remarks about the weather, said: "Mr. T——, I did
not quite understand your remark at dinner; if you can do so, please
explain." After a long silence, he replied: "Well, you will find it
out sooner or later, and I do not know that I am violating any confidence in telling you now, *this ship is a Slaver.* Yes: that is just
what she is, and belongs to a company of Spaniards who are represented here by the eldest of the Spanish passengers, who will be
the captain at the proper time; the other Spaniard will be his mate.
They purchased this ship two months ago, and have had all sorts
of difficulties ever since with the custom-house. She sails under the
American flag, and is supposed to be owned by a commission house
in New Orleans, who are the agents there of the Spanish company.
They wanted to obtain papers permitting the ship to go to the
African coast; just now everything destined there is regarded with
suspicion and the Spaniards wanted to go in ballast to seek a cargo
of palm-oil, camwood, and any other merchandise offering. The
custom-house authorities declined, for various reasons, to issue the
papers. In the meantime, the ship had been loaded with empty
casks and a quantity of staves in the rough from which to manufacture other casks, if necessary. The question of getting sufficient
supplies of food aboard was a very delicate one, for food could not
profitably be carried as freight to that locality, and it was not required in barter. Then the Spaniards proposed to equip her as a
whaling-ship, with her whaling-ground from Bermuda to the Cape
of Good Hope. This would permit her occasionally to call on the

African coast for water and fresh food-supplies, yet would require a much longer period to complete the trip. Just at this time the commission house heard of the purpose of the McDonogh commissioners to send the ex-slaves, via Baltimore, to Liberia. After considering the matter it was determined to offer this ship as a means of transportation at a very moderate price. If they had dared to do so, they would have been willing to pay a handsome premium. The offer was accepted and the date fixed. The Spaniards now had a legitimate cargo for the African coast, and easily procured the necessary papers for a trading point on the Congo River, stopping at Liberia on the voyage out. I can also tell you that your presence here is not pleasant for Captain C——, for he had about determined to run down on the south side of Cuba with these negroes, leave them at a place he knows of, and continue on the voyage. Now, this cannot be done, unless you come into the arrangement; but I do not think he will say anything to you about it. You are a stranger and we are constantly in sight of and speaking vessels, and it would be easy for you to say a few words which might spoil the entire expedition."

Next morning early, as the captain and the doctor were taking coffee on deck, in the course of general conversation, the captain remarked: "What a valuable lot of negroes these are; all the men have some trade or vocation which makes them most desirable on any plantation. The women are all experienced in their duties; they would bring a round sum in Cuba; and Cuba is very near, and I know where they could be landed without much risk."

The doctor at once replied: "Captain, these negroes must be landed at their destination in Africa, and as long as I can, I will not permit any change of programme."

As if to disarm any suspicion, the captain said: "Of course, they must be landed in Liberia, I was only regretting that so much money is just thrown away."

During the mate's watch which followed, he asked the doctor what the captain had said, for on his return to the cabin there had been a long and stormy conversation with the Spanish gentleman, who would not be persuaded that there was very little risk in landing the negroes in Cuba, whether the doctor consented or not. On learning the details of the conversation between the captain and the doctor, the mate replied: "Well, that matter is now decided, for we are sailing southeast, instead of southwest, and that means we will not stop at Cuba this part of the trip."

"Now," said he, "this is my second voyage of this kind; the first was from New York to Africa and Brazil, and as slavery will probably be abolished in Brazil, and coolies are getting cheaper than negroes in Cuba, this is probably the last slave ship; and if we are successful, we will land the last cargo of slaves. To begin, you must understand that there are necessary one person as head manager, and three agents, each one with an assistant to replace the principal in case of accident, sickness or death. The head resides in Havana. One agent, with his assistant, the Spanish captain and his friend, on board with us, went to the United States to purchase the fastest sailing-vessel that money could buy, and he found, in New Orleans, the Baltimore clipper ship *Rebecca*, near five hundred and fifty tons, carrying sky-sails, studding-sails to royal yards, and stay-sails to royals, with a record of fourteen knots to windward, sailing inside of four points from the wind. She was fitted out with new sails, cordage, extra spars and yards, and a large supply of material with which to make other sails at sea, and to replace uncertain stays, running rigging, etc. The custom-house officers seemed to be suspicious of her and watched everything connected with the ship very closely. Just at this time the offer to the McDonogh commissioners was made to take the negroes as passengers and arrangements were completed. Now began the purchase, in large quantities, of rice, white beans, pork and biscuit, which were ostensibly for our passengers. With a long hose, all the casks were filled with water from an opening below the water-line in the ship's bow, a supply of lumber was obtained, and bunks constructed between decks the whole length of the ship's hold, and for several times the number of passengers expected; a large cooking furnace was also built on deck. Another agent and his assistant sailed some months ago for the coast of Africa, and have purchased and contracted to carry on shares as many negroes as can be stowed on board. The place where they are to meet is known on board only to the Spaniards; another agent and his assistant are established as fishermen on an unfrequented island on the south side of Cuba, I know that much. There, with a companion or two, they fish, for the markets, so as to require a regular camp and a small vessel. They will be ready, when we arrive, to inform us when and where to land the cargo. The head, in Havana, keeps everything in working order, and it is his particular business to fee the customs officials and keep them away from where they are not wanted. One ounce of gold, seventeen dollars, per head, is the fee he pays to the officials for every negro landed, who divide among themselves, according to previous arrangements."

Life on board was a very pleasant one, as our ship was splendidly provisioned with every delicacy necessary to our comfort; and with beautiful weather, the run in the Gulf Stream was full of interest. Each day experiments were made, by changing the size and character of sails, to develop the greatest speed. All the masts were examined and put to their utmost strain; new stays and preventer-stays were added until it was no longer doubtful about the masts being able to support any strain. The ship could easily make three hundred and twenty to three hundred and forty miles daily, running as close to windward as she could sail. Being in the southeast trades, she would run twelve hours on east-north-east tack and twelve hours on the south by west tack, and in the twenty-four hours' run make a net gain, east, of thirty miles.

The negroes soon became accustomed to the motion of the vessel, but the length of the voyage tired them, and they repeatedly said that when they got ready to return to Louisiana they would walk around by land, as they had had enough of sailing. To keep them employed, the women were engaged to mend and launder the officers' clothing; and as their utensils were all stowed away in the lower hold, it was necessary to extemporize others. The washing and drying were easily accomplished, but the ironing was done by putting hot coals in a tin bucket and rubbing that over the pieces—with not much of a success, however.

On July 1, 1859, there was a terrible storm of wind and rain, and the sea was very rough. Cape Palmas was in sight; Monrovia, the capital of Liberia, being situated on it. The mist obscured all objects near the water and when it cleared, a small steamer hove in sight and fired a blank shot for the *Rebecca* to come to. She hoisted the American flag and sailed on, followed by the steamer, which proved to be the English cruiser *Viper*, which approached as near as could be safely done and sent an officer on board. He politely stated his mission and was invited below, where the ship's papers were produced and shown him, as an act of courtesy—for the ship was now within the limits of the Liberian Government. The officer pleasantly observed that he knew the vessel as soon as it was in sight and with other cruisers had been on the lookout for her for some time; that his government, by the last mail steamer to St. Paul de Loanda, had notified the cruisers that the ship *Rebecca* was suspected. She had been described with such accuracy that there could be no mistake. He thought she then had an outward bound cargo and was much chagrined to find that it was inward bound and at its destination. After a short stay he left and steamed away to the south.

A long canoe, manned by four apparently naked negroes, then came out from the shore, through a very rough sea but without much apparent effort. Coming alongside, they climbed over the rail and jumped down among the passengers. They were naked, except for a piece of cloth tied around the loins, fine specimens of muscular development, short and stout, tattooed down the forehead to the end of the nose and on the cheeks with a dark-blue pigment. They were kroomen, a tribe dispersed along the coast, employed by ships to load or obtain water, or as pilots—and seldom exported. A wail as from Hades arose from the passengers; who were filled with consternation and terror at sight of the kroomen, and the sailors, taking advantage of the situation, went among the poor negroes and told them it was now time for them to take off their store clothes and get ready to go ashore—just like these people whom they had come to live with.

The ship was anchored at a place assigned by the kroomen and a message was sent ashore, but a storm delayed the arrival of an official until the next evening. His appearance quieted the negroes like oil on troubled waters. This agent was an enthusiast and soon gave them to understand that the garden of Eden was an ill-conditioned suburb compared to Monrovia.

July 4th was observed as a "fete" day and the officers of the ship were invited to dine with the President of the Republic and his ministers.

That evening, the missionary, the only white man living in the negro republic, took the doctor aside and told him there was considerable doubt as to the character of the *Rebecca*, and on reaching the ship, he told the officers they were suspected. A council was held at once and arrangements were made for the landing next day of the passengers and their effects. The English gunboat had just returned to Monrovia and was anchored but a short distance from the ship and her company was not desired longer than possible.

Next morning a fleet of sloops, canoes, and yawls came alongside early. The Spanish captain then told the doctor he could go with the vessel as far as the Congo River, where he might meet the mail steamer, and this offer he accepted. By noon the passengers and their effects were landed and the captain had returned with ship's papers, etc. The anchor was hoisted and a southerly course was made. The English cruiser at once followed, but as the *Rebecca* sailed twelve miles to his eight, before dark the Englishman was out of sight.

The Spanish captain now appeared on deck, a short, swarthy, black-whiskered man, with a cold, determined look, dressed in open shirt with a large silk handkerchief around his neck, white trousers, with a large red sash wrapped several times around his waist, a wide soft hat—a typical bandit. His assistant followed in almost similar costume and went forward and rang the ship's bell; the crew was called to the afterdeck, where the Spanish Captain A—— addressed them, in Spanish and English:

"Men, I am now the captain of this ship; this is my first mate," introducing his assistant; "the other subordinate officers are retained in their positions; the late captain and mate will be respected and advised with. The object of this voyage is a cargo of negroes to be purchased in Africa and landed in Cuba; the trip is full of peril, but if successful, full of money. If there is one of you who desires to go ashore, the ship will stop at a place where he can be safely landed and double wages to date given him."

All expressed themselves anxious to sign new articles and the wages were declared, if the voyage was successful, to be: For the American captain and first mate, $5000 each; second mate, $3500; carpenter, $3000; each sailor, $1500. The crew numbered twenty-three, all told, Turks, Greeks, Italians, Spaniards, Scotch, Yankees, and Danes.

It was plain that the Spanish captain did not trust Captain C——, and although they were courteous to each other, there was an entire absence of familiarity. The crew had the same feeling, and on one occasion while Captain C——, suspended in a bow-line over the stern, was inspecting the rudder hinges, the sailor at the wheel took out his knife and made a movement as if to sever the rope and drop the captain into the sea, but the doctor saw the movement and sharply called the Spanish captain's attention to the intended treachery.

The ship was some weeks in advance of the time for her intended arrival at a point agreed upon and so they sailed leisurely along until one day's sail from Mayumba, which is about two hundred miles north of the mouth of the Congo River. This portion of the coast was carefully guarded by the United States, English, Portuguese, and Spanish steam and sailing vessels, so that in approaching the coast there was considerable risk of being overhauled. Although the ship's papers were regular to a point on Congo River, yet the vessel might have been seized as suspicious and subjected to a return to Sierra Leone; and there, the matter fully investigated by a court organized to condemn and confiscate.

One day her movements were so regulated that, by sailing all night toward the coast, she would be, at daylight, fifteen miles distant. A yawl was then lowered and the Spanish captain with two sailors entered it, provided with two days' supplies and compass, and pulled away for land. The ship at once returned to sea with the understanding that forty days after she was to return to the place where the Spanish captain had expected to land. The Spanish mate was now in command and put to sea, four hundred miles from land, then sailed back one day, and the next returned to sea, for the entire period of forty days, never coming within two hundred miles of the shore. This was a very quiet and uneventful cruise; on two occasions only, were vessels sighted, which proved to be whalers and were given a wide berth.

At daylight, on the morning of the fortieth day, the ship had approached the coast near enough to see distinctly objects along the shore, but seeing no living creature, a man was sent aloft to be sure no vessel was in sight and the ship ran along the coast a few miles, until a negro was seen waving a large white flag, with a red cross its entire length and width; this was the signal and in a short time several negroes could be seen dragging the ship's yawl to the water from its place of concealment. In an hour, Captain A—— was again on board. It was plain that something had gone wrong; the agent and assistant had arrived much later than anticipated; both had been ill with African fever and were at a trading post on the Congo River, trying to get well. British cruisers had passed almost daily and could be expected at any moment. A council was again held in the cabin; the ship put to sea and it was determined that, as the ship's papers were regular and permitted going to the Congo River, she would proceed there at once and await events.

Light winds and strong currents delayed arrival at the trading station, which was about seventy miles from the mouth of the river. On reaching moorings a boat with two white men in it was found; one of whom was recognized as the agent's assistant, who informed the captain that the agent had died of consumption and African fever. His assistant was slowly convalescing and all trading operations had been suspended until his recovery or the arrival of the ship. His companion in the boat was a trader, at whose post he had found a home. The ship was now in for a delay of some time, as Spaniards move slowly, and so she was anchored about seventy-five yards from the shore on the left bank going up stream.

One day a man-of-war's long boat was seen coming up the river with an officer and ten men; they anchored almost immediately under the bow of the *Rebecca* and there they remained as long as the ship lay in the river. They were from the British gunboat *Tigris* and had spoken the *Vixen*,—another gunboat, which had gone farther south in search of the ship. The *Tigris* lay at the mouth of the river to intercept any attempt that might be made to leave with a cargo of negroes. Again the Spanish captain left the ship and was gone for many days. As it was necessary to replenish the supply of water, this was done with a hose through an opening in the bow, without the boat's crew knowing anything about it, although but a few feet distant.

One day a trader from the interior came aboard with the information that a disease declared to be smallpox had broken out in the barracoons where the negroes intended for the ship were being collected, and asked what could be done about it. The doctor had in his pocket-case a vaccine crust enveloped in adhesive plaster, and going with the Spaniard he journeyed two days up the river and was then carried southward, many miles into the interior, in a hammock slung between two poles with two men at each end of a pole. This route was circuitous to avoid the annoyance of other tribes who would levy heavy tribute. On reaching the barracoon, it was found to be an enclosure about three hundred feet square, fenced with bamboo about eight or nine feet high, a thatched roof running entirely around it and extending perhaps ten feet toward the center. It was a very frail structure to be used as a place of confinement, but sufficient to shelter from sun and rain and heavy dews, which were very cool. These barracoons were permitted in this locality by neighboring chiefs, because it enabled them easily to dispose of their captured slaves, and, being so far in the interior, they were safe from unauthorized visitors. A few negroes were found by the doctor to be suffering from smallpox, contracted from a tribe which frequented the coast, having intercourse with kroomen who had contracted in it St. Paul de Loanda. The infected were separated and new barracoons erected for them, as well as for the uninfected, in a distant locality. The old barracoons were burned and as far as the vaccine virus could be extended, it was used. From those vaccinated a new supply of virus was obtained. The disease was arrested there.*

Enough negroes had been purchased and contracted for to be transported on shares, to load the ship; and her departure was only a question of when they could be put on board without risk of smallpox reappearing among them. The negroes were then to be sent by easy marches to a place half a day's journey from the seacoast, where they would remain until the time agreed upon to move

* From the factors the doctor learned something about the manner in which the slave trade was carried on at that time. A trader, Portuguese always, procured consent from a head of a strong tribe to establish himself among them and paid liberally in presents for the privilege. Consent obtained, a barracoon was at once built and each member of the tribe was a self-constituted guardian to protect it; a scale of prices was agreed upon for negroes, according to age and sex, averaging two fathoms or four yards of calico, one flint-lock musket, one six-pound keg of coarse powder, one two-gallon keg of rum, some beads and brass wire; an English value of about eight dollars gold for each negro captured by this tribe from neighboring and weaker ones. There had been a lower rate of prices until within a few years when competition had slowly increased the rates.

to the coast. This last march to the coast was done at night, so that they had ample time to arrive before daylight. The ship was due at daylight and if she could not reach the coast at that hour, the whole business was to be postponed for a week and the negroes immediately returned to the half-day station, rested and cared for.

When the doctor returned to the ship on the river, he found that quiet preparations had been made to leave at a moment's notice; and fresh supplies of poultry and fruit had been taken aboard. The Spanish captain alone knew the locality where the negroes would be met and it was impossible for any sailor to have given information of value to the English in their boat under the bow of the ship.

Rather than risk African fever on the Congo River during a stay for an indefinite period, together with a spirit of adventure, considerable curiosity and a great confidence in his good luck, prompted the doctor to accept an invitation from the Spanish captain to remain with the ship. They learned that a Portuguese man-of-war had visited the mouth of the river and, finding the English gunboat *Vixen* there, had gone on to the north. This made things very much mixed; one cruiser south, one at the river's mouth and one north, and the Portuguese was the worst one of all. At that time, if a vessel was captured with negroes on board, she would be taken to Sierra Leone; the sailors being landed at or near the place of capture to look out for themselves. If the ship had a flag and could be identified, the officers were transferred at Sierra Leone to their respective governments for trial, the negroes sent ashore, an attempt at colonization made, and the ship sold and broken up; but if no nationality could be established, the officers were imprisoned for a term at Sierra Leone, with or without civil trials. If the Portuguese made a capture, every officer and sailor was sent to their penal settlements, and that was the last ever heard of them. The American government had the sailing man-of-war *Vincennes* stationed there.

One morning, early, about October 1, 1859, the anchor was raised and the ship sailed down the river. Her papers yet protected her, for she had ostensibly made an unsuccessful mercantile venture and was returning home. The English yawl was taken in tow and the officer in command was invited on board. It was a pleasant trip to the mouth of the river, which was reached in the afternoon. The gunboat steamed alongside to get her officer and learn the ship's destination and on being informed, "United States," someone remarked, "Oh, of course! perhaps!" The course during the evening and night was northwest towards the United States. This was to get off shore and ascertain the strength of the wind at that season and also to see what speed could be made. At daylight the course was shaped south and all hands were employed in removing every trace of name from bow, stern and smallboats. The white ports on the ship's side were painted out and every paper or scrap that could be found was, with the American flag, weighted and thrown overboard.

"Now!" said the captain, "we have no name, and no nationality; we are nobody and know nothing. If we are captured, every mouth must be sealed, in that only can we escape the severe penalties."

For four days and nights they cruised about, keeping the distance of nearly one hundred and fifty miles from land. On the afternoon of the fourth day, having taken accurate observations of the position at sea, the course was shaped for the coast; every light was extinguished but that of the binnacle, which was hooded so that the man at the wheel could see the compass and yet the light could not be seen; an extra watch was kept and at three o'clock next morning, the ship was within two miles of the shore in latitude 6° 10', South, previously agreed upon. So correct were the chronometers and the estimation of wind and current, that there was no error in the calculations; they could hear the roar of the breakers, but there was not light enough to see the shore. As it grew lighter they could see the low shoreline, which appeared to be broken into small hillocks of sand sparsely covered with a scrubby vegetation.

A number of small craft resembling oyster boats could be seen outside the breakers and after a satisfactory scrutiny of the horizon from the masthead, a signal, a large white flag with a red cross,

CAPTURE OF THE SPANISH SLAVER "MIDAS," JUNE 27, 1829, ON THE GREAT BAHAMA BANK,
BY H.M. SCHOONER "MONKEY"

From the colored aquatint, after the painting by W. J. Huggins, in the Macpherson Collection

THE HARBOR OF HAVANA, CUBA

From a drawing by J. W. Hill, made about 1850

was hoisted, and as it blew out it was answered from the shore. Soon the beach seemed to swarm with moving objects. A number of long, black objects left the shore and, when through the breakers, they stopped at the small craft outside and it could be seen that negroes were being transferred to the boats outside the breakers, from canoes, which ran out with from four to six in each. As the sloops were filled they sailed for the ship and, ladders having been arranged, the negroes were soon coming over the ship's side; as each one reached the deck he was given a biscuit and sent below. The sloops soon were flying to and fro and a great number of negroes were already on board at 2 P.M., when the lookout at the masthead shouted: "Sail ho! away to the southward."

From the deck nothing could be seen but a danger signal was hoisted at once to hurry all aboard faster. In a short time a little black spot would be seen from the deck. Smoke! A cruiser! Another signal, a blood-red flag, was hoisted, informing those ashore of the kind of danger. If possible the bustle ashore was increased; the ship's boats were lowered and they aided materially. The approaching vessel had seen the ship and the volume of smoke increased. She could now be seen with the naked eye and was recognized as the *Vixen*. A signal from shore that a very few remained was hoisted. Another hour passed, and the vessel was certainly within three miles. The boats were then recalled and the entire fleet of sloops soon sailed toward the ship. The boats were hoisted in and lines were thrown to the sloops now alongside. Just then the *Vixen* changed her course slightly and fired a solid shot, which passed to leeward. At this the Spanish captain cried out: "Let go!" The pin holding the staple in the anchor chain was cut and the chain parted. Sail was hoisted rapidly, the negroes in the sloops climbed over the ship's side, and as the sloops were emptied they were cast adrift with their single occupant, a krooman. They scattered like frightened birds.

It seemed a long time getting headway on the ship and everybody was looking very anxious, as other sails were set; studding-sails were added, stay-sails hoisted and a large square sail on the mizzen-mast from the deck to topsail. The *Vixen* was now within a mile and she seemed to have wonderful speed; again she changed her course and there followed a puff of smoke. That was too close for comfort, as the splashing sea showed where the ball ricocheted and went very near. However, the ship seemed to have gained some in distance during this manoeuvre and the wind grew stronger the farther she got from land. A cloud of black smoke showed that a grand effort was being made by the gunboat to recover the distance lost while changing her course to fire. The *Rebecca* was now easily going ahead and the distance between grew greater and soon the wind was so strong that it was necessary to take in the lofty studding-sails. Another hour and it was getting near night, with the cruiser at least five miles astern, still holding on, hoping something would happen to disable the ship yet. Night fell, but she continued her course without change until midnight, when it was changed to south-south-west until daylight, so that if something should happen to the masts, she would be far from the route of the gunboat in case it still followed us. At daylight the course was west by north and the south-east trade-wind was driving the ship along at fourteen knots an hour.

There were a number of strange white men aboard; Spaniards, representing the barracoon from which some of the negroes were taken on shares,—one-half for the ship, the other half for the owner, whose representative would purchase merchandise in the United States or England, and ship to St. Paul de Loanda in the mail steamer, and from there in small sloops to destination. Among the sailors were a number of strange faces, the crew of a captured vessel. They were glad to have a chance to return.

During the embarkation the doctor was engaged in separating the negroes who did not appear robust or who had received some trifling injury in getting on deck, sending them to an improvised hospital made by bulkheading a space in the rear of the forecastle. The others, as they arrived, were stowed away by the Spanish mate; so that when all were aboard there was just room for each to lie upon one side. As no one knew what proportion were men, all were herded together. The next morning the separation took place; the women and girls were all sent on deck and numbered about four hundred. A close bulkhead was then built across the ship and other bunks constructed. The women were then sent below and enough men were sent up to enable the carpenter to have room to construct additional bunks. A more docile and easily managed lot of creatures cannot be imagined. No violence of any kind was necessary; it was sometimes difficult to make them understand what was wanted, but as soon as they comprehended, immediate compliance followed.

The negroes were now sent on deck in groups of eight and squatted around a large wooden platter, heaping-full of cooked rice, beans and pork cut into small cubes. The platters were made by cutting off the head of flour or other barrels, leaving about four inches of the staves. Each negro was given a wooden spoon, which all on board had amused themselves in making during our forty-day trip. Barrel staves were sawed into lengths of eight inches, split into other pieces one and a half inch wide, and then shaped into a spoon with pocket-knives. A piece of rope yarn tied to a spoon and hung around the neck was the way in which every individual retained his property. As there was not room on deck for the entire cargo to feed at one time, platters were sent between decks, so that all ate at one hour, three times daily. Casks of water were placed in convenient places and an abundant supply was furnished day and night. When night came they were stowed in their new quarters, the men amidships, the women in the apartment bulk-headed from the men aft; the hospital forward. Looking down through the hatches they were seen like sardines in a box, on the floor and in the bunks, as close as they could be crowded. Large wind-sails furnished a supply of fresh air, and the open hatches sufficient ventilation.

A muster was made the next day to verify the lists held by each party represented. Each factor had a distinguishing brand; some a letter, others a geometrical figure; and every negro was branded with a hot iron on the left shoulder, a few days before shipment, by his owner or representative. They were all young, none less than twelve or fourteen, and none appeared over thirty years. They numbered, all told, nearly twelve hundred.

The captain then selected about twenty of the strong men and clothed them with a sack which had holes cut in it for head and arms. These men were called *camisas* (shirts) and were required to do the scrubbing and cleaning between decks, etc., and given daily a small allowance of rum. The women were divided into squads and sent on the after-deck for an hour for each squad. This changing kept up until night; the men were confined to the main-deck between cabin and forecastle and sent in squads of as many as could get on deck at once. As they came up on the first trip, each morning, every one plunged into casks of salt water and ran about until dry.

Notwithstanding their apparent good health, each morning three or four dead would be found, brought upon deck, taken by arms and heels, and tossed overboard as unceremoniously as an empty bottle. Of what did they die? and always at night? In the barracoons it was known that if a negro was not amused and kept in motion, he would mope, squat down with his chin on his knees and arms clasped about his legs and in a very short time die. Among civilized races it is thought impossible to hold one's breath until death follows. It is thought the Africans can do so. They had no means of concealing anything and certainly did not kill each other. The duties of the *camisas* were also to look after the other negroes during the day and when found sitting with knees up and head drooping, the *camisas* would start them up, run them about the deck, give them a small ration of rum, and divert them until in a normal condition.

The negroes had brought on board with them several small monkeys, which were, to them, a constant source of amusement. Another and almost perpetual pastime was the exploration of each other's head. The ship was now far away from land, making fourteen knots each hour and had no fear of any molestation for some time to come. The negroes seemed to tire of the monotony of things and some grog was daily distributed to the men and native songs and dances were constantly going on. The ingenuity of everyone was taxed to provide a new source of amusement; a special watch was put at each hatch to render any assistance in the event of sickness and to prevent intrusion by the sailors. The throwing overboard of the dead did not seem to affect them in any way, as it was their belief they returned to Africa after death away from home.

It was interesting to note the tribal distinctions among them. Tattooing was not general, but the teeth were either drawn or filed in most fantastic arrangements, generally to a point like saw teeth, or every other one was filed half-way down. The nose, lips and ears had perforations of different sizes, and a mark of distinction appeared to be the cicatrices of numerous short incisions in the skin of arms, breast and legs, sometimes of irregular shapes with attempts at geometrical figures. The colors of their skin varied also from a shining black to griffe.

It was now nearly the end of October and the ship was rapidly approaching the Caribbee Islands. Maps were examined and, after some discussion, it was thought safest to run between the French islands of Martinique and Dominique and so the course was shaped for the fifteenth degree of latitude, being midway. One morning the mountains of each could be seen, appearing about twelve miles distant. Thus far not a sail had been sighted and in passing, although at considerable distance, all the negroes were sent below so that the ship might appear to be an ordinary merchantman. A course was kept about one hundred miles south of Porto Rico, San Domingo and Hayti, until near the extreme western end of Hayti. While about midway between Hayti and Jamaica, the lookout discovered a steamer far to the westward and as its course was not yet known, sail was shortened. After half an hour it was seen that the steamer's course was almost east, so that she would intercept the ship and the course was changed slightly. All the negroes were sent below as well as the greater part of the white men. It was desirable to pass so far distant that the absence of a name on the bow of the *Rebecca* would not be noticed. The steamer was very slow and probably was the English mail steamer from Kingston, touching at Hayti and San Domingo. She eventually passed about five miles distant, and breathing more freely after her disappearance, all sail was again made, the negroes sent on deck, and an extra biscuit given each one as a thank offering.

The ship was soon north of Jamaica, but there was a dangerous place to pass, Cape de Cruz, the extreme southern point of Cuba, and on the eastern end. The course was now northwest. Vessels from the United States approach very closely, thereby saving distance to Trinidad, a prominent port on the south side of Cuba, where sugar and molasses were largely exported. It was known that an American cruiser was stationed here to intercept slavers and it was very inexpedient to run a race with her. Accordingly the speed of the ship was so governed that she would run by the dreaded locality late at night and distant about fifty miles.

The destination of the ship now became known. South-southeast of Puerto Principe, Cuba, there is a chain of six little islands running parallel with and about twenty-five or thirty miles distant from the island. The second one from the western end is the largest. It has a scrubby growth of mangrove bushes about eight feet high, a few cocoanut trees, and a most valuable spring of fresh water. It is less than a mile wide and nearly three miles long, of coral formation and but a few feet above the level of the sea.

It was necessary that the ship approach the island after midday, so that the negroes could be discharged and the vessel disposed of before dark. By burning it at night the light would have attracted greater attention than in the day, and during the day it might have been supposed some brush was burning ashore. The place was a regular highway for all vessels approaching and leaving the south of Cuba.

November 3d, 1859, the ship was but fifty miles distant at daylight, with light winds, making a headway of about eight miles an hour. About ten o'clock, some few miles ahead an American bark was sighted bound in the same direction. It never would have done to approach her near enough to be spoken, for the captain would, in all probability, have invited himself aboard to have a chat for an hour or two. Sail could not be shortened, for it would have attracted attention. What should be done? The captain called the carpenter, who, with the assistance of the crew, brought on deck two large water casks. The head of each was knocked out, ropes secured to the rim, and then the casks were lowered astern, so that they would drag with the open end toward the ship; as soon as the ropes tightened the speed was reduced so much that the bark rapidly drew ahead and in an hour could not see what was going on aboard the ship.

It was now mid-day and the chain of islands was in sight. The position of the one sought had been calculated very closely, but the casks had retarded speed so that the ship would reach the island later than had been expected. At mid-day another observation was taken and the island located exactly—about fifteen miles distant. As the ship approached, a signal flag—a large white one with a red cross—was hoisted to the top of the mainmast. Some time elapsed without a sign of any living creature on the island. The ship was more than six weeks behind the most liberal estimate of time, and the Spaniards began to fear that those assigned to meet the ship had given up all hopes of a successful voyage and had gone to the mainland. Just as the gloomiest views seemed to be about realized, two men appeared running through the thin undergrowth to the water's edge, waving their hats and gesticulating wildly. A shout of recognition was the return salute. The ship was sailed to within half a mile, and anchored in fourteen fathoms of water. The four boats were lowered in a hurry and the landing of the negroes began. More than two hours were needed to land all of them, with a sufficient number of large sails for shelter and also food supplies.

Meanwhile, the carpenter had been sent below to scuttle the ship; all the combustible material aboard was collected in the forecastle, between decks, and in the cabin, liberally saturated with oil, turpentine and paint, and as the last of the crew left the ship the match was applied to each heap, and before the boats reached the shore, she was on fire from stem to stern. The rigging soon burned and the upper masts fell one after the other, still held to the ship by the heavy stays. She gradually sank and before an hour there was nothing left on the sea to indicate the destruction of the *Rebecca*.

As the negroes were landed they were hurried back far enough to be out of sight of any passing vessel, the scanty growth of mangrove affording ample hiding. After dark the sails were so spread and secured as to shelter the negroes from the dews, which were cold after the warm days. These tents were taken down before daylight, as they could have been seen by a passing vessel. Great was the joy of the Spaniards at being ashore in a place of security, for they felt tranquil about the part yet to come. Immediately after all were ashore the fishing sloop was despatched to the mainland with intelligence of their arrival. The island was of coral formation and covered with thin soil and very little grass. It was covered with mangrove bushes and there were about a dozen cocoanut trees, stunted in growth but with a good supply of fruit, yet green.

The joy of the negroes was great at being ashore and so bountifully supplied with food and water. Each day vessels passed, but none near enough to discover the island's secret.

Before the sloop left there was considerable discussion among the sailors about their pay, they wishing to be paid before the negroes were sent to the mainland, and the Spaniards desiring that the remaining risks should be shared by all alike and all paid at the final destination. The matter was compromised by the Spaniards agreeing to pay those who demanded it. Four days after the sloop left, two small schooners arrived bringing money for those who demanded it, and they were paid in Spanish doubloons. The negroes were now transferred to the two schooners and although they had been closely packed in the ship they were now jammed together in the hold, as none could be allowed on deck. The officers were divided and were permitted to remain on deck in the little space that could be found.

Sail was made for Trinidad, about seventy-five miles distant, and before dark the harbor was reached amid a fleet of vessels. A custom-house boat met the schooners and less than one hundred yards from an American bark assigned an anchorage. The schooners had the appearance of ordinary coasters and did not attract any attention. At ten o'clock that night a bright light was seen on the beach at the extreme east end of the harbor and the schooners made sail for it, but on reaching the point were told that arrangements were not complete for transportation and could not be before the next night, so they returned to the anchorage and kept busy all night distributing biscuits and water to the negroes, who were hungry and restless. The night air was cold and to keep warm, the doctor stood in the open hatch with his chin on a level with the deck, keeping his body in the warm air below while he breathed pure air. To go below for only a few minutes was terrible because of the impure air.

Morning came slowly and again every care was taken not to betray in any way the character of the vessels. Sail after sail passed, coming and going. At last the sun went down, the air became cool, and night again obscured everything. At ten o'clock the light reappeared and the schooners made for it, showing a single lantern, which was extinguished as they approached. The schooners ran ashore in about three feet of water and the negroes hurried ashore without noise, wading.

In the darkness could be seen a long line of wagons, two-wheeled, with an open frame of poles and cords extending around the body of the wagon about three feet high. The women and youngest negroes were put in the wagons, the framework supporting them from falling and enabling many more to crowd in. When the wagons started, the negro men followed on foot. The route led over a mountainous country, through coffee plantations, into the interior and the traveling was slow for some time. At 7 A.M. the plantation of Don S. B—— was reached, which was the destination, nearly twenty-three miles from the coast. The negroes were sent to an inclosure to be fed and rested and the officers were escorted to the residence of the proprietor, where all had a bath, change of clothing and a good breakfast.

The doctor was seated on the veranda smoking, when a Catholic priest and an assistant arrived and passed on to the inclosure. Shortly after came a wagon filled with clothing and being curious the doctor followed. Inside the inclosure the negroes were drawn up in rows. Their brands were examined and they were separated into lots representing each mark. The priest, assisted by his young man, passed along in front, the young man registering the name the priest had given each as they were baptized. As the priest finished one lot they were at once furnished with clothing, the women with a sort of loose gown of coarse cotton cloth and the men with a long shirt, and then sent off in different directions. Don S. B—— said that there were but twenty-five of the new arrivals on his plantation, the others having been delivered to the planters who had already contracted for them, paying $350 for each.

The Spaniards now began to interest themselves in behalf of the American captain, mate, and the doctor. The laws of Cuba required every person landed to be provided with a passport or permit, the latter being issued under certain conditions for one month, at the expiration of which the holder would be arrested if on the island; this permit, if the person was satisfactorily identified and vouched for, could be renewed from month to month. The Americans had arrived without the knowledge of the government and had neither passport nor permit. These permits for one month were now purchased by the Spaniards from an accommodating official, at a cost of one doubloon (seventeen dollars) each, and the Americans concluded to go now to Havana, that place offering more opportunities for leaving the island than the smaller ports. The doctor's permit represented him as a machinist, the captain's, as a carpenter, and the mate's, as a merchant.

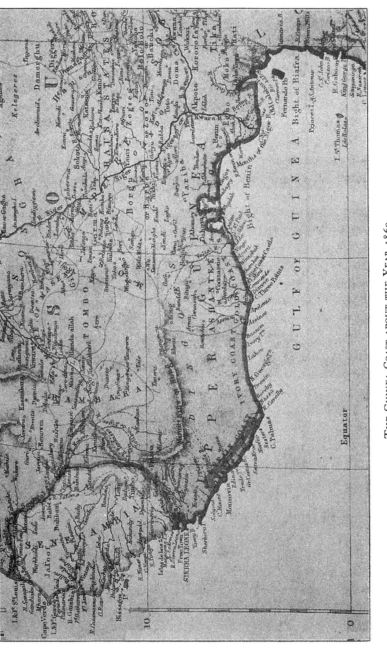

THE GUINEA COAST ABOUT THE YEAR 1860

From Black's *Atlas of the World*, Edinburgh, 1867

At three o'clock on the morning of the fifth day after their arrival they started for Trinidad to take the coast steamer to Batabano, stopping at Cienfuegos, Casilda, and other points. They were escorted by their Spanish friends, all on horseback with old-fashioned trappings, holsters and pistols. The steamer left soon after they reached the wharf and there were several passengers who scrutinized them very closely. On the evening of the following day the Americans reached Batabano, the terminus of a railroad across the island to Havana, and late in the evening were in Havana and at the American Hotel.

Two weeks later, a steamer from New York to Panama arrived, with some accident to her machinery which delayed her several days. The doctor went out to her, shortly after her arrival, and saw that a number of her passengers were going ashore to visit the city during the delay of the ship; they could get a permit at a certain place on the wharf and remain ashore if they desired. A happy idea came to him and he went ashore with them and asked for a permit to visit the island during the stay of the vessel; it cost twenty-five cents. He then went to the Captain-General's office, to the passport department, and stated that he was a passenger on the steamer in the harbor from New York to Panama, destined to San Francisco; that he was an engineer going to California and while visiting the city on permit had met a planter with whom he had made arrangements to take off his sugar crop; that some new machinery was needed in the sugarhouse, which could only be procured in the United States in time for use that season, and that it would be necessary for him to return to New Orleans by the Panama steamer now due. He therefore asked for a passport, as the steamer could not take him without one. The clerk said such things were of frequent occurrence and soon had a passport ready. Hurrying to the hotel, the doctor related his experience to the American captain and mate, who concluded to try their luck in the *rôle* of homesick and discontented gold-seekers anxious to return to their home in the States. Both of them got into a boat, were taken out to and around the ship and returning, obtained their permits, and together went to the pass-port office declaring themselves disgusted with the idea of going to California and desiring to go back home, via New Orleans, on the steamer reported due in a day or two. They obtained their pass-ports and came to the hotel, where, in a well-closed room, a bottle of wine was opened and a toast drank to the success of the scheme for reaching home.

Two days after they were aboard the Panama steamer and two days later in New Orleans where the doctor sent the following message to his parents in Natchez, Mississippi: "Just returned from the coast of Africa, safe and well."

INDEX

A CATALOG OF SELECTED
DOVER BOOKS
IN ALL FIELDS OF INTEREST

A CATALOG OF SELECTED DOVER
BOOKS IN ALL FIELDS OF INTEREST

CONCERNING THE SPIRITUAL IN ART, Wassily Kandinsky. Pioneering work by father of abstract art. Thoughts on color theory, nature of art. Analysis of earlier masters. 12 illustrations. 80pp. of text. 5⅜ x 8½.   23411-8

ANIMALS: 1,419 Copyright-Free Illustrations of Mammals, Birds, Fish, Insects, etc., Jim Harter (ed.). Clear wood engravings present, in extremely lifelike poses, over 1,000 species of animals. One of the most extensive pictorial sourcebooks of its kind. Captions. Index. 284pp. 9 x 12.   23766-4

CELTIC ART: The Methods of Construction, George Bain. Simple geometric techniques for making Celtic interlacements, spirals, Kells-type initials, animals, humans, etc. Over 500 illustrations. 160pp. 9 x 12. (Available in U.S. only.)   22923-8

AN ATLAS OF ANATOMY FOR ARTISTS, Fritz Schider. Most thorough reference work on art anatomy in the world. Hundreds of illustrations, including selections from works by Vesalius, Leonardo, Goya, Ingres, Michelangelo, others. 593 illustrations. 192pp. 7⅛ x 10¼.   20241-0

CELTIC HAND STROKE-BY-STROKE (Irish Half-Uncial from "The Book of Kells"): An Arthur Baker Calligraphy Manual, Arthur Baker. Complete guide to creating each letter of the alphabet in distinctive Celtic manner. Covers hand position, strokes, pens, inks, paper, more. Illustrated. 48pp. 8¼ x 11.   24336-2

EASY ORIGAMI, John Montroll. Charming collection of 32 projects (hat, cup, pelican, piano, swan, many more) specially designed for the novice origami hobbyist. Clearly illustrated easy-to-follow instructions insure that even beginning papercrafters will achieve successful results. 48pp. 8¼ x 11.   27298-2

THE COMPLETE BOOK OF BIRDHOUSE CONSTRUCTION FOR WOODWORKERS, Scott D. Campbell. Detailed instructions, illustrations, tables. Also data on bird habitat and instinct patterns. Bibliography. 3 tables. 63 illustrations in 15 figures. 48pp. 5¼ x 8½.   24407-5

BLOOMINGDALE'S ILLUSTRATED 1886 CATALOG: Fashions, Dry Goods and Housewares, Bloomingdale Brothers. Famed merchants' extremely rare catalog depicting about 1,700 products: clothing, housewares, firearms, dry goods, jewelry, more. Invaluable for dating, identifying vintage items. Also, copyright-free graphics for artists, designers. Co-published with Henry Ford Museum & Greenfield Village. 160pp. 8¼ x 11.   25780-0

HISTORIC COSTUME IN PICTURES, Braun & Schneider. Over 1,450 costumed figures in clearly detailed engravings–from dawn of civilization to end of 19th century. Captions. Many folk costumes. 256pp. 8⅜ x 11¾.   23150-X

THE CLARINET AND CLARINET PLAYING, David Pino. Lively, comprehensive work features suggestions about technique, musicianship, and musical interpretation, as well as guidelines for teaching, making your own reeds, and preparing for public performance. Includes an intriguing look at clarinet history. "A godsend," *The Clarinet,* Journal of the International Clarinet Society. Appendixes. 7 illus. 320pp. 5⅜ x 8½. 40270-3

HOLLYWOOD GLAMOR PORTRAITS, John Kobal (ed.). 145 photos from 1926-49. Harlow, Gable, Bogart, Bacall; 94 stars in all. Full background on photographers, technical aspects. 160pp. 8⅜ x 11¼. 23352-9

THE ANNOTATED CASEY AT THE BAT: A Collection of Ballads about the Mighty Casey/Third, Revised Edition, Martin Gardner (ed.). Amusing sequels and parodies of one of America's best-loved poems: Casey's Revenge, Why Casey Whiffed, Casey's Sister at the Bat, others. 256pp. 5⅜ x 8½. 28598-7

THE RAVEN AND OTHER FAVORITE POEMS, Edgar Allan Poe. Over 40 of the author's most memorable poems: "The Bells," "Ulalume," "Israfel," "To Helen," "The Conqueror Worm," "Eldorado," "Annabel Lee," many more. Alphabetic lists of titles and first lines. 64pp. 5³⁄₁₆ x 8¼. 26685-0

PERSONAL MEMOIRS OF U. S. GRANT, Ulysses Simpson Grant. Intelligent, deeply moving firsthand account of Civil War campaigns, considered by many the finest military memoirs ever written. Includes letters, historic photographs, maps and more. 528pp. 6⅛ x 9¼. 28587-1

ANCIENT EGYPTIAN MATERIALS AND INDUSTRIES, A. Lucas and J. Harris. Fascinating, comprehensive, thoroughly documented text describes this ancient civilization's vast resources and the processes that incorporated them in daily life, including the use of animal products, building materials, cosmetics, perfumes and incense, fibers, glazed ware, glass and its manufacture, materials used in the mummification process, and much more. 544pp. 6⅛ x 9¼. (Available in U.S. only.) 40446-3

RUSSIAN STORIES/RUSSKIE RASSKAZY: A Dual-Language Book, edited by Gleb Struve. Twelve tales by such masters as Chekhov, Tolstoy, Dostoevsky, Pushkin, others. Excellent word-for-word English translations on facing pages, plus teaching and study aids, Russian/English vocabulary, biographical/critical introductions, more. 416pp. 5⅜ x 8½. 26244-8

PHILADELPHIA THEN AND NOW: 60 Sites Photographed in the Past and Present, Kenneth Finkel and Susan Oyama. Rare photographs of City Hall, Logan Square, Independence Hall, Betsy Ross House, other landmarks juxtaposed with contemporary views. Captures changing face of historic city. Introduction. Captions. 128pp. 8¼ x 11. 25790-8

AIA ARCHITECTURAL GUIDE TO NASSAU AND SUFFOLK COUNTIES, LONG ISLAND, The American Institute of Architects, Long Island Chapter, and the Society for the Preservation of Long Island Antiquities. Comprehensive, well-researched and generously illustrated volume brings to life over three centuries of Long Island's great architectural heritage. More than 240 photographs with authoritative, extensively detailed captions. 176pp. 8¼ x 11. 26946-9

NORTH AMERICAN INDIAN LIFE: Customs and Traditions of 23 Tribes, Elsie Clews Parsons (ed.). 27 fictionalized essays by noted anthropologists examine religion, customs, government, additional facets of life among the Winnebago, Crow, Zuni, Eskimo, other tribes. 480pp. 6⅛ x 9¼. 27377-6

THE BEST TALES OF HOFFMANN, E. T. A. Hoffmann. 10 of Hoffmann's most important stories: "Nutcracker and the King of Mice," "The Golden Flowerpot," etc. 458pp. 5⅜ x 8½. 21793-0

FROM FETISH TO GOD IN ANCIENT EGYPT, E. A. Wallis Budge. Rich detailed survey of Egyptian conception of "God" and gods, magic, cult of animals, Osiris, more. Also, superb English translations of hymns and legends. 240 illustrations. 545pp. 5⅜ x 8½. 25803-3

FRENCH STORIES/CONTES FRANÇAIS: A Dual-Language Book, Wallace Fowlie. Ten stories by French masters, Voltaire to Camus: "Micromegas" by Voltaire; "The Atheist's Mass" by Balzac; "Minuet" by de Maupassant; "The Guest" by Camus, six more. Excellent English translations on facing pages. Also French-English vocabulary list, exercises, more. 352pp. 5⅜ x 8½. 26443-2

CHICAGO AT THE TURN OF THE CENTURY IN PHOTOGRAPHS: 122 Historic Views from the Collections of the Chicago Historical Society, Larry A. Viskochil. Rare large-format prints offer detailed views of City Hall, State Street, the Loop, Hull House, Union Station, many other landmarks, circa 1904-1913. Introduction. Captions. Maps. 144pp. 9⅜ x 12¼. 24656-6

OLD BROOKLYN IN EARLY PHOTOGRAPHS, 1865-1929, William Lee Younger. Luna Park, Gravesend race track, construction of Grand Army Plaza, moving of Hotel Brighton, etc. 157 previously unpublished photographs. 165pp. 8⅞ x 11¾. 23587-4

THE MYTHS OF THE NORTH AMERICAN INDIANS, Lewis Spence. Rich anthology of the myths and legends of the Algonquins, Iroquois, Pawnees and Sioux, prefaced by an extensive historical and ethnological commentary. 36 illustrations. 480pp. 5⅜ x 8½. 25967-6

AN ENCYCLOPEDIA OF BATTLES: Accounts of Over 1,560 Battles from 1479 B.C. to the Present, David Eggenberger. Essential details of every major battle in recorded history from the first battle of Megiddo in 1479 B.C. to Grenada in 1984. List of Battle Maps. New Appendix covering the years 1967-1984. Index. 99 illustrations. 544pp. 6½ x 9¼. 24913-1

SAILING ALONE AROUND THE WORLD, Captain Joshua Slocum. First man to sail around the world, alone, in small boat. One of great feats of seamanship told in delightful manner. 67 illustrations. 294pp. 5⅜ x 8½. 20326-3

ANARCHISM AND OTHER ESSAYS, Emma Goldman. Powerful, penetrating, prophetic essays on direct action, role of minorities, prison reform, puritan hypocrisy, violence, etc. 271pp. 5⅜ x 8½. 22484-8

MYTHS OF THE HINDUS AND BUDDHISTS, Ananda K. Coomaraswamy and Sister Nivedita. Great stories of the epics; deeds of Krishna, Shiva, taken from puranas, Vedas, folk tales; etc. 32 illustrations. 400pp. 5⅜ x 8½. 21759-0

THE TRAUMA OF BIRTH, Otto Rank. Rank's controversial thesis that anxiety neurosis is caused by profound psychological trauma which occurs at birth. 256pp. 5⅜ x 8½. 27974-X

A THEOLOGICO-POLITICAL TREATISE, Benedict Spinoza. Also contains unfinished Political Treatise. Great classic on religious liberty, theory of government on common consent. R. Elwes translation. Total of 421pp. 5⅜ x 8½. 20249-6

PERSPECTIVE FOR ARTISTS, Rex Vicat Cole. Depth, perspective of sky and sea, shadows, much more, not usually covered. 391 diagrams, 81 reproductions of drawings and paintings. 279pp. 5⅜ x 8½. 22487-2

DRAWING THE LIVING FIGURE, Joseph Sheppard. Innovative approach to artistic anatomy focuses on specifics of surface anatomy, rather than muscles and bones. Over 170 drawings of live models in front, back and side views, and in widely varying poses. Accompanying diagrams. 177 illustrations. Introduction. Index. 144pp. 8⅜ x11¼. 26723-7

GOTHIC AND OLD ENGLISH ALPHABETS: 100 Complete Fonts, Dan X. Solo. Add power, elegance to posters, signs, other graphics with 100 stunning copyright-free alphabets: Blackstone, Dolbey, Germania, 97 more–including many lower-case, numerals, punctuation marks. 104pp. 8⅛ x 11. 24695-7

HOW TO DO BEADWORK, Mary White. Fundamental book on craft from simple projects to five-bead chains and woven works. 106 illustrations. 142pp. 5⅜ x 8. 20697-1

THE BOOK OF WOOD CARVING, Charles Marshall Sayers. Finest book for beginners discusses fundamentals and offers 34 designs. "Absolutely first rate . . . well thought out and well executed."–E. J. Tangerman. 118pp. 7¾ x 10⅝. 23654-4

ILLUSTRATED CATALOG OF CIVIL WAR MILITARY GOODS: Union Army Weapons, Insignia, Uniform Accessories, and Other Equipment, Schuyler, Hartley, and Graham. Rare, profusely illustrated 1846 catalog includes Union Army uniform and dress regulations, arms and ammunition, coats, insignia, flags, swords, rifles, etc. 226 illustrations. 160pp. 9 x 12. 24939-5

WOMEN'S FASHIONS OF THE EARLY 1900s: An Unabridged Republication of "New York Fashions, 1909," National Cloak & Suit Co. Rare catalog of mail-order fashions documents women's and children's clothing styles shortly after the turn of the century. Captions offer full descriptions, prices. Invaluable resource for fashion, costume historians. Approximately 725 illustrations. 128pp. 8⅜ x 11¼. 27276-1

THE 1912 AND 1915 GUSTAV STICKLEY FURNITURE CATALOGS, Gustav Stickley. With over 200 detailed illustrations and descriptions, these two catalogs are essential reading and reference materials and identification guides for Stickley furniture. Captions cite materials, dimensions and prices. 112pp. 6½ x 9¼. 26676-1

EARLY AMERICAN LOCOMOTIVES, John H. White, Jr. Finest locomotive engravings from early 19th century: historical (1804–74), main-line (after 1870), special, foreign, etc. 147 plates. 142pp. 11⅜ x 8¼. 22772-3

THE TALL SHIPS OF TODAY IN PHOTOGRAPHS, Frank O. Braynard. Lavishly illustrated tribute to nearly 100 majestic contemporary sailing vessels: Amerigo Vespucci, Clearwater, Constitution, Eagle, Mayflower, Sea Cloud, Victory, many more. Authoritative captions provide statistics, background on each ship. 190 black-and-white photographs and illustrations. Introduction. 128pp. 8⅞ x 11¾. 27163-3

PIANO TUNING, J. Cree Fischer. Clearest, best book for beginner, amateur. Simple repairs, raising dropped notes, tuning by easy method of flattened fifths. No previous skills needed. 4 illustrations. 201pp. 5⅜ x 8½. 23267-0

HINTS TO SINGERS, Lillian Nordica. Selecting the right teacher, developing confidence, overcoming stage fright, and many other important skills receive thoughtful discussion in this indispensible guide, written by a world-famous diva of four decades' experience. 96pp. 5⅜ x 8½. 40094-8

THE COMPLETE NONSENSE OF EDWARD LEAR, Edward Lear. All nonsense limericks, zany alphabets, Owl and Pussycat, songs, nonsense botany, etc., illustrated by Lear. Total of 320pp. 5⅜ x 8½. (Available in U.S. only.) 20167-8

VICTORIAN PARLOUR POETRY: An Annotated Anthology, Michael R. Turner. 117 gems by Longfellow, Tennyson, Browning, many lesser-known poets. "The Village Blacksmith," "Curfew Must Not Ring Tonight," "Only a Baby Small," dozens more, often difficult to find elsewhere. Index of poets, titles, first lines. xxiii + 325pp. 5⅜ x 8¼. 27044-0

DUBLINERS, James Joyce. Fifteen stories offer vivid, tightly focused observations of the lives of Dublin's poorer classes. At least one, "The Dead," is considered a masterpiece. Reprinted complete and unabridged from standard edition. 160pp. 5³/₁₆ x 8¼. 26870-5

GREAT WEIRD TALES: 14 Stories by Lovecraft, Blackwood, Machen and Others, S. T. Joshi (ed.). 14 spellbinding tales, including "The Sin Eater," by Fiona McLeod, "The Eye Above the Mantel," by Frank Belknap Long, as well as renowned works by R. H. Barlow, Lord Dunsany, Arthur Machen, W. C. Morrow and eight other masters of the genre. 256pp. 5⅜ x 8½. (Available in U.S. only.) 40436-6

THE BOOK OF THE SACRED MAGIC OF ABRAMELIN THE MAGE, translated by S. MacGregor Mathers. Medieval manuscript of ceremonial magic. Basic document in Aleister Crowley, Golden Dawn groups. 268pp. 5⅜ x 8½. 23211-5

NEW RUSSIAN-ENGLISH AND ENGLISH-RUSSIAN DICTIONARY, M. A. O'Brien. This is a remarkably handy Russian dictionary, containing a surprising amount of information, including over 70,000 entries. 366pp. 4½ x 6⅛. 20208-9

HISTORIC HOMES OF THE AMERICAN PRESIDENTS, Second, Revised Edition, Irvin Haas. A traveler's guide to American Presidential homes, most open to the public, depicting and describing homes occupied by every American President from George Washington to George Bush. With visiting hours, admission charges, travel routes. 175 photographs. Index. 160pp. 8¼ x 11. 26751-2

NEW YORK IN THE FORTIES, Andreas Feininger. 162 brilliant photographs by the well-known photographer, formerly with *Life* magazine. Commuters, shoppers, Times Square at night, much else from city at its peak. Captions by John von Hartz. 181pp. 9¼ x 10¾. 23585-8

INDIAN SIGN LANGUAGE, William Tomkins. Over 525 signs developed by Sioux and other tribes. Written instructions and diagrams. Also 290 pictographs. 111pp. 6⅛ x 9¼. 22029-X

THE STORY OF THE TITANIC AS TOLD BY ITS SURVIVORS, Jack Winocour (ed.). What it was really like. Panic, despair, shocking inefficiency, and a little heroism. More thrilling than any fictional account. 26 illustrations. 320pp. 5⅜ x 8½.
20610-6

FAIRY AND FOLK TALES OF THE IRISH PEASANTRY, William Butler Yeats (ed.). Treasury of 64 tales from the twilight world of Celtic myth and legend: "The Soul Cages," "The Kildare Pooka," "King O'Toole and his Goose," many more. Introduction and Notes by W. B. Yeats. 352pp. 5⅜ x 8½.
26941-8

BUDDHIST MAHAYANA TEXTS, E. B. Cowell and others (eds.). Superb, accurate translations of basic documents in Mahayana Buddhism, highly important in history of religions. The Buddha-karita of Asvaghosha, Larger Sukhavativyuha, more. 448pp. 5⅜ x 8½.
25552-2

ONE TWO THREE . . . INFINITY: Facts and Speculations of Science, George Gamow. Great physicist's fascinating, readable overview of contemporary science: number theory, relativity, fourth dimension, entropy, genes, atomic structure, much more. 128 illustrations. Index. 352pp. 5⅜ x 8½.
25664-2

EXPERIMENTATION AND MEASUREMENT, W. J. Youden. Introductory manual explains laws of measurement in simple terms and offers tips for achieving accuracy and minimizing errors. Mathematics of measurement, use of instruments, experimenting with machines. 1994 edition. Foreword. Preface. Introduction. Epilogue. Selected Readings. Glossary. Index. Tables and figures. 128pp. 5⅜ x 8½.
40451-X

DALÍ ON MODERN ART: The Cuckolds of Antiquated Modern Art, Salvador Dalí. Influential painter skewers modern art and its practitioners. Outrageous evaluations of Picasso, Cézanne, Turner, more. 15 renderings of paintings discussed. 44 calligraphic decorations by Dalí. 96pp. 5⅜ x 8½. (Available in U.S. only.)
29220-7

ANTIQUE PLAYING CARDS: A Pictorial History, Henry René D'Allemagne. Over 900 elaborate, decorative images from rare playing cards (14th–20th centuries): Bacchus, death, dancing dogs, hunting scenes, royal coats of arms, players cheating, much more. 96pp. 9¼ x 12¼.
29265-7

MAKING FURNITURE MASTERPIECES: 30 Projects with Measured Drawings, Franklin H. Gottshall. Step-by-step instructions, illustrations for constructing handsome, useful pieces, among them a Sheraton desk, Chippendale chair, Spanish desk, Queen Anne table and a William and Mary dressing mirror. 224pp. 8⅛ x 11¼.
29338-6

THE FOSSIL BOOK: A Record of Prehistoric Life, Patricia V. Rich et al. Profusely illustrated definitive guide covers everything from single-celled organisms and dinosaurs to birds and mammals and the interplay between climate and man. Over 1,500 illustrations. 760pp. 7½ x 10⅛.
29371-8

Paperbound unless otherwise indicated. Available at your book dealer, online at **www.doverpublications.com**, or by writing to Dept. GI, Dover Publications, Inc., 31 East 2nd Street, Mineola, NY 11501. For current price information or for free catalogues (please indicate field of interest), write to Dover Publications or log on to **www.doverpublications.com** and see every Dover book in print. Dover publishes more than 500 books each year on science, elementary and advanced mathematics, biology, music, art, literary history, social sciences, and other areas.